THE BOOK OF THE
VIOLIN

THE BOOK OF THE
VIOLIN

Edited by Dominic Gill

RIZZOLI
NEW YORK

FRONTISPIECE:
Louis Guéné, *Violon du Roi*: painting by François l'Aîné
Dumont, 1791

First published in the United States of America in 1984 by
RIZZOLI INTERNATIONAL PUBLICATIONS, INC.,
712 Fifth Avenue, New York NY 10019

Copyright © Phaidon Press Limited 1984

ISBN 0-8478-0548-4
LC 84 42683

Designed by Gwyn Lewis
Picture research by Elizabeth Agate

Printed and bound in Spain by Eraclio Fournier, S. A.
Vitoria

Contents

Preface

If the name once more did not carry such unlooked-for associations, and if the task were not patently impossible to achieve in the space of 100,000 words, this book, like its companion *The Book of the Piano*, might have been called *The Complete Book of the Violin*. Comprehensiveness, at any rate, has been a guideline from the start; and the other guideline has been balance. *The Book of the Violin* covers, or touches on, nearly every aspect of the violin, its history and pre-history, its repertoire, its makers and performers, from the earliest times to the present day. But to have been led down too many sidetracks and byways, however fascinating, would have meant omitting too much of central importance; to have attempted to list every name and every fact would have resulted in a cumbersome and unreadable *catalogue raisonné*.

There are therefore certain conscious omissions: chief among them a thorough investigation of the role of the violin in chamber music—a huge topic which, to be adequately represented, would call for a book at least half as long again. There are other, too, which have been the subject of many difficult decisions, appraisals and reappraisals: in any book of such ambitious scope, some reader will find some favourite fact or name left out. But few, I hope. A glance at the Index, as well as the Contents Page, will show just how comprehensive the book remains.

The Discography is another matter. There the selection has been unavoidably, and unashamedly, subjective: the reader is directed to the introduction at the head of the list. A number of the records are no longer to be found in current catalogues; but it is gratifying to see how often the best of them are regularly reissued, and surprising, too, how often the reader, once alerted to the existence of a rarity, can make exciting discoveries of his own.

It has been a general policy, so that *The Book of the Violin* shall be accessible to those unable to read music, only to include music examples which also make a general visual point. Dates of birth and death are often included in the text when they help to clarify the historical perspective or argument. But in the Index most proper names are dated—so the Index may also be used as a handy reference guide for dates alone. The Glossary and Bibliography are short guides: to reading, and to further reading.

The Chronology of Violinists, like the Discography, makes no claim to completeness. But there has been a consistency, as well as a kind of poetry, involved in the choice all the same. The history of the violin is also the history of many hundreds of violinists of the first rank: great artists, justly esteemed, who have made an original and invaluable contribution to the story of music. This book could not possibly list them all. But within that rank there is also a body of violinists which it may seem almost invidious to identify—but which stands out nonetheless: the magicians of the first rank, those violinists who force us (even against our will) to make a further division between greatness and genius; not just the many violinists who have together forged a tradition, but the violinists without whom it is impossible to imagine a violin tradition at all. There will be argument as to whether one name or another in the list should have appeared there; but there are, I think, no notable omissions—except of violinist-composers like Paganini, Vieuxtemps and Wieniawski, who are treated separately in the main text, and of early names from the pre-recording age (David, Marsick, de Bériot, Bull and Ernst come immediately to mind) whose legends are secure, but whose actual quality is by now almost impossible to estimate.

Prologue

Previous page: Detail of angel musicians from *The Virgin and Child with Saints*: painting by Bartolommeo Montagna (d. 1523).

Left: African musical bow (*umuduli*) with gourd resonator.
Centre: Jamaican three-string bamboo violin.
Right: Bedouin *rebab*.

Viola da gamba, viola da braccio, violone da gamba, violone da braccio, violone, violon, viole, viola, violetta—names for string instruments, all played with a bow, at around the same period of the early sixteenth century during which we know the violin first emerged. The first four letters of every name are the same: a close-knit family might be supposed from the common root.* Yet where does the familiar modern violin stand in the list? Are any, or all, of them violins? Are any, or all, of them even related to the violin?

The ancestry of the violin, as well as the answers to such questions, are touched on at various points in the following pages: but if the reader always expects precise elucidation, he will be disappointed. In the matter of *exactly* how, where and why the violin was first invented, contemporary historians of the sixteenth and early

seventeenth centuries have left us entirely in the dark. The unkindest cut of all is delivered during the first century of the life of the violin by Michael Praetorius, who, in his *Syntagma musicum* of 1619 (see also p. 60), leads the reader to the brink, then leaves him standing there. The subject is dismissed with a tantalizing shrug, and no more comment than the following words: '. . . and since everyone knows about the violin family, it is unnecessary to indicate or write anything further about it'.

Perhaps Praetorius was merely concealing his ignorance; perhaps, after all, he was telling the truth. Whatever the case, what anyone knew then, nobody knows now. As the violin historian David Boyden (to whom all writing since 1965 about the early years of the violin, and therefore many of these chapters, are gratefully indebted) remarks with understandable feeling in his *History of Violin Playing*: 'Had [Praetorius] passed on his detailed knowledge of the sixteenth-century violin, oceans of ink and countless hours spent in research might have been saved in the intervening centuries.' If the early history of the violin sometimes seems confusing, it is precisely because, enfolded in such a historical mist, it is often confused.

Music is as fundamental as the whistling of the wind, the snapping of a twig, or the cry of the human voice. Whatever stage of social or cultural evolution a people has reached, it has already become acquainted with

Viola, viella and *vidula* in medieval Latin = 'bowed instrument' (whence also the many forms of 'fiddle': *vielle, videl, fydel* etc., and the *fydelstyk* with which they were played). The etymology is obscure, but the root is probably the Indo-European *jyā* or *bjyā* = 'bow(string)', whence the Greek *biós* (βιός = 'arc' or 'bow')—and thus various forms of 'bowing' or 'bending' (Old High German *biogan* = 'to bow' or 'to bend', as also the related modern German *biegen*, Italian *piegare* and French *plier*). Via the interchangeable 'b' and 'v', *bio-* gives *vio-*. The letter 'l' after the root may derive from the Greek *ulé* (ὕλη = 'wood') and the adjectival prefix *ulo-* (= 'wooden'). *Bio + ulo* (= 'bow' + 'wood' or 'bowed wood') becomes *vio + (u)lo*, already nearly *violon*, or violin. Further links such as those suggested by Herbert Whone (see p. 211) with the Greek βίος (= 'life') and with the Latin and German roots *vol-* and *vil-* (= 'will') are attractive but more tenuous.

Indian *ravanastron*.

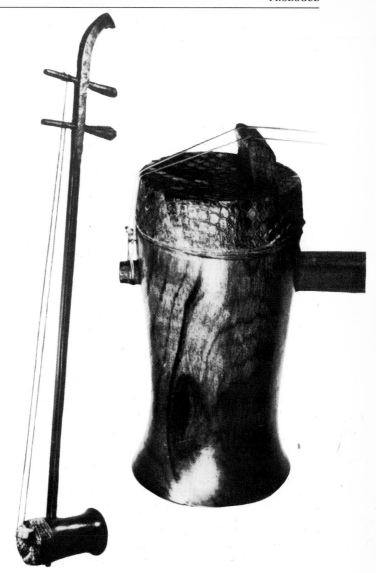

music. The aesthetic of that music may not be common to all: in Japanese Zen philosophy, natural sounds—wind in a bamboo forest, the click of stone on stone—are as inherently musical as any man-made noise; the complex rhythmic patterns of African drumming are fraught with meanings of quite another order than those (if any) perceived by European ears; to the African tribesman who attaches a hollow gourd to the centre of his bow to amplify the sound of the vibrating string, that sound is music. From the twanging bow-string to a solo violin sonata by J. S. Bach is a large step indeed; but structurally and acoustically it is only a small step from the hollow gourd to the more elaborate forms of sound-box.

For all the great differences of culture between Africa on the one hand and Greco-Roman civilization on the other, they had at least one thing in common: their basic techniques of producing musical sounds. The ancient Greeks, pioneers in the fields of philosophy, poetry, rhetoric, the visual arts, architecture and the theory of music, knew only two main melodic instruments apart from the voice: the reed-flute and the lyre—the latter essentially a sound-box and frame, variously shaped, strung with two or more gut or hair strings, and plucked with a plectrum or with the fingers. (The ancient Greek *kithara*, remote ancestor of the guitar, was essentially a larger and more powerful lyre, which instrument it supplanted in post-Classical Greece. The single-string monochord, said to have been invented by Pythagoras, had no sound-box, and was more scientific than musical instrument.)

In ancient Greece, this type of instrument was only used to enhance the effect of song and poetry. But when we come to consider the ancient nations of Asia, we find an innovation of the greatest importance to the development of music: the bow. The bow alone enables the player of a stringed instrument to progress beyond single, rapidly decaying plucked notes, drawing from his strings sounds of any duration, and, where required, an *increasing* as well as decreasing intensity. The introduction of the bow gave a new range of expression to music: the power, in the same manner as the voice but independent of it, to rouse, excite or soothe the listener with sustained and thrillingly varied tones.

The first bow may have been just that: a hunting bow. Experiment will have suggested better results from woven silk, or from the tail hair of a horse (common among Asian peoples, especially in India and Persia, as binding material). In Asia, the sound-box consisted either of an open drum (made from a gourd or hollowed tree-trunk) or a hollow bamboo stem. A separate finger-

board was as yet unknown: higher and lower notes were produced by pressing the fingers against the strings to shorten and lengthen them. (In the case of some of these early instruments—the Persian *kemangeh*, for example—the bow was not passed over the strings, but merely pressed against them, while notes were produced by moving the instrument itself.) In other forms, a skin-covered drum served as the body of the instrument: the Persian *rebab*, for instance, had a single string made of hair, tensioned with a peg, stretched across a skin-covered belly.* The *kemangeh rumy*, another type, had

*Some claim that the prototype of this sort of instrument is the Indian *ravanastron* (see p. 18 and pp. 22–23), still in use today, and according to legend invented by Ravanon, King of Ceylon, in the third millennium BC, travelling from India to Europe by way of Persia and Arabia during the Crusades. Other scholars believe that a bowed instrument like the *crouth trithant*, mentioned in a sixth-century poem by Venantius Fortunatus, Bishop of Poitiers, had existed in Europe for many centuries before the Crusades. Whatever the lineage, both the *crouth* and the *ravanastron* are likely to have a common origin: Asia was the original home of both the Celtic and the Teutonic tribes, and it would be surprising if they had not brought with them to the West either bowed instruments themselves, or at least a recollection of their Asian prototypes.

Minstrels at a feast (fiddle, hurdy-gurdy, harp psaltery): from a thirteenth-century French Bible.

Below: Angels playing the crwth: detail from a stained glass window (1447) in Beauchamp Chapel, St. Mary's Church, Warwick.

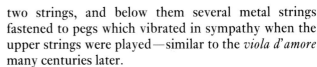

A modern Cretan rebec.

two strings, and below them several metal strings fastened to pegs which vibrated in sympathy when the upper strings were played—similar to the *viola d'amore* many centuries later.

The Arabian *rebab*, developed from the Persian *rebab* (see also p. 18), marked another important advance. Here we see, for the first time, a sound-box in the form of a rectangle or trapezoid, with sides corresponding to the ribs of the later lute. During the years following the Moorish invasion of Spain in the eighth century, the *rebab* became known in western Europe by the name of rebec; a further advance in design at this time was the addition of rosettes cut into the tapering end of the instrument's body, which served as sound-holes.

At the religious ceremonies of the Celtic tribes, the harp used to play an important role: tales of the Druids' skill in accompanying their songs on the harp have been handed down from generation to generation of Welshmen. But the Celts also revived another instrument of Asian origin, the *crouth* or *crwth*—which takes

Spanish rebecs: miniature from the thirteenth-century *Cantigas de Santa Maria.*

German *Minnesinger* with fiddle: from the *Mannessische Liederhandschrift, c.* 1320.

its name from the Greco-Roman lyre (called in Latin *testudo* and in Greek *chelys* = 'turtle'), originally constructed from a turtle-shell covered with skin, by way of the German *Rotta* (Old High German *Hrôta, Hrôtta* or *Chrotta* = 'turtle' or 'toad').

The *crouth* was a large rectangular covered frame fitted with strings, originally of rather awkward shape and difficult to handle. The shape was gradually modified: the sound-box became narrower, with more gently curved lines, reminiscent of the Greek lyre, and anticipating the medieval and Renaissance rebec. The most significant developments were a narrow neck, and—an entirely new feature—a bridge fixed to the body, whose fitting necessitated the addition of two round holes cut in the belly on either side of the strings, as a function of the design and also to allow access for the maker's tools. The most remarkable feature of this bridge was the unequal height of its feet: the left foot under the lower strings was short and rested on the belly, while the foot under the high string was as high as the ribs,

passing through the right sound-hole and resting on the back of the instrument.* The *crouth*'s bridge, therefore, can be seen as the prototype of the soundpost of our modern string instruments (see family tree on pp. 22–23, and further on p. 35).

The Teutonic tribes of northern Europe had also taken over the *crouth*—possibly even before the Celtic tribes of Scotland, Wales and Ireland, or (as another legend has it) after the Celtic missionary Winfried Gallus, who converted many of the Teutons to Christianity, had introduced them to the instrument by bringing Celtic harpists and *crouth*-fiddlers with him to the continent. One later invention of definitely Teutonic origin, however, and an intriguing distant cousin to the violin,

*A rebec of the kind still played in Greece today (see opposite) shows this same bridge design. Acoustically it makes sense: the lower strings resonate on the relatively supple belly, while the tones of the high string are reinforced by the much more rigid back.

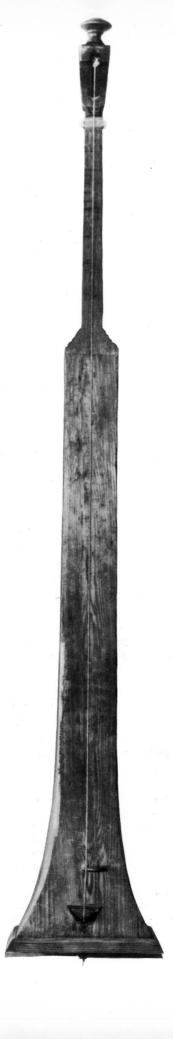

was the *Trumscheit*, a bowed elaboration of the Greek monochord.

In its original fifteenth-century form, the *Trumscheit* (or 'drum wood') had an elongated body with ribs, formed like a trapezoid, with a narrow neck and a single string stretched over a 'drum bridge'—a tiny 'shoe' whose heel was fixed to the belly of the instrument with a tack. The string rested on that point of the bridge corresponding to the uppermost back of the shoe, and the pressure of the string on the bridge as a result was so strong that it vibrated as the string was bowed, producing a kind of drum-roll on the soundboard. The sound was not unlike a trumpet's: by pressing the finger gently on the string while bowing—in rather the same way the modern violinist plays harmonics—a shrill, penetrating flageolet-like note could be produced. The *Trumscheit* came to be called '*tromba marina*' or '*trompette marine*' in Italy and France, and 'marine trumpet' in England. Another name was 'nuns' trumpet', since for many years, even until the late nineteenth century, it was used as a substitute for the trumpet in convents (the puzzling 'marine' may derive from a corruption of 'Mary' or 'Maria': there is no evidence that the *Trumscheit* was ever put to nautical use). Berlioz, writing in 1859, called it 'a triton's conch, capable of frightening asses', reflecting the general nineteenth-century view; but in earlier centuries, a surprising number of composers, including J.-B. Lully and Alessandro Scarlatti, had used it for special effects in their scoring, especially in theatrical works.

The string-instrument family, and therefore the ancestors of the violin, whether close cousins or distant relatives, are so numerous that they cannot possibly all be mentioned here. But one other is worth special note, since it is the only string instrument that was both a close relative of the violin and yet played without a bow. The hurdy-gurdy (*Leier*, *Radeleier* or *Bettlerleier* in German, *vielle à roue* in France) was of Eastern origin, finding its way to Europe early in the Middle Ages through Byzantium and Muslim Spain. It had a body with ribs similar to that of the primitive medieval fiddle (see below)—but its three strings were stretched not across a bridge but across a wooden, sometimes leather-covered, resin-coated wheel. Fitted to the 'neck' was a keyboard with tangents which stopped the string or strings when they were depressed (some instruments also had the notes of the scale marked on the keyboard, a practice later adopted by members of the lute family, but found here for the first time).

Hurdy-gurdies came in all sizes: small enough to be carried around the player's neck on a cord, or so large

Boy playing a *viola da gamba*: chalk drawing (once attributed to Carracci) by Bartolommeo Cesi (1556–1629).

(the *organistrum* hurdy-gurdy used in cloisters and monastic schools) that two or more people were needed to hold them. The mechanical sophistication of the hurdy-gurdy was such that only the most rudimentary instruction was needed to produce a recognizable tune: by the fifteenth century it was a familiar sight at every level of European society, played by court musicians at the palace, and by minstrels and beggars on the village green. Its popularity was long-lasting: Haydn, Mozart and Donizetti used it occasionally, and beggars' monkeys continued to dance to its strains well into the nineteenth century; the sound can still be heard today, especially in certain regions of northern France. Every age will have had its hurdy-gurdy virtuosos. But from the Middle Ages onwards the real virtuosos of the easily

portable, sound-sustaining string-box used a bow: and their instrument was the fiddle.

The word 'fiddle' (and its many associated forms: see p. 18) is perhaps the most loosely defined and confusing in the whole of our story, since it has been used at one time or another to describe almost every kind of string instrument under the sun. One of the earliest references, by the ninth-century German poet Otfried von Weissenburg, for example, refers to the '*fidula*' as a plucked instrument; but by and large, during the Middle Ages and Renaissance, writers used it either as a generic term for all bowed instruments, signifying anything from 'bowed lute'* to rebec to *crouth* to viol—a practice which continued even after the birth of the violin itself, thus compounding the confusion—or more specifically for what is termed today the 'medieval fiddle', a bowed instrument, usually rectangular or oval, with anything from three to six strings, one of them sometimes a drone-string, with or without frets on its fingerboard, and played as a rule high on the body, against the chest or on the collar-bone.

This was the instrument of the *Minnesänger*, minstrels and troubadours: the *Fiedel* or *Geige* in Germany, the *fidel* in England, the *fele* in Scandinavia, the *vielle à archet* in France. It was lightweight and portable, and so travelled easily; its bright tones could lend extra colour to special church occasions, and to dramas both liturgical and secular; together with the shawms and trumpets, it was the characteristic instrument of feasts and dancing.

In late fifteenth-century Italy, important developments in fiddle design took place which did not spread far at the time: the fiddle with a drone-string developed into the *lira da braccio*, while the droneless type with indented sides can be seen as one of the immediate precursors of the violin itself. In northern Europe, however, the medieval fiddle continued longer in use, until it was eventually overshadowed by the Renaissance viol, a very different type of instrument that was also played with a bow.

*'Lute' is yet another word plagued by unstable meaning. In its modern Western sense it denotes a plucked instrument with a flat belly of elongated oval shape and a deeply curved back, a fingerboard turned backwards at the tuning pegs at an angle of nearly 90 degrees, and as many as fourteen double strings. Its origins are Arabic (the name comes from the instrument known as the *ūd*, which means, literally, 'wood'), and it flourished in Europe in many different forms from the Middle Ages until the eighteenth century. The word has also consistently had a wider generic sense, the source of much confusion, covering a wide range of instruments. In this broad sense, the Indian *sitar*, the Japanese *shamisen*, the Syrian *ūd*, the ukelele, banjo and guitar are all 'plucked lutes'; the Indian *sarangi*, the Chinese *ching-hu*, as well as the lyre, rebec, viol and violin, are all 'bowed lutes'.

Although in the broadest sense it belongs to the same family, combining characteristics of the pear-shaped rebec and the medieval waisted fiddle (both of which are closely related to the violin), the viol is a distinct new development, and establishes a family branch of its own. It is more unlike the violin than any of its cousins: it has a fingerboard with frets (as compared with the violin's smooth fingerboard); a flat (as opposed to a slightly convex) back; narrower, more sloping shoulders; it is strung with between five and seven strings. More fundamental still, the viols revived the ancient playing position of 'a gamba' ('at the leg')— either on the lap or knees, between the knees, or for the larger viols, on a stool or on the floor.

During the late fifteenth century, the viol design quickly spread from the Iberian peninsula (where it originated is not known: but the *a gamba* position, which had disappeared from the rest of Europe, survived in Spain throughout the fourteenth and fifteenth centuries) through the Balearic islands and Sardinia to Italy, and from there to the rest of Europe, reaching England and France during the early 1500s. And the introduction of the viol also marks this prologue's turning point: for it was just at this time that an unknown Italian genius, somewhere near Milan, conceived and built the first violin.

No one knows the name of that Lombard genius—if indeed he was a single person, and if it was in Lombardy that he produced his new design. (There are references to the violin in France and Poland between 1529 and 1545, but the main weight of evidence points to northern Italy as its birthplace.*) We can only say with certainty that by about 1550 the four-string ('true') violin must have been a familiar part of the European musical scene, since the instrument and its tuning were described in detail by Philibert Jambé de Fer in his *Epitome musical* of 1556 (see p. 17). We also know that a three-string violin, tuned to the pitches of the lower three strings of the true violin, had preceded it by about a generation, for such an instrument appeared in north Italian paintings between 1508 and 1530. It is most likely that the other members of the violin family (viola, cello) made their appearance at the same time—a fresco of Gaudenzio Ferrari of 1535, for example, shows the three-string violin and viola with a cello (whose strings cannot be distinguished) together as a family; and Jambe de Fer's treatise also describes a parallel four-string family.

Opposite: The first known representation of the complete violin family (violin, left; cello, centre; viola, right): detail of a fresco (*c.* 1535) by Gaudenzio Ferrari in the cupola of Santa Maria delle Grazie, Saronno.

Below: The earliest known picture of a violin: detail of a fresco (1505–8) by Garofalo in the Sala del Tesoro, Palazzo di Ludovico il Moro, Ferrara.

One more side-glance is relevant. (Readers who care nothing about terminology, and less about etymologies, should proceed directly to page 17, where the pre-history of the violin is recounted briefly, and where the instrument itself is brought to life by a violin maker's hands.) Almost as baffling as the origins of the violin are the many different words used in different countries and at different periods to denote it. Around the year 1500, for example, the word *viola* did not mean 'alto violin' as it does today, but rather (in accord with its derivation) a bowed instrument of any kind, or more specifically a Renaissance fiddle. After the emergence of the violin around 1520, however, the word *viola* was used to denote an instrument of either the viol or the violin families; and when the Italian writer sought to distinguish the two, he used the same word with different qualifiers. Thus *viola da gamba* ('leg viola') referred to the viol family, and *viola da braccio* ('arm viola') referred to the violin family—particular members within each family being further designated by terms like 'soprano' or 'alto'. *Soprano di viola da braccio* would therefore have meant 'soprano arm viola', or violin.

The eventual emergence of the single, unambiguous Italian word '*violino*' ('little *viola*'), first recorded in 1538, was an obvious step; and by the 1550s, to the exquisite relief of later musicologists and historians, it had established itself everywhere in Europe to denote, finally and irrevocably, the violin. But there had to be a catch. '*Violino*' and its associated forms became quickly established *nearly* everywhere in Europe—except in France. In France alone, a special word arose, nearly the same, but crucially, puzzlingly different. '*Violino*' meant 'little *viola*' = violin; but on the face of it, the French form '*vyollon*' or '*violon*' seemed to have been formed not from this diminutive but, on the contrary, by adding the augmentative '-*on*' or '-*one*', as if it had come from the Italian '*violone*' ('large *viola*'). By one of the quirkier paradoxes of musical linguistic history, in fact it had.

The paradox is best explained by remembering that in Italy at this time, in the early 1500s, the augmentative word *violone* ('large *viola*') was used to denote the class of viols as a whole; while the later (1538) diminutive

*The first known documentary reference to the violin, in an official record of the General Treasury of Savoy, records a payment of 6 *scudi* on 17 December 1523 for the services of '*trompettes et vyollons de Verceil*' (the French name for Vercelli, a Piedmont town under Savoy rule about forty miles west of Milan).

term *violino* ('small *viola*' = violin) had not yet appeared in general use.* In the treatise from which the quotation at the head of the next chapter is taken, Jambe de Fer said that one of the earliest Italian names for the violin, in addition to the term '*viola da braccio*' just mentioned, was also '*violone da braccio*'—and this joining of '*da braccio*' to '*violone*', just as to '*viola*', would certainly have been a useful and likely way for the Italians in the early 1500s to have distinguished the new violin played 'on the arm' from the plain viol-family *violone* played 'at the leg'.

The French at that time, however, were the political rulers of northern Italy, and French was the official language of Savoy and Piedmont. When the French chroniclers of those regions came to describe the new violins, they merely adopted the Italian '*violone da braccio*'; but since there was already a French word ('*viole*') in common usage for the viol, they had no use for the distinction provided by '*da braccio*' and '*da gamba*', and the '*da braccio*' was dropped as redundant—leaving '*violon(e)*' to mean 'violin'.

The one word with a secure meaning from the start is '*violino*', which was always used in Italy to denote an instrument of the violin family—almost always the true violin, only occasionally the alto violin (or modern viola). After the middle of the sixteenth century, the terminology of the instrument became stable: '*violino*' was constant in Italy, '*violin*' in England, '*violon*' in France, and '*Violine*' or '*Geige*' in Germany (speculation about the derivation of '*Geige*' could fill another chapter on its own). '*Violetta*', at first a little viol, briefly used in Italy as a synonym for *violino*, came to mean 'alto violin', or viola, before its use died out in the nineteenth century.

And so we have reached the violin: magnificent child of the *lira da braccio*, the rebec and the fiddle. We look back today on a tradition of more than four centuries, during which, among bowed instruments, the violin has reigned supreme—as soloist, chamber player, and lifeblood of the orchestra. Its appearance is deceptively simple: behind that familiar, functional shape lies a story, told in the following pages, of some eighty separate pieces of wood, each one fashioned individually and assembled to form what is acoustically the most com-

plex, the most responsive and 'alive', of all musical instruments. In complexity of sound, indeed, and in emotional appeal, the violin's only rival is its model, the human voice. But in its ability to sustain a tone, unbroken, coloured by so many nuances of expression and intensity, the violin is unrivalled. That is the secret of its versatility—the very range of mood and effect that this little instrument, tucked under the chin, can summon, from the most strident and dramatic to the exquisitely lyrical and tender. And that is why no other, even the chameleon piano, can boast of so large, important and varied a repertory—if all forms of solo, chamber and concerted music for the violin are taken into account.

It is right that the final focus of a prologue should shift from the past to the present, and that its last words should be those of one of our own age's great violinists, Yehudi Menuhin, writing of the instrument he holds:

The handling and playing of a violin is a process of caress and evocation, of drawing out a sound which awaits the hands of the master. It is enticing and fascinating, passive if you wish, but ready to respond at the slightest touch. A beautiful violin contains that infinite potential—of sound, flexibility, colour, intonation, pitch and volume—which awaits the music and the musician . . .

Paradoxically, however, tactile contact with the violin is strictly limited. There is the delicate contact between the chin and the chin-rest; between the collar-bone and the lower violin edge; and between the thumb and finger of the left hand and the neck (except when the hand rises to the higher positions well above the neck). But otherwise contact is restricted to the working surface of the fingerboard, and it is on this that the violinist spends his lifetime of concentration. There are no visible mileposts and, blindly but surely, he must discover in this field of action, limited in space, the infinite scope which mastery reveals. Accuracy of placement of fingers, accuracy of touch and vibration, accuracy of each motion, vertical or horizontal or sideways, rolling or oscillating—these are the means with which he can express the whole gamut of human emotion and evoke the response of his audience wherever they may be . . .

With his right hand he must develop an equally sensitive feel for the stick, for its weight and resistance, for the quality of the sound which each type of motion achieves—whether the bow is floating or exerting its weight and pressure, whether his hold is loose or gripping, and whether the bow, within its narrow range, moves farther from or closer to bridge or fingerboard . . . This power to dominate the realms of space comes from the triumph of subtlety and degree. The strength of a violinist's performance, his attack and incisiveness, are derived in the first place from the delicacy of his sensation. If he can develop an awareness of the millionth of a grain rather than of an ounce, of an ounce rather than of a pound, he is on the way to becoming a violinist.

---

*The point is therefore not just a minor etymological one, since the French *violon* (= violin) is so easily confused with the Italian *violon(e)* (= viol). The similarity has been a source of misunderstanding for centuries. Even in the nineteenth century, the distinguished scholar François-Joseph Fétis, for example, misled a whole generation of researchers by mistranslating from an early sixteenth-century treatise the Italian term *violoni* (= viols) as *violons* (= violins).

The Anatomy of the Violin

We call viols those with which Gentlemen, merchants and other virtuous people pass their time . . . The other type is called violin; it is commonly used for dancing . . . I have not illustrated the said violin because you can think of it as resembling the viol, added to which there are few persons who use it save those who make a living from it through their labour.

Philibert Jambe de Fer, Epitome musical des tons, sons et accordz, es voix humaines, fleustes d'Alleman, fleustes à neuf trous, violes, & violons. Lyons, 1556

Previous page: 'Musica' from the cycle of frescoes (1492–
c. 1495) in the Sala delle Arti Liberali, Borgia Apartments,
Vatican, by Bernardino Pinturicchio.

Origins

In the sixteenth century the violin was barely respect-
able, regarded as the common instrument of dance
music and for the most part played by 'professional'
musicians who had the social status of servants. It was
not until after 1600 that the violin properly achieved
its modern stature as the most perfect of all bowed
instruments. Its exact historical origins remain unclear,
and there is still lively argument among the many
researchers who have attempted to trace them. In this
respect this chapter will confine itself to a brief
description of the families of instruments which could
be considered as ancestors of the violin.

There is one theory that the first bowed instrument
was the Indian *ravanastron*: a two-stringed instrument
consisting of a cylinder of hollow wood with a piece of
snake-skin stretched over one of the openings on which
rested a bridge. The two strings were tuned a fifth apart.
Its invention is attributed to Ravanon, king of Ceylon,
who ruled in the third millennium B.C. The descendants
of the *ravanastron* appeared in Europe during the
Crusades, coming from India by way of Persia and
Arabia. Another theory suggests that a plucked or
bowed instrument existed in northern Europe long
before the crusades, variously known as *crot*, *cruit* or
crouth, which had anything from two to six strings and
a smooth, unfretted fingerboard and from which later
developed the Welsh lyre-like *crwth* (and later still the
Irish *timpán* frame harp).

Very little at all is known about the development of
the instrument between these very early examples and
the fourteenth century—at which time we find various
types of instrument which can be considered the most
probable recent ancestors of the violin: the rebec, also
called *rybybe*, *rebab*, *rubeba* or *ribeca*, which had a
smooth fingerboard over which were stretched three
strings tuned in fifths; and the fiddles (generally with
three strings, but in certain regions with four, five, or
six) variously named *ficula*, *fidel*, *fithele*, *fideile*, *phidil*,
fele, *viddle*, *vièle*, *vielle*, *viula* and *vihuela*—broad terms
used from the middle ages onwards to describe either
(especially before 1300) any kind of string instrument,
or more specifically (the meaning intended here) a
bowed instrument, usually rectangular or oval,
sometimes with a fretted fingerboard, and normally held
high on the body, against the chest or on the collar-bone.

The family tree on pp. 22–23 shows how the bowed
instrument families of both violins and viols (for viols,
see pp. 13–14) might have developed, but controversy
will always rage among scholars as to which instrument
has most influenced the development of which family.

My own, possibly oversimplified but realistic judgement is that these primitive instruments were really only
different aspects of one large family—the differences
being mostly regional and aesthetic rather than musical.
Certainly they all produced the same type of sound, and
were used at different periods and in different regions
interchangeably to play the same types of music.

The earliest fiddles were usually made by cutting the
body, neck and pegbox from a single plank of wood
and then scooping out the inside of the body. By the
fifteenth century this method of construction had been
replaced by sawing out the body, leaving only the sides,
and then applying a flat top and bottom whose edges
overlapped the sides. The shape of the body could be
either rectangular or oval.

Evolving from the fifteenth-century fiddle came the
lira da braccio, which had six or seven strings, an arched
top and back, and a shape more closely resembling that
of the violin, with an upper and lower bout and deep
indentations at the waist ('middle bouts') to make room
for the tilt of the bow. The *lira da braccio* also had a
soundpost set inside the hollow body between the top
and back which served to increase the volume of sound
the instrument could make, and also to help the
structure support a heavier tension on the strings. A
combination of features of the *rebec*, *fidel* and *lira da
braccio* leads us directly to the violin.

Not only is its ancestry unclear, but it is also uncertain
who invented the first violin. It is not known, for example, whether in fact the first violins were viola-sized
instruments like their immediate ancestor the *viola da
braccio*, or whether perhaps (as is more likely) the whole
family of violins—violin, viola and cello—emerged at
the same time. Although the violin family as we now
know it lacks a true tenor member, it is clear that a tenor
viola did once exist: Monteverdi specified its use, and
several examples of a *tenore* exist in museums today, but
the instrument was apparently awkward to hold and to
play and so became extinct. The double bass does not
strictly belong to the violin family at all, but is a
degraded form of the *violone* (in its sixteenth-century
Italian meaning: see p. 15), a member of the family of
viols.

Brescia and Cremona appear to have been the first
important centres of violin making, and Andrea Amati
(*c*.1511–80), Giovan Giacobo dalla Corna (*c*.1484–
c.1550) and Zanetto da Montichiaro (*c*.1488–*c*.1565) are
three makers among several who have been credited as
the 'inventors' of the instrument. The earliest known
documentary evidence* of the existence of a violin

*See footnote on p. 15.

proper, however, is dated 1523, which is before Amati's professional career began. So it is safer to consider Amati as no more than the first famous maker.

The anatomy of the violin in its modern orchestral form has remained virtually unchanged since about 1830, at which time most of the original violins of the 'Golden Age' of violin making from 1690 to 1750, including virtually all of the great eighteenth-century instruments, were rebuilt to meet the demands of the composers and players of the day for a much greater volume of sound and a greatly extended treble compass. Between 1830 and 1860 such specialist craftsmen as Jean-Baptiste Vuillaume in Paris and the Hills in London took apart and literally rebuilt almost every instrument in existence which was considered to be worth the trouble.**

The illustration on pp. 20–21 shows the components of the modern violin. The following table shows a summary of the alterations which were made in the early nineteenth century to change the violin from its original to its modern form.

Table of Approximate Measurements

	Original	'Modern' adaptation
Length of neck	125 mm	132 mm
Width of neck at nut	25 mm	24 mm
Width of neck at body	34 mm	33 mm
Back angle of neck	0–2°	5–7°
Length of fingerboard	220–240 mm	270 mm
Thickness of bass bar	4.5 mm	5.5 mm
Bass bar height at bridge	7 mm	10 mm
Length of bass bar	240 mm	270–80 mm
Diameter of soundpost	4.1 mm	6.5 mm
Height of bridge	27–28 mm	32–34 mm

(The curvature of bridge and fingerboard increased)

The *neck* was lengthened and reset into the violin at a steeper angle to give a more comfortable holding position; and the *fingerboard* was lengthened, thus extending the compass of stopped (i.e. not harmonic) notes up to a^4 (the top A of the modern piano). The *bridge* was set a little higher with more curvature both on the top of the bridge and on the fingerboard (this actually made triple-stopping more difficult and for the first time

**It was Vuillaume who rebuilt the 'Messiah' (see illustration on p. 45) and the 'Lady Blunt' Stradivarius violins. With a true craftsman's instinct and foresight, he preserved the original bass bars and necks (the original neck of the 'Lady Blunt' was sold in 1979 together with the instrument; the 'Messiah' is displayed, with its original bass bar beside it, in the Ashmolean Museum, Oxford).

forced players to arpeggiate three-note chords). The *bass bar* was lengthened, and its height under the bridge increased, primarily in order to withstand the greater pressure of modern strings. The *soundpost* was also increased in diameter, which not only gave more strength to the violin belly but a more robust tone over the whole range.

The differences between the original or Baroque and the modern violin are best visually demonstrated in profile drawing (fig. 2). Note the very thick wedge-shaped neck of the Baroque instrument, which although clumsy in appearance, considering that the violin was supported on the collar bone of the player without the aid of chin or shoulder rest, allowed him to shift position with relative ease without dropping his instrument.

The fingerboard needed to be only as long as the compass of the music of the day dictated. There was therefore a gradual progression from the earliest violins with absolutely straight necks and short fingerboards through the 'transitional' violins of the late eighteenth century, whose necks and longer fingerboards tilted back slightly, perhaps 2 or 3 degrees from the horizontal, so as better to accommodate the music of the Classical period, to the modern instrument with its neck tilted at an angle of about 5–7 degrees. The very high positions of the modern fingerboard also required that the neck should be of even thickness as far up the violin as possible, so that the left hand could move up the fingerboard in a straight line.

I know of only one surviving original soundpost, discovered in an unaltered violin in the Paris Conservatoire. It had dropped and fallen to the end-block of the violin and attached itself to a lump of glue which must have been soft at the time. The diameter was 4.1 mm. Compared to the thickness of 6.5 mm (at least) of the modern post, this seems to be very thin. The stringing of early violins (see p. 37 *et seq.*), however, was so much lighter than that of the modern violin that the body was quite adequate to withstand the tension applied to it.

The relatively straight neck and wedged fingerboard of the Baroque violin also meant a lower bridge height than that of the modern instrument. There is no standard height for an original bridge as this was dependent on both the thickness of the fingerboard wedge and the height of the arching of the top (belly) of the violin. The earliest violins tended to have very high arches. It was Stradivarius who started the trend towards the flatter-bellied violins—thus achieving a broader and larger sound, although sacrificing at the same time some of the sweetness of tone found in the

The modern violin

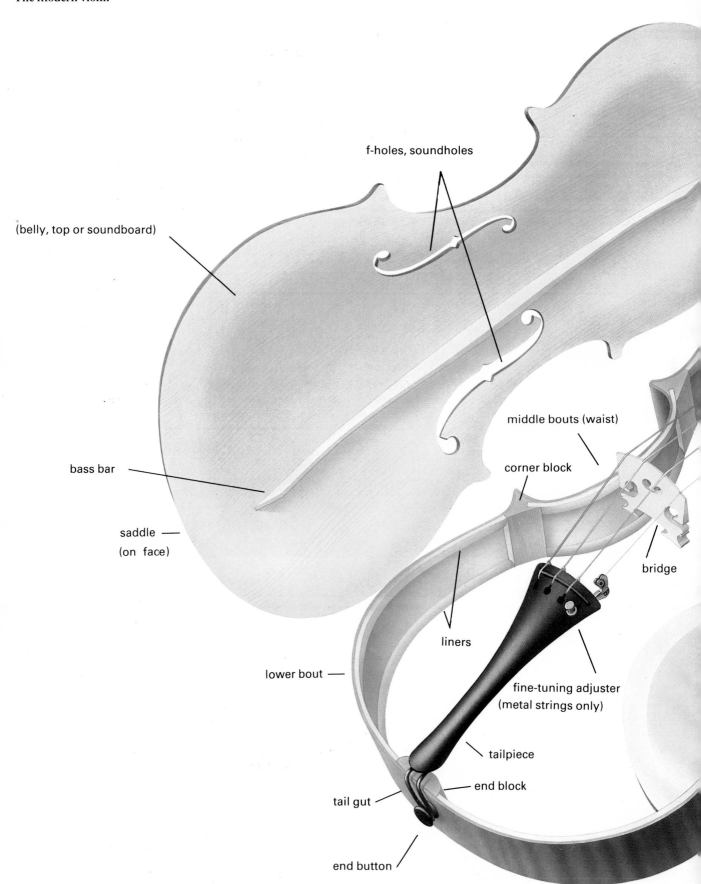

f-holes, soundholes

(belly, top or soundboard)

bass bar

saddle —
(on face)

middle bouts (waist)

corner block

bridge

liners

lower bout —

fine-tuning adjuster
(metal strings only)

tailpiece

end block

tail gut

end button

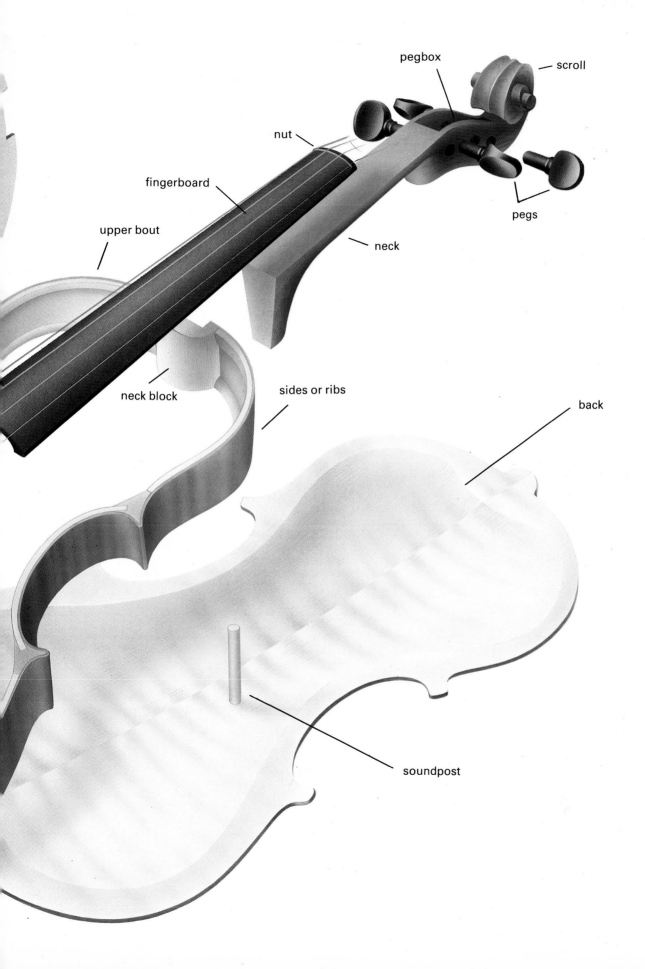

pegbox

scroll

nut

fingerboard

upper bout

neck

pegs

neck block

sides or ribs

back

soundpost

Family tree, showing the lines of development of the viol and violin families.

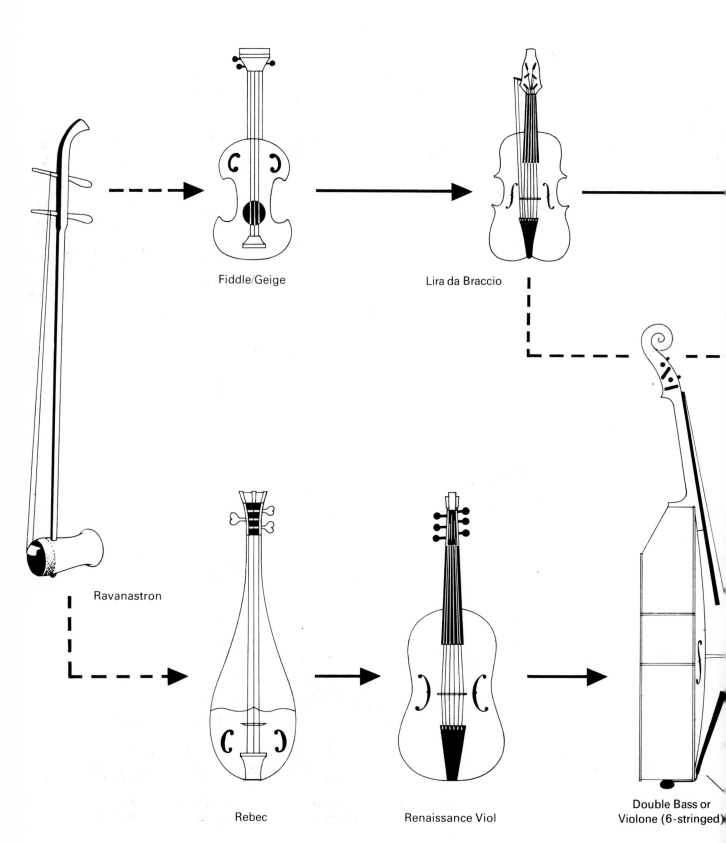

Fiddle/Geige

Lira da Braccio

Ravanastron

Rebec

Renaissance Viol

Double Bass or
Violone (6-stringed)

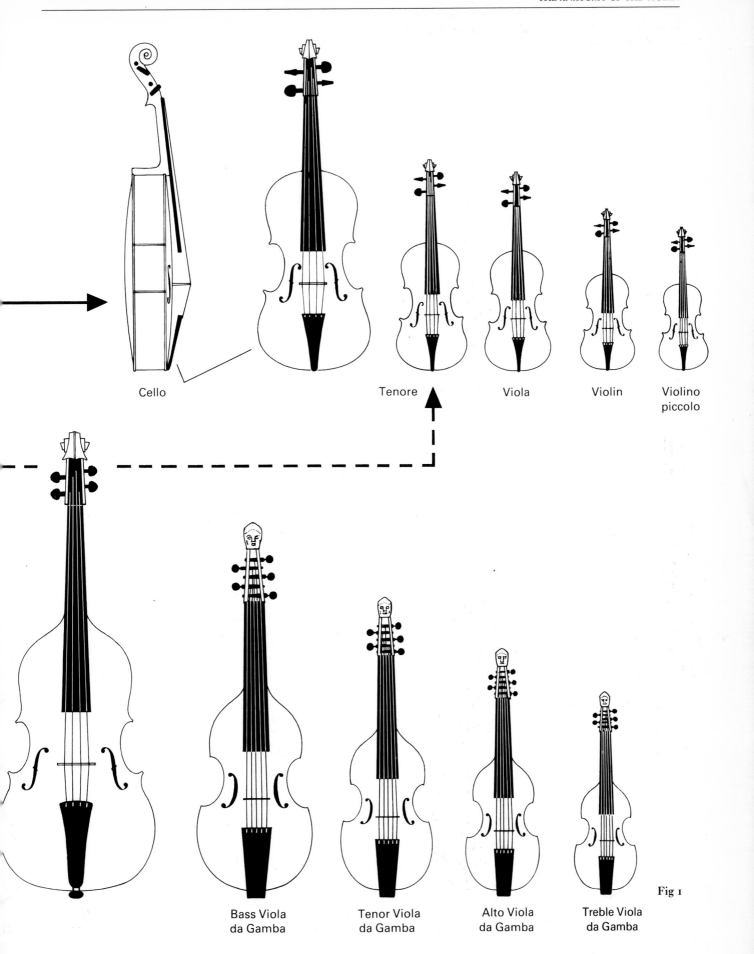

Cello

Tenore

Viola

Violin

Violino piccolo

Bass Viola da Gamba

Tenor Viola da Gamba

Alto Viola da Gamba

Treble Viola da Gamba

Fig 1

Comparative set-ups of the Baroque (above) and the modern (below) violin.

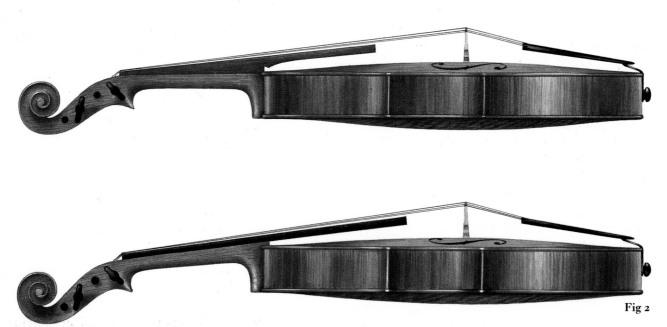

Fig 2

high-arched instruments of Nicolo Amati, Jacob Stainer and others.

The bass bar serves not only to support the sound-board (belly) under the bridge but also to conduct sound transmitted through the bridge along the length of the instrument. There was no standard height and length for a bass bar; each maker had his own idea of the optimum dimensions. German violins, with their higher arching curves, tended to have smaller bass bars in all dimensions than the Italian. The development of modern high-tension stringing made it necessary to strengthen this component, so that bass bars today are of more or less standard size.

The Set-up

All the preceding details of string-tension, height of bridge and size of soundpost come under the general term of the *set-up* of the violin. Given a perfectly-made violin, an even slightly imperfect set-up can result in the instrument simply not sounding or working at its best. Each musical period requires a different and quite critical set-up of its own, or the balance of the instrument becomes disturbed. As well as the set-up for the music there is the set-up for the instrument: extremely small changes in the position of a soundpost, for example, can make very great differences to the way in which an instrument responds. The dimensions of the bridge, its thickness, and the hardness of the wood selected all make quite audible tonal differences to the sound of the instrument. The type of strings used, and the height at which those strings lie above the fingerboard, will affect not only the player's comfort when handling the instrument but also his ability to play in tune on all parts of the fingerboard. Setting up a violin, therefore, requires a very fine appreciation of the nuances of tone appropriate to the individual musical expression of the player.

It must be pointed out that the changes which the violin underwent between 1570 and 1830 should not be called 'improvements'. The violin was designed and modified to suit the requirements of the music of its day. Seventeenth- and eighteenth-century music was written for combinations of instruments which were all required to form a perfect blend with one another. The harpsichord was as much at a disadvantage in ensemble with a pianoforte as the Baroque violin would be today playing in the string section of a modern symphony orchestra. The converse also applies: the modern violin is far too dominant when played with the harpsichord, and a harpsichord cannot even be heard above a modern cello. The musical punctuation of Baroque music is much easier to express with an original instrument, and dynamic relationships automatically become more natural. So perhaps the two forms of the violin, old and new, have become virtually different instruments which are not interchangeable in their proper contexts.

The Woods

The woods used in the making of the violin are with only very few exceptions the same throughout all the various schools of violin making. The *soundboard* (also called *top* or *belly*) is made of pine, spruce or fir

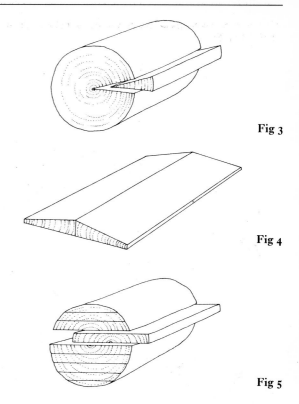

Fig 3

Fig 4

Fig 5

(commonly *Pinus sylvestris*, *Picea excelsa*, and *Abies pectinata*), and is almost invariably made from two pieces perfectly matched and joined in the centre. The *back* is made of maple (*Acer platanoides*) usually from Switzerland, Bohemia or Hungary, or of sycamore, often from Scotland. It can be highly figured or completely plain, sometimes in one piece, most often in two. The *sides* (ribs) are made from maple or sycamore to match the back, and are best reserved from the same piece of wood.

Neck	maple or sycamore
Fingerboard	ebony
Bridge	Bosnian maple
Pegs	rosewood, boxwood or ebony
Bass bar	spruce or pine
Soundpost	spruce or pine
Purfling	ebony–maple–ebony, laminated in three alternate strips (modern makers often use fibre)
Blocks and Liners	willow, spruce or pine
Saddle and Nut	ebony

Of the above components the nature of the wood used in the soundboard (belly), back and ribs is of specially critical importance to the sound and quality of the instrument. The pine trees must grow at very high altitudes about 2500 metres above sea level and in a soil which does not encourage rapid growth. The average age of a tree suitable for instrument making is 200 years. The ideal spacing of the annular rings is between 1 and 2 mm, which would produce a tree a little less than one metre in diameter. The trees must be cut in winter when the sap is no longer rising and, once felled, cross-cut into butts of various lengths depending on whether the wood is to be used to make a cello or a violin. The wider-grained wood closer to the root where the trunk might be about 1.2 metres in diameter is most suitable for the bass instruments, while wood nearer to the top is suitable for the violin.

After felling, the butts are cleaved into 'quarters', and only if the butts have split perfectly straight and true is the wood worth any further consideration. The annular rings, which show as hard red lines, consist of impacted resin and are the summer growth of the trees, whereas the softer white area between the rings is winter carbohydrate growth. It is these impacted resin lines which conduct the sound along the soundboard, and for this reason selection should be for a good strong resin line in the wood. The carbohydrate growth acts as a damper and helps to control the acoustic behaviour of the soundboard.

Since the days of factory production, violin wood has often been mechanically sawn, but in the golden age it was, as it is still today by the most discriminating makers, always split by hand radially into wedges. This process is known as quartering (fig. 3). Perfectly quartered wood has more rigidity and strength than wood sawn even slightly away from the quarter. The maker is always seeking for minimum thickness without loss of strength, which provides greater control when he decides on the final thickness required to achieve his tonal aims.

The back of the violin acts more as a reflector than a resonating board. For this reason density becomes the most important factor in selection. Highly figured maple produces a beautiful looking violin, but does not necessarily guarantee the production of a fine sound. Plain wood was often used by all the great makers in the past. For both back and belly the process of quartering the timber is the same. Once the wood is split into a wedge, and if a single wedge is not large enough to form a back, it must be divided again along the length to provide two equal wedges which when opened out like a book are joined together (see fig. 4). It is also acceptable and often preferred for flat-cut backs (fig. 5) to be used in one piece. When this flat method of cutting is used, the resultant wood is more flexible, since the annular rings (its chief strengthening component) will be lying sideways. Makers invariably compensate for this lack of ultimate rigidity by leaving flat-sawn backs a little thicker. Quartered backs in one single piece are very beautiful and preferred by many makers: the maple tree in particular often grows to very large diameters and a wide quartered section is not difficult to obtain.

The wedges should then be left for at least five years to dry. Nowadays the drying process is sometimes hurried by the use of the kiln—an entirely unsatisfactory compromise, because such fast dehydration of the timber cannot be matched by the equally necessary, but slow, oxidation of the resins within the wood. Wood dried in this way absorbs moisture at an exaggerated rate once the wood has been removed from the kiln. The working texture of the fibres in the wood also changes and its strength is affected. Some makers believe that the use of very old wood, dried for fifty years or more, is ideal. My own observation is that such wood is usually too dry and brittle, and loses some essential properties of elasticity; the resulting instruments seem to be temperamental in their behaviour, excessively responsive to small changes in climate and humidity.

The ribs (sides) of the violin are best taken from excess maple on the back, but can come from another section of the tree provided that the character of the grain matches the back. The neck comes from a block of matching maple large enough to accommodate the dimensions of the beautiful *scroll* head and curved *pegbox* which will be carved out of it. The modern violin fingerboard is of solid ebony which wears well under the pressure of metal strings. The fingerboard of the Baroque violin was shorter and much lighter, usually made of maple wood covered by a thin veneer of ebony. The tailpiece was often treated in a similar manner.

The Construction (Cremonese Method)

The size of the violin had become virtually standardized by the end of the seventeenth century, and although there were some experiments with larger models (for example, Amati's 'Grand' model and Stradivari's long model), by about 1700 most makers had settled on the following measurements:

Length of body	355 mm
Depth of ribs	28–30 mm average
Width at upper bout	170 mm
Width at waist	112 mm
With at lower bout	208 mm

Variations in size between makers from the seventeenth century to the present day mostly relate to the type and configuration of the arching soundboard (belly) and back, and the depth of the ribs, thus affecting the internal air space and dynamics of the function of the soundboard as a vibrating plate. The highly arched instruments of the early Amatis, for example, and those of Jacob Stainer of Absam had an exceptional tonal sweetness and a very soprano top-string sound. The flat-arched instruments of Antonio Stradivari and Giuseppe Guarneri (nicknamed 'del Gesù') had a more robust sound and a broader bass tone than the higher-arched earlier models.

The maker must first decide on the kind of instrument he wishes to make, and then proceed to make drawings and patterns of its shape. Like all members of its family, the violin is made with the aid of a *mould* or *form*. Many of Stradivari's own forms, which were made from hard woods, have survived and are housed today in the Civic Museum in Cremona, together with many of his original templates, drawings and tools.

The mould used in Italy was invariably of the solid inside type, although other schools and makers have used other methods (for example, building on a flat board of wood on which the outline has been drawn or on an outside fitting mould). Because so much survives from the original workshop of the great maker Antonio Stradivari (1644?–1737, also commonly known by the Latinized form of his name, Stradivarius), I intend to illustrate the Italian method.

By this method, the inside mould was cut to the exact shape of the inside of the violin with recesses cut out to receive the corner blocks, end block and neck block, and strategically placed holes were drilled into the mould to allow some form of clamping to be applied. The mould is usually made up in two layers which together amount to the exact height of the ribs; one layer, much narrower than the other, can then be removed when the back liners are due to be glued in place. If the mould is made in one piece, its thickness is about two-thirds the height of the ribs.

The corner and end *blocks* must now be temporarily attached to the mould with a spot of glue and shaped to continue the line of the mould and to provide the exact configuration for the ends and corners of the instrument. The blocks are usually made from willow, although spruce or pine is also used.

The *ribs* are planed to an even thickness of approximately 1.8 mm by using a toothed plane—the toothing marks being continually removed with a metal or glass scraper. This kind of planing is necessary when figured wood is used, because the figure can only be satisfactorily planed with a conventional blade with motions *across* the grain. The ribs of the violin, however, are too narrow to allow such cross-grain planing. The ribs are then bent over a very hot iron, having first been dampened either by immersion in warm water or by means of a damp cloth on the bending iron. The tight

A Stradivarius mould.

Thickness gauges (top) and purfling cutters (below) from Stradivari's workshop.

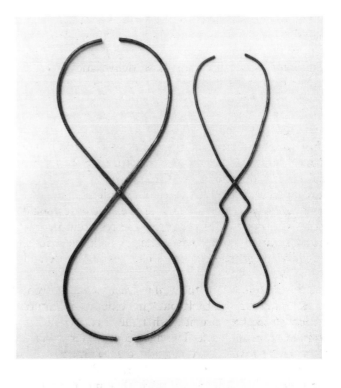

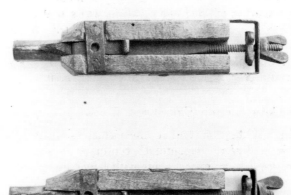

curves of the waist are very difficult to bend without breaking: the heavier the figure in the wood, the more difficult they are to bend. To facilitate this a very flexible piece of steel or a canvas strap is used, the ribs being sandwiched between the bending strap and the bending iron itself. Particular care must be taken throughout the bending process not to scorch the wood. Once all the sections of the ribs have been accurately bent, they can be attached to the mould and glued firmly onto the blocks.

At this time the *neck* and *scroll* must be prepared. This is accomplished in separate stages, and it is important to follow these stages in sequence.

A set of three templates is required: the first showing the side view of the neck and shoulder including the maximum width of the eyes of the scroll; the second showing the length of the scroll as if rolled out like a carpet; and the third showing the sides of the pegbox and the position of the pegs. These templates may also be cut into more than one piece (see fig. 6).

Violin ('Charles IX') by Andrea Amati, Cremona 1564.

Violin by Andrea Amati, Cremona 1574.

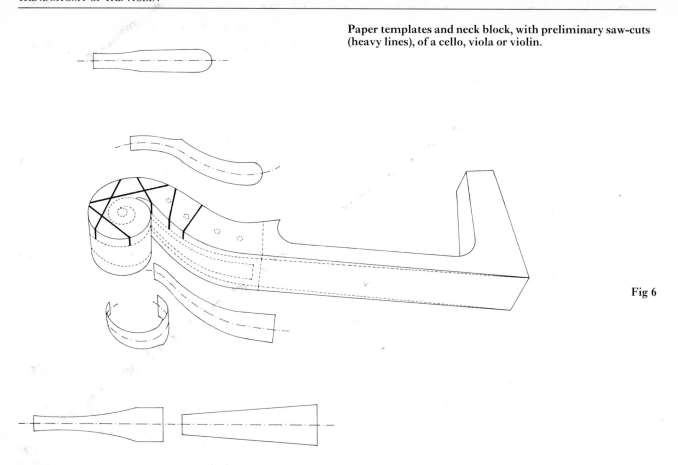

Paper templates and neck block, with preliminary saw-cuts (heavy lines), of a cello, viola or violin.

Fig 6

The side template is then marked on to the selected block of perfectly squared wood, and the outline is cut with a band or bow saw to the full width of the scroll. A centre line is drawn all along the cut-out block, back and front, and the shape of the back and top of the scroll and top of the pegbox are then drawn on to the block. A series of saw cuts are then made at specific places along the scroll which meet the drawn lines both top and bottom; after removing as much excess wood as possible without crossing any drawn lines, the work then proceeds with the aid of various gouges.

It is very difficult to describe the cuts which are made with the gouge. So much is in the eye of the individual craftsman: but the balance of the scroll depends on not exaggerating the hollows too much, and the channels carved into the back of the scroll should never form a perfect round at the bottom but be left a little flat. The eyes of the scroll should not be left too long or too thick (wide in diameter); at the same time the curls leading up to the eyes should not be too full, or the eyes will not protrude sufficiently when viewed from the front and back. The bell of the scroll as it curls under to the peg box must not reach maximum flare until the last possible moment. All these factors, and many still more subtle, combine to make a scroll which flows and pleases the eye from every conceivable viewing angle, and which is a piece of sculpture in itself.

The *pegbox* is hollowed out by drilling numerous holes to within approximately 4.5 mm from the bottom,

and then carving these out with a spoon gouge and flat chisel (it is always advisable to drill pilot holes for the pegs before hollowing the pegbox to prevent breaking out when the drill later passes through the pegbox walls).

Now the taper of the *neck* should be cut, and the neck can be roughly shaped. Modern necks are attached to the neck block by means of a dovetail joint, which should be prepared at this stage. The final shaping of the neck can take place after the soundbox of the body is assembled, with the fingerboard temporarily tacked to the neck (but removed again before varnishing). In Stradivari's time the neck was attached flat on to the block with glue and secured by three iron nails from inside the block. This required that the neck should be attached before the box was complete.

Once the ribs have been firmly set to the blocks and all excess wood has been removed to form the corners and the exact height of the ribs properly throughout, then the back *liners* are applied. In the case of the full-depth, two-piece mould, the shallower top piece is now removed, leaving space to apply and clamp the liners. The liners, made like the blocks of willow, spruce or pine, are applied in rectangular section. Those around the upper and lower bouts are butted up against the corner and end blocks; those around the waist are set into the corner blocks, to prevent them from springing away if the glue should ever fail (see fig. 7).

Once the glue holding the liners has dried, the frame

Corner block, showing butted and mortised liners.

Below: Arching templates used to gauge the contours of the back and front.

of the instrument (ribs and liners) is more rigid and can be removed from the mould to allow the liners to be shaped with a knife to their final aerodynamic form, merging into the ribs at the inside surface and leaving a good platform on to which the back can be glued firmly. The corner blocks now also receive their inside shaping to continue the inside contour smoothly. While the back is being prepared, the sides with their shaped liners attached can be temporarily clamped back on to the mould to keep them in perfect shape.

To prepare the *back*, the two wedges of split wood described earlier are jointed and glued, and the final shape cut out with a bow saw or band saw; an even rim thickness is scribed with a marking gauge 4–4.5 mm from the bottom. A set of six templates is required for carving the outer surface of the back: one showing the contour over the full length, and five half-templates showing the contour in various positions across the back (fig. 8). The rough shaping of the complex curves of the back is commenced by using a curved gouge to cut a channel across the grain along the line of each template. The longitudinal shape is carved first and the transverse sections follow until the back has deep gouged grooves in all the five positions of the templates. These shapes are then blended one into the other by eye and touch. The rough marks left in the wood by the gouges are then smoothed with a very shallow gouge and finished off with tiny curved-bottom planes, using the toothed iron and scraper method previously mentioned in connection with the ribs. Surface finishing is not done until the entire soundbox has been fitted together. Instead of sandpaper, which was not used in Stradivari's time, dogfish skins were commonly employed to bring the surface of each part of the violin to a perfect smoothness. Even today it is detrimental to the appearance of the wood to use sandpaper, as this clogs the grain and flattens the fibre in such a way that light no longer reflects well from it. A fine thin metal scraper leaves the wood glistening, enhancing its natural beauty.

Many makers insert the *purfling* into the back before hollowing out the inside. If this procedure is used, special attention must be paid to the exact and final shape of the back. The purfling consists of a lamination of three alternate layers of ebony/maple/ebony, making a strip approximately 1.4 mm wide and 2 mm deep. The line of the purfling must be first scribed with a gauge specifically designed for the purpose. This scribing should only suffice as a guide for the knife, which will be used to deepen the line to a depth of approximately 1.5 mm, forming a channel which is dug out with a small chisel with a cranked end. The purfling must be pre-

bent for the waist curves and points, and mitred together where it meets in the corners. There is a tradition that the apex of the mitre should be shaped into a 'bee sting' —a sharp projection of the point often accomplished by making a cut to continue one edge of the purfling and filling the cut with black mastic (a compound of ebony dust and glue). The purpose of purfling is primarily to strengthen and frame the outline of the instrument; but a secondary function could be even more important—to help prevent cracks from running up the instrument.

The back must now be hollowed to a pattern of thicknesses previously decided by the maker. This is achieved first by drilling away as much excess wood as possible and then removing the remainder with the aid of curved-bottom planes and scrapers. The final thickness of the back plate varies according to the chosen pattern: the thickest area is just under the soundpost or centre section of the back, not only in order to provide extra strength where the soundpost bears down on it, but also because it is at this point that the greatest sonic energy is concentrated, which would be in danger of dissipating too quickly if the back were too thin.

The average thicknesses of back and front plates by Stradivari are shown in fig. 9—but these would vary in practice according to the density and weight of the piece of wood selected. Some makers decide upon the final

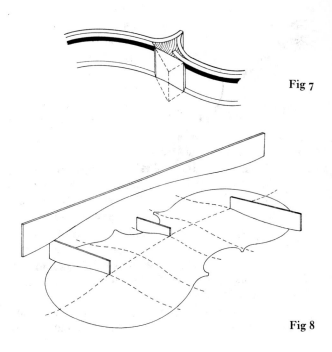

Fig 7

Fig 8

Violin by Giovanni Paolo Maggini, Brescia *c.* **1600.**

Violin ('The Alard') by Nicolo Amati, Cremona 1649.

Measurements made by Sacconi of average thickness of front and back plates of Stradivarius violins.

Method of clamping on front and back plates.

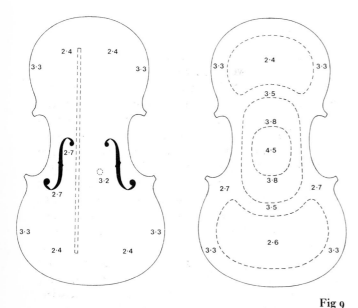

Fig 9

thickness by 'tuning' the plates and listening to the tone when the wood is tapped with the knuckle, or by bowing the edge of the plate to produce a tone. The thicker the wood, the higher the note produced by tapping or bowing. It is essential that the back and front plates are separated by at least a half tone, otherwise a serious imbalance in the harmonic response of the instrument will result.

The edges of the rims may now be rounded and the back prepared for gluing on to the ribs. This is first done without glue: once the centre is lined up so that the rims protrude equally all around the instrument, a small hole is drilled in the back over the end and neck blocks, into which a small piece of maple dowel is inserted. This will effectively prevent the back from slipping out of alignment while the gluing is taking place, using any of the various types of manufactured clamp available for gluing the back to the ribs (see fig. 10). The shape of the body is now stabilized, and the mould can be safely removed.

The preparation for shaping the *soundboard* or belly plate is essentially the same as that used for the back. It is rare for a violin to have the same contours for both back and soundboard, so the sets of contouring templates are normally different. The thicknesses are less for the soundboard and generally vary less within its shape (see fig. 9). The area immediately surrounding the *f-holes* (soundholes) is left a little thicker to prevent unwanted vibration.

Once the contouring is completed, there remain two additional and critically important stages before the soundboard is ready to be glued into place: the placing and cutting of the f-holes, and the making and fitting of the *bass bar*.

Every maker has his own characteristic f-hole design (see fig. 11), and many theories exist concerning their significance. Generally speaking, the centre or bridge position between the f-holes is the exact point of balance of the soundboard, and the distance between them crucially affects its acoustic behaviour: a maker will conduct numerous experiments before settling on the ideal position for his particular model. The procedure for cutting the f-holes begins with the placing of the top and bottom eyes. These are perfectly round, and are bored from both sides using a tool which closely resembles an apple-corer with a central guiding pin. A paper or thin wooden template would be used to join the two eyes; excess wood can then be sawn out using the fine blade of a fret saw, and the final shaping skilfully accomplished with a knife. The tiny notches denote the alignment position of the centre of the bridge.

The bass bar consists of a piece of pine wood perfectly split and fitted longitudinally to the underside of the soundboard, thus allowing the entire soundboard area to be used for the production of bass tones (see illustration on pp. 20–21). An important secondary function is to provide strength to oppose the downward pressure of the strings on the bridge feet.

There was no fixed dimension for the bass bar in the seventeenth and eighteenth centuries. Various schools advocated various sizes, of which a number have fortunately survived. We have clear evidence, for example, that the average bass bar dimensions used by Stradivari were: length, 50 mm away from the upper and lower ends of the belly; height, 6–7 mm under the bridge; width, 5 mm. This is very small when compared with the standardized dimensions of the modern bass bar: length, 7/9ths of the body length (approx. 39.5 mm

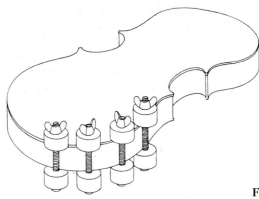

Fig 10

$\int\int\int\int\int$ Fig 11

Sound holes by (left to right) Andreas Amati 1574, Nicolo Amati 1649, Jacob Stainer 1656, Joachim Tielke 1670, Antonio Stradivari 1710, Guarnerius del Gesù 1742.

away from the upper and lower ends of the belly); height, 10 mm; width, 5.5 mm.

Some makers prefer to select wood for the bass bar which is dense and therefore quite heavy. The intention is to provide some inertia to help 'hold down' the sound and give it greater duration. The bar must be very precisely fitted, but there is some argument as to the best placing: whether ot not, for example, the angle at which it stands should be at right-angles to the centre or inclined perpendicular to the curvature of the soundboard; and whether the bar should fit perfectly to the inner surface when dry, or be slightly sprung i.e. cut so that the ends will not lie on the belly without being forced into place, so providing some upward pressure against the foot of the bridge. My own view is that the 'sprung' procedure should be avoided, since artificially created stresses produce nodal points which are likely to cause undesirable resonances known as 'wolf-tones'. The earliest violins had bass bars which were integral with the belly—in other words, the maker did not carve the belly away at the position he required the bass bar to be. In these cases there would have been no stress. Although this practice was continued in Europe for quite a long time, Italian makers generally favoured a separate bass bar.

Before attaching the soundboard to the body, an upper set of liners are required which match those between ribs and back. The body is now ready to receive the soundboard and the neck.

The *soundpost* has been called the soul of the violin (and indeed the French word for the soundpost, *l'âme*, means exactly that). This small rod of pine wood joins the soundboard to the back, and is fitted about 6–7 mm behind the foot of the bridge on the treble side. Its functions are to conduct sound through the instrument to the back, to help support the soundboard under the bridge, and to control the response of the instrument. It is a very sensitive component which will alter the tone of the violin dramatically if moved or incorrectly fitted.

A soundpost should be fitted so that the ends lie perfectly flush with the transverse curves of the underside of soundboard and back. It is a 'slide fit', which must be neither too loose, or the post will fall out, nor too tightly wedged, or the sound becomes nasal and sharp. When the post is moved back away from the bridge foot, the sound becomes gentler in the treble; closer to the bridge, the sound is sharper and more authoritative. Great skill is needed to fit and place a sound post correctly, and it is often moved many times, all the while experimenting with the musician, to achieve the best possible tonal balance of the violin.

The Glues

The glues used in violin making are invariably of the gelatin type—derived either from rabbit skins or horse hooves. It is essential to use a glue which is to some extent hygroscopic (tending to absorb moisture), and which will yield with the natural expansion and contraction of the wood under various climatic conditions. Use of inflexible modern resin glues could result in serious damage to an instrument which wants to expand in very humid weather. Certain components of the violin (for example the fingerboard) are subject to wear, and must be periodically replaced; the glue with which these are attached must therefore be detachable with relative ease.

There are at least four grades of gelatin glue in my shop, ranging from entirely transparent pure gelatin, which is appropriate for certain non-structural repairs, to dark brown horse-hoof gelatin used for heavy joints where a dark-coloured glue line need not be avoided and strong, reliable structure is essential.

The Varnish

It has long been claimed that the formula of Cremonese instrument varnish was kept secret by its makers and has now been lost. Some have even credited the wonderful tone-quality of the Cremonese violin to the quality of its varnish; but the main praise of eighteenth-century Italian varnish has always been of its visual beauty—an amazing transparency and reflectivity combined with a wonderful depth of colour ranging from golden to dark brown, orange to deep red-brown. A good violin can be spoiled by adding an inappropriate, inflexible varnish; but a poor violin will not be improved by using a beautiful and flexible varnish—it merely becomes less poor than if it were covered with boat-deck varnish!

Italian violins were finished in two distinct stages. It can be observed on great instruments that have suffered wear over the centuries that a ground or undercoat sealer was applied which is virtually indestructible and has withstood the ravages of time and use with extraordinary resilience. It is this yellowy-brown base which has preserved the great instruments, leaving the wood clear and clean. The research of modern masters (e.g. Simon Sacconi) has revealed traces of silicates in the wood which could have become imbedded from the abrasive (dog-fish skin) or from particles of glass (it was common seventeenth- and eighteenth-century practice to add ground glass to the varnish to provide added refraction and, if the glass was lead-based, to help the varnish dry

Letter to a patron from Antonio Stradivari, Cremona, 12 August 1708: *Most illustrious, most reverend and worthy patron: I beg you will forgive me the delay with the violin, occasioned by the varnishing of the large cracks, that the sun may not re-open them. However, you will now receive the instrument, well repaired, in its case, and I regret that I could not do more to serve you. For my work please send me a Filippo.*

It is worth more, but for the pleasure of serving you I am satisfied with that sum. If I can do anything more for you, I beg you will command me, and kissing your hand I am, most illustrious and reverend Sir, your most faithful servant A.S.

more quickly). However, it is my theory that this sealer could just as easily have been a mixture of potash and sand to form potassium silicate—a waterglass which would vitrify in the fibre of the wood and provide an indestructible sealant base. The effect of potassium silicate on maple and pine is, as it happens, to turn the wood exactly this yellowy-brown colour.

The second stage is the application of the layers of coloured varnish. A likely theory as to the type of varnish used in the seventeenth and eighteenth centuries was presented by Dr. W. Fulton, who suggests that a pine resin varnish was made by cooking the resin (Venetian turpentine or colophony) to very high temperatures—the higher the temperature, the darker the resulting colour in shades from amber to dark brown. Rich reds could be easily obtained by cooking the resin in an iron pot that contained traces of rust (ferric oxide)—could those beautiful Cremonese reds have been the result of nothing more than a happy accident? Once cooked, the resin would be reheated with linseed oil until it reached the right consistency, and then thinned with a suitable solvent for use.

Certainly the above-described varnish, when well made, produces all the qualities of flexibility and transparency that a good varnish should. It also passes one of the important tests of a Cremona varnish in so far as it fluoresces a bright salmon colour under long-wave ultraviolet light (also called 'black light'). All of the many theories and recipes, however, are too numerous to set down here, and varnish formulae became ever more complex with each succeeding generation. The fashion for using oil varnishes which require long drying times was set aside in the nineteenth century in favour of quick-drying spirit varnishes. These are, however, more brittle and less deep in appearance, and have been regarded by some as stifling to the tone of the violin.

Varnishing is completed with several layers of coloured varnish applied until the desired shade is reached, followed by several coats of clear varnish which, when dry, will be rubbed with pumice and tripoli powders and so burnished until the surface is silken to the touch. A good oil varnish always feels slightly waxy, and even on old violins it is often possible to leave fingerprints in the varnish which only clear away with time.

The Final Stage

Once varnished, the violin is ready for the permanent attachment of the *fingerboard* and the fitting of the *tuning pegs*, the *nut*, the *tailpiece* and the *bridge*.

The dimensions of the bridge, and its fitting, are both of great importance to the resulting tone. Stradivari cut his bridges from maple of a similar density and type to that used for the back and ribs. Modern bridges are frequently cut from very slow-grown Bosnian maple. The eighteenth-century bridge had many variations of shape and pattern, especially as regards the cut-out portions of the wood. Modern bridges are of a fairly standard design and are generally quite tall compared to their eighteenth-century counterparts. The most important factor is the fitting of the bridge feet, which must lie perfectly over the contour of the soundboard. The earliest bridges had solid thick feet. Stradivari's bridges had flanged feet, but were otherwise left quite heavy. Modern bridge feet are often cut away so that only a very thin flange lies on the soundboard (see

The back of a Guarnerius del Gesù violin of 1731 (left) in normal light and (right) under 'black' (ultra-violet) light, showing how only small areas of the original Cremonese varnish (fluorescing yellow-pink) remain. The wood is still in pristine condition protected by the silicate-based ground.

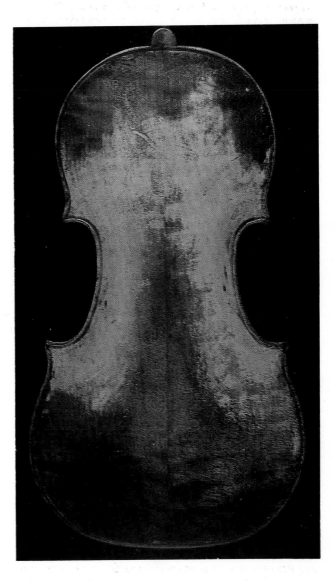

fig. 12). It is probably not advisable to allow the flanges of the feet to become too thin: for this is the point of transmission of sound into the body of the violin and any deviation from a perfect fit must result in loss of transmission. Should any distortion occur in the flanges, the bridge would then be 'point loading' the soundboard at the centre of the feet.

The curvature on the top of the bridge and fingerboard are more exaggerated on modern violins to facilitate use of the heavier Tourte bow (see also pp. 50–52) with its rather thick ribbon of hair. The fingerboard and bridge curves are shaped with a slight inclination towards the treble string. The tailpiece of ebony is attached to the violin by means of a piece of gut (or today, nylon) around the end *button*.

The Strings

It is well known that up to the middle of the nineteenth century violins were strung with gut, but very little has been written about the development of the strings, or about the ideas of the famous makers of the time with regard to how best to string the violin.

Several sets of instructions for making gut strings survive. The procedure involves taking the intestines of sheep (sometimes rams were preferred and sometimes castrated rams or 'wethers' were specified), removing all weak extraneous material by a combination of soaking and rubbing, and thus producing from them a thin membraneous material which when taut looks like fine plant fibre. As many of these fibres as necessary are combined to make up the final string diameter and then

Violin bridges (from top): reconstruction of a Stradivarius bridge; ink-decorated Stradivarius bridge; bridge attributed to Tartini; modern violin bridge.

Fig 12

twisted on hooks into a cylindrical shape. When dried, this is a normal or plain gut string.

Variations of this technique can be used to produce other kinds of gut string. The Venice Catlin or 'roped gut' string was made by taking several strands of plain gut string and twisting them while wet into a rope-like mesh, which could be polished when dry to equalize the diameter throughout the string. Craftsmen specializing in the making of gut strings made their appearance in the fifteenth century, and as the bass range of instruments increased, so the techniques for making suitable strings varied. There is evidence to suggest that by the beginning of the sixteenth century roped gut strings were being produced in Munich—although until string makers in Bologna started making them around 1660, they were too expensive for general use. The English names for these roped gut strings were Katlyns, Catlings, Cattelins, or Catlins; in the seventeenth century they were generally called Venice Catlins, since the trade in them had started in Venice. During the second half of the seventeenth century, English musicians commonly used Venice Catlins for the strings tuned from about a sixth below the highest string to about an octave below that, and thicker unpolished strings called 'Lyons' (after the French string-making centre) for the lower notes.* At this time, plain gut strings from Rome developed a reputation (which lasted until well into the present century) for high quality at the right price.

The general method of stringing in the sixteenth century, therefore, was to use Romans (plain gut) for the high notes, Catlins (roped gut polished) for the middle, and Lyons (unpolished thick rope gut) for the low bass notes.

The introduction of the roped-gut string produced a very strong G-string sound of clear but not very closely focused pitch and rather 'froggy' tone-quality. At first it was not very popular. Praetorius said that he did not like it, and Monteverdi avoided it; but during the seventeenth century soloist improvisers learned to exploit it effectively, and the strong, virile roped-gut sound came to be more widely appreciated, in particular by the Italians. (Clear evidence survives that Stradivari used a roped-gut G-string 2.5 mm in diameter.) Its rich bass quality even prompted some composers to specify the violin as bass accompaniment to other instruments. Leopold Mozart complained about the ludicrous prac-

*Venice Catlins and Lyons were originally different in appearance, Catlins having a characteristic smooth surface; but during the eighteenth century the name Catlin became devalued, and was often used to signify thin gut strings of any kind.

Two possible reconstructions of eighteenth-century stringing: Italian (above) 1, plain gut E; 2, plain high-twist gut A; 3, Catlin D; 4, Catlin G. French (below) 5, plain gut E; 6, high-twist gut A; 7, open wound D; 8, close wound G.

tice of using a violin to provide *continuo* for a cello solo!

Another technique of string making, introduced in the mid-seventeenth century, was that of overspinning—which involved winding a strand of thin silver wire around the gut string, either very closely so that the gut was completely covered by the wire ('close-wound'), or more loosely ('open-wound'). It is not known exactly where or by whom the technique was invented: but it is probable that windings were first applied to the bass strings of the violin, to give a richer and more closely focused sonority to the bass of the instrument, by dealers or instrument makers in France around 1660.

Overspinning was mainly confined to the G-string, although in France an overspun open-wound D-string was also used—a practice well documented around 1700, but abandoned later in the eighteenth century, probably as a result of the introduction of *portamento* as an important aspect of playing style, and the difficulty the player would therefore have in sliding the finger along the rough, open-wound string.

In summary, therefore: before about 1660, violinists had no choice but to use four gut strings. In the late seventeenth century,* and throughout most of the eighteenth century, French violinists used an overspun close-wound G-string and an open-wound D (in addition to the usual close-twisted plain gut A-string and thin plain gut E)—while the Italians appear to have retained a preference for all-gut stringing.** In Germany and England most players also continued to use all-gut stringing, although an overspun close-wound G-string was occasionally fitted. With the development in the second half of the eighteenth century of *portamento* playing, on an instrument whose neck was set at a steeper angle, and with heavier-tipped, Tourte-type bows, players of most countries changed to the type of stringing generally used throughout the nineteenth century—which is to say, gut on the three upper strings and an overspun close-wound G.

*Recent research suggests that there was also an intermediate stage in the development of the overspun string. Very close examination of accurately drafted seventeenth-century oil paintings indicates that a metal filament, probably of brass, may have been wound in alternate strands with the rope core of the gut bass strings to provide a smooth open-wound-type string. This was most likely also a French innovation.

**Italian paintings of the violin in the eighteenth century usually show a progressive increase in string thickness from treble to bass, and no change of string colour. The silver-wound G-string was of a distinctly different colour from a gut string, and also noticeably thinner than the gut D-string above it—identical colouring and progressive thickening thus imply all-gut stringing.

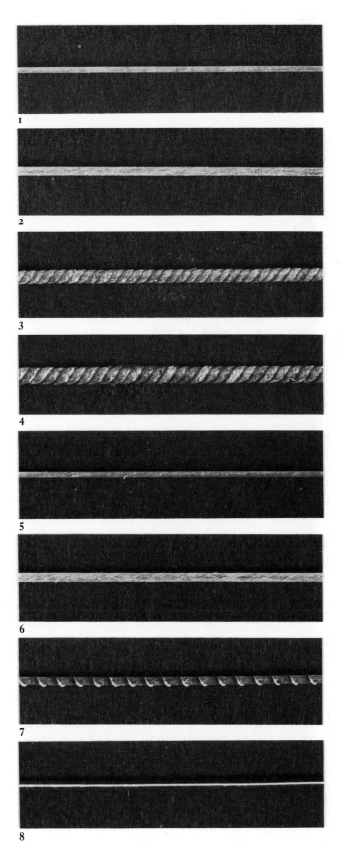

1

2

3

4

5

6

7

8

Inlaid violin by Antonio Stradivari, Cremona 1683.

Violin by Antonio Stradivari, Cremona 1702.

The ideal tensioning of strings has always been a matter of considerable argument. There were basically two opinions: one advocating equal tension on all four strings, which gave a sensation of evenness under the bow when moving from string to string; and another favouring a much higher-tension E-string and quite low tension on the overspun G. Since the evidence concerning pitch in the seventeenth and eighteenth centuries is inconsistent and inconclusive (we know only that the various pitches of the time were almost certainly lower than modern pitch), it is difficult to assess precisely the tension applied on the bridge of the violin until the nineteenth century, when such measurements were first recorded.

We know, however, that during the seventeenth, eighteenth and early nineteenth century strings were thicker than they are today. In 1832, Louis Spohr noted that 'generally speaking, in order to obtain a rich and powerful tone, a violin should be furnished with the largest set of strings it will bear . . .'; and it is certain that, since a thick string requires a higher tension than a thinner string to produce the same note, pre-nineteenth-century string tension will have been proportionately higher, even given the differences of dimension and set-up, than it is today.

During the middle of the nineteenth century, indeed, string tension appears to have increased, reaching a peak of about 35–44 kg, perhaps as a result of the need felt by many performers for greater volume and power in the new, larger concert halls. By the end of the third quarter of the nineteenth century, tensions had relaxed again, probably somewhere near to the present-day average of 30 kg: a practical step, and a reaction to an over-reaction, for it must be said that increasing string tension increases the effort required to play the violin, and makes quick, clean articulation far more difficult.

Metal stringing on violins was advocated and practised as early as the late sixteenth century. In 1619, Praetorius wrote that a violin strung in metal had a beautiful soft sound (the metal will have been iron and brass, and the pitch relatively low). Until the late nineteenth century, however, there was no metal string material available that could reliably be tuned as high as gut; according to Carl Flesch (1923), it was only in the early years of this century that the two violinists, Willy Burmester and Anton Witek, pioneered the use of a metal E-string in public performance (both suffered from extreme perspiration problems, which they hoped a metal E-string might help alleviate). The practice became widespread during the first World War, and in the following years use of the gut E-string gradually diminished until by 1945 it had almost disappeared (although a few violinists, of whom Fritz Kreisler is the most famous, resisted the introduction of metal and con-

Opposite: Carving planes from Stradivari's workshop.
Below: Stradivarius inlay patterns.

tinued to play with an E-string made of gut). Once metal E-strings had passed into general use, all kinds of metal windings and cores were experimented with; but it was not until the late 1940s and 1950s, and the introduction of more flexible rope-metal cores, that full stringing with all-metal strings was fully accepted by some professionals.

Decoration

Viols have traditionally been decorated in many elaborate ways, but violin decoration is comparatively rare. Fashionable Brescian, French and English makers in the seventeenth century sometimes placed a double line of perfoling on the soundboard, or sometimes a series of loops to form a design on the back in the style of the viol makers. Occasionally the scroll was replaced, especially in Germany, by a beautifully carved head, often depicting a mythological beast. The great maker Jacob Stainer often carved a lion-like head on his violins; but the greatest master of this type of ornamentation was the Hamburg maker Joachim Tielke (1641–1719), many examples of whose exquisitely carved violin heads still survive.

Stradivari made a number of violins whose scrolls and ribs were beautifully inlaid with intertwining vines and floral shapes. On the comparatively rare occasions that he inlaid the body of a violin, the purfling was always

executed in the form of a double line, with the wood channeled out between, and a continuous string of alternating elongated ivory diamonds and dots set into the channel embedded into black mastic. On some of his decorated instruments the design was accomplished simply by painting in black and varnishing over—but in most cases the design was carved out with a very fine veining chisel and filled with black mastic. On occasion Stradivari also decorated a bridge with inked designs (see fig. 12).

Innovators

Throughout the violin's history, its makers have attempted to design new violins based on the acoustical theories prevailing at the time. Some of these innovations deviated very considerably from the form of the violin as we know it, and were motivated by scientific curiosity, rather than by musical demands. Probably the most famous of such innovators was the French scientist and acoustician Félix Savart (1791–1841), who designed a trapezoidal violin which had no arching and straight soundholes. His designs were approved by the Academies of Sciences and Arts but were never adopted by any makers. François Chanot (1787–1823) designed a violin with a reversed (i.e. downward-turned) scroll and a flat, guitar-shaped soundboard, whose strings were fixed to the soundboard in the same way as the

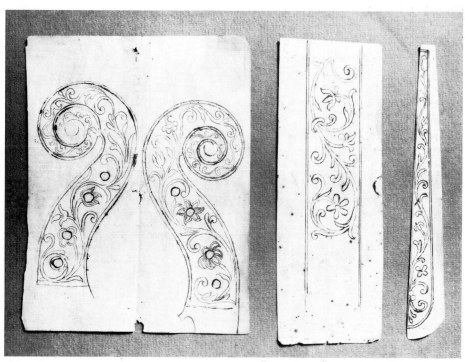

Violin by Pietro Guarneri, Mantua 1703.

Violin ('The Messiah') by Antonio Stradivari, Cremona 1716.

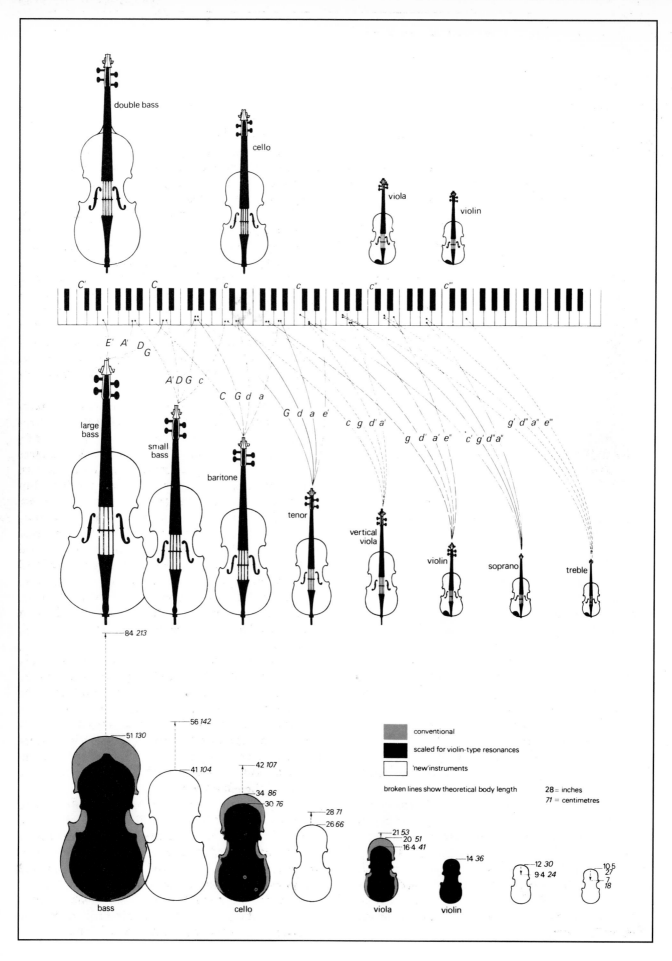

double bass

cello

viola

violin

C'   C   c   c'   c"   c'''

E' A' D G

A' D G c

C G d a

large bass

small bass

baritone

G d a e'

tenor

c g d' a'

vertical viola

g d' a' e"

violin

c' g' d" a"

soprano

g' d" a" e'''

treble

84 *213*

56 *142*

51 *130*

41 *104*

42 *107*

34 *86*
30 *76*

28 *71*
26 *66*

21 *53*
20 *51*
16 4 *41*

14 *36*

12 *30*
9 4 *24*

10.5
27
7
18

conventional

scaled for violin-type resonances

'new' instruments

broken lines show theoretical body length   28 = inches
71 = centimetres

bass   cello   viola   violin

The new family of violins designed by Dr Carleen Hutchins.

guitar. The soundholes were not f-shaped, but merely slits which followed the curve of the sides.

Violin vagaries of the nineteenth century are too numerous to list in detail. In 1856, one Thomas Howell took out a patent on a design for a new violin which had foreshortened upper bouts, an extra-long fingerboard to aid playing in the high positions, and a bridge attached to the soundboard well away from the chin. Others were more eccentric: violins made of leather, *papier maché*, silver and brass, a violin with an added horn like a trumpet, and many more of every conceivable shape. None has withstood the test of time.

Among the innovators of the twentieth century, Dr. Carleen Hutchins deserves special mention for two very important lines of research. Her design and development of a new Concert Violin, more powerful than the standard full-size violin of 14 inches but retaining the tonal quality of the classical violin, have resulted in an instrument 15 inches long with slightly wider upper bouts and substantially wider and longer lower bouts, whose string length and internal air space, however, remain the same as the standard violin's. This has been achieved by calculating the internal air space contained in the average standard violin and narrowing the rib height accordingly on the new 15-inch model. The f-holes are slightly larger than on the standard violin, and the bridge and bowing positions are an inch further away than usual from the player's face. The increased area of the soundboard produces an increase in volume, while the narrow ribs help to retain the brilliance, and even to emphasize it.

Dr. Hutchins's main line of research, however, has been the development of an entirely new family of violins, made up of eight instruments (see opposite), constructed on the basis of mathematical design and electronic acoustical testing combined with classical violin-making skills.

The range of the new family extends from the low tones of a seven-foot contrabass violin to the high tones of a tiny treble violin tuned an octave above the classical violin. Spaced at approximately half-octave intervals over this range, the new instruments are not intended to replace the older stringed instruments but to augment and complement them, thus achieving a richer and smoother balance within a large symphony orchestra.

Time will tell if composers and musicians can ever unite to exploit the exciting possibilities of a new family: by doing so, perhaps most significantly of all, composers could finally eliminate the many compromises they have been forced to make by the lack of a true tenor voice in the modern violin family.

The Good and the Great

If the violin maker has made a violin using the finest materials and principles of construction, and has set up the instrument well, it must be assumed that he will have made at least a 'good' instrument. Evaluation of sound-quality—especially in such vague and general terms as 'poor', 'good', 'very fine' or 'great'—is by its nature highly subjective, and must depend to a large extent on how easily and naturally a player can 'express' himself with a certain instrument. In the final analysis, however, even though individual tastes vary enormously, most virtuosos will agree whether or not a particular instrument is a 'great' instrument. What then constitutes a great instrument? How can one maker consistently produce very fine or even great instruments, while another who applies identical principles produces merely good ones?

There is no simple answer. That the greatest makers should not merely have made the occasional fine instrument, but produced instruments consistently throughout their working lives which all violinists agree to be great, is essentially as mysterious as the existence of the oeuvre of any great artist in any medium. But we can hazard guesses of a sort, even if they seem more like poetical commentary than explanation. The genius of the great makers must have lain above all in their intimate understanding of the materials they worked with; but still more important, in the very clear ideal of sound which the makers will have carried with them, and within themselves, at every stage of the making, from the first moment they held in their hands each piece of wood destined to become part of an instrument, to the last drop of varnish.

Innovations in particular can only produce truly meaningful results when the changes have arisen as the culmination of ideas flowing from the composer to the musician and thence to the maker; innovation for its own sake, or to satisfy the maker's own sense of self-importance, has always proved negative and unproductive. Stradivari was at once a great maker and an innovator who responded to the requirements of the music and the venues of his day.

In modern days, a few have come to violin making on their own; most have learned their craft through a school. Fewer still of these have had the privilege of an apprenticeship wherein they can share to a progressively greater degree the close relationship which should always exist between musician and maker—a rapport essential to the realization that the violin maker's function is, at base, no more and no less than to provide a service for the music and musicians of his time.

The Bow

Opposite: *Boy Playing the Violin*: painting by Hendrik
Terbrugghen (1588–1629).

It has been said that without the bow the violin is
useless. Perhaps so, but then without the violin the
bow is even more useless. Both of these statements are
important truisms, for they point out the strong inter-
dependence between bow and violin. Quite simply, it
is inconceivable that one could exist without the other—
and indeed there is not a shred of evidence throughout
history to indicate otherwise.

That is not to pretend that the relationship between
the violin and bow has always been an equal one, for
such parity has only really occurred in the second half
of the twentieth century. Previously the bow had been
viewed as an accessory: an important accessory, needless to say, but an accessory nevertheless. In consequence no serious study of the bow, its makers, its
functions and its value as a work of art was undertaken
much before the beginning of our century. There are
occasional references to a few earlier individuals who
were sufficiently intrigued by the art of the bow maker
to put together collections of various sizes and degrees
of importance; but in general bows were assigned a
function not dissimilar to that of horse-shoes. Both are
clearly necessary; but when worn out or broken, they
should be replaced with a minimum of fuss. And
because it was not considered worthwhile even to
attempt to repair a broken bow, the traditions of the
seventeenth- and eighteenth-century bow makers were
largely lost. Fortunately, with the appearance of
improved glues and repair techniques this sad state of
affairs has been almost completely reversed in our time.

For the average person, or indeed the average violinist, the bow remains a complete mystery. Ask six players
what qualities a fine bow should possess and you will,
more than likely, get six different answers. (It is of more
than passing interest that players' opinions of violins
are far less confused. There are good reasons for this,
which I will discuss in more detail at the end of the
chapter.) Before embarking on a chronological voyage
to see how the bow developed from the seventeenth to
the twentieth century, it will be useful to familiarize the
reader with the standard names given to the various
parts of the bow. As can be seen from the accompanying
diagrams, the modern bow maker must be master of
many trades because his craft requires skills in wood-
working and metalwork as well as an aptitude for artistic
decoration using precious metals and mother-of-pearl.
But the physical make-up of the bow has not always
been so complex. In fact, as the name itself implies, the
earliest bows were the quintessence of simplicity.

Bow making did not become a separate and specialized craft until the middle of the eighteenth century.

Before this time bows were made in violin makers'
workshops, not by the principals but by apprentices.
Consequently the identities of the majority of
eighteenth-century and of all seventeenth-century bow
makers will forever remain unknown to us. Without
names and dates, therefore, the categorization of trends
and periods for early bows must remain a matter of
astute conjecture. Less ideally, this process can easily
descend to the level of biased guesswork; and
unfortunately it is precisely such a state of pseudo-
academic endeavour which prevailed throughout most
of the nineteenth and early twentieth centuries. In short,
the past study of the art of the bow maker is often not
much more than a collection of anecdotes and rumours.
This is a pity, since it is clear that the facts about bows
(as indeed about almost everything else) are much more
interesting than the fiction.

Most of the various types of bows in common use

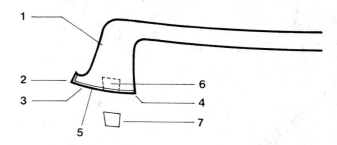

The head of the bow: (1) ridge, (2) peak or point, (3) face, (4) plate
or tip, (5) tip liner, (6) mortise, (7) plug

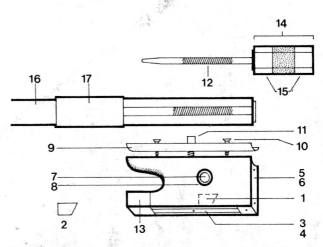

The frog of the bow: (1) mortise, (2) plug, (3) slide, (4) slide-liner,
(5) heel, (6) heel-plate, (7) eye, (8) ring, (9) underslide,
(10) underslide screws, (11) screw-eye, (12) screw, (13) ferrule,
(14) button, (15) bands or rings, (16) wrapping, (17) thumb grip

'A Display of the Successive Ameliorations of the Bows of the Seventeenth and Eighteenth Centuries': from *Notice of Antonio Stradivari* by François Joseph Fétis.

during the seventeenth and eighteenth centuries have become known to us by the names of the famous players who are said to have advocated them initially. However, even here, history is not at all clear and we have largely to accept the namings on trust. The set of drawings opposite first appeared in Fétis's book, *Notice of Antonio Stradivari*, and has been reproduced countless times since. Apart from the crudeness of the drawings this chart obviously supports the contention that the leading virtuosi participated in the development of these bows not as craftsmen but as expert consultants. It is quite normal that this should have been so, since to this day it is not unusual for a bow maker to enlist the aid of a good violinist to evaluate the merits of new ideas. The fact is that most bow makers are not players, and one way or another rely on a certain amount of outside expertise.

No one looking at the drawings taken from the Fétis book could be blamed for thinking that the early bow was a crude, utilitarian implement. But while these bows may not be as sophisticated as their modern counterparts, they most certainly are not primitive. In fact their

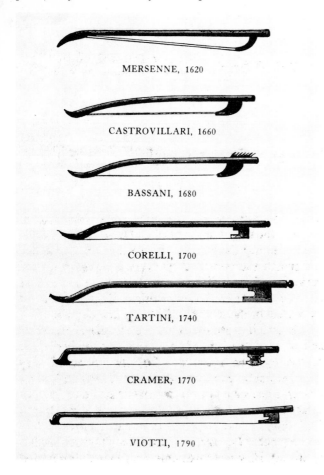

MERSENNE, 1620

CASTROVILLARI, 1660

BASSANI, 1680

CORELLI, 1700

TARTINI, 1740

CRAMER, 1770

VIOTTI, 1790

relationship to the Baroque violin was as functional as that of the modern bow to the modern violin and its music. It is indeed the realization that period instruments were built to play the music of their times, and vice versa, that has inspired the current revival of past performance practices on authentic instruments, spearheaded by groups such as Concentus Musicus of Vienna, La Petite Bande of Brussels, Aston Magna of New York, and the Academy of Ancient Music and the English Concert, both of London. The efforts of these groups as well as their many followers constitute a kind of practical musicology which is unparalleled by any of the past methods of study. In order to set the record straight, and as a kind of belated apology for the Fétis drawings, I include here some photographs of eighteenth-century bows which speak eloquently for themselves.

It is important to remember that these bows were engineered, as it were, to serve the needs of the music of their time. Distinctive qualities of articulation and sound production were inherent in the making of these sticks: any idea that their makers were somehow groping about in a fog of uncertainty, hoping to 'discover' the modern bow, should be laid to rest once and for all. It has always been the basic requirement for any performer to be perfectly familiar with the capabilities of his materials: to know what his bow will or will not do. Composers have long taken advantage of such performing expertise and have mostly tried to write music which exploited the resources of the instruments of their times. Indeed most early Baroque composers were fine performers in their own right, and it would be foolhardy to accuse them of ignorance.

But art is not static, and towards the middle of the eighteenth century certain tangible new trends began to develop. Music moved more and more frequently out of the private *chambres de concert* into larger halls; this in turn meant that the intimate sound of Baroque instruments seemed increasingly small-toned and ineffective. Both performers and instrument makers were sensitive to such changes, and, in the case of the bow, the second half of the eighteenth century witnessed some remarkable transformations. In terms of the modern bow, these were arguably the most important fifty years in the entire development of the bow. And it was the work of the Tourtes, both father and son, which led the way for all others to follow. While they did not work in isolation, in fact quite the opposite, there is an understanding of concept coupled with superb craftsmanship which quite simply places their work on a higher level than that of their contemporaries. Nor should it be forgotten

Violin bows (from top) by unknown maker *c.* 1700; unknown
maker *c.* 1750; unknown maker *c.* 1752; viola bow by
Thomas Smith (working *c.* 1756); Louis Tourte (Tourte *père*)
c. 1760; John Dodd *c.* 1780.

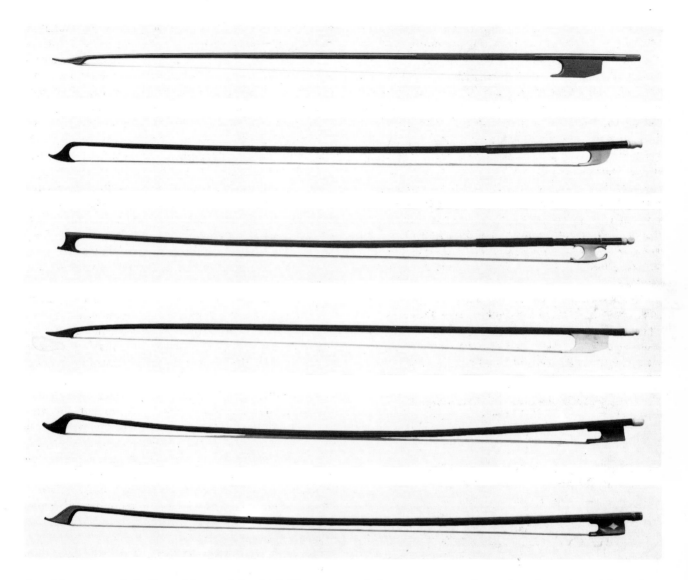

that this was a period of transition and that both Tourtes
would have divided their output, at least before the turn
of the century, almost equally between old and new style
bows. That neither their transitional or modern bows
have ever been improved upon by any other makers
speaks volumes about their rare talents. Past writers
have dubbed the son, François Xavier Tourte, the
Stradivarius of bow makers: a title which is actually
more meaningful and less glib than it might at first seem,
for both the Tourtes set standards which have not only
remained unsurpassed, but have been rarely equalled,
to this day.

The development of the bow in the eighteenth century can be followed by observing the changes which
affect the *head*, *shaft*, and *frog*. In retrospect, it can now
be seen that the overall trend was to decrease the height

of the outcurve arch, to lengthen the stick and to
equalize the height of the head and frog. By the middle
of the century the hair and stick were almost parallel,
and shortly thereafter makers began bending an inward
curve into the middle or upper half of the shaft. This
curve, called the *camber*, was initially of little depth, but
by the end of the century it had acquired a symmetrical
profile which centred around the middle of the shaft
and touched the hair when relaxed. At the beginning
of the eighteenth century, bow length could vary
anywhere between 24 and 28 inches (61–71 cm), more
or less, since standard measurements had not yet been
established. By the end of the century, bow length
(including the adjuster) was generally fixed at slightly
over 29 inches (74 cm), but rarely more than $29\frac{3}{8}$ inches
(74.6 cm). Bow measurements are generally calculated

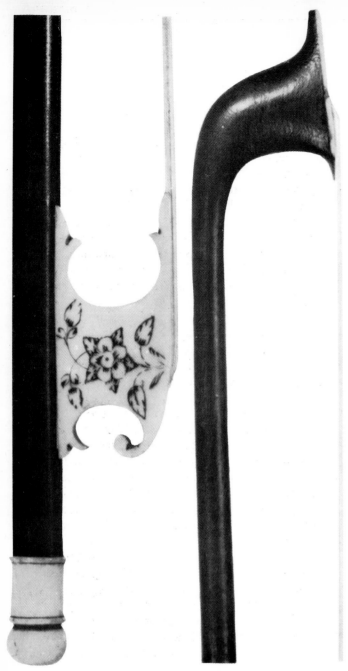

action of the modern bow enormously different to that of its Baroque counterpart. Its variety of length notwithstanding, the outcurve design prescribes that the most stable part of the bow will be the middle. Thus it should not be surprising that music of the Baroque is characterized by the constant presence of quick-moving notes, which is precisely what the bow of the time did best. Of course, this is not to say that the Baroque bow was the determining cause of style in Baroque music, but it was most certainly a factor.

As the shaft of the bow both lengthened and flattened during the second half of the eighteenth century, so the area of stability was extended in both directions. But while this vastly improved the bow's sustaining qualities, it did so at the expense of articulation. Thus in a nutshell, even at the risk of over-simplification, the early bows can be viewed as *articulators* while the modern bow serves as a *resonator*. That is to say, such are the essential qualities inherent in the two types of bow—without necessarily denying a broader view than the definition would seem to imply. The crucial variable, and one which should never be underestimated, is the skill of the performer.

Possibly the most uncomfortable period of development for the bow was the third quarter of the eighteenth century—the so-called 'transitional' period. Bow makers at this time were no doubt trying to sort out the tug-of-war between the accepted past traditions of their masters and the progressive musical demands of the Classical and Roccoco composers, so it is hardly surprising that there is evidence of a certain floundering of purpose among them. When one considers that so much was undecided, and that the weight, camber, length and even the materials from which bows were made were far from having been standardized, it is no wonder that transitional bows present such a confusing picture. The essential message, however, is clear: no matter what problems of balance and lazy response may plague these bows, they invariably possess good sustaining qualities.

Even at this late date, the profession of bow maker was still mainly anonymous. One of the earliest known branded bows is a transitional type stamped TEIN-TURIER on the butt. It dates from somewhere in the third quarter of the eighteenth century and illustrates several interesting things. The stick is made of pernambuco, not of the more accepted snakewood or ironwood, and the style is definitely forward-looking. However, the most curious aspect of this bow is the name of the maker. It is well known that it was an accepted practice in the eighteenth century to boil pernambuco wood to create

on an 'extremity to extremity' basis, but unfortunately vary so greatly from maker to maker that it is not really possible to present one set of fixed or ideal figures. (Depending on the location of the frog on the shaft, the hair length can vary in a similar way.)

The process of flattening and lengthening the shaft directly influenced the development of the head. The earlier long and pointed heads were simply a continuation of the line of the outcurved stick: any other design of head would have been absolutely illogical. As the arch dropped, however, the angle of the head to stick had to be increased to prevent the head from pointing upwards. Although the many varying head profiles seem to obscure the issue a little, in fact the head and shaft of the modern bow are basically cut at right angles to each other. This, coupled with the fact that the frog is also seated on the shaft at right angles, renders the

Vivaldi's cadenza for the third movement of his violin
concerto in D (RV212a).

an orange-purple dye, and *teinturier* translates in English to 'dyer'. Unfortunately nothing is known about this man except his ironic name, Jacques Le Teinturier, and that he lived in Rouen around the middle of the eighteenth century.

In contrast to the well-established practice by which violin makers labelled their work, bow makers, being suppliers of accessories, appear not to have branded their wares until the second half of the eighteenth century. Even so, it took virtually another hundred years before the stamping of bows became a universal practice. The earliest brands show only the maker's surname, for example, TEINTURIER, GAULARD or TOURTE L. As their craft gained importance over the years, bow makers' brand stamps included more detail (although the small size of the butt naturally limited the scope). Nevertheless, we find that by 1850 a typical brand would include the maker's surname, his initial(s) and city of residence, for example, F. N. VOIRIN A PARIS. Before the middle of the nineteenth century, bow makers appear to have branded their work only randomly; and that most celebrated bow maker of all time, François Xavier Tourte, is not known ever to have stamped any of his bows.

It took the combined talents of the Tourtes, father and son, to launch the modern bow. Although the son, François Xavier, has long been highly regarded, his father, whose Christian name is assumed to have been Louis, has been rather unfairly ignored by comparison. In point of fact Tourte *père* was a consummate craftsman who deserves full credit for having provided a truly remarkable apprenticeship for his son.

The influence of the work of François Xavier Tourte has been profound on all subsequent bow making. All of the French bow makers of the first half of the nineteenth century did their best to copy his bows. Exceptionally talented makers like Persois, Eury, Henry and Peccatte all looked to the bows of Tourte as their ideal. He was the first bow maker to achieve fame in his own time: and most significantly, his bows were not regarded as accessories but as valuable acquisitions. Had it not been for the Tourtes' timely emergence, bow making might have had to suffer many more years of anonymity.

Before continuing with the remainder of the nineteenth century we should pause briefly to consider the development of the frog. The moveable frog with its screw and nut mechanism made its appearance some time near the beginning of the eighteenth century. Before this the two most common types of frogs in use were either the clip-in model which was pressed into a fixed position, or a moveable type without the screw mechanism which made use of a '*cremaillière*' to prevent the frog from sliding forward. In the case of the latter type, a band of metal was looped over a series of notches either recessed or superimposed on the butt. Both of these types belong more correctly to seventeenth-century bows and are rarely seen today outside museum collections.

Throughout the first three quarters of the eighteenth century the frogs remained proportionally lightweight, although they did increase in size and weight as the century progressed. Because the bow was generally held at some distance away from the frog, neither end of the stick felt excessively imbalanced. But as the century progressed and tonal demands increased, the bow hand

Violin bows (from top) by Louis Tourte (Tourte *père*), Paris
c. 1770; François Tourte (Tourte *le jeune*), Paris *c.* 1790;
François Tourte (Tourte *le jeune*), Paris *c.* 1820.

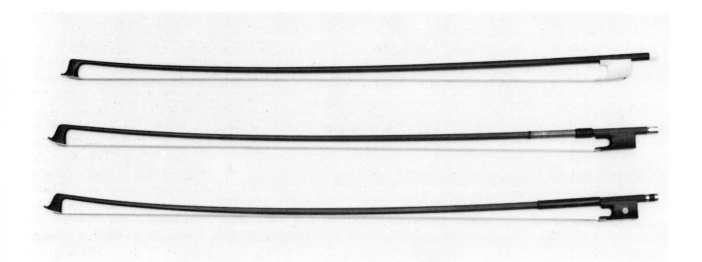

moved closer and closer to the frog to allow greater
leverage. While the lower hand positions succeeded in
opening up a wider range of sonorities, the effectively
longer stick now created a kind of gravitational
imbalance. To compensate for this, bow makers began
to add metal parts to both the frog and the adjuster to
act as ballast. And since the hand, by the early
nineteenth century, was beginning to cause considerable
frog wear, these metal reinforcements also served to pro-
tect the wooden surfaces. No one maker can be singled
out as the actual inventor of the ferrule, the heel plate,
the seating slide, or the adjuster bands, in spite of anecdotes which claim the contrary.

The nineteenth century was to bow making what the
years between 1650 and 1750 were to Italian violin making. Curiously enough, almost all of the great bow
makers were French and worked either in Paris or Mirecourt. Why the greatest violin makers were Cremonese
and the greatest bow makers were Parisian remains a
mystery—perhaps it was simply a quirk of fate, or possibly the traditions of violin making during the seventeenth and eighteenth centuries in Italy had become so
thoroughly established that the emergence of the
modern bow at the close of the century held no great
fascination for them. In the case of the French, their
background in violin making was not nearly so strong
and hence their craftsmen could reasonably be expected
to be more adventurous. No doubt, the challenge of
developing a more modern bow also appealed to the
Gallic inventive instincts, which were especially strong
in France in both the arts and sciences during the
nineteenth century.

It has been often said that it was François Xavier

Tourte who first established the parameters of the
modern bow. In essence this is true, but we should not
assume therefore that the bow ceased to develop at this
point. Far from it. Early nineteenth-century bows were
designed for acoustical requirements far less intense
than those of our time. The demand for stronger and
broader string sound has increased steadily, and instrument and bow makers have striven to meet the challenge. Generally speaking, Tourte bows tend to be
lightweight by modern standards: few of his violin bows
exceed an overall weight of 60 grams. Most makers who
followed the Tourte model tended to make their own
bows more heavily wooded to increase their weight; but
in all other respects the Tourte concept reigned supreme
for the first half of the nineteenth century. Dominique
Peccatte, Nicolas Eury, Nicolas Maire, François Lupot,
Joseph Henry, and Persois were among the leading
lights to honour the Tourte pattern. By the middle of
the century, however, a quiet revolution was in the making. The angular head and frog so characteristic of the
Tourte bow was being softened in its outline; but it was
not until the appearance of François Nicolas Voirin that
the Tourte bow was challenged in any fundamental way.

Voirin created, in essence, a radically different bow.
The profile of the head was slimmed down and the progression of camber moved closer to the head. Purely in
terms of elegant craftsmanship the bows of Voirin and
his principal followers, Alfred Lamy, Louis and Claude
Thomassin and Charles Nicolas Bazin, established new
standards of excellence. But more important still, the
change of camber produced playing qualities quite different from those of the Tourte school. Basically, the
new style of camber yielded a stronger stick, which in

Violin bows by (from top) James Tubbs, London; André Vigneron, Paris; James Tubbs, London; Eugène Sartory, Paris; Dominique Peccatte.

turn enabled the Voirin school to reduce the thickness of the shaft and lighten the overall weight of the bow. Indeed every aspect of these bows, the lightness of the head and shaft as well as the finely-worked frogs and adjusters, seems to have been designed to reduce weight while preserving strength.

From the fact that the Voirin concept remained the vogue with the French, Germans and English until the turn of the century, it can safely be assumed that violinists of the time preferred its lightness, grace and balance to the more rugged qualities of the Tourte-Peccatte design. Be that as it may, the early years of the twentieth century witnessed a return to favour of the heavier bow, and bow makers began to discontinue their lightweight bows. However, it is interesting to note that they did not discard the elegant Voirin model, but instead simply increased its weight, thereby creating a new type of

action which was to hold sway during the first half of the twentieth century.

Before leaving the subject of nineteenth-century bow making in France, proper homage should be paid to the great luthier Jean-Baptiste Vuillaume, and his influence on bow making in his country. Vuillaume was trained as a violin maker in Mirecourt, and, to the best of our knowledge, did not serve an apprenticeship in bow making. Nevertheless his keen interest in the craft prompted him to hire a long succession of the finest French makers to make bows for his shop. These bows were stamped with Vuillaume's brand, but in reality he made none of them. Among the distinguished bow makers who passed through his shop we can count Dominique, François and Charles Peccatte, Joseph Fonclause, Pierre Simon, Persois, Guillaume Maline and F. N. Voirin. There is no question that all of these makers benefited from

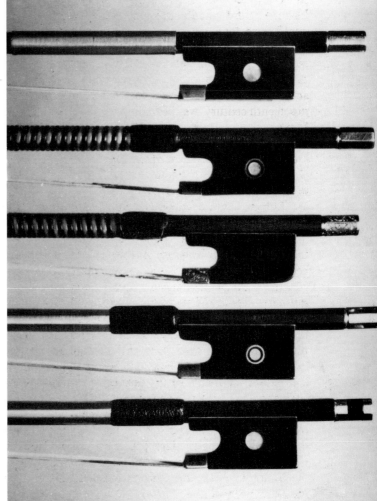

Opposite: François Tourte: engraving from *Gallerie des violons et luthiers célèbres morts et vivants* (1819).

Below: The frog of a metal bow by J. B. Vuillaume.

Vuillaume's keen interest and advice, and the experience gained in his workshop enabled them to fashion bows which virtually defined the state of the art for all time, or at least for as long as the violin remains an acoustical instrument. Vuillaume was not only a master violin maker but an inventor and a shrewd businessman. Although many of his innovations, like the self-rehairing bow, the metal bow and the round-edged frog, have not survived the test of time, all were sensible developments and show that he was hardly ever content with the status quo. He was also so intrigued by the magical playing qualities of the bows of François X. Tourte that he instigated research which produced a formula to describe mathematically the taper of the shaft of the Tourte bow. Again, although the validity of this formula has recently been questioned, it does not diminish the sincerity of his purpose.

While Vuillaume can be said to have established the first large-scale bow-making workshop, the British firm, W. E. Hill & Sons, took this concept several steps further. Apart from promoting his round-edged frog, Vuillaume made no demands on his bow makers to alter their individual styles. The Hills, on the other hand, designed their bow from start to finish by combining historical insight with the practical expertise of their early craftsmen; and thus by the turn of the century succeeded in formalizing a uniquely vigorous approach to bow making which subsequent makers followed with distinction. The Hill bow is essentially English in character, drawing substantially from the traditions of the Dodd and Tubbs families, and invariably exhibits the highest possible standards in quality control and craftsmanship. If Vuillaume can be regarded as the catalyst of nineteenth-century French bow making, then the Hill tradition must be viewed as nothing less than the life-blood of bow making in twentieth-century England. One is hard pressed to name any notable twentieth-century English bow maker who did not receive his training at the Hill workshops. It is safe to say that without the influence of Vuillaume and Hill, the development of bow making would have been severely retarded.

At this point it is relevant to pause for a moment to examine another essential, but non-structural, component of the violin bow: the hair. Hair is to bows as strings are to violins: without the one, the other is useless. Horse-hair has been preferred to all other kinds of hair, probably since before the Middle Ages, on account of its length, strength and ready availability (it was also evidently an advantage that the diet of hair-producing horses could be monitored to ensure the growth of healthy tails). It has been said that hair from North American horses tends to be stronger and more robust than that of Asian horses, which often is finer and of a silkier texture. Before the hair can be used it has to undergo a vigorous process of cleaning and sorting. Ideally, every hair should be as uniformly cylindrical as possible; but since horse-hair is a natural product and prone to irregularities of growth, in practice no more than five per cent of the hair taken is actually suitable for bow hair.

Among makers and players, the traditional preference has long been for white hair. This is partly due to the fact that the whiteness of rosin powder blends better visually with white hair, and partly because black hair tends to be rather too coarse. The best grades of bow hair are only cleaned and double drawn, never bleached: chemical bleaching renders the hair more brittle and thus increases its chances of breaking in use. Due to the relative scarcity and thus the high price of top-grade white hair, there have been a number of experiments with synthetic substitutes. The great Polish virtuoso Bronislaw Huberman (1882–1947), for example, tried a fine-gauge wire, but with only mixed results. More recently various nylon substitutes have been proposed—not without success in some of the cheaper grades of school bows. Professionals, however, by and large prefer natural white horse-hair, since they find that it produces the smoothest and most cohesive tone quality.

Returning to French bow making in the first half of the twentieth century, we find that Eugène Sartory and Emile A. Ouchard were the leading exponents of the fortified Voirin model. Bows by these makers and their followers are sturdily built and almost always have very strong shafts: characteristics which make them ideal orchestral bows, but perhaps also a little unyielding for solo work. Consequently, there has been a definite swing back to the ideals and principles of the Tourte-Peccatte school among contemporary bow makers; and although nothing lasts forever, it can reasonably be predicted that this trend will continue at least to the end of our century.

As will have been noticed, nothing so far has been said about German, and relatively little about British, bow making. British bow making in the nineteenth century was dominated by the two families of Dodd and Tubbs. The best-known of these, James Tubbs, appears to have been an eccentric man who produced a very large number of highly individual bows. For the player,

they take some getting used to, and the majority admit to being baffled by their action and balance. John Dodd, who was roughly contemporary with François Tourte, also made some fine bows, although their measurements and quality were never very consistent.

Little is known about bow making activities in Germany before the nineteenth century. During the nineteenth century the French were the undisputed leaders of the field, and possibly this intimidated the Germans to a certain extent since most of their work can be categorized as utility grade. A few makers achieved something above that level, most notably Ludwig Bausch, as well as the Knopf, Nürnberger and Pfretzschner families; but even they could hardly be said to compare with the best of the French. In our own time, however, there has been a certain renaissance in German bow making, and some of their contemporary work has been enthusiastically received.

The case of Italian bow making, or rather the lack

of it, during the nineteenth and twentieth centuries remains something of an enigma. Certainly the Italians made all of their own bows during the seventeenth and eighteenth centuries—but these were anonymous works of which only a handful survive today in museum collections. It may be that the Italians' apparent lack of interest in bow making is quite easily explained: they preferred to make violins! Whatever the case, there has never existed a single native Italian bow maker with an international reputation.

No mention either has been made so far of American involvement in bow making, and this is because efforts to produce fine bows in the United States have surfaced only comparatively recently. Earlier in the century a number of leading dealers in New York, Philadelphia and Chicago employed good bow makers—but their principal job was to carry out repairs and produce the occasional reproduction. One of the earliest American bow makers was John Alfred Bolander Jr., who recently celebrated his ninetieth birthday in retirement in California, and who has been called affectionately the 'Grandma Moses' of American bow making because his style is so individual. A new chapter in American bow making began in 1960 when William Salchow returned from his apprenticeship in Mirecourt, France. Originally a cellist, Salchow deserves credit not only for having produced a significant body of fine work closely modelled after the great Parisian *archetiers*, but perhaps more importantly, for having taught the art of fine bow making to a number of promising young American craftsmen. It is no exaggeration to say that the best bows currently made in America compare favourably with the best anywhere in the world.

At the beginning of this chapter I mentioned the fact that most violinists (and for that matter violists and cellists) find it more difficult to choose the right bow than the right violin. This should not be surprising since the bow is subjected to so many more diverse muscular influences than the violin. The violin itself is manipulated with far less complex movements than the bow, which operates on many levels and extensions and whose co-ordination is never less than problematic. For better or worse, we live in a right-handed world, and it is clear that the most complex tasks involving the playing of stringed instruments, whether bowed or plucked, have been assigned to the dominant hand since the earliest of times. Had the ancients felt that fingering was more complex than bowing or plucking, then there is no doubt that the right hand would have been assigned this task.

The value of fine bows has risen dramatically over the last two decades. In the 1970s alone bows appreciated tenfold. To quote a typical example, a Hill bow priced at £100 in 1970 in London had a retail value ten years later of at least £1000. Such prices seem astronomical to most players today; and as a final irony we should not forget that most nineteenth-century bow makers died paupers because they were literally unable to make a living from their art. For make no mistake, a fine bow is as valid a work of art as is a fine Stradivarius or Guarnerius. The belated recognition accorded to fine violins and bows is certainly long overdue, but in many ways it still comes too soon for the violinist of average means. The central problem is one of price. Since the best nineteenth-century bows now cost upwards of £10,000, it is clear that only the most fortunate among us will ever be able to purchase a fine bow by Tourte, Peccatte, Eury, Henry or Simon. That is a matter for regret, since bows by these as well as many other great makers possess a power of articulation and nuance which entirely belies their construction of something as mundane as a stick of wood.

Will there ever be another François Xavier Tourte or Dominique Peccatte?—in theory at least, the possibility cannot be ruled out. One of the biggest problems facing the contemporary bow maker is an ever-dwindling supply of fine-quality pernambuco, snakewood and ironwood. While a fine maker can do marvellous things with ordinary grades of wood, there is no question that a great bow is the result of extraordinary skill and intuition applied to exceptional material. The same observation naturally also applies to violins, but fine grades of maple and pine are somewhat easier to obtain. In other respects the future looks rosy for the contemporary bow maker. Provided that the problem of wood supply can be solved and that the traditions of the great nineteenth-century bow makers are thoroughly assimilated, there is no question that a ready market awaits those whose bows can meet the standards.

Like fine wines, fine bows possess truly individual personalities which demand to be appreciated in their own right. They certainly cannot be rushed into submission. It takes time and patience to discover the hidden potential of a great bow. But once this is accomplished, the violinist can rightly expect that the tonal spectrum of his violin will be greatly enhanced. Some bows seem to produce a 'darker' sound, while others—though such judgements are highly subjective—may tend towards a 'soprano' quality. Similarly, remarkable variations in action occur in all fine bows. Not only are violins and bows interdependent, but a clever match between the two can produce sensational results.

The Baroque Violin

In the evening as she [Mary Queen of Scots] wished to sleep,
five or six hundred scoundrels of the town serenaded her
with wretched violins and small rebecs, of which there is no
lack in this country; and they began to sing psalms than
which nothing more badly sung or out of tune could be
imagined. Alas, what music and what repose for her night!

Brantome, 1561

It is a kind of disparagement to be a cunning fiddler. It
argues his neglect of better employment and that he has
spent much time on a thing unnecessarie.

Owen Feltham, 1631

Previous page: Orpheus: Ivory relief by Christoph Angermair, d.1630.

Recitation with *lira da braccio* accompaniment: wood-cut from the epic 'Morgante maggiore' by Luigi Pulci, Florence, *c.* 1500.

I THE SEVENTEENTH CENTURY

Emancipation: The Solo Violin in Italy

One of the strangest occurrences in musical history is the emancipation of the violin. From its function as a provider of lively, popular but definitely down-market dance music, it was transformed within an astonishingly short space of time into a vehicle of the highest, most sophisticated art. The change took place in Italy in the last years of the sixteenth century; by 1607 Claudio Monteverdi could use a violin duet in the central invocation of his *favola in musica*, Orfeo, to express Orfeo's plea to the mighty spirit Charon: '*Possente spirto e formidabil nume*'.

This was a sudden change. We can be in no doubt—in spite of the many unanswered questions as to its origins—that the violin was a familiar instrument in the middle of the sixteenth century. Praetorius in *Syntagma Musicum* (1619) wrote disarmingly that 'since everyone knows about the violin family, it is unnecessary to indicate or write anything further about it', a remark which has left subsequent historians tantalizingly in the dark. By the last decades of the sixteenth century, Italian writers already had an elevated notion of the instrument's origin, if an account from Bernardi's *Ragionamenti musicali* (1581) quoted by Emanuel Winternitz is to be believed:

The violin was invented by Orpheus, son of Apollo and Calliope. The ancient poetess Sappho invented the bow fitted with horse-hair, and was the first to use the violin and viola in the way they are used today; and this happened 624 years before the coming of our Lord Jesus Christ.

Possibly this legendary belief led Monteverdi to associate the instrument with Orpheus in his drama, supplanting the lyre of Striggio's original text.

But the facts of the matter are more complex. There are elements in the violin drawn from the Renaissance fiddle and from the rebec, both essentially popular instruments. There are also elements of the *lira da braccio*, a noble instrument, larger than the violin, usually with seven strings, which was often used to accompany the recitation or singing of poetry at Italian courts. This link is interesting, as the *lira da braccio* featured, we know, in the earliest Orpheus drama with singing, the play by Angelo Poliziano (1471). Baccio Ugolino, who played Orpheus, accompanied himself in performance on the *lira da braccio*. Another virtuoso performer on this instrument was Alessandro Striggio, who was described in 1567 as one who was able to play four parts at once on the instrument with such lightness and such

musicality that his listeners were amazed. Striggio's son, also called Alessandro, was Monteverdi's librettist.

The rise of the violin in Italy coincides precisely with the development of monody and with the establishment of the *basso continuo* technique which was to survive as long as the musical Baroque. In this sense the violin is the Baroque instrument *par excellence*. Of course, revolutions rarely happen as quickly as their makers at the time or their subsequent analysts like to imagine, and the careful researches of David Boyden, Howard Mayer Brown and others have demonstrated the extent to which the violin was used in pre-Baroque Italian music—especially in *intermedii*, those early proto-operatic entertainments—and also the extent to which there was an important tradition of virtuoso solo instrumental writing in this same pre-Baroque period.

That tradition of virtuoso display is associated chiefly with the art of ornamentation and particularly with that of diminution: the addition of a florid solo line to the homophonic texture of a madrigal or motet, and the elaboration of a musical figure or phrase with short note-values. And it was undoubtedly in such works that the techniques of brilliant writing for strings, using such lower instruments as the *viola bastarda* and the *viola da gamba*, was developed. Still, it is not unrealistic to date the emancipation of the violin from around the year 1600, and to treat its specially demonstrative style as a sign of the changing taste of the age.

The whole impetus behind the growth of both vocal monody and instrumental solo writing was the independent, creative musician. Gone (or rather, supplanted in fashion) was the discourse on equal terms found in the madrigal and the motet. The elaborations of the ornamentation treatises at the end of the sixteenth century point towards a new musical world in which the soloist is paramount, and the establishment of the *basso continuo* provided literally a foundation for this new art. Caccini's *Le nuove musiche* of 1602 celebrated this change in vocal music (and his instructions about singing have much to teach the contemporary violinist as well). The violin is given marked solo parts in the canzonas and soloistic motets of Giovanni Gabrieli (*c.* 1553/6–1612)—though these *violino* markings seem to refer to an instrument slightly lower in range; but the violin unequivocally emerges as a solo sonata instrument in the 1610 collection of pieces by Giovanni Paolo Cima (*c.* 1570–?after 1622).

Opening Flourishes

Cima's collection of 1610, published in Milan, is devoted chiefly to sacred music: *Concerti ecclesiastici*, a Mass and two Magnificats. Nestling among these grand pieces are six small sonatas, of which the first is for solo instrument and bass. Its wide-leaping intervals and sharp, brittle scales proclaim it as a modest but important inauguration of the violinistic style which was to dominate the early Italian sonata. A more melodic approach to the violin may be heard in the remarkable piece which was included in the posthumous collection of pieces by Giovanni Gabrieli, *Canzone e sonate*, published in 1615. This *Sonata con tre violini* presents the apparatus of the Baroque style almost fully formed: a slow-moving bass line, over which the instruments exchange fragments of material. The melodic range is quite narrow, and the phrase-lengths are short. With those two qualifications, however, Gabrieli's piece can be seen as a model for the violin composition of the period.

Though we will be concerned here chiefly with music for solo violin, it is important to recognize that there was no essential difference of technique between a solo piece (sometimes confusingly called *sonata a due* because of the presence of a bass line) and the trio sonata (which, also confusingly, usually involves four performers, two on the upper lines, one playing the bass line and one realising it at the keyboard) or larger ensembles like Gabrieli's.

The liveliest advances in violinistic writing were made by the period's greatest genius. Not only in *Orfeo* but also in his dramatic madrigals and even in his *Vespers* collection of 1610, Claudio Monteverdi (1567–1643) pushed the idiom of the instrument forward. The *stile concertato*, undoubtedly inspired by the somewhat naïve battle-pieces of the previous century, was an invention of Monteverdi's which was ideally suited to the newly emancipated violin. Its fierce, scuttering figurations can be heard to splendid effect in the dramatic madrigal *Il Combattimento di Tancredi e Clorinda* and, later, in the magnificent scene in *Il Ritorno d'Ulisse* when Ulysses draws his bow on his wife's suitors. Monteverdi also used violins in his *Scherzi musicali* and in other large scale pieces such as the mini-opera *Il Ballo dell'Ingrate*. This style of violin playing was widely imitated: Heinrich Schütz took it to Germany, where it became the basis of a far-reaching attempt to match human emotions with musical phrases or figures. Monteverdi's art, indeed, here provides one basis for the whole aesthetic of the Baroque.

The extent to which Monteverdi's music—and doubtless, too, the technique of those players who performed it, for the composer-performer link has always been strong in the violin repertory—inspired lesser composers may be heard in the music of Dario Castello (*fl.* 1620s) and Giovanni Fontana (?–*c.* 1630). Castello published the first book to be devoted wholly to sonatas in 1621, describing the pieces as *Sonate concertate in stilo moderno*; he seems himself to have been a wind player, but his writing for violin is brilliant. His sonatas characteristically alternate fast and slow sections in the manner of the canzona, but his fast sections are full of very difficult passage-work. In a preface which appeared when the book was reprinted in 1629, Castello implored his players not to give up at a first attempt; he explained that his idiom is a result of 'the new style which everyone is attempting to observe'. Other striking features in these early sonatas include passages marked *tremolo*, indicating repeated notes slurred under a single bow.

The sonatas of Giovanni Fontana were not published until after his death; they appear in a volume bequeathed to the church of Santa Maria delle Grazie in Florence and were published in 1641. They were undoubtedly written before the 1640s, and show striking contrasts between the old-style formalism of the canzona with its imitative opening, and the free idiom of vocal monody which dominates the second and sixth of the set. Here there are recitative-like largos and showy allegros which sound as if they were derived directly from vocal declamation.

The most important of these early Italian violin composers, however, is Biagio Marini (*c.* 1587–1663): his influence, like that of Monteverdi, went beyond his native land. He worked as a violinist at St. Mark's in Venice under Monteverdi, and then in several Italian towns, from where he travelled widely around Europe. In his first published collection of 1617, a real violinistic idiom is developed: *tremolo* is indicated for the first time (seven years before Monteverdi requested the same device) and slurs are also marked. While some of the pieces, such as the solo sonata *La Ponte*, are somewhat basic, the two trio sonatas *La Foscarina* and *La Agguzzona* are far more adventurous.

The title of this collection is brief but significant: *Affetti musicali*, musical emotions. Here, as in Monteverdi, the violin is used to characterize human feeling. The title of Marini's next important string collection, op. 8, is anything but brief: *Sonate, symphonie, canzoni, pass'emezzi, baletti, correnti, gagliarde, e retornelli, a 1.2.3.4.5 & 6. voci, per ogni sorte d'instrumenti. Un Capriccio per sonar due violini a quattro parti. Un ecco per tre violini + alcune sonate capricciose per sonar due a tre parti con il violino solo, con altre curiose + moderne inventioni.* This brilliantly varied assembly of music is, as the last phrase of the title implies, consciously experimental. There is a beautiful *Sonata in ecco* for three violins in which two of the violinists stand a way off, like the echo singers in Monteverdi's *Vespers*: the resonant acoustic of a huge church is almost necessary to make Marini's figurations overlap with genuine echo. There is a solo sonata in which Marini avoids making a cadence for the whole of its eighty-one bars. There is another which changes style continually. Perhaps the most famous of the set in terms of developing violin technique is the *Sonata per sonar con due corde*, which involves the use of double-stopping, and also includes many marks of expression: *tardo, presto, forte, piano*, a selection of trills, and the use of the word *affetti* as an expression mark (which remains something of a puzzle: it may indicate some type of *tremolo* effect).

Why has this outstanding repertory of music for early violin remained so little known? There is a simple answer, which is that the rapid, crisp articulation and true, piercing tone required by these Italian pieces is difficult, if not impossible, to realize on the modern (that is, essentially, the nineteenth-century) violin. Only with the revival of violins in their original form, as described earlier, has it become possible to let this music speak with its true accents.

Advancing Technique: Italian Virtuosos

During the seventeenth century Italian violinists and composers advanced the technical language of the instrument with surprising speed. Marco Uccellini (*c.* 1603–1680), who worked in Modena, pushed the range of the instrument upwards, making use of the sixth position to reach a high G on the top string. He seems, from the dedication of his op. 4, to have played on the fact that his name was also that of the birds (*uccelli*), and perhaps strove to imitate their song in some of his long melodic lines. Some scholars, however, have noted his liking for 'piquant chromaticisms and false relations', not especially bird-like traits, and it is certainly more important to stress the way in which his harmonic style provides a link between early and later Italian idioms. In Uccellini the archetypal sequence of harmonies which modulate through the cycle of fifths is to be found: the bass line runs, for instance, G-C-F-B flat-E flat, and so on, and each time a seventh chord above pushes the music towards its temporary new home before returning it to the key it started from or to a near relation. Such modulatory technique was to underpin much of the harmonic language of Corelli. Uccellini also used unusual keys, such as B major, B flat minor and E flat minor; it is interesting to speculate on how purely he could have tuned these very rare keys on his instrument: presumably, by avoiding open strings altogether, (which is easy to do at least in E flat minor). Another of Uccellini's innovations, perhaps suggested by the imitative elements of Monteverdi's *stile concertato*, is contained in the sonata *Tromba sordina per sonare con Violino solo*, which appears at the end of his op. 5: for this trumpet-like piece, the strings of the violin have to be re-tuned to different pitches from normal, a practice called *scordatura* which will become very important when we consider the violin music of Central Europe.

Before Rome became the focus of Italian violin music in Corelli's time, activity was concentrated in the northern towns, particularly Venice and Bologna. In Venice, a new generation of violinist-composers in contact with Monteverdi's pupils wrote attractive, if scarcely important, music. Giovanni Legrenzi (1626–90) was a typical example: well known as an opera and as a church composer (he was *maestro di cappella* at St. Mark's in Venice from 1685), he nevertheless put some of his most forward-looking ideas into his collections of instrumental music, almost all of which are for violins (though it is interesting to note that in his op. 10 of 1673 he indicated that the music could also be played on viols, a rare suggestion at this late date). In Legrenzi's striding, confident themes we can hear the developing language of tonality: typical formulations include the strongly-accented tonic note, rising or falling with a scalic figure to the dominant, followed by an arpeggio or a fanfare-like broken chord, with occasionally an expressive chromaticism before the fugal answer enters. We are not far here from the fugue subjects of Bach and Handel, and indeed Bach wrote a fugue on a subject which is attributed to Legrenzi (BWV 574), though scholars have not yet tracked it down.

The interaction of performance and composition in this period becomes increasingly important. Under Legrenzi the *cappella* of St. Mark's reached its largest ever constitution, and Stephen Bonta has suggested that some of the pieces in his op. 8 and op. 10 might have been conceived for orchestral performance. In Bologna, the orchestra at the San Petronio chapel was a strong attraction to composers. Maurizio Cazzati (*c.* 1620– 1677) came there in 1657, and among his pupils was G. B. Vitali: both had a significant effect on the progress of violin music. Anne Schnoebelen has described the activities of Cazzati at San Petronio in two excellent articles ('Cazzati *vs.* Bologna', *Musical Quarterly*, January 1971; 'Performance Practices at San Petronio', *Acta Musicologica*, 1969) which leave a vivid impression of the feuding and arguments which marred his occupancy of the post. Cazzati's extravagance in importing outside instrumentalists was undoubtedly one cause of friction between him and his colleagues; Schnoebelen suggests that the founding of the famous Accademia Filarmonica in Bologna in 1666 may have been in direct opposition to Cazzati's activities.

Like Legrenzi, Cazzati wrote much sacred music, but made his most individual contribution to the development of string writing. He has been judged a composer of mediocre inspiration and craftmanship, yet his solo and trio sonatas which appeared as op. 50 (1669) and op. 55 (1670: they were probably published by Cazzati himself, as his feuds extended to the Bologna music publishers) are important insofar as they extend the idiomatic language of the violin. Dance rhythms make an appearance, as do parts intended for larger *ripieno* groups which point forward to the *concerto grosso*.

Cazzati's most famous pupil, Giovanni Battista Vitali (1632–92), was a cellist, who played in the Accademia as well as at San Petronio. His extraordinarily original output, however, looks back to Marini's experimental adventurousness. After an innocuous series of trio and ensemble sonatas, he published in 1689 his only two solo sonatas in a treatise called *Artificii musicali ne quali si contengono in diverse maniere, contrapunti dopii, inventioni curiose, capritii, e sonate* (op. 13). This includes some very odd pieces in which Vitali demonstrates his interest in obscure matters of theory, especially of rhythm and tuning. 'He deserves not to be called a musician who knows not how to handle the recondite secrets of his art in whatever style', he writes in his preface. So there is a trio sonata which uses three time signatures: 'the first violin sounds in *tempo ordinario*,

the second violin in *dodecupla*, and the violone sounds in *tripla*': that is, one part in 4/4, one in 12/8, and one in 3/4, though the same metrical pulse is used for all of them. And there is a *balletto* in which one part is written in F sharp and the other in the enharmonic key of G flat. Vitali's experiments with tuning extend to a Passacaglia which he describes as *per Violino che principia per B. molle, e finisce per Diesis*: it begins in a flat key and ends in a sharp key, moving from E flat around a circle of fifths to end in E major, using on the way both A flat and G sharp in different harmonic contexts. Again, the imminent world of J. S. Bach—the ascending modulatory canon of *The Musical Offering*— is hinted at.

Vitali's son Tomaso Antonio (1663–1745) should be parenthetically remembered here for a famous Chaconne which it seems likely he never wrote. It was supposedly one of the earliest works to achieve fame in the violin schools of the nineteenth century, when Ferdinand David edited and arranged it. David changed a substantial amount of the violin writing to match the expected virtuosity of nineteenth-century players, elaborating the end of the work to provide a brilliant climax (he could not accept that, as in Bach's more famous Chaconne, the end might return to the simplicity of the beginning). Some modern editors, restoring the original version of the work, have reclaimed it for Vitali; but it bears little relation to his other music, and must be attributed at present to that prolific master, Anon.

More important strides towards the violin language of the high Baroque were taken by Pietro degli Antonii (1648–1720), whom William Newman praised as an 'unexcelled melodist in the noble style of the late seventeenth century . . . a master of the finely drawn line, whether continuous or broken up into short utterances in the manner of a recitative'. The interesting aspect of Antonii's music, especially in his op. 4 (1676) and op. 5 (1686) sonatas, is the way in which he re-introduces a vocal inflection to the violin line, an inflection which had been largely missing during the development of idiomatic string styles and ensemble techniques. These lyrical traits are emphasised by his choices of marking, for example *Adagio affettuoso*, *Aria grave*, and *Aria posata*.

Through the work of all these arguably minor composers centred around Bologna, the ground is prepared for Arcangelo Corelli (1653–1713)—who when he moved to Rome still called himself '*il Bolognese*'—to sum up and bring to a new height of expressiveness the violinistic language of the high Baroque.

Ballet and Masques: the Violin in France and England

France and England were both slow to follow the lead established by Italy in turning the violin from a popular instrument into the herald of a newly demonstrative musical age. In France, the violin made its first formal, independent appearance in *Circé, ou le Balet comique de la Royne*, which was given one evening in October 1581 from 10 o'clock until 3.30 the next morning, with music by the Italian Balthazar de Beaujoyeux (*c.* 1535—87) leading an ensemble imported from Italy. These two sets of instrumental dances for *violons* are the first examples of violin music to have been printed anywhere, and the detailed descriptions of the extravagently lavish staging of the ballet show that they would have been played on stage by violinists costumed 'in white satin enriched with gold tinsel, feathered and provided with egret plumes': a degree of authenticity to which revivals of French Baroque music have not yet aspired.

The violin took a long time to escape this association with the dance. In 1630 the theorist Trichet wrote that 'violins are principally destined for dances, balls, ballets, masquerades, serenades, morning songs [*aubades*], feasts and all joyous pastimes, having been judged more appropriate for these kind of pastimes than any other sort of instrument.' Its connection with outdoor performance is also noted by Trichet, who recalls the custom that 'formerly one accompanied the bride and groom to the church with the sound of oboes and returned them to their home with the sound of violins'—perhaps a prefiguring of the violin's later romantic role in serenading.

The instruments which found favour in France were lutes, viols, and harpsichords, 'instruments of repose destined for serious and tranquil pleasures whose languid harmony is the enemy of all action and who demand only sedentary Auditors' (Michel de la Pure writing in 1668). Violins were not likely to gain entrance to that scene. But as the dance became increasingly important at court, so too the violin became valued as an incisive leader of the dance-band: de la Pure suggested that 'the Glory of the Violin is only to play the measure and tempo accurately as soon as the Entrée commences.'

Beaujoyeux's band of Italian violinists did not establish themselves at court, and by 1590 many of them had returned home. But there were sufficient French performers to fill the gap and by 1609 there were already 22 *violons ordinaires de la chambre du Roy*. This suggests that the violin had been emancipated from the category of outdoor music provided by the *écurie*, the stable. But in 1626 Louis XIII established the famous band of *24 Violons* as a separate administrative unit, and at this point the violins lost their place in the *chambre*. This *Grande Bande*, as it was usually known, mirrors directly the transformation of the violin from a popular to a sophisticated instrument: François Lesure has established that many of the French players came directly from the popular street bands of the *Confrérie de St. Julien des ménétriers*.

Though the *24 Violons* is often called the first modern orchestra, it is important to realize that its layout was quite different from that of the modern string orchestra. Its basis was the violin, playing the top line, and the *basses de violon* playing the bottom line. There were no second violins: the central three parts were all played by violas; their function in filling up the harmonies was recognized in their collective title '*parties de remplissage*'.

So for many years the solo potential of the violin lay undeveloped in France, as the instrument took its place in the many ballets devised for the entertainment of the court. Its idiom was simple and its technique not especially advanced: virtuosity was more tellingly demonstrated on the bass viol, which Marin Marais (1656–1728) and his colleagues brought to a height of perfection. When André Maugars visited Italy in 1638 he was amazed by the brilliance and skill of the ten or twelve violinists he heard in Rome. The French theorist Marin Mersenne, one of the first to acknowledge the possibilities of the violin, pointed out in 1637 that most French violinists used only the upper two strings of the instrument, which seems difficult to believe until one considers the limited range of dance music as the top line of a five-part ensemble.

In England, a traditional British compromise between old and new styles helped to assist the albeit slow progress of the violin. For while the viol consort retained its pre-eminence at the end of the 16th century as a vehicle for serious musical discourse, the 'broken consort' also became popular. In this mixed instrumental grouping colouristic variety was prized above all; the most famous example of the form, Thomas Morley's *First Book of Consort Lessons* (1599), was scored for treble lute, pandora, cittern, bass viol, flute and treble viol, with the violin indicated as an alternative to the treble viol. In music which used the style of the dance, the violin quickly became established as an alternative to the treble viol. John Dowland's *Lachrimae* (1604) were 'set forth for the Lute, Viols or Violons, in five parts'. In Anthony Holborne's *Pavans Galliards, Almains and other Short Aeirs* (1599), violins, viols or

Claudio Monteverdi: portrait by Bernardo Strozzi (1581–1644).

Seventeenth-century itinerant musicians in Venice: painting from a Venetian manuscript.

'other musicall wind instruments' are indicated.

But this use of the violin also shows how slow England was to develop an idiomatic style of writing for the instrument. Several years ago (in *Music and Letters*, October 1956) Thurston Dart suggested that some of the fantasies of Orlando Gibbons, for instance, had top parts which were specifically written for violins. In *Early Music*, July 1983, Oliver Neighbour suggests that the use of violins could indicate 'some more public 'context' for the music. The working of these pieces, however, is essentially abstract, a long way from the idiom of the Italians. David Boyden's conclusion (in his *History of Violin Playing from its Origins to 1761*) is that 'it is unlikely, both for musical and political reasons, that in England before 1650 there existed a substantial body of violin music that treated the violin in a way comparable to the advanced practices of the Italian composers'. It is possible, though, to make an exception for the music of William Lawes (1602–45), who designed some of his consorts for two violins, bass viol and *obbligato* organ. Here the violin adopts some of the

techniques of the 'division viol', with diminutions and running passages which are very different in idiom from dance music. Lawes's dense, almost Beethovenian counterpoint is well served by the clarity of the violin: the superb 'Royall' consort, also called 'The Greate Consort', a collection of 66 dances in various suites, existed in various different versions, but Murray Lefkowitz believes that the music is written in four real parts, with two violins on the top two lines. Lawes stands between two musical ages, the old age of the Renaissance, and the new age, rather cautiously slow to arrive, of the English Baroque.

Imitations and Mysteries: Central Europe

The climax of early Baroque writing for the violin is to be found neither in Italy, France or England, but in the far less well-known regions of Central Europe. Here, the export of Italian writing began early with Biagio Marini and Carlo Farina, whose eccentric *Capriccio stravagante* (1627), which aimed to imitate the

A *Violon du Roi* in court costume: engraving by N. Arnoult, 1688, and (below) musicians in the *Chambre du Roi* at Versailles: engraving by Trouvain, 1696.

Opposite: A string orchestra (perhaps containing some of 'the King's twenty-four violins') playing in Westminster Hall during the banquet to celebrate James II's coronation on 23 April 1685.

Below: Johann Heinrich Schmelzer: copy (1842) by Ferdinand Groer after an unknown engraved portrait.

Joueur de violon de chez le Roy

Se vend a Paris chez N. Arnoult rue de la fromagere a l'Image S. Claude aux halles avec Privilege du Roy

QUATRIEME CHAMBRE DES APARTEMENS

sound of animals with its truly extravagant *col legno*, *pizzicato* and other indications, may have provided hints as to how the violin's possibilities could be extended. A German, Nicolaus Bleyer, is credited with one of the first known pieces for violin and *continuo* from this area—a set of variations on the famous tune *Est-ce Mars*. Johann Staden (1581–1634) and his pupil Johann Erasmus Kindermann (1616–55) both contributed early works to the repertory. Kindermann in particular continued the tradition of eccentricity: in one trio sonata the second violin part has to be discovered by reading the first violin part backwards (another foretaste of Bach's puzzles in *The Musical Offering*); and another is called *Giardino corrupto*, in which numbered instructions have to be followed to find the second's part from sections of the first's. More significantly, Kindermann wrote in *scordatura*, indicating different tunings for the violin strings, and this technique was to become an important expressive resource in this area of Europe.

One of the most influential early composers for the violin in Central Europe, and a creative figure of the

highest worth whose music has all too often been overlooked, is Johann Heinrich Schmelzer (c. 1620–80). He worked as a violinist and Vice-Kapellmeister at the Imperial Court of Leopold I (himself a keen musician) in Vienna, and was appointed Kapellmeister just before his untimely death from the plague. In 1660 Müller's *Reise-Diarium* praised him as 'the famous and nearly the most distinguished violinist in Europe', and it must indeed have been a skilled player who was able to master his *Sonatae unarum fidium* (1664), the first ever publication of solo violin sonatas in Germany or Austria. Here the Italian technique of variation is exploited in a succession of brief, constrasted sections. But the *sonata prima* from that set also shows remarkable resourcefulness, with agile figures that bounce up octaves and down tenths, and one variation written entirely in trumpet-call arpeggios. The *sonata terze* includes striking echo effects, an *Adagio* with double stopping, and an extremely florid central section which races up into the leger lines. Schmelzer's love of instrumental colour led to his including the violin in ensembles which prefigure the variety of Bach's Brandenburg Concertos: among the collection *Sacro-profanus concentus musicus* of 1662 are ravishing canzona-type pieces which use the violin alongside the cornett, bassoon and trombone as a virtuoso soloist.

The Austrian tradition established by Schmelzer was carried on throughout Central Europe. His most famous associate was Heinrich Biber; but also important were the South Germans Johann Jakob Walther (c. 1650–1717) and Johann Paul von Westhoff (1656–1705), who rapidly brought German violin playing to a technical level which equalled that of Italy. Walther's influential *Hortulus chelicus* (1688) included one sonata with the most unusual title *Aria in Forma di Sonatina*, and a hilarious extravagance in the tradition of Farina called *Serenata a un coro di violini, Organo Tremolante, Chitarrino, Piva, Due Trombe e Timpani, Lira Todesca, et Harpa Smorzata, per un Violino Solo*, in which a solo violin and *continuo* imitate all those various instrumental sounds. In other pieces Walther imitates birdsong, and, as Schmelzer also did, wrote a sonata on the cuckoo's

67

call. Other pieces in his *Scherzi* (1676) point the way to a new virtuoso tradition, however, and earned for Walther the dubious accolade from Fétis of 'the Paganini of his century'.

Westhoff also used programmatic devices in his sonatas, and must have been himself a fine player because he won the approval of Louis XIV in Paris; the King is supposed to have named a war-like movement from Westhoff's sonata '*La Guerre*': not, we might think, a startlingly imaginative act. But Westhoff's important claims to fame are his Suite (1683) and his recently rediscovered set of Partitas (1696), which are written for unaccompanied violin and point us towards the achievement of Bach's Sonatas and Partitas.

Other such unaccompanied works may be found in the output of Heinrich Ignaz Franz von Biber (1644–1704), who slightly predates Walther and Westhoff, but is musically the most important of all seventeenth-century violinists. Walther disliked the art of *scordatura* and wrote against it in one of his prefaces, but for Biber it was a foundation of his very considerable art. Biber came from a Bohemian background, and wrote his early work at Kromeriz Castle, where a large number of his autograph manuscripts are preserved. He then became a member of the Salzburg Kapelle, where he would have worked with Georg Muffat. His *Sonatae violino solo*, containing eight sonatas, appeared in 1681; a number of superb ensemble pieces for two violins, often tuned in *scordatura*, can be found in such collections as *Harmonia artificia-ariosa* (1712).

A work which may be taken here as the climax of seventeenth-century violin writing, however, is the collection of sixteen 'Mystery' sonatas which Biber probably completed about 1676. Their purpose must remain uncertain, but there was a special celebration

of the mysteries of the Rosary in Salzburg Cathedral each October, and it seems likely that Biber performed them as postludes to the Rosary services there. Biber's Mystery sonatas are programmatic in a way not encountered in the simplistic war-pieces and cuckoo songs of his contemporaries and predecessors. He aims not merely to imitate a sound but to provide a meditation on an event. Each of the first fifteen sonatas uses a different *scordatura* tuning of the violin (making the works almost impossible to play as a sequence unless one has a variety of violins to hand) and is prefaced by a woodcut illustrating the scene. In the first, 'The Annunciation', the angel's descent is depicted in brilliant flourishes, Mary's acceptance in a profound, double-stopped *Adagio*, and the angel's disappearance with equally florid passagework. The second, 'The Visitation', uses a dance-suite to depict the quickening excitement as Mary communicates her tidings. 'The Birth of Jesus' opens with an eloquent, slow movement called *Sonata*; 'The Presentation in the Temple' takes the appropriately ritualistic form of a *Ciacona* with vigorous cross-strong bowing. Nothing here is literally depicted—musical considerations come first—but 'The Scourging of Jesus' has heavy repeated notes in the solo part, and 'Jesus's lament on the Mount of Olives' has 'sobbing' double-stopped chords.

'The Crucifixion' is announced in a solemn *Praeludium* where Biber for the first time uses triple stopping as well as angular dotted rhythms; 'The Resurrection' is brilliantly depicted in a flurry of ecstatic figuration which gains a fanfare-like quality from the remarkable tuning of the strings D-G-D-G. (The original editor of the sonatas could not believe this tuning and so suggested an alternative which made nonsense of the music.) The chorale *Surrexit Christus Hodie* is introduced triumphantly here. The trumpet-style writing is continued in 'The Ascension', where the strings are now tuned to a C major chord C-E-G-C so that the energetic fanfaring has a natural sparkle and glint. But the most glorious effect in these sonatas comes at the opening of

Ex. 2 *Mystery Sonatas*

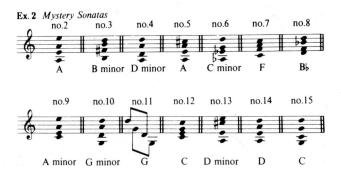

Violin and lute: detail of a painted frieze (late sixteenth century) in the great chamber of Gilling Castle, Yorkshire.

Below: Florentine musicians: painting by A. D. Gabbiani (1652–1726).

The opening bars of Biber's Mystery Sonata XVI.

no. 13, 'The Descent of the Holy Ghost', where the top two strings are tuned a third apart so that exquisite chains of double-stopped strings can depict the fluttering of the spirit and its descent. In the last two accompanied sonatas the Assumption and the Coronation of Mary are portrayed.

The last of these Mystery sonatas is quite unexpected. It is prefaced by a picture of a guardian angel leading a small child (a feast also celebrated in Salzburg Cathedral during October), and consists of an unaccompanied Passacaglia for violin solo. It takes the familiar descending four notes of so many ground basses, and from the first hypnotic addition of an uncertain, repeated off-beat phrase, elaborates the bass line with consummate skill. It reaches a piercing climax on repeated top Ds, then the theme is heard descending unaccompanied in the treble and the music sinks to a pause: it gathers strength, rushing up scales and arpeggios, and with a final flourish of battle-like repeated notes, the theme is triumphantly repeated with triple-stopping. Nothing finer than this Passacaglia was written for the violin in the seventeenth century, and nothing like it was to be heard again until the Chaconne of Bach's D minor Partita.

II THE EIGHTEENTH CENTURY

High Baroque

When Arcangelo Corelli dated his op. 5 sonatas 1st January 1700, it was surely a conscious declaration that a new musical era had begun. And these solo sonatas, too, introduce a new mature age of the violin. They were to become by far the most influential sonatas of their time, and by the end of the century would have appeared in no fewer than forty-two different editions, carrying the school of Corelli forward into the age of the Romantic violin. Corelli's pre-eminence sprang partly from his personal reputation, partly from the fact that his music created a stable style, and partly from the coincidence that his activity and the growth of the music publishing industry came together in the first years of the new century.

Corelli was renowned as a performer; about him are told the first of those romantic tales of passionate involvement with music-making which will later be associated with C. P. E. Bach and, of course, with Paganini. Galliard wrote in 1709: 'I never met with any man that suffered his passion to hurry him away so much whilst he was playing on the violin . . . [he] gives in so much to what he is doing that he doth not look like the same man . . . [his] eyes will sometimes turn as red as fire; his countenance will be distorted, his eyeballs roll as in an agony . . .' Yet outwardly Corelli seems in his portraits appropriately archangel-like, and the English historian Hawkins said he was 'remarkable for the mildness of his temper and the modesty of his deportment'. He must indeed have been transformed in performance. Corelli's solo violin sonatas make considerable demands on the player, but none as eccentric as those of the late seventeenth-century Central European tradition. He often asks the soloist to play the first two opening entries of a fugue subject in double-stopping, or gives him a virtuoso cadenza using cross-string *bariolage* writing over a sustained bass note. But Michael Talbot places their style in perspective with his comment that 'if Corelli's idiom often seems predictable, over-simple or even commonplace, it is paradoxically as a result of his very originality as perceived by his contemporaries who, by appropriating and developing its most advanced features, turned what were once exciting novelties into dry clichés.' And David Boyden surely isolates the

Violino Solo.
Passagaglia.

ARCANGELVS CORELLIVS FVSIGNANO dictus BONONIENSIS.
Liquisse Infernas Iam Credimus Orphea Sedes / Et terras habitare, huius sub imagine formæ. / Divinus patet Ipse Orpheus, dum numine digna / Arte modos fingit, vel chordas mulcet utramque / Agnoscat Laudem, meritasque BRITANNVS honores.
H. Howard pinx. / J. Smith Anglus fecit.

SONATA III

Arcangelo Corelli: mezzotint by J. Smith after Hugh Howard (1675–1737).

Below: Written-out embellishments in the Roger edition of Corelli's op.5 (1715).

reason for their extraordinary success when he writes that Corelli's pieces 'were so idiomatically written for the violin that they almost played themselves.'

Corelli's op. 5 sonatas raise the important question of the extent to which printed editions of violin music in this period contained all the information necessary to performance. We noted at the very beginning of this survey that the use of modern instruments makes the realization of the music of Marini and his contemporaries difficult; so too a literal approach to musical notation, as established in the nineteenth century, makes the performance of Corelli's music quite unconvincing. It was expected that the slow movements would be extensively ornamented, and that all the movements would be appropriately graced with trills and cadential flourishes. But to what extent these practices were codified is uncertain, and how rigorously they were applied is a matter for debate. Fascinating evidence survives, however, in the case of Corelli's op. 5. Perhaps around 1715 Estienne Roger, the French music publisher active in Amsterdam, published Corelli's op. 5 in what he described as a 'new edition engraved with the same format as the four first works of Corelli, with the embellishments marked for the Adagios as Mr. Corelli wants them played, and those who are curious to see the original of Mr. Corelli with his letters written on this subject can see them at Estienne Roger's.'

This publication provides elaborate ornamentation for the Adagios of the first six sonatas, mostly in the form of running scales and turns, which transform their character. We cannot be certain whether Corelli wrote them, or whether he simply approved of them in principle. And the question also has to be asked: if practices like this were so common, why did Roger feel the need to publish this detailed and explicit example? Some scholars have doubted that the graces can be relied upon; Robert Donington suggests that 'someone perhaps heard him [Corelli] on one occasion play something like this, and wrote down the approximation as well as he remembered it, which was not very well.' Donington approves the ornamentation of the first sonata, but remarks that 'in the following five sonatas, the ornamentation gets to be more and more clumsy, incomplete and inconsistent, in fact at times really rather ugly'. This may be a judgement based on modern taste; David Boyden accepts them as authentic, and believes moreover that the edition probably appeared during Corelli's lifetime, before the publication by Walsh in London in December 1711 of the op. 5 sonatas 'with ye Graces'.

The story of Corelli's op. 5 as a model for Baroque ornamentation does not end here, however, for further

like Corelli, was a brilliant performer: a vivid description of his playing is given by von Uffenbach in 1715:

Towards the end [of the opera] Vivaldi played a solo accompaniment admirably, adding at the end a free fantasy which quite frightened me, for it is scarcely possible that anyone ever played or will play this way, for he placed his fingers but a hair's breadth from the bridge, so that there was barely room for the bow, doing this on all four strings with imitations at incredible speed.

In his early solo sonatas, from op. 2 (1712), Vivaldi shows how skilfully he can manipulate figures and phrases which are particularly well suited to the violin, reiterating them and laying them out in those large-scale patterns which were to function with even greater effectiveness in his concertos.

Vivaldi pays his debt to Corelli with a couple of references to the older master's op. 5, modelling the opening of his second sonata on Corelli's famous first sonata, as did Vitali and Albinoni. Vivaldi's op. 2 takes Corelli's *sonata da camera* as its point of departure, rearranging the familiar dance forms so that sometimes the *giga* begins the sonata. There is some fiery writing in the *Capriccio* of the ninth sonata and in the similarly titled movement in the twelfth sonata; more serious is the *Adagio* of the second sonata, cast as a recitative in an unusual foreign key. Like so much of Vivaldi's music, this set was published in London, and pirated editions were also available in Amsterdam. The fact that so much new music was rapidly available throughout Europe must have radically altered the speed with which composers and performers could learn from each other.

New heights of skill

The two decades following Vivaldi's op. 2 saw the publication of collections by Geminiani, Somis, Veracini, Tartini and Locatelli, in all of which the idiom of Corelli is developed, or some would say dissipated. Geminiani we shall consider later. Giovanni Battista Somis (1686–1763) is a figure of an interest disproportionate to his musical accomplishment, for he forms a crucial personal link between Baroque and Classical styles. He studied for three years with Corelli, and perhaps with Vivaldi as well, and he passed on that teaching to some of the leading French figures of the century, including Leclair, Guillemain and Guignon. He also taught Gaetano Pugnani, who in his turn taught Viotti, the famous founder of the nineteenth-century French school. Of Somis's fame as a performer we have sadly few reports: when he played at the *Concerts Spirituel* (a Parisian con-

elaborations appeared later in the century. Geminiani's have survived, as have those of his pupil Matthew Dubourg; both of these alter the fast movements as well as the Adagios, and create free improvisatory fantasies with the material that takes them far from Corelli. Nicola Matteis is reported also to have made a set, for it is mentioned by Quantz, but that has disappeared.

The flowering of violin music in Italy from the roots established by Corelli was very rapid. Back in Venice, Tomaso Albinoni (1671–1751) published several sets of sonatas. He, like T. A. Vitali is celebrated for a piece he did not write: that infamous *Adagio*, based on a single-line fragment of his own music, elaborated in luscious nineteenth-century style by his biographer and editor, Remo Giazotto. More indicative of his importance is the fact that Albinoni's music was used by J. S. Bach both to learn the Italian style himself and to teach it to his pupils: two themes from Albinoni's op. 1 sonatas were borrowed by Bach as subjects for keyboard fugues, and one sonata from op. 6 survives complete with a realization of the *basso continuo* by H. N. Gerber, which Bach has corrected in his own hand. (It is published in Spitta's biography of Bach.)

A stronger development of Corelli's idiom is found in the wonderfully demonstrative violin writing of Antonio Vivaldi. With Vivaldi the art of the violin concerto is resoundingly established, and the instrument is carried on to a public platform where it felt increasingly at home: very soon the concerto would begin to supplant the sonata as the vehicle for advanced violin writing (see *The Violin Concerto*, p. 159). Vivaldi,

The Concert: painting by Pietro Longhi (1702–85).

Francesco Maria Veracini: engraved frontispiece to his
Sonate accademiche (1744).

cert series founded in 1725), the *Mercure de France*
merely praised the 'precision and brilliance of this great
master'. Hubert le Blanc, in the course of a fierce
defence of the viol '*contre les entreprises du violon*' tells
us more illuminatingly that Somis displayed 'the
majesty of the most beautiful bow-stroke in Europe . . .
A single down-bow lasts so long that one is made breathless thinking of it.' In his music, too, Somis is important
as a transitional figure. Boris Schwarz has noted that
the opening Allegros of his sonatas are extended into
something we can recognize as 'an incipient sonata form
in the Classical sense', with an exposition, digression,
and shortened recapitulation. And he brought together
elements of the old church and chamber sonatas, combining them to form a new type of abstract sonata genre.

'The Beethoven of the eighteenth century' was Tor-
chi's surprising accolade for Francesco Maria Veracini
(1690–1768), a cosmopolitan and volatile figure who was
employed in Dresden, appeared in England, and led an
extremely complicated life. M. G. White and John
Walter Hill in *Music and Letters* (1971, 1975) have
disentangled some of his activities, and Hill discusses
his depressive traits, his attack on his wife with a dagger,
and his attempted suicide. His playing was undoubtedly
virtuoso, but drew differing reports. Charles de Brosses
in 1739 wrote that 'his playing is just, noble, knowledge-
able and precise, but a little lacking grace'. Burney said
that 'the peculiarities of his performance were his bow-
hand, his shake, his learned arpeggios, and a tone so
loud and clear that it could be distinctly heard
throughout the most numerous band of a church or
theatre.' He published a set of twelve sonatas in 1716,
and another, op. 1, in 1721; his most famous set,
however, is the *Sonate accademiche* (1744), which Hill
suggests were written for Italian private concerts
(*accademie*) rather than being especially academic in the
conventional sense. Veracini uses many unusual movement titles—*Aria Schiavonna, Cotillion, Schozezze,
Polonese*—and the whole collection is more miscel-
laneous than his op. 1, which had been carefully
designed as a cycle with six minor-key chamber sonatas
and six major-key church sonatas. In his preface to
op. 2, Veracini suggested that players could choose two
or three movements from the four or five provided 'to
comprise a sonata of just proportions'. As so often, the
last of the collection is exceptional. It is a Passacaglia
on the descending chromatic fourth, announced by the
violin and taken up by the *continuo*. Veracini marks the
opening *Largo assai e come sta*—that is, 'do not add
ornamentation'—and then interpolates a *Capriccio
Cromatico*, a more cheerful movement based on the

same theme, and a long D major *Ciacona* before returning to the material of the opening.

Another outstanding Italian figure beside Vivaldi and
Veracini is Giuseppe Tartini (1692–1770), who is said
to have been inspired by having heard Veracini play at
a concert in Venice. He was *primo violino e capo di
concerto* at St. Anthony's basilica in Padua, a post which
allowed him considerable freedom to travel and perform
abroad. Burney contrasted his modest, unassuming
character with that of the more boastful Veracini; his
letters confirm that he was solicitous of the welfare of
others. In Tartini's sonatas the changes noted in the
music of Somis are consolidated: there are often three
movements, slow, fast and faster; the texture is increasingly homophonic; and the Allegros have a binary
design that hints at sonata form. There is a rather lyrical,
almost swooning style in some of the slow movements
which ensured that Tartini's music survived into the
nineteenth century as a vehicle for violinists; but those
performers were probably not aware of the extraordinary decorated versions of some of the slow movements
in his op. 2 which are preserved in a manuscript now
at the University of California, Berkeley. In the manner
of Roger's decorations for Corelli's op. 5, these present
three different versions of the third sonata's opening
movement with extremely detailed ornaments, trills and

Violinist: charcoal drawing by Giovanni Battista Piazetta (1682–1754)

Tartini elaborations in J. B. Cartier's treatise *L'Art du violon*.

elaborations. One example at least of multiple elaborations in Tartini's music was known to the nineteenth century, however, since it was reproduced in the tutor, *L'Art du Violon* (1798), by J. B. Cartier (see p. 114), where Tartini's famous 'Devil's Trill' sonata appeared for the first time in print (first, except for the devilish trill itself, which Leopold Mozart used to demonstrate a point in his 1756 *Versuch einer gründlichen Violinschule*: see also p. 92).

From this pedagogical use of Tartini's music, it might be guessed that he had an important teaching role: in fact his instruction was vital for a new generation of violinists. Tartini founded a violin school in 1727 or 1728 which drew violinists from most of Europe. It appears likely that Tartini's instructions were widely disseminated, for some of Leopold Mozart's 1756 treatise is drawn from the posthumously published *Traité des agréments* of Tartini. Tartini also taught harmony and counterpoint, and speculated into the theory and practice of music: one of his teaching aids, *L'Arte dell'Arco a sino cinquanta variazioni per violino …*' was based on the famous Gavotte from Corelli's op. 5 no. 10, and was also included in Cartier's treatise in 1798. Once again a direct line between the violin

Above: Giuseppe Tartini: oil painting by unknown eighteenth-century artist.

Below: Pietro Locatelli: engraving by Cornelis Troost.

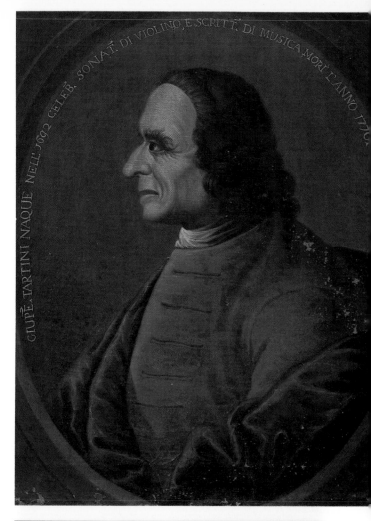

practice of the end of the seventeenth and the beginning of the nineteenth centuries can be demonstrated.

The last of Corelli's famous, or notorious, followers was Pietro Antonio Locatelli (1695–1764), one of the most brilliant performers of the mid-eighteenth century, whose varied musical output has been overshadowed by a small number of pieces in which he developed the violin's technique far beyond the range of the probable. Contemporary reports of his performance are intriguingly divided: some praised the sweetness of his *cantabile* (De Brainville opined that his gracing of the *Adagio* from Corelli's op. 5 no. 4 would make a canary fall from its perch in a swoon of pleasure), while others marvelled at the strength of his attack (Dampier thought he must surely wear out twelve violins a year). For Burney his music 'excited more surprise than pleasure'—but then Burney did not like even Geminiani's music.

The root of the trouble with Locatelli is the amazing set of concertos issued in 1733 as his op. 3 under the title *L'Arte del violino*, which includes twelve concertos with twenty-four unaccompanied *Caprices* 'ad libitum'. The *Caprices* are in the nature of cadenzas to the concertos, but they can scarcely ever have been used as such, since they are almost as long as the movements they would have had to fit into. In the concertos, Locatelli emphasizes writing in extremely high positions on the E-string, and in the *Caprices* such writing is diversified with all manner of technical effect, *bariolage* and cross-string writing which gives the violin its widest ever range up to that time. As late as the fifth edition of *Grove's Dictionary*, there was a feeling that such adventurousness was somehow morally indefensible: Grove quoted *arpeggiando* passages from *Le Labyrinthe*, and thundered: 'This savours strongly of charlatanism, and it is astonishing to find a direct pupil of Corelli one of the first to introduce such senseless feats of execution into the art of violin playing'. (To be fair, that passage originated at least as early as the second edition of Grove in 1910, and was left uncorrected through to the fifth: *The New Grove* circumspectly remarks that the op. 3 works 'are by no means his most representative'.) Nevertheless, Locatelli's innovations fall into the pattern of those explored by Tartini and Veracini, and in France by Leclair, and they are undoubtedly the inspiration of Paganini's own *24 Caprices*: their musical effectiveness is unquestionable, and Locatelli still holds a secure place in the violinist's repertory.

Vanitas: painting by Pieter Claez (*c.* 1597–1640).

Restoring the violin: France and England

In France, a very few composers made the sudden leap in violin playing from the accomplished ensemble writing of Lully to the extraordinary solo style of Leclair. The credit for introducing the sonata style to France is acknowledged to be due to one composer, François Couperin, who claimed it loudly at the time. His innovations were made in the form of the trio sonata rather than the solo sonata, but his well-known declaration in the preface to the publication of *Les Nations* in 1726 should be reproduced:

. . . The first sonata in this collection was also the first that I composed and the first that was composed in France . . .

Charmed by those of Signor Corelli, whose works I shall love as long as I live, much as the French works of Monsieur Lully, I attempted to compose one, which I had performed in the concert hall where I had heard those of Corelli. Knowing the greediness of the French for foreign novelties above all else and lacking confidence in myself . . . I pretended that a kinsman of mine had sent me a sonata by a recent Italian composer . . . I rearranged the letters of my name so that it became an Italian name . . . The sonata was devoured eagerly and I felt vindicated by it . . .

Couperin's juxtaposition and reconciliation of the French and Italian styles in his *Apothéose de Lully* is famous, and set the idiom which prevailed for some time in France. His sonatas rarely introduce the most virtuoso elements of violin playing, and rely instead for their effect on a detailed and precise realization of ornaments.

Couperin was followed by such striking players as François Duval (*c.* 1673–1728), who was famous for his performances of Corelli's music, and Jean-Féry Rebel (1666–1747). Rebel played in and later directed the *24 Violons*, and the five sonatas at the end of his *Recueil de douze sonates* are among the earliest French examples, along with those of Elisabeth Jacquet de La Guerre and Sebastien de Brossard. Like Couperin, Rebel gave his sonatas titles, and also mixed French and Italian styles judiciously, if we are to believe Freneuse: 'Rebel has indeed caught some of the flare and fire of the Italians; but he has had the good taste and sense to temper these by the wisdom and gentleness of the French, and he has abstained from those frightening and monstrous cadenzas that are the delight of the Italians.'

The link between these composers and Leclair is provided by such figures as Jean-Baptiste Senaillé (*c.* 1688–1730), another member of the *24 Violons*, who

Jean-Marie Leclair: engraving by Jean-Charles François after Alexis Loir, 1741.

Below: The opening of Leclair's sonata no. 6 from his *Quatrième livre de sonates* (1745).

published many sonatas, received a royal privilege to issue 'sonates françaises', but also appeared in Italy at Modena, where he served at the court for two years. Michele Mascitti (1663–1760), a pupil of Corelli's, settled in Paris, as did Giovanni Ghignone (1702–74), who took the name Jean-Pierre Guignon and composed sonatas in the three-movement form of the Italian opera sinfonia. It is typical of the age that Guignon and his rival Jean-Baptiste Anet appeared together at a *Concert Spirituel* in a competition between French and Italian styles. A contemporary wrote that Guignon's playing 'is of an admirable lightness, and he claims that the agility of his bow renders the public a double service, which is to keep listeners from drowsiness by his fire, and to train by the study of his performance soloists who are stopped by no difficulty'.

More interesting musically are the compositions of Louis-Gabriel Guillemain (1705–70), which are clearly in the mould of the early classic sonata, with first-movement plans that include thematic contrast, formal development and recapitulation. In his *Amusements pour le Violon seul* (1762) he contributed to the small but important genre of unaccompanied violin pieces, already noted in the music of Westhoff and Biber.

Jean-Marie Leclair (1697–1764) forms the climax of this French Baroque school of violin playing, and leads the way towards the Classical era: he continued to exert a powerful influence on performers beyond the end of the eighteenth century. Leclair achieves what Couperin had aimed at: the reconciliation of French and Italian styles. In his sonatas the fast movements tend to be Italianate in style, but the slow movements introduce something of the French *cantabile* idiom. Busy figuration abounds, but the technical demands are not excessive, except, perhaps, in the famous sixth sonata from his fourth book. Here the unusual arpeggio figuration of the opening has to be explained in detail by the composer in the printed edition: 'In order that the passage at the beginning of this movement have its desired effect, each chord must be played with the top note first, and the three strings held simultaneously. The small notes indicate a sort of continuous *tremblement* which must project from each chord and should be played as quickly and as loudly as possible . . .' Double and triple stopping abounds, and the Gavotte in the same sonata is written in two parts almost throughout. But eloquence is always Leclair's aim, and these sonatas achieve a powerful, direct expressiveness which is rarely encountered in the French music of this period.

In England the spread of the sonata, and of the violin, had to wait until the Restoration of Charles II in 1660.

The Division-Violin:
CONTAINING
A Choice Collection of Divisions to a Ground for the
TREBLE-VIOLIN.

Being the first Musick of this kind ever Published.

LONDON, Printed by J. P. and are Sold by John Playford, near the Temple-Church: 1685.

Thereafter, they spread together like wildfire (the second quotation at the head of this chapter shows how poorly regarded the violin still was in England in the early part of the seventeenth century). The historian Sir John Hawkins wrote that 'to say the truth, the Italian style in music had been making its way into this kingdom even from the beginning of the seventeenth century . . . In compliance therefore with this general prepossession in favour of the Italian style, Jenkins composed twelve sonatas for two violins and a bass . . . the first compositions of this kind by an Englishman.' Those particular publications of John Jenkins (1592–1678) have not been traced, but he will stand well at the beginning of the line of English violin composers. Like William Lawes he introduced the violin into his consort music, but gave it idiomatic lines to play which suited the character of the instrument.

The style of Italian violin playing was introduced into England after the Restoration with the formation of a band of twenty-four violins modelled on that of the French court. Soloists such as Nicola Matteis began to make an impression in London, and he published several collections of 'Ayres for the Violin' which are a very varied rag-bag of currently fashionable styles. The less sophisticated aspect of the violin is still evident

in these pieces, as it was in John Playford's enormously popular compilation *The Division Violin*, which first appeared in 1684 and was often reprinted. Most of the pieces here are dances or sets of variations, and though an advanced style of violin playing is occasionally hinted at, the technical demands are mostly fairly limited. It includes some music by Thomas Baltzar (*c.* 1630–63), born in Lübeck, employed in Sweden, the most illustrious of the foreign virtuosos who preceded Matteis; he loved convivial company, and is said to have died from excessive drinking. He was praised by Anthony Wood, who 'saw him run his fingers to the end of the finger-board of the violin and then back insensibly, and all with alacrity and in very good tune, which he nor any in England never saw the like before'. Baltzar's variations in *The Division Violin* are relatively elaborate, with Italianate figurations.

Not until Henry Purcell, however, did England produce a native composer skilled in the methods of the Italian sonatas. Roger North says that Purcell followed Matteis in his adoption of Italian forms, and Purcell certainly owed to direct Italian influence in the famous introduction 'To The Reader' in his 1683 sonatas. He writes that he has 'faithfully endeavoured a just imitation of the most fam'd Italian masters; principally,

Below: Henry Purcell: portrait in black chalk, attributed to John Closterman (1660–1711).

Opposite: *A Young Man Playing the Violin*: painting by Peter Lely, *c.* 1640.

to bring the seriousness and gravity of that sort of Musick into vogue and reputation among our Countrymen, whose humour, 'tis time now, should begin to loath the levity and balladry of our neighbours . . .' There seems to be implied in this an attempt to move away from the popular image of the violin to something more serious; certainly the gloriously effective writing for violin in both the 1683 set and the posthumous 1697 set of ten sonatas in four parts demonstrates a complete command of contemporary technique.

The eighteenth-century violinist Matthew Dubourg, on the other hand, was scathing about Purcell's achievement, and wrote in *The Violin*: 'Purcell knew only Basani, Torelli, and predecessors of Corelli; the capabilities of the violin remained unknown to him, and his sonatas will hardly escape being characterised as barbarous'. (A judgement which goes to show the danger of placing technical accomplishment above musical worth, an ever-present danger when discussing violin music and violin players.) But in fact these sonatas integrate the Italian style with the imitative, carefully-worked style of the English viol fantasia, and so stand as one of the greatest examples of that particular blending of new and old idioms which has distinguished English music from Dunstable to Elgar.

Italians in London

In the early years of the eighteenth century, Italian violinists came to England in large numbers. As Roger North put it: 'And the best utensill of Apollo, the violin is so universally courted, and sought after to be had of the best sort, that some say England has dispeopled Italy of violins and no wonder, after the great master made that instrument as it were with human voice, saying to his schollars—*Non udite lo parlare?* (Do you not hear it speak?) . . . But how long this humour will hold without back-sliding into ballad-singing I cannot forsee . . .'

Among these Italians the most important were three pupils of Corelli. Pietro Castrucci (1679–1752) played in Handel's opera orchestras; Giovanni Stefanno Carbonelli—who is unaccountably omitted from *The New Grove*—led the same opera orchestra with such skill that he was introduced as a character into one of Sir Richard Steele's comedies, appearing to play a violin solo. He published one set of sonatas. A surviving handbill for a concert at Drury Lane in 1722 gives a good impression of the circumstances in which violin music was heard in public at this time. 'Signor Carbonelli's Concert' was arranged in three groups: first a concerto for two trumpets; a new concerto by Albinoni 'just

brought over'; a song; and a concerto composed by Signor Carbonelli. Then a concerto for the 'base violin'; a song; and 'by desire the eighth concerto by Archangelo Corelli'. The final group consisted of another concerto by Carbonelli, a solo on the arch-lute, a song, a new concerto on the 'little flute' by Woodcock, a solo by Carbonelli (probably the showiest piece of the evening), and finally another two-trumpet concerto.

The third pupil of Corelli to appear in London was Francesco Geminiani, who arrived with Veracini in 1714. His op. 1, published in 1716, was later revised with detailed markings, providing an important source of performance-practice documentation. Geminani's debt to Corelli was repaid in transcriptions of the master's music for the new form of the *concerto grosso*, and his imitation of Corelli's op. 5 no. 1 in his own op. 1 no. 1. Handel himself accompanied Geminiani when he played at court in 1716. Many reports of his playing are complimentary, but Geminiani has suffered because his style found favour with neither of the music historians of England in this period, John Hawkins or Charles Burney. Burney reports rumours that Geminiani was unsuccessful as a leader of the orchestra

in Naples because the players could not follow his eccentric tempos. But a Mrs Delany, who heard Geminiani play in Dublin at the age of 72, reported that 'the sweetness and melody of the tone of his fiddle, his fine and elegant taste, and the perfection of time and tune make full amends for some weakness of his hands . . .'. Hawkins claims too that musicians were astonished by Geminiani's harmonic surprises (which he suggests most improbably that Geminiani derived from a study of the music of Gesualdo): the players 'not choosing to deviate from the good and wholesome rules which they had been taught in choirs . . . shook their heads and hung their harps upon the willows.'

In fact Geminiani's idiom, while showing an advance over that of Corelli, is by no means as complex as those of contemporary Italians, and his technical devices, too, are relatively restrained. But he does demand enormous agility from the player, in crossing strings, and leaping more than an octave: he was one of the few violinists who could play his music, which perhaps contributed

to its poor reputation. He was even more important as a theorist than as a player, and his contribution to the teaching of the violin will be considered in the following chapter (see pp. 92–94).

A few native English composers made contributions to the violin repertory at this time: Richard Jones (*c.* 1730s) published some sets of pieces which have been reprinted in modern editions. Michael Festing (?–1752) was a pupil of Jones and Geminiani who became Master of the King's Musick and director of the Italian opera orchestra. Like several of his contemporaries he preferred the word 'solo' to describe the sonata for a single instrument; 'sonata' meant trio sonata in his usage. His solos exploit the full range of the instrument and are vividly dramatic, with strong contrasts. John Stanley (1713–86), the blind organist, followed the same terminology in his *Eight Solos* (1740). Thomas Arne (1710–78) contributed a set of trio sonatas op. 3, and William Boyce (*c.* 1710–79) wrote very popular trio sonatas which remained in the repertory for many years.

Opposite *The Enraged Musician*: engraving by William
Hogarth (the violinist is thought to be Castrucci), *c.* 1741.

Perhaps they were heard at the concerts of Thomas Britton, well-known as the Musical Small-Coal Man, who promoted a series of public concerts in a small room over his shop (lit by a window 'no bigger than the bung-hole of a cask', as Ned Ward reported). Pepusch wrote a sonata called 'Smalcoal' for him, and Britton's very impressive library contained violin music by Walther, Biber, Cazzati, Albinoni and Vivaldi, as well as a copy of Corelli's op. 1 marked 'used at this Assembly for many years'. This demonstrates how widely violin music travelled around Europe.

Handel

The violin sonatas of George Frideric Handel (1685–1759) are few in number: though he exploited the violin to brilliant effect in the *concertino* parts of his *concerti grossi* and in the sinfonias, *ritornelli* and arias of his operas and oratorios, he was less interested in writing chamber music for the instrument. The situation of his solo sonatas has been extremely confused because the editor of the *Händel-Gesellschaft*, Friedrich Chrysander, grouped together fifteen sonatas which he included in Handel's 'op. 1': not all of these are authentic. Terence Best (in *Music and Letters*, October 1977), has clarified matters. Roger published 12 sonatas as Handel's op. 1 in about 1722, and Walsh reprinted the set around 1732. But nos. 10 and 12 of these sets are different, and neither pair of sonatas 10 and 12 is now thought to be by Handel. Of the rest, only the A major sonata op. 1 no. 3 is undoubtedly a work for violin: it contains a singing *Andante*, an energetic *Allegro* with plenty of the cross-string figuration Handel used so effectively elsewhere, an eloquent decorated *Adagio* and a final Gigue. However the E minor sonata for recorder, op. 1 no. 1, also exists in a version in D minor for violin. And the sonata in G minor op. 1 no. 6, described as 'oboe solo', is indicated as a violin solo in the autograph in the Fitzwilliam Museum, Cambridge (where it follows the D minor arrangement in the same source).

To these three authentic violin sonatas two more may be added: the early, lively G major sonata from around 1707 included by Terence Best in the recently published Series IV volume 18 of the Halle Handel Edition, and the D major sonata which is usually called 'op. 1 no. 13'. This nonsensical description is Chrysander's; in fact the work was written as late as 1750 and is nothing to do with either original op. 1 publication. It is an exceptional work, representing Handel's style at its most mature. The opening gesture is unforgettable: the violin, rising up the notes of the D major triad, suddenly extends itself and lands not on a D but on an E, and then extends the phrase by ascending another D major broken chord and landing on a high B. The magnificent final *Allegro* was to serve Handel again as a sinfonia in his last oratorio *Jephtha*.

Before Bach

To return to the area of central Europe whence Handel came to England will enable us to trace the Baroque violin as far as its greatest master, Johann Sebastian Bach. It is misleading, however, to view Bach's predecessors only as lesser lights who led towards him: they merit performance and study just as their Italian contemporaries do. One key to the slow progress of music in the German areas in the early years of the seventeenth century is the disruption caused by the Thirty Years War which broke out in 1618. As Heinrich Schütz wrote: 'Among the other free arts the noble art of music has not only suffered great decline in our beloved fatherland as a result of the ever present dangers of war; in many places it has been wholly destroyed, lying amid the ruins and chaos for all to behold.' The war ended in 1648, and Schütz was among the leaders of those who restored the arts to their rightful place in the area. His strong links with the Italian school of Monteverdi and Gabrieli helped to ensure that the innovations of their violin writing were imported into Germany: Schütz himself used them in his concerted vocal pieces (though he never wrote sonatas), and passed their idiom on to his pupils.

In northern Germany, Johann Rosenmüller (*c.* 1619–84) is an outstanding example of a composer who turned Italian idiomatic devices to his own expressive ends, creating in his multi-sectional sonatas for several string instruments a splendid variety of form and colour. His pieces include *battaglia* fanfares in C major, sombre fugues, and slow movements in recitative style with sudden pauses and rhetorical declamations. Dietrich Buxtehude (*c.* 1637–1707) is best known as an organist, but he also wrote several resourceful solo sonatas and ensemble sonatas. An especially interesting work is the B flat major sonata for violin, *viola da gamba* and *continuo*, which anticipates later eighteenth-century three-movement form and shares thematic material between treble and bass instruments. A close associate of Buxtehude's was Jan Adam Reincken, who published the collection *Hortulus Musicus* in 1688. He, too, is chiefly important as an organist, but the six sonatas in his collection demonstrate characteristics of both solo sonata and suite, and are intended for use in church or chamber.

In Southern Germany the most important pre-Bach figure was Johann Pachelbel (1653–1706). He links the Bohemian tradition of Schmelzer and Biber with that of Bach, for he knew Schmelzer and used *scordatura* in his music; he also knew Buxtehude and Daniel Eberlin (who was Telemann's father-in-law) and thus unusually linked the Protestant north of Germany and the Catholic south. In his keyboard music many of Bach's techniques are suggested; in his violin music he rather looks back to the style of Biber, placing a single solo violin above a group of low instruments, as in his G major Suite (which uses two violas), or his Aria and variations in A major, which uses two gambas beneath the solo violin. His music has a glorious richness and substance of content, though the use of the violin is not in itself especially adventurous. Undoubtedly Pachelbel's most famous work, the Canon in D for three violins and *continuo*, has in modern arrangements for string orchestra been absurdly transformed and separated from its sprightly companion Gigue. One performer of the original version, Reinhard Goebel, has recently suggested that the piece might be by Biber.

While Bach drew inspiration from the German composers of keyboard and ensemble music who preceded him, perhaps a more important stimulus to his instrument style during his lifetime was his contact with

the glittering court of Dresden, which he visited in 1717 and where he subsequently made strenuous efforts to obtain an appointment. In Dresden he became acquainted with Jan Dismas Zelenka, a fascinating composer who wrote in a dense contrapuntal style for the oboe but little for the violin; Johann David Heinichen (1683–1729), who had studied in Leipzig and wrote some twenty-five solo sonatas; and Sylvius Leopold Weiss, the lutenist. Possibly the most significant contact was with Johann Georg Pisendel (1687–1755), who had studied in Italy with Torelli and Vivaldi. He was respected by audiences and composers alike: Albinoni, Vivaldi and Telemann all wrote works specifically for him to play, and he was admired as an orchestral director—apparently he marked bowing and expression marks in the orchestral parts, an early example of this now routine practice. He taught both J. G. Graun and Franz Benda.

It may be that in Dresden in 1717 Johann Pisendel played Bach his sonata for unaccompanied violin. We have already seen how rare this form was, being attempted only by Westhoff, by Biber in his Passacaglia, and by a couple of other composers. Pisendel's sonata demonstrates a style which Bach was to develop in his own solo sonatas and partitas. There is an opening *Largo*, with all possible ornamentation written into the music, where chordal declamations interrupt the flow

Opposite: The rehearsal of an opera: painting by Marco
Ricci (early eighteenth-century). The characters include
Heidegger (seated extreme right), the violonists John, James
and Michael Festing (left) and the cellist Andrea Caporale.

Below: George Frideric Handel: portrait by Thomas
Hudson, 1756.

so that he could be in the midst of the sound. His first biographer Forkel reported:

As the greatest expert and judge of harmony he liked best to play the viola, with appropriate loudness and softness. In his youth, and until the approach of old age, he played the violin cleanly and penetratingly, and this kept the orchestra in better order than he could with the harpsichord. He understood to perfection the possibilities of all stringed instruments . . .

But apart from the brilliant violin solo in the fourth Brandenburg Concerto, and some later solos in the cantata arias, there is no violin music in his output which approaches the sonatas and partitas in their range of difficulty. And yet there is nothing showy or demonstrative in these pieces in the Italian sense: their demands are unfailingly subordinated to musical results.

The many technical problems posed by the multiple-stoppings in these sonatas and partitas have been solved in a variety of ways by modern performers. The strangest misconception, which flourished for some time, was that on a violin of Bach's period it would have been possible to play all four strings at once and so sound Bach's written-out four-part chords in glorious organistic harmony. This was never the case: the short bow, relaxed hair tension and flattened bridge of Bach's time gave a far greater agility and subtlety in moving from string to string, but a quadruple-stopped chord still had to be played by touching three strings and sustaining only one or two of them. Nevertheless, strenuous efforts were made to invent a 'Bach bow' which could play these works 'precisely as written', and a monstrous arc with a huge curvature in which the violinist could tighten or relax the hair during the performance was created. This bent its way across all the strings so that they could sound together. (Far more useful advice in adapting Bach's music to the modern violin is given by Joseph Szigeti in his book *Szigeti on the Violin*.) There is yet to be a player who has mastered the art of the Baroque violin to a sufficient extent to give a performance of these works in period style which can stand beside the greatest performances on modern instruments; but already the attempts that have been made have revealed much about the original concepts of phrasing and articulation in the music.

Three of the six pieces are Partitas, in the free form of the dance suite: three are sonatas in the slow-fast-slow-fast arrangement of the old church sonata (though there is no real evidence, as some commentators have suggested, that they were used in church). The works were written down in Cöthen in 1720, but they may

of rhapsodic melody. Then there is an *Allegro* in binary form, such as Bach was to use in his dance movements, and finally a *Giga* with a virtuoso variation. Although the idiom perhaps points forward more firmly than Bach's, it is close enough to suggest a direct line of inspiration: possibly Bach designed his pieces for Pisendel to play.

Contrapuntal climax

To look at the fair copy which J. S. Bach prepared in 1720 of his *Sei Soli a Violino senza Basso accompagnato* is a moving experience. Bach's fluent, dramatic, perfectly poised musical calligraphy is exquisitely laid out on the page; as was his custom, every page of manuscript is used to the utmost, with extra staffs to complete the movements added at the bottom of the pages where necessary. The writing is impeccably clear, and there are very few signs of erasures and alterations. Doubtless Bach was copying from previous manuscripts, though experience suggests that he was probably modifying as he copied. But the sheer command of technique and expression in these highly unusual forms still leaves one breathless: no wonder that nineteenth-century musicians, baffled by the extraordinary scope of these pieces, decided they need the assistance of piano accompaniments, which both Schumann and Mendelssohn duly provided.

Bach, we know, played the violin skilfully, and used also to play the viola when he directed the orchestra,

Fuga.

87

The Palace of Cöthen: engraving _c._ 1650.

well have been begun at Weimar, where it seems that Bach did more violin playing himself. The first sonata, in G minor, includes one of the massive fugues that dominate this set, a work Bach liked so much that he transcribed it for organ. Its hammer-stroke chords illustrate perfectly the kind of resonance Bach expected from his instrument, with the fugal line supported by accompanying chords underneath or on top. The preceding _Largo_ traverses a quite simple harmonic framework, but the sweeping decorations elaborate the outline in great detail. The Siciliano is written like a trio, with a melodic bottom line accompanied by harmonious thirds and sixths above, which might sound like a pair of flutes. Then, as will happen often throughout this set, the com-

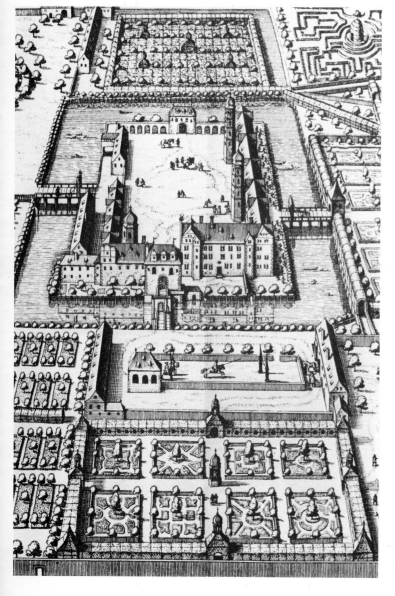

plexities of multiple-stopping are dissolved in a triple-time _Presto_ of brilliant, perpetual, single-line motion.

The second sonata, in A minor, also includes a fugue, one that found favour even with Bach's contemporary Johann Mattheson (who on another occasion mocked the word-setting in Bach's cantatas.) He quoted the fugue's subject:

Who would believe that these short notes would be so fruitful, as to bring forth a counterpoint of more than a whole sheet of music paper, without unusual extension and quite naturally? And yet the skilled Bach who is particularly gifted in this form, has set just this before the world; indeed, he has also introduced the subject here and there in inversion.

Mattheson's brief account does less than justice to the fantastic resourcefulness with which Bach works his two-bar fragment, alternating between two, three and four-part writing, reducing it to a single line of figuration for the fugal episodes and then building up the entries again; the fugue's modulatory scheme and plan of entries and episodes are perfectly constructed down to the final, intense two-bar flourish at the close. The opening _Grave_ is similar in its decorated style to the _Largo_ of the first sonata; the _Andante_, by contrast, sings its Vivaldi-like melody over pulsing repeated notes which would have been touched in on the lower strings. This time the final _Allegro_ is in common time, with indications of _forte_ and _piano_ echoes; again it eschews complexity in the continual drive of its single line.

The third sonata, in C major, presents the most astonishing of the three fugues of this set; it is said to be the longest fugue in terms of bar numbers that Bach ever wrote. The solid, four-square theme is built on a Lutheran chorale melody, _Komm, heiliger Geist_, which is given a bold descending chromatic line as countersubject. The massive plan of the fugue includes four separate expositions, the second in _stretto_ (with the entries occurring at twice the speed of the first exposition) and the third, at the precise centre of the work, in which the theme is treated in inversion. In the episodes, single lines wing their way around the thematic material, and grow to huge climaxes built on cross-string writing—the continually repeated low Ds at the climax of the second section and low Gs at the climax of the third ring out almost like sustained notes (the same technique is used at the most powerful moments in the D minor harpsichord concerto, undoubtedly derived from a violin concerto). The _Largo_ which follows this fugue has to be a relaxation; but the _Adagio_ that precedes it, with its insistent dotted rhythms and repeated,

Concert at the Schloss Ismaning: detail from an oil painting
by Peter Jakob Horemans, 1731.

angular quadruple-stopping, screws up the tension. The final *Allegro assai*, an exultant triple-time movement, makes superbly effective use of cross-string writing.

The three Partitas are more varied in plan: the first in B minor offers an *Allemanda*, Courante, Sarabande, and a final *Tempo di Borea*, each with double (or variation). The third, in E major, opens with the brilliant *Preludio* which Bach later elaborated in the Sinfonia to his Cantata no. 29, *Wir Danken Dir, Gott* (but how striking it is that the orchestration offers nothing that cannot be imagined from the line of the solo violin!); then there is a *Loure*, a well-known *Gavotte en Rondeau*, a pair of Minuets and a bourrée, and final Gigue. At first, the D minor Partita, the second of the three, looks as if it will have the same plan as no. 1. It opens with a

sturdy *Allemanda* and *Corrente*, both unusually free of multiple-stopping, a short *Sarabanda* and a powerful *Giga* with arching arpeggiated lines. But then comes the overwhelming surprise: a *Ciacona* of the utmost grandeur, in which the old descending tetrachord (the subject used by Biber in his unaccompanied Passacaglia) is elaborated with infinite resourcefulness. Every technical possibility is exploited here to expressive ends. The plan is not unfamiliar from the keyboard chaconnes of the French school of Fux and Muffat: two sections in the minor, enclosing a central section in the major. But Bach manages to make those two transition points from minor to major and back again unforgettable, with the F sharp at the first transition point, and the B flat at the second point each heard in the opening chord

to emphasize the change. *Arpeggiando* playing is called for (Bach did not indicate how he wished this to be realized, which is why various performances can sound very different at this point), and in one D major passage the fanfare-like writing of the North Germans is transformed. The climax is built over the reiteration of the open A-string against sequences of increasing strength: the lines soar upwards with a sense of infinite power that was not to be recaptured in music until the end of Beethoven's opp. 109 and 110 piano sonatas. There is a final flourish, and the Chaconne theme returns with the same powerful simplicity as at the beginning.

Musicians through the ages have revered this Chaconne as a supreme example of musical art. Brahms, attempting to capture the sense of self-imposed limitations in the work, transcribed it for piano left hand, transferring its sonorities into the tenor register of the keyboard. Busoni, less aware of its limitations but penetratingly understanding its musical substance, changed it into a flamboyant Romantic masterwork which stretches the limits of the piano as Bach did those of the violin. Bach's great biographer Spitta was surely wrong in referring to this piece as a triumph of the spirit over substance. It is surely, in a way that only Bach could have achieved, a perfect joining of spirit with substance, so that the very challenge of realizing the music on the violin becomes a central part of the musical experience.

Pointers forward

It might seem appropriate to close this survey of the Baroque violin with the massive achievement of Bach's six solos. But in fact another group of his works provides a more significant pointer to the future. His sonatas for violin with *obbligato* keyboard are the first important members of a musical family whose offspring was to dominate the years of the Classical violin. For in these works, perhaps under the influence of the splendid new harpsichord acquired in Cöthen from Berlin (which may also have inspired the rewriting of the harpsichord part of the fifth Brandenburg Concerto), Bach raises the keyboard part to a level of importance it had never previously been given.

His method is to write trios for two instruments: the right hand of the keyboard player and the violinist make a duet on equal terms, while the left hand of the keyboard player provides the *continuo* bass line. It is possible that another bass instrument reinforced this line; when the keyboard player's right hand was unoccupied with his solo, figures in the bass line indicate that he would have filled in the harmonies in the *continuo*

player's normal fashion. In the G major sonata the keyboard even has a movement to itself: in one source, the Courante from the E minor Partita, in another, a vigorously worked solo.

The sharing of material varies in the different sonatas. In the opening B minor sonata (BWV 1014) the violin's line in the *Adagio* is quite distinct from the harpsichord's; only later does it adopt the same six-note quaver pattern. The following fugue is in three equal parts; the next *Andante* is skilfully written so that although the violin has long sustained notes, the harpsichord (which cannot sustain) avoids them. The second sonata (BWV 1015) in A major opens with an exquisite canon in two parts marked *dolce*, with a freely imitative bass line; the second *Andante* is also a canon, worked over a *staccato* walking bass. The fast movements here are concerto-like in their structure and musical language.

The opening *Adagio* of the third sonata (BWV 1016) in E major reverts to an elaborate singing line for the violin with fully realized chords for the harpsichord; in the second *Adagio*, marked *ma non tanto*, the harpsichord emerges from its chordal opening to share the violin's triplets. The two bustling Allegros are both imitative. In the fourth sonata, BWV 1017 in C minor, the harpsichordist keeps a continuous figuration in motion through both slow movements: the first is a Siciliano, the second an *Adagio* in E flat major. The oddest opening movement is that of the fifth sonata in F minor, where the violinist seems merely to be adding occasional extra counterpoint to an already complete keyboard texture: in this the approach of the Classical 'accompanied sonata' is clearly foreshadowed. The balance is redressed, however, in the highly original *Adagio*, where it is the violin which provides a sustained chordal background to the harpsichordist's flourishes. The sixth sonata in G major (BWV 1019) opens with one of the most magnificently worked concerto-type movements and closes with another, in which the duetting of violin and harpsichord is placed against a syncopated bass line.

As so often, Bach, in bringing the art of his time to perfection, does not merely look backwards but points to the future. In his unaccompanied violin music he was to inspire future generations of violinists to new—and at times extremely un-Bach-like—achievements; and in his accompanied violin sonatas he was to provide a model for a host of later and regrettably lesser composers; not until Mozart developed, through his long line of pieces, the violin and keyboard sonata was the promise of the form to be fulfilled.

The Classical Violin

Previous page: the violinist: chalk drawing by J. A. Portail (1695–1759).

Opposite: The Mozart family: Nannerl and Wolfgang are at the keyboard, while Leopold holds his violin. Mozart's mother (d. 1778) is represented in a portrait (c. 1775) on the wall: painting by Johann Nepomuk della Croce, c. 1780.

Below: Francesco Geminiani: portrait by William Hoare (1706–92).

Techniques and Treatises

At first sight, it appears strange that two major treatises on playing the violin, one summarizing the Baroque tradition, and one already looking forward to the Classical tradition, both date from the same decade. Francesco Geminiani's *The Art of Playing on the Violin* first appeared in 1751; Leopold Mozart's *Versuch einer gründlichen Violinschule* (translated as 'A Treatise on the Fundamental Principles of Violin Playing') appeared in 1756. Both include much similar information, but in terms of the instruction it gives about bow strokes and articulation, Leopold Mozart's tutor is by far the more advanced. It seems that Mozart probably compiled his book in ignorance of Geminiani's, and believed it to be the first of its kind.

The appearance of both tutors in the same period should alert us to the growing professionalism and sophistication of the art of the violin. Neither tutor was the first; earlier, there had been many books of instructions by Michel Corrette and others, but their fundamental role was by and large to enable a gentleman amateur to obtain, without too much effort, a basic schooling in the violin which would enable him to play his part in ensemble music (an exception is the recently discovered *Musicalischer Schlissel* of 1677 by Johann Jacob Prinner, so far unpublished, which gives detailed instructions for the technique of playing string instruments, and is in advance of its time, in particular in its advice concerning violin grip).

In Geminiani and Leopold Mozart the aim is very different: it is to preserve and disseminate for a wide variety of students the essence of private training, to enable the young violinist to attain to professional status. Other writers, notably Georg Muffat, had provided instructions for orchestral playing, giving important information on the conventions of the time, on the speed of dance movements, and so on, but that was not primarily an instruction in violinistic technique. That these two treatises of the 1750s were quickly followed by pirated, altered and otherwise rearranged versions of them, and also by several new treatises, demonstrates the growing enthusiasm for the instrument as the era of the Classical violin begins.

It is tempting to take a treatise at face value. Without a precise knowledge of the surrounding circumstances, however, it is dangerous to pronounce that a certain statement mirrors the practice of the age, and then to copy it literally. A treatise may convey the normal practice of the time; on the other hand, it may have been written down because it contradicted the normal practice of the time with which the writer disagreed.

The writer may wish to emphasize some fundamental premises which he feels are being lost sight of in his time; he may wish to correct faults of technique he sees in players around him. By the 1750s the art of musical history and historiography, soon to flourish, had scarcely begun: Charles Burney and John Hawkins began to publish their histories in 1776. We cannot expect such a perspective on the music of the past as we take for granted in later writings.

There is another possible way to view the treatises of Geminiani and Leopold Mozart: not first as expressions of old and new styles, but as expressions of the rival Italian and German schools of playing, with the most significant tutor that followed them, that of L'Abbé le fils (*Principes du Violon*, 1761), as a representative of the French school. We have seen in the previous chapter how Italy swept all before it in its development of the Baroque violin and its idiomatic style for the instrument, and also how the first half of the eighteenth century saw the establishment of a rival French school of virtuoso performance, which reached its climax in the music of Leclair. One of the threads in the story of the Classical violin in the much shorter period of the second half of the eighteenth century will

be the establishment of that French style as the leading violinistic school in Europe, with a position at the end of the century that influenced the violin music of the whole of the nineteenth century.

Francesco Geminiani's practical instructions were probably compiled when he was living in England, though the musical examples in his book, curiously, are all titled in Italian, with separate page numberings. It is possible to see them as efforts to reassert the preminence of Italian practices over those fashionable in Europe in the 1740s; for in his Preface, Geminiani expresses himself in terms which would have been thought not merely conventional (as a superficial reading might suggest to us) but philosophically conservative in significant ways. In a way that anticipates some of the later declarations of Sir John Hawkins when inveighing against newer music, Geminiani asserts in his opening sentence the purpose of musical discourse:

The intention of Musicke is not only to please the Ear, but to express Sentiments, strike the Imagination, affect the Mind, and command the Passions. The Art of playing the Violin consists in giving that Instrument a Tone that shall in a Manner rival the most perfect human Voice; and in executing every Piece with Exactness, Propriety, and Delicacy of Expression according to the true Intention of Musick.

And just in case we have missed the implied criticism of wilder contemporary practices, Geminiani spells them out:

But as the imitating the Cock, Cockoo, Owl and other Birds; or the Drum, French Horn, Tromba-Marina, and the like; and also sudden shifts of the Hand from one Extremity of the Finger-board to the other; accompanied with Contortions of the Head and Body, and other such tricks rather belong to Professors of Legerdemain and Posture-masters than to the Art of Music, the Lovers of the Art are not to expect to find any thing of that Sort in this Book.

We may overlook the fact that the earliest imitative pieces were written by Italians such as Carlo Farina; Geminiani is undoubtedly referring to central European pieces such as those of Walther (see above, p. 67). As for technical feats and showiness of performance, we can only speculate as to whom he had in mind—perhaps the disciples of Locatelli?—but it is clear that he espouses a sober approach to his art which was becoming increasingly out of fashion in the entertainment-conscious days in which he lived. Philosophically, there would have been many who believed that music's intention was indeed only to please the ear: in that argument, a large measure of the eighteenth-century's disagreement about the meaning of music was summed up.

Below: Frontispiece to Leopold Mozart's *Treatise on the Fundamental Principles of Violin Playing*, 1756.

Right: Frontispiece from *The Compleat Tutor for the Violin*, c. 1765.

Further evidence of Geminiani's unfashionably serious approach can be found later in his book, in his instructions on improvisation and *vibrato*. He insists that 'playing in good Taste doth not consist of frequent passages but in expressing with Strength and Delicacy the Intention of the Composer . . . were we to make Beats and Shakes continually without suffering the pure note to be heard, the Melody would be too much diversified.' This might be taken for a severely restricting instruction were it not for the evidence which survives in the form of Geminiani's elaborations of Corelli's sonatas. The restraint Geminiani was urging must have been in response to the excesses of his age.

In some areas Geminiani was ahead of his time: David Boyden has noted that his instruction with regard to the fingering of chromatic passages was so perceptive that it had to be rediscovered in the twentieth century. His whole approach to shifting the fingers into the higher positions on the fingerboard is experimental and imaginative. This was one of the fundamental problems of eighteenth-century violin technique. Unless the player gripped the instrument with his chin, as Prinner suggested (see footnote, p. 96), the hand actually had to support the weight of the instrument. Hence

position-changing posed a problem. It was just possible to move up the fingerboard with comparative ease, but moving down was more complicated. Shifts in position had to be accomplished when an open string was being played, or at the ends of phrases. This, taken with the evidence of the eighteenth-century bow and instrument, suggests that continuous *legato* was not practised, and that short bow strokes were used, producing shorter musical phrases.

As the century passed, this style of playing became increasingly unsuited to the new musical idioms that arose. In particular, the Classical era's emphasis on a singing line of melody implied the use of much longer sustained bow strokes on the violin, a technique to which the old instrument and especially the old bow were unequal. Hence the development of a new kind of bow which could achieve that expressive end, and the modification of the violin's shape. A transitional approach can clearly be seen in some of Leopold Mozart's instructions, for he emphasizes from the start that the violin should be played with a 'manly' stroke, and he explores the relatively uncharted technical waters of continuous trills, trills in thirds and sixths, and a huge variety of bow strokes designed to give maximum variety and colour to the performance.

Below: Title-page of the French edition of Geminiani's treatise.
Right: Title-page of *Principes du Violon* by L'Abbé le fils, 1761.

It is noticeable that in his treatise Leopold Mozart is far more ambitious than Geminiani in his treatment of the background to the subject. He shows a familiarity with the writings of all manner of early theorists, including Glarean and Gaffurius, such as the historians of a couple of decades later were to draw on. He feels the need to base his practical instruction in theoretical dogma, and his historical presentation is far more rigorous than that of Geminiani's, for he travels through the basis of notation and music history before he arrives at violin technique.

Another striking aspect of Leopold Mozart's remarks which bears on the changing circumstances in the second half of the eighteenth century is his emphasis on the importance of orchestral technique as against solo performance. In his concluding chapter, he makes the point that anyone can play a solo tolerably well in his own wayward manner, but to take part in an orchestral performance a good violinist

must have great insight into the whole art of musical composition and into the difference of the characteristics; yet, he must have a specially lively adroitness to be prominent in his calling with honour, in particular if he wishes in time to become the leader of an orchestra. Perhaps

there are, however, some who believe that more good orchestral violinists are to be found than solo players. They are mistaken. Of bad accompanists there are certainly enough; of good, on the other hand, but few, for nowadays all wish to play solo . . . Few solo players read well, because they are accustomed to insert something of their own fantasy at all times, and to look after themselves only, but rarely after others.

It should also be noted that Mozart, like Geminiani, advises against the thoughtless, showy elaboration of material; but his complaint is not so much against the modern style as against those who essay it without sufficient preparation. One of his caveats is still valid:

. . . not only must one observe exactly all that has been marked and prescribed and not play it otherwise than as written; but one must throw oneself into the affect to be expressed and apply and execute in a certain good style all the ties, slides, accentuation of the notes, the forte and piano; in a word, whatever belongs to tasteful performance of a piece, which can only be learnt from sound judgement and long experience.

The developing history of violin technique, comprehensively researched by David Boyden for the period up to L'Abbé le fils's treatise of 1761, has yet to be fully researched and published for the period up to the end

Vos yeux commencent nos tourmens,
Et vos doigts charmans
Achèvent leur ouvrage.

From J. B. de Laborde's *Choix de chansons*, vol. 2, 1773: an engraved collection of *chansons* for which illustrations were commissioned from leading French illustrators of the day.

the hand in the high positions, the violin has no support, and must necessarily fall unless by long practice the advantage of being able to hold it between thumb and index finger has been acquired.' In the chin position 'the violin remains unmoved in its place even during the strongest movements of the ascending and descending hand.'*

These comments emphasize that the second half of the eighteenth century was a period of rapid development in performance styles. It would be easy to say of the violin—as many say of the piano—that as a certain style was being striven towards, and was finally attained in the first decades of the nineteenth century, so that style should be applied in retrospect to the music of the eighteenth. But that is to neglect the challenge which the more limited instruments and performance styles held for the composers of the eighteenth century. With the violin as with the piano, composers wrote for the resources that were available, and the more we discover of those practicalities the nearer we may come to understanding their idiom.

So the increasing prominence of the violin in public performance, the skill of orchestral players and soloists alike, the growth of professionalism as exemplified in these treatises, and the burgeoning of both skilled and unskilled performance—all these perspectives will be important when considering the repertory of the Classical violin.

Away from the Limelight

The period of the Classical violin, then, was a period of rapid development and change. But it is also noticeable that for a significant period during the eighteenth century the violin's importance as a solo instrument in the field of chamber music declined. The wealth of solo sonatas for violin which we surveyed in the preceding chapter is not matched by those surveyed here. It is unfortunately outside our scope here to survey the development of the violin's repertoire in orchestral and ensemble music: another book, and as many pages again, would be needed to chart the orchestral style which sprang from the excitement of the Mannheim school and which was taken over by Mozart in his symphonic writing, or to chronicle how the violin became a voice in perhaps the most sophisticated and perfect musical form produced by Western man, the string quartets of Haydn, Mozart and Beethoven.

*On the other hand, Prinner's treatise referred to above condemned players who rested the violin on their chest, and suggested a chin grip as early as 1677, indicating that practices varied widely in different parts of Europe.

of the eighteenth century. For this was a period of extremely rapid change both in musical styles and concert-giving techniques, and there can be—as we shall see in connection with the introduction of new-style bows—much argument as to when exactly changes were begun. This affects performance practice in a way that scarcely arises before 1750.

To take one example: consider the problems concerning the way the violin is held. Geminiani in his text (and in its French translation which appeared a year later) suggests holding the violin against the collar-bone; this is one stage more advanced than the old position, used for dance music, of placing it against the breast. But confusingly, the famous picture, supposedly of Geminiani (see p. 95), issued with the French version of his treatise, shows him holding it under his chin in a central position. This is more advanced again. Leopold Mozart says that the collar-bone position does not give sufficient security, and advises that it be held on the left collar-bone with the right-hand part of the violin under the chin (not a position one sees very often among period-instrument players today). It is not until the French treatise of L'Abbé le fils that the normally accepted method of holding the left part of the violin underneath the chin is taken as the norm. As Mozart says, the collar-bone position is somewhat difficult and inconvenient for players, as 'during quick movement of

Jean-Joseph Cassanea de Mondonville: pastel portrait by
Maurice Quentin de Latour (1704–88).

Pierre Gaviniès: engraving from *Gallerie des violons et luthiers célèbres morts et vivants* (1819).

As a solo instrument in the Classical period, the violin was demoted because of changing fashions. In particular, the rise of the keyboard as a solo instrument favoured by amateurs and dilettantes as well as by professionals caused a change in the balance of instrumental power. The particular suitability of the keyboard to the Classical sonata, and the secondary place of the violin, are both reflected in the statement of the French writer François Castil-Blaze at the end of this era, in 1821:

The sonata is composed for a single instrument that plays accompanied by a bass or viol if his instrument such as the violin or flute has not the means of making a complete harmony heard. But the piano, the harp, and even the guitar can get along without this support. The sonata suits the piano best of all, on which one can play three or four distinct voices at the same time, and even more. It is also on this instrument that it has gone furthest in its astonishing progress.

(*Dictionnaire de musique moderne*, 1823, trans. William Newman)

As we noted at the end of the previous chapter, Bach's sonatas for violin with *obbligato* keyboard mark a new style, but its premise of equality between violin and keyboard was not generally followed. Instead the genre of the 'accompanied sonata', in which the violin is present chiefly as an adjunct to the keyboard, became increasingly prevalent. Also fashionable, however, was the duet for two violins, of which the Breitkopf Catalogue (that

remarkable guide to musical taste in the years 1762–87) lists some 450 examples. These were for the private amusement of dilettantes, but also for teaching purposes. It is interesting that the treatise of L'Abbé le fils already referred to gives all its examples in the form of violin duets, presumably for teacher and pupil to play together: these include dance suites arranged from the music of Rameau as well as more purely technical exercises. All the outstanding teachers of the violin in the second half of the century wrote music in this form.

The same genre of accompanied sonata was anticipated in the music of Mondonville, whose *Pièces de clavecin en sonates, avec accompagnement de violon* op. 3, published in Paris about 1734, suggested a similar subordination of the violin to the harpsichord. A different approach was taken by Michel Corrette (himself the author of an influential early treatise, *L'Ecole D'Orphée*) when he suggested in his sonatas op. 25 of 1742 that the accompaniment could be either included or omitted. It would seem, however, that it was the fashionable Johann Schobert in Paris who first published a set of sonatas in 1760 with the instruction 'which can be played with violin accompaniment'. Thereafter, the genre spread like wildfire; the cello as well as the violin was provided as an optional extra part in many publications, which varied in importance—it was often dispensable.

Looking through the published violin sonatas of Johann Christian Bach, for example, one rarely encounters a movement where the violin does more than tastefully complement the keyboard, usually by adding thirds and sixths, or occasionally smiling a sweet echo in an appropriate gap. C. P. E. Bach, who wrote brilliant sonatas in the old style for violin and keyboard (including a B minor sonata which strikingly echoes his father's famous flute sonata in the same key) also wrote accompanied sonatas with easy keyboard parts, published in 1776 and 1777, but these show a rather more pointful approach to the string parts.

So what kept the art of the solo violin alive during this period? There were already enough technical problems in the works of Locatelli to provide a challenge for the rest of the century: as one writer has remarked, if there are any more feats of execution in Paganini than in Locatelli, that is not because they were impossible for Locatelli but only because he had not thought of them. But a few composers require mention here alongside those Classical masters who revivified the art of the violin sonata: they were chiefly virtuosos and teachers who continued the French dominance of violin playing.

Joseph Boulogne Saint-Georges: engraving by W. Ward after Mather Brown.

Pierre Gaviniès (1728–1800) stands in the direct line of brilliant violin virtuosos following Leclair (the succession is indicated in the title of Fayolle's survey of 1810: *Notices sur Corelli, Tartini, Gavinies, Pugnani et Viotti*). We hear of him playing with L'Abbé le fils one of Leclair's unaccompanied duets, and making successful appearances at the *Concert Spirituel*. The Mozart family heard him in 1763–4; he directed the *Concert Spirituel* orchestra as leader, and organized it from 1773 to 1777. Contemporary reports of his playing are effusive. In his seminal history of French violin playing, *L'école française de violon*, the musicologist Lionel de La Laurencie noted that Gaviniès was especially famous for his bow control, projection of melody, ornamentation, and dynamic range. He made much use of the violin's lowest register; the middle movements of his sonatas are often called '*Romance*', and flow with the easy charm typical of this period.

Gaviniès's most famous contribution to violin literature falls right at the end of our period, following his appointment as professor of violin at the influential new Paris Conservatoire in 1795. Perhaps his *24 Matinées* had been written some years before their publication in 1800, but they sum up the manner in which a newly accomplished style of French violin playing had subsumed and transformed the art of Locatelli's 24 *Caprices* and had prepared an idiom for the new age of Paganini.

Among Gaviniès's pupils who also composed for the violin were Baudron, Capron, Guénin, Leduc and

Paisible. Nicholas Capron wrote popular pieces based on familiar tunes; Simon Leduc (1748–77) was a more important composer who developed the expressivity of French violin writing with much use of Italian markings (*Molto flebile espressivo affettuoso*, he marks in his op. 1). Marie-Alexandre Guénin (1744–1835) showed his following of fashion by writing sonatas for keyboard '*avec accompagnement du Violin*'; but in many of these pieces the violin actually has a prominent leading role, sometimes marked 'solo'. (La Laurencie described some of this school of violinist-composers as inaugurating a 'Mozartism before Mozart'. Though it is doubtful how much of an influence this had on Mozart himself, it is certainly true that some of the melodic and harmonic characteristics of his music are mirrored—with far less resourcefulness—in the French composers of this period; but with the coming of the Italian Viotti to Paris, all that tended to be obscured.)

Among the most interesting of these French violinist-composers was Joseph Boulogne de Saint-Georges (1739–99), who was born on the island of Guadeloupe to an African mother and a French father. His father took good care of his education, and trained him in fencing and violin playing, but the latter activity came to predominate when Gossec founded the *Concert des Amateurs* in 1769 and asked Saint-Georges to be his orchestral leader. He took over as Director in 1773. During his extremely colourful life he fenced with a transvestite before the Prince of Wales in London and was thrown into prison for suspected corruption. What is important about his three surviving violin sonatas is their avoidance of subservient violin writing: keyboard and violin are treated as equals. Their technical demands are equal to those of his elaborate concertos, some of which have recently been published in facsimile* by the Johnson Reprint Corporation.

* In his interesting performance notes for that reprint, Gabriel Banat compares some of Saint-Georges' figurations first with Gaviniès, and then with Beethoven in his quartets and violin concerto. Some of Saint-Georges' writing is so elaborate that Banat floats the suggestion that the new Tourte-type bow (see pp. 50–53), with its ability to keep an even pressure on the string and to draw a continuous sound from it, might already have been in use by Saint-Georges' time: 'The misconception that the advent of the modern bow did not occur until about 1800 with François Tourte, and that Viotti was the first to use it, was perpetuated by the Belgian musicologist and composer François-Joseph Fétis. According to Jacques Français, Louis Tourte, the father of François Tourte, and possibly Edward Dodd '*le vieux*' and other anonymous makers, had by this time [1775–80] produced bows which in their design and therefore in their performing ability were identical to bows we employ today.' That case must be regarded as unproven, at least until Français publishes his research, but it serves well to illustrate the pressure which performing musicians now feel when dealing with the music of this period to push the clock forward towards the resources of the future.

Pietro Nardini: portrait by an unknown eighteenth-century artist.

Gaetano Pugnani in the court dress of a violinist to the Sardinian court at Turin. He is holding the manuscript of the first violin part of one of his six trio sonatas: portrait by an unknown artist, *c.* 1754.

Italy

In Italy the period during which pre-eminence passed to the French nevertheless saw some significant figures who followed Tartini (see p. 74). Burney met Carlo Antonio Campioni (*c.* 1730–88) in Florence in 1763, and remarked on his collection of ancient music and on his wife—'a lady who paints very well, and who is likewise a neat performer on the harpsichord'. Campioni's music transfers some of the violin's advanced techniques to the keyboard, and one of his keyboard sonatas has an independent *obbligato* part for violin. Domenico Ferrari (1722–80) was highly praised by Dittersdorf, who was not easy to please (he called some of Mozart's music 'too highly spiced'), and he wrote violin music full of brilliant Locatellian techniques as well as using harmonics in one sonata (op. 1 no. 5). Although his use of continuo bass is typical of the Baroque, his treatment of melody and harmony points towards the emerging Classical style.

The most famous of Tartini's pupils was Pietro Nardini (1722–93). Leopold Mozart declared in 1763 that 'the beauty, purity and evenness of his tone and his *cantabile* cannot be surpassed, but he does not execute any great difficulties'. Burney in 1770 wrote that 'his style is delicate, judicious and highly finished . . . he seems the completest player on the violin in all Italy'. But it was left to Christian Schubart to extol him most effusively: 'The tenderness of his playing is indescribable . . . He detached the notes very slowly, and each seemed like a drop of blood from his tender soul . . . One has seen ice-cold aristocrats weep when he performed an *Adagio*'. Mozart heard his playing in 1763 and 1770. He contributed an important work to the small genre of the unaccompanied violin solo: his *Sonate énigmatique* uses a curious notation on two staves to delineate treble and accompaniment lines in the textures; it also very unusually employs *scordatura*, tuning the violin strings differently from normal custom. The musical interest of his sonatas is not large, but their *allegro* movements anticipate the plan of Classical sonata form, and his opening adagios continued to be performed with ornamentation, for they appeared in Cartier's famous anthology (see later, p. 114).

'The celebrated performer on the Violin, Lolli, came into England at the beginning of 1785', wrote Burney; '. . . so eccentric was his style of composition and execution, that he was regarded as a madman by most of his hearers. Yet I am convinced that in his lucid intervals he was in a serious style a very great, expressive and admirable performer. In his freaks nothing can be imagined so wild, difficult, grotesque and even

ridiculous as his compositions and performance.' Antonio Lolli (*c.* 1730–1802) has roused a great deal of controversy, and there is an echo of *Grove's* dismissal of Locatelli in Wasielewski's declaration that his compositions were 'the most valueless and characterless product of eighteenth-century violin literature'. The critic Hanslick called him 'the forerunner and prototype of Paganini'; his playing certainly seems to have been more interesting than his music, though his works compare favourably with those of many other eighteenth-century violinist composers who, regardless of talent, were expected to provide their own repertory.

Lolli is included by the Italian theorist Rangoni, writing in 1790, as one of a trio of violinists in whom the finest elements of Tartini's art is kept alive. The first was Nardini; the last was Gaetano Pugnani (1731–98), of whom Rangoni wrote:

Among the top-ranking violinists I distinguish Pugnani by the animated and vibrant eloquence throughout his melody. This great sonata composer, whose . . . modulations are clear, concise and energetic, like the sentences of a philosopher and an orator.

Vue du theatre dressé a la Cour pour Le divertissement de l'Opera donné a S. A. R. Madame La Princesse de Piedmont.

Desseigné par Le Ch⁰ Dom. filippo Juvarra P⁰ Architecte de S. M.　　　　　　　　　　　　　　*Gravé par Antoine Aveline à Paris*

Pugnani appeared in London, knew J. C. Bach as well as Dittersdorf, but spent much of his time in Turin, where he followed his teacher Somis as violinist of King's Music. Boris Schwarz notes that Pugnani showed a great interest in developing the use of the modern bow, which he may have discussed with Tourte and his son; he also used thicker strings on his violin. But it is in his music that Pugnani shows the most interesting signs of approaching the Classical language, by his use of contrasted subordinate passages in fast movements, and modulation to open the development.

Pugnani's innovations were carried forward by another Italian, the much more widely famous Luigi Boccherini (1743–1805); his violin sonatas, however, form a tiny part of his huge output, and he was much more concerned with his own solo instrument, the cello. There are a couple of early sets of accompanied keyboard settings; with his predecessor Sammartini, he may be said to prepare the way for the most important composer whose violin music we have to consider here, Wolfgang Amadeus Mozart.

It is difficult to feel that any of Mozart's predecessors in the form of the 'accompanied' sonata match the quality of his work. The sonatas of J. C. Bach in this genre have already been mentioned, and there were many other Englishmen and immigrants practising this form in London in the second half of the eighteenth century. Carl Friedrich Abel (1723–87) left some 106 sonatas of which many are of the accompanied type. The

pre-eminence of the Mannheim school, including Johann Stamitz (1717–57) and Carl Stamitz (1745–1801), in developing the Classical language is no longer accepted without some qualification, and the violin was not widely used there as a solo instrument; Boccherini and Sammartini made important advances, as did the French school. A more fertile source of Mozart's style can perhaps be found in those Viennese composers who preceded him: Matthias Georg Monn (1717–50) wrote few violin sonatas, but Georg Christoph Wagenseil (1715–77) left two sets of accompanied sonatas for keyboard with violin which were published in London.

If we are to look for violin music which consciously influenced Mozart, then there is only the frankly uninteresting music of his father Leopold, and more intriguingly the music of a Bohemian composer Josef Mysliveček (1737–81) whom Mozart met in Bologna in 1770. His accompanied sonatas show a startling resemblance to Mozart's early style, and indeed Mozart praised them, recommending his sister to learn them from memory and perform them 'with much expression, gusto and fire': 'for they are sonatas which are bound to please everyone, which are easy to memorize and very effective when played with the proper precision'. The influence of Czech folk music in Mysliveček's music has also been noted, and some commentators have attempted to show that his style exerted a strong influence on Mozart's early work. But as *The New Grove* cautions wisely: 'a more exhaustive study of the

Opposite: An opera performance in the Royal Palace, Turin, 1722.

Wolfgang Amadeus Mozart: silverpoint drawing by Doris Stock, April 1789.

development of the Viennese Classical style will have to be undertaken before such a claim can be properly evaluated'.

Mozart

In fact, the development of the Viennese Classical style can almost be traced in the violin and keyboard works of Mozart himself, since he wrote examples in the form throughout his creative life, and they provide a telling and comprehensive survey of his development in one particular field. His first four sonatas, K.6–9, were published in Paris in 1764 as opp. 1 and 2. Leopold Mozart wrote enthusiastically of 'the furore they will make in the world when people read on the title-page that they have been composed by a seven-year-old child', but it seems likely that Leopold himself contributed to their composition. With their cheerful Alberti basses in the piano and modest contributions from the violin, these sonatas are not really remarkable, yet it is notable how, even so early, Mozart makes the violin at least contribute something to the texture: a little echo in K.6, imitative textures in K.8. The chiming sixths have been anticipated in J. C. Bach's accompanied sonatas, but the sturdiness of K.7's first movement and its perky little second minuet surely have Mozart's own imprint. It is most unusual to find the second minuet of K.8 in the key of B flat minor; all these sonatas, including the last G major K.9 (which is the least inventive), end with a pair of minuets.

The sonatas K.10–15, which also include *ad libitum* cello parts, should perhaps be mentioned here; they appeared in London in 1765. But the next set of violin sonatas proper is K.26–31, published in the Hague a year later as Mozart's op. 4. Already in K.26 in E flat, the violin imitates the keyboard entry, though it then confines itself to brittle repeated notes—which may help to explain why composers often asked that in such accompanied sonatas the violin should use a mute. The final movement of this sonata is a witty *Rondeau* in which the violin acts as if it were a tutti section. A more interesting sharing of material occurs in the first movement of K.28 in C, where shooting scales answer each other in keyboard and violin; in the second movement, an *allegro grazioso*, the violin is given an equal share in the thematic material. There is a little more imitative work in the D major sonata K.29, though in K.30 in F major most of the attention is on the keyboard player's elegant cross-hand writing. Typically Mozartian is the energy and essentially simple harmonic framework of K.31 in B flat; this sonata is concluded by a movement

in a form which will become familiar, the theme and variations, though the violin is allowed little in the way of an independent contribution.

The sonatas K.55–60 are now believed to be spurious: Alfred Einstein for a while thought they might be by Joseph Schuster, whose violin sonatas Mozart praised in a letter home ('They are not bad. If I stay on I shall write six myself in the same style, as they are very popular here'). But that has now been disproven, and the works remain anonymous. For the next authenticated set of sonatas we must move on more than a decade to those published in Paris in 1778, again as op. 1. The first three were probably written in Mannheim in early 1778, and the remaining three added in Paris in the summer. At once here we can observe the emancipation of the violin from its accompanying role. It announces the open, singing melody of the sonata K.301 in G, and though it frequently joins in the accompaniment during the sonata, it has a tune of its own in the middle section of the final triple-time *Allegro*. The first movement of

this sonata shows a form closer to the *ritornello* structure of the concerto than to sonata form.

The opening of the E flat sonata K.302 is familiar from Mozart's symphonic style at this time: an elaborated, vigorous descending arpeggio. Here the violin has horn calls and energetic triplets, and there is a most marvellous transition back to the second subject in the recapitulation. Although absolutely no violinistic tricks were needed (which would put the music out of reach of the amateur), Mozart is already exploiting the instrument's special possibilities. In the finale it doubles the keyboard an octave below. The third of this set, K.303 in C, unusually has a slow introduction which most ingeniously first stabilizes the key of C, then leads away from it to a cadence towards G, and introduces the *Allegro* with maximum instability by taking the G, sharpening it, and leading from E minor into A minor. The *Adagio* recurs in mid-sonata (like that in Haydn's

'Drumroll' symphony and one of the pieces from Schuster's set) and this time leads a C to C sharp and then D minor. A confident C major is nevertheless restored before the close, and the final Minuet is tonally unremarkable.

Though these sonatas have their impressive moments, nothing in them prepares us for the shock of the E minor sonata K.304, which is among Mozart's most impressive creations in any form. It may be unwise to link it directly with the period following the death of his mother in Paris in July 1778; it can be dated, however, to within a month both of his bereavement and of that other outburst in the minor mode, the A minor piano sonata K.310. E minor is a most unusual key for Mozart; indeed the only parallel for the key and expressive content of this remarkable sonata is Haydn's *Trauer* symphony no. 44 of around 1772: could Mozart have known it? Like the finale of that symphony, this sonata's

Opposite: Autograph of the first page of Mozart's F major sonata K377.

first movement opens with a suppressed, tortured unison, and then bursts out *forte*. Mozart's resourcefulness (and also his avoidance of predictable sonata contrasts) is exemplified by his wonderfully varied treatment of this opening unison theme. After the initial outburst, the violin takes it up over a smooth keyboard accompaniment; it returns in canon, in G major, modulating to B, to cadence the first half. The piano opens the development alone with the theme, where it forms the basis of a short but highly expressive imitative section with strong dissonances. The master-stroke comes at the moment of recapitulation, however: Mozart gives the phrase to the violin alone, but as it reaches the highest note, he sends the piano crashing in with an extraordinary chord (which can only be described as an altered 6/5), in a rhythmic figure which is repeated three times to harmonize the rest of the theme. Even then Mozart has not quite finished with his surprises: as a coda, the theme enters again, quietly in the violin, over another fluctuating accompaniment of infinite peace.

The minuet which ends this strange sonata is scarcely less remarkable. Its spirit is almost Baroque, and its material uses the Baroque descending tetrachord to underline its harmonies. After a hushed transition, an ineffably simple melody *dolce piano* appears—for this minuet has become a rondo—transposed down an octave *sotto voce*; but before the sonata ends, there is a sudden outburst of energy in Mozart's most strenuous public manner, with swirling unison arpeggios and a hammered chord from the violin.

After this, the succeeding sonatas come as an anticlimax. The A major K.305 is a cheerful, bouncy affair, using the splendidly unexpected key of E minor in place of E major in the development. Its variations (the first Mozart had written since K.31) are highly decorated. In the last of the set, K.306 in D major, the early manner of the J. C. Bach-style accompanied sonata is inflated by the quasi-orchestral effects familiar from the piano sonatas of the time. An interesting feature of the slow movement, an *andantino cantabile*, is the instruction '*mezza voce*'— which here probably means 'of medium loudness', rather than the specifically violinistic indication *mezza di voce* (meaning the swelling of the note as the bow is drawn across the strings) which eighteenth-century theorists often mention. There is a brilliant piano cadenza in the finale which confirms its predominance in this work. From the same year, 1778, comes a little C major sonata dated 11 March, and intended for the daughter of Mozart's landlord in Mannheim, Thérèse Serrarius. Mozart's autograph (in the New York Public Library) is scribbled with

documentation, including his own reminder 'Pour Mademoiselle Thérèse'. It is a chirpy piece.

Mozart's next set of violin and keyboard sonatas was published in Vienna in 1781, and includes that C major work as well as a sonata in B flat K.378 which may date from Salzburg in 1779 or (according to the latest research) perhaps early 1781: Einstein suggests a link with a melody from *Die Entführung* in its slow movement. It is striking to find, even at this date, the sonatas published as *Six sonates pour le clavecin ou pianoforte, avec l'accompagnement d'un violon*, as if the violin were still dispensable. But Mozart's publisher Ataria was doubtless bowing to contemporary fashion, and if a few pianists without violinists in attendance nevertheless bought the works, he would not mind; the set was dedicated to a pianist, Josepha von Aurnhammer. That the adventurous idiom of this music and the independence it provided for the violin still surprised Mozart's contemporaries may be gathered from the review this set received from Cramer's *Magazin*:

These sonatas are the only ones of this kind. Rich in new ideas and in evidences of the great musical genius of their author, very brilliant and suited to the instrument. At the same time the accompaniment of the violin is so artfully combined with the clavier part that both instruments are kept constantly on the alert; so that these sonatas require just as skilful a player on the violin as on the clavier . . .

The violin is least in evidence in the first sonata of the published set (probably the first of the new four to be composed), K.379 in G. The piano part is extremely elaborate and showy, which makes the story Mozart tells in a letter to his father about this work all the more remarkable:

Today (for I am writing at 11 o'clock at night) we had a concert, where three of my compositions were performed— new ones, of course . . . a sonata with violin accompaniment for myself, which I composed last night between eleven and twelve (but in order to be able to finish it, I only wrote out the accompaniment for Brunetti and retained my own part in my head) . . .

This extraordinary process has been documented by Erich Hertzmann, who showed how Mozart used a form of shorthand to notate his own part. The form of this sonata is in fact most unusual, and seems to have provided a direct model for Beethoven in his E flat piano quartet of 1785. Mozart writes a sonata-form movement, this time a fast one. Throughout the sonata, only the major and minor of G are used.

The next two sonatas to be written in this set are both

in F, and as this would have been unacceptable in a publication, Mozart inserted the earlier sonata in C between them. In fact, they are strongly contrasted. In the first the violin reverts to an accompanimental role, most imaginatively so in the gloomy, slow semiquavers which underpin the theme of the *Andante*. The second F major sonata K.377 is one of Mozart's happiest, most exuberant inventions. Again he makes a positive virtue of the violin's traditional accompanimental role by making that accompaniment actually mean something. The piano's striding sequential theme is a strong, splendid creation; but the addition of the violin's throbbing triplet accompaniment makes it irresistibly exciting. When the violin takes over the tune, the piano's triplets are arpeggios, not repeated notes; the triplet movement is sustained without a single pause through each half of the first movement. After that exhausting exercise, a quieter slow movement is indicated; Mozart writes a theme and variations announced by the piano on an exceedingly simple melody animated by turns; some of the variations remind one of the deeply-felt last movement of the string quartet K.421. The finale is an unusually shaped *tempo di minuetto*, with two contrasted *trio* sections in the centre.

The remaining two sonatas are as contrasted as the two F major works. The E flat major sonata K.380 opens portentously with crashing chords and a strange unac-

companied flourish for the keyboard treble, but it soon relapses into more conventional duettings. The final *Rondeau* sounds like a sketch for a piano concerto. (The last of the set is the G major work that was written first.)

There are two variation sets contemporary with the publication of this set: one in G major K.359 and another in G minor K.36, both written in Vienna in June 1781, and both using French songs popular at the time. They are both pleasant but not unusual works of their kind. Of more interest are a group of uncompleted fragments from around the same time, printed in an *appendix* to the New Mozart Edition. The little Andante and Allegretto in C, ascribed to 1782, may however be much later, from 1788. The B flat sonata K.372 was completed by Stadler from a fragment dated 24 March 1781: it is an extrovert, impressive work.

The 1782 fragments may be associated with Mozart's struggle to achieve Constanze's hand in marriage, and perhaps also with his exposure to learned styles at the house of Baron van Swieten. The very odd Andante and Fugue in A major K.402 is a minuet which leads to a sober fugue; the minuet is finely wrought, but the fugue is rather dry and not as successful, for example, as the C minor Fugue for string quartet or piano duet. Eric Blom says that 'it dates from the time when Constanze urged fugal writing upon Mozart, and it is not the only work of the kind written in the year of their marriage

which shows a certain lack of interest'. Einstein, more on Mozart's side, suggests it shows that Mozart 'begins to realise that Constanze's love for fugues is not altogether genuine'. Another sonata fragment in A, K.Anh 48, may date from this time. Datable to August or September 1782 in Vienna is the magnificent fragment in C minor, perhaps inspired by Bach's C minor Fantasia for harpsichord or more generally by its style, for which Mozart provided the beginnings of a violin accompaniment. It is usually played today as a solo piano piece. (The New Mozart Edition includes two further tiny fragments, of an A major sonata K.Anh 50, and a G major sonata K.Anh 47, which is of interest for showing how Mozart sketched in the essential sections only of a piano part.)

Before turning to the fine three sonatas which are Mozart's major contribution to the form, let us mention here chronologically the last of his violin sonatas, the little *Kleine Klavier Sonate für Anfänger mit einer Violine*, dated Vienna, 10 July 1788. This must have been written for a particular purpose, and shows every sign

of having originally been a piano solo work. It includes some beautiful chromaticism in the final variations, but is otherwise not outstanding.

We know quite precisely the origins of the B flat sonata K.454. Mozart wrote to his father on 24 April 1784:

We now have with us the famous Strinasacchi from Mantua, a very good violinist. She has a great deal of taste and feeling in her playing. I am at this moment composing a sonata which we are going to play together on Thursday at her concert in the theatre.

Apparently Mozart had the same deadline problem as with an earlier sonata, and played his own part from memory with a blank sheet of music paper in front of him at the piano. Regina Strinasacchi was about twenty and a distinguished player, with music by Saint-Georges, among others, in her repertory. For her Mozart wrote a superbly rich, powerful sonata, with a slow introduction worthy of the weightiest symphony. There is an unprecedented breadth in the violin's

Opposite: Portrait of a court musician with instruments: detail of a painting by Peter Jakob Horemans, 1722.

Regina Schlick-Strinasacchi, for whom Mozart wrote his violin sonata in B major K454: silhouette by an unknown artist, 1795.

Below: Title page (1784) of Mozart's piano sonatas K333 and K254 and the violin sonata K454 'accompanied by a violin *obbligato*'.

majestic line, which descends over low pulsing chords from the piano. In the fast section, Mozart indulges a favourite whim by taking a little unimportant figure from the cadence of the first section to open the development (compare the immensely powerful example in the G minor piano quartet). The singing *Andante* in E flat is again on a very large scale, with decorations when the theme returns which give a good notion of Mozart's ornamentation practices.

The sonata in E flat K.481 is dated Vienna, 12 December 1785; it was published by Hoffmeister, and the reason for its composition is not known. The first movement introduces the famous 'Jupiter' theme at one point in the coda; the central *Adagio* in A flat is extraordinary. It is in the form of a rondo with two episodes and varied repeats of the main theme, but in the middle it slides into A major for a version of the theme which takes on (like the E major episode in the Minuet of K.304) a sadness even greater than that of the minor mode. The enharmonic modulation back to A flat (which in one bar involves the right hand in A flat and the left in A major) is chilling, and the coda which shifts eerily and unpredictably from A flat and back to A is weird in the extreme.

The A major sonata K.526 was written during work on *Don Giovanni*. It is dated 24 August 1787, and presents one of Mozart's very rare first-movements in triple time (the early G major string quartet and the E flat major symphony are other examples). This is an exceptionally tight construction worked out with great skill, and there is a closer integration between violin and piano writing than anywhere else in his output. The *Andante* starts as a bare melody over piano octaves, like one of Haydn's piano trios; but it is soon deflected into the most remarkable harmonic byways, attaining a waywardness soon after the start of the development that makes one feel, as at some of Mozart's strangest moments, that a carefully ordered world is about to disintegrate completely. But the anguished long notes of the violin over the piano's flat, dissonant chord sequences eventually fade, and the music pulls itself back together again—as Mozart could always do, even at his most despairing.

The superb finale is in the *moto perpetuo* tradition established by the first movement of the F major sonata, but here the movement is halted from time to time to make the wit even more apparent. Few pieces of Mozart's can actually cause an audience to laugh with them, but this is one; the joke is extended through many episodes. Here the boundaries between the melody and accompaniment are dissolved because we cannot be sure

any more which is which: is the violin's darting, syncopated line the main material, or is that provided by the piano's rushing quavers? The integration is complete, and Mozart has finally moved all the way from those first conventional sonatas in which his father may have had a hand to the most enduring achievement in the keyboard-and-violin music of his time.

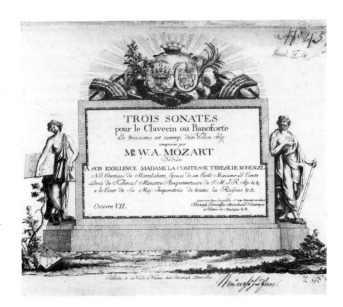

Beethoven

Mozart made the most important contribution to the Classical violin sonata: Haydn left only one isolated work, and even Beethoven's works do not span his creative output in the same way as Mozart's. Nevertheless, Beethoven's output is significant and has established a permanent place in the repertory, unlike the countless other similar pieces which were published at the end of the century. And from the beginning, of course, Beethoven wrote for a true partnership of violin and piano, returning to the model which Bach had provided many decades previously.

Before Beethoven's first published violin sonatas, he wrote a few smaller works: a set of twelve variations on *Se vuol ballare* from Mozart's *Le Nozze di Figaro* Wo.40 is the most inventive, and dates from 1793 in Vienna. There is a Rondo in G, Wo.41, written the following year in Bonn, and arrangements of Six German Dances Wo.42. Beethoven gave a reason for publishing the *Figaro* variations in an entertaining letter of June 1794:

I should never have written down this kind of piece, had I not already noticed fairly often how some people in Vienna after hearing me extemporise of an evening would note down on the following day several peculiarities of my style and palm them off with pride as their own. Well, as I foresaw that their pieces would soon be published, I resolved to forestall these people.

Beethoven's first set of three sonatas, his op. 12, were published in 1799 (though they were probably written one or two years earlier) and dedicated to Antonio Salieri. The title-page still announced '*Tre sonate per il clavicembalo o forte-piano con un violino composte*'—but the usage is merely conventional. It was just at this period that Beethoven made a joke in a letter that 'I cannot compose anything that is not *obbligato*, seeing that, as a matter of fact, I came into the world with an *obbligato* accompaniment.' That the language of these sonatas was still ahead of current usage may be judged from the puzzled reception the sonatas had in the Leipzig *Allgemeine Musikalische Zeitung*:

The critic, who heretofore has been unfamiliar with the pianoforte pieces of the author, must admit, after having looked through these strange sonatas, overladen with difficulties, that after diligent and strenuous labour he felt like a man who had hoped to make a promenade with a genial friend through a tempting forest and found himself barred every minute by inimical barriers, returning at last exhausted and without having had any pleasure. It is undeniable that Hr. Beethoven goes his own gait; but what a bizarre and singular gait it is! Learned, learned and always learned—and

nothing natural, no song. Yes, to be accurate, there is *only a mass of learning here, without good method*; obstinacy, but for which we feel but little interest; a striving for strange modulations, an objection to customary associations, a heaping up of difficulties on difficulties till one loses all patience and enjoyment.

The opening of the first sonata in D major bears a resemblance to that of Mozart's E flat sonata K.302, but the similarity is only superficial. Mozart's arpeggio figure is here subjected to nervous twists and pauses, and the development begins with a dramatic drop from the key of A to F, with a theme taken from its own codetta. This section moves into D minor, making the return of the D major opening—the tonic is retained here—all the more brilliant. The most notable features of the second movement's theme and variations are the transformation of the simple theme into a stormy third variation in the minor, and the pulsing accompaniment to the final variation which evaporates to nothing. In the quirky rondo finale, Beethoven's sense of humour is evident: after all the energy expended on the argument and development, the music becomes stuck on a little unaccompanied rhythmic tag for the violin, which the piano echoes, which the violin echoes in a different key, which the piano . . . finally they agree on almost the most remote note possible (a high F natural in D major) and suddenly a crashing D major cadence arrives.

In the A major sonata op. 12 no. 2 the ghost of the accompanied sonata is evident in the skipping opening, for which the violin provides triplets to a piano melody, as did Mozart in his F major sonata. But the melody is soon exchanged—or partly so, as it soon falls beneath the violin's range and the piano has to rescue it. Beethoven generates enormous tension from the slide down in C major for the development's opening, and from the elongated return to the opening. There are surprises, too, in the gentle *Allegro piacevole* which concludes the sonata, for Beethoven uses an enharmonic twist to shift the music into strange keys. And if the opening movement of the op. 12 no. 3 sonata in E flat is fundamentally unclouded, the central movement, marked *adagio con molt'espressione*, is a wonderful anticipation of the depths of his later piano writing, with a wide variety of figuration and styles in the keyboard part.

The essential element in the A minor sonata op. 23, which was published in 1801 with a dedication to Count Fries, is its brevity of utterance. The cell of the first theme is only a bar long, repeated in sequence; the whole movement is very terse and concise. Textures are sharp and open; the *presto* marking (which will recur

in the 'Kreutzer' sonata) is very unusual. The central movement is not especially slow, but is marked *andante scherzoso, più allegretto*: it includes an impressive fugato. The final *Allegro molto* must surely be a conscious or unconscious echo of that in Mozart's A major sonata, but it is worked out with typically Beethovenian eccentricity, even to the echoed cadential ornament in the middle; the chordal episodes almost take the listener to the development section of the 'Jupiter' symphony's finale.

The fifth sonata is the famous 'Spring' sonata in F op. 24; like the fourth it was written for Count Fries (after a voyage in Italy in 1799) and was published in 1801, but it was given a later opus number. Whereas the fourth emphasizes brief, taut phrases, this glorious opening movement is notable for its expansiveness and relaxation. A resemblance between this opening theme and the theme of Clementi's sonata op. 25 no. 4 (published in 1790) has been noted by Harold Truscott, and between it and a concerto melody of Rodolphe Kreutzer by Boris Schwarz, but these resemblances serve only to point up the wonderful balance of Beethoven's own formulation, with its sweeping, unexpected rise of an octave at the end. The relaxation and warmth do not inhibit a symphonic-style argument, however. For the first time, Beethoven introduces a Scherzo into his violin sonatas: and a brilliantly witty one it is too, with rhythmic displacement between violin and piano ensuring that we never quite know where we are: the coda calls our bluff as the synchronization gets worse but the musical sense improves.

The op. 30 sonatas of 1801–2 were dedicated to the Emperor Alexander I. Beethoven received no reward at all until 1814; when the Empress of Russia that year gave Beethoven fifty ducats for a small Polonaise, she was reminded that nothing had been given him for op. 30, and added a hundred ducats. The central *Adagio* in op. 30 no. 1 was described by Wilhelm Lenz as an 'impressive Italian-style cantilena': the style certainly owes something to Pugnani and Nardini. The finale now associated with the 'Kreutzer' sonata was originally attached to this work, but it is more happily completed by the *Allegretto con variazioni* which now form the last movement, which at times anticipate the 'Diabelli' variations in their spare humour, and sometimes also the severe language of the late piano sonatas (for example, in the fugal variation V).

The op. 30 no. 2 sonata is in Beethoven's characteristically serious key of C minor. In the way it opens with a piano unison and then throws that melody over a pulsating accompaniment, it is slightly reminiscent of Mozart's E minor sonata K.304. But the working out here is grandiose and passionate, unusually so for this date. The first movement is superbly balanced, with its tense *fugato* and huge antiphonal chords leading to a powerful climax in the centre of the movement: the opening theme is emphasized in unison by both piano and violin and then leads back through a very slow passage to the return of the theme in the violin. This large-scale sonata not surprisingly includes a Scherzo movement, and the finale's innocent theme is prepared

Opposite left: George Polgreen Augustus Bridgetower (1779–1860): drawing by Henry Edridge.

Opposite right: Rodolphe Kreutzer: portrait by Antoine Paul Vincent, 1809.

Pierre Rode.

by rumble of drums to lift the curtain: the little drumroll motif is resourcefully used throughout to most exciting effect.

The sonata op. 30 no. 3 in G is one of the least often performed, but Nigel Fortune in *The Beethoven Companion* is enthusiastic about it: 'there is no other Beethoven sonata remotely like it, and it is one of his wittiest and most delightful works. Again he seems at once to revitalize the past and to point to the future. He finds an anticipation of the nineteenth-century romance, Schubert and even Schumann in the central movement, and the *perpetuum mobile* finale is an entirely personal re-creation of a Haydn rondo, with slight Lydian, folklike overtones in the subject, plenty of tonic pedal and at bar 177 an outrageous switch to E flat, complete with till-ready accompaniment.' The violinist Joseph Szigeti called it 'one of the most harmonious works of the set'.

With the 'Kreutzer' sonata op. 47, we reach the point where the violin sonata bursts its bounds, where the music of the chamber is taken out on the largest scale to become a concerto for two instruments suitable only for the public concert hall. In this sonata the emancipation of the violin with which we began two centuries ago is gloriously achieved. Beethoven admitted as much when he described it as *'in un stilo molto concertante quasi come d'un concerto'*. He had played the work with George Bridgetower, but after a quarrel dedicated the work to the famous virtuoso Rodolphe Kreutzer. He, however (according to Berlioz), declared it 'outrageously unintelligible', and never played it. (Beethoven's links with the French school of violin playing are important, and have been explored by Boris Schwarz in *The Musical Quarterly*, October 1958.)

Whether or not Kreutzer played 'his' sonata, it is one of the most impressive works in the violin's repertory, and its huge scale of utterance strikingly anticipates that of the 'Eroica' in Beethoven's symphonic output, which followed soon after in 1803. The opening, in double and triple stopping for violin alone, is immediately arresting; the first fast section, marked *presto*, has a titanic fury broken by pauses and hesitations, and it is massively extended like the first movement of the first 'Rasumovsky' quartet. Tovey comments merely that 'the rich set of ornate variations follows with exactly the right contrast of tone; while the happy and witty finale is the only possible outcome of the other two movements which is neither trivial nor sententious'. But it is also possible to feel that nothing here matches the demonic inspiration of the first movement, immortalized in Tolstoy's famous story about the power of music:

A terrible thing, this sonata, especially the opening *Presto* . . . Why does it do what it does? Music makes me forget my true situation. Under the influence of music I seem to feel what I do not feel, to understand what I do not understand, to be able to do what I am not capable of doing . . .

The Kreutzer Sonata

Beethoven's association with the French school of violin playing also provided the inspiration for the completion of his last violin sonata, written in 1812 for the famous violinist Pierre Rode. He may have begun the work earlier, but he took Rode's playing into account at least in the finale, for he wrote to Archduke Rudolph:

In writing it, I must consider Rode's style of playing. We are fond of rushing passages in our finales, [some translations have 'we like to have fairly noisy passages in our finales'] yet that does not suit Rode and—it really troubles me somewhat.

Rode's technique was surely not taxed by this G major sonata, however, even if late in life his powers were somewhat reduced. The opening phrase floats in as if from nowhere on the violin to be picked up from the piano and fashioned into a melody. The song-like *Adagio espressivo* is in E flat, as similar to the 'Pathétique' piano sonata's slow movement as the rhythms of the opening movement recall the fourth piano concerto. The scherzo is spiky and witty; the final *Poco allegretto* opens in the old-fashioned manner of the accompanied sonata but then develops through many brilliant episodes to a climax in which the violin is just for a couple of bars, in a rush to the top of the E string, mercilessly exposed.

Towards a new century

It would be misleading to end the story of the Classical violin with Beethoven. True, he was writing the greatest music for the instrument as the century turned, but he was not the most influential, or in purely violinistic terms the most important, composer of his period for the instrument. Influence was to be found at the beginning of the new century in the hands of those French violinist-composers with whom we have noted Beethoven's links in his later sonatas: Kreutzer, Rode, and a third, Baillot. All three drew their inspiration from Giovanni Battista Viotti, the great Italian violinist, pupil of Pugnani; these four names provide the link between this chapter and the next.

Viotti was the last of the Italian school of violinists who descended directly from Corelli. But more important, by spending a decade in residence in Paris from 1782 to 1792, he transformed the French violin school of Leclair and Gaviniès, and in adding to it the accomplishments of the Italians, laid the foundation for a new style of violin playing which dominated the early nineteenth century. This work was accomplished mainly through the example of his concertos, which were widely imitated. Beethoven learnt from them. Mozart added wind parts to one of them, and the lesser composers followed their style of composition. Viotti wrote some twenty-nine concertos, Kreutzer nineteen, Rode thirteen, Baillot nine. By 1800 the older concerto repertory was obliterated, and the concerto of the Parisian school reigned supreme as the model of its kind.

One other significant publication from this period provides an apt climax to the whole history of the violin surveyed so far. Jean-Baptiste Cartier was another member of the French violin school, a colleague and friend of the famous trio. He studied with Viotti but was less well known as a performer. He was however widely esteemed as a teacher, and it must have been in connection with his teaching activities that he assembled *L'art du violon*, a huge collection of sonatas and isolated movements published in Paris in 1798 and enlarged in 1803 (this edition has been made available in a modern reprint).

The contents of Cartier's anthology summarize the art of violin playing through the period we have been discussing. Even through a period which saw a revolution in musical language unparalleled since the end of the Renaissance, a period in which much old music was laid to rest to await 'rediscovery' in the following century, the violin's repertory remained remarkably constant. Corelli's op. 6 concertos may have been forgotten by orchestras, but his op. 5 no. 7 sonata is preserved by Cartier. Gathered here we find works by countless minor composers—Aubert, Guignon, Cupis, Bonporti, d'Auvergne, Zarth, Vachon and others. But there are also classics of the Baroque repertory: from Locatelli's op. 3, Leclair's op. 9 no. 1, Geminiani's op. 1 nos. 1 and 6;; Nardini's odd *Sonate énigmatique*, and a whole set of his sonatas preserved with fantastic elaborate written-out ornamentation in countless alternatives, providing a compendium of eighteenth-century improvisational technique.

For the first time, Cartier published in full the famous 'Devil's Trill' sonata by Tartini, of which Leopold Mozart had quoted the most difficult bits (Baillot appears to have owned this manuscript). For the first time, too, there was the complete set of fifty variations that Tartini based on Corelli's much-varied Gavotte from op. 5. Most remarkable of all, almost at the end of Cartier's collection, after an unaccompanied fugue by Stamitz, stands the great Fugue in C major from Bach's sonata in C for unaccompanied violin. This was drawn from a copy owned by Gaviniès: it was the first time any of Bach's unaccompanied music had been printed. So, in spite of changing taste and changing fashion, the history of developing performance on the violin ensured that the musical wheel turned full circle back to the work which was the climax of our survey of the musical Baroque. Unlike choral singers who had never heard the *St. Matthew Passion*, the adventurous violinist did not need a Mendelssohn to revive Bach; all his sonatas and partitas were published by 1802. The extraordinary continuity in the history of the violin was demonstrated once again.

The Nineteenth Century

Previous page: Joseph Joachim and Clara Schumann: chalk drawing by A. Menzel, 1854.

Preamble

By 1800 music was growing noisier, more intense and more strenuous. It was being composed, not for performance chiefly in court drawing-rooms, but in public concert-halls before large audiences who paid to hear everything, and wanted it to be more stirring, less intellectual, instantly and massively admirable, stunning in brilliance, rich and grand in melodiousness. The concert halls were there: the Gewandhaus in Leipzig, for instance, prototype of the nineteenth-century concert hall, opened for business in 1781, and the Handel celebrations of 1784 in London, which started a vogue for monumental choral sound, were quick to influence the continental taste for music.

Composers were ready to accommodate the public taste. The French Revolution, and afterwards Napoleon, encouraged monumental music with a dash of military bravado. In all of this, we today think of Beethoven as key figure: so he was (though in this book he is discussed elsewhere), but there were many others, especially Italians in France (Paisiello, Cherubini, Rossini), cultivating similar moods, some with every success. The clarion call to *la gloire*, among Napoleon's foes as well as his allies, was musically for louder instruments: the violin had already answered that call with the instruments, more robust yet still greatly sensitive, being made in Mirecourt and Nancy, and eventually in Paris, by such families as Médard, Lupot and above all Vuillaume, a school of violin-makers closely linked to Cremona, able also to modernize older Cremonese violins for the requirements of modern music and large auditoria (see also p. 19: it is only in the 1980s that we have begun seriously to doubt the wisdom of modernizing so many of those violins).

In Paris Louis Tourte had designed and made a stronger, more efficient violin bow, which was quick to supplant its more flexible predecessor (see p. 53). All existing musical instruments underwent similar transformation around 1800, for the same purpose, and with the same result, which was the emergence of a new, unprecedentedly amazing virtuoso generation of solo executants. The glory of their predecessors, the castrati of Baroque opera, was fading; in the wings, waiting to take over, were the instrumental superstars, chiefly the pianists and the violinists. They not only performed the repertory, but composed it themselves, or influenced the other composers who wrote for them. The violin music, with which this chapter is concerned, is split between two categories: on my left, Paganini and his side, whose glory was great, but ephemeral—of them all, perhaps the only great composer, for this moment of posterity, was Franz Liszt. On my right is Joseph Joachim, whose admirers found him, until his last years, as consummate a technician as Paganini, and also the most profound of musical interpreters. For posterity his chief importance was his influence on others. It was an earnest influence, anti-virtuoso: Brahms, Dvořák and Max Bruch were three of his many protégés. But Joachim's side must also include those other violinists who worked with composers of serious intention, David, Ysaÿe, Brodsky. None of all these was a Frenchman, nor was Viotti. But nineteenth-century violin playing, and therefore music for the violin, had its roots in Paris, where its founder was the Italian Giovanni Battista Viotti, who systematized the teaching and style, then travelled Europe and made it standard everywhere, with variations through his descendant pupils. Hardly any great violin music came from France until the century was well advanced. Yet I cannot help suggesting that some of the nineteenth century's most enjoyable violin music came from France, even if it is not played as often as the German repertory.

France and Belgium

The importance of Paris as the European centre of violin schooling, in the first half of the nineteenth century, was not disputed—unless by citizens of Brussels, where a parallel school was launched by Charles de Bériot in 1843, along Parisian lines. Good violin playing nonetheless all stemmed from Paris, and from Viotti as musical patriarch. The lineage was impeccable, the international spread almost evangelic, as a teacher-pupil genealogical tree will show (see following page). Almost all the violin music mentioned below can be traced back to one of these pupils of the Corelli school. The French school of violin playing had its centre at the Paris Conservatoire, which was founded in 1795, and in 1811 opened its concert hall (seating 1,055 people) where orchestral concerts were regularly given from 1828 under François Habeneck (1781–1849), the founder of efficient orchestral training for the nineteenth century, with its more powerful instruments and more fervent music. Habeneck was a violinist, as the tree shows, and string-coaching was his speciality. Berlioz's story of the pinch of snuff at the first performance of his *Grande messe des morts* was given credence when Habeneck tried to stop Berlioz from giving concerts in the Conservatoire hall: he recognized a rival conductor who might prove dangerous. But Habeneck taught Beethoven's music to Parisian concert audiences, and his orchestral pupils travelled far and wide, teaching others the new violin method.

Viotti (1755–1824) came from a poor family in Piedmont, but was taken into the house of a noble lady who recognized the boy's exceptional talent, and had him taught by Pugnani. When he arrived in Paris in 1782, almost as much stir was created by his Stradivarius violin as by the way he played it. Although he was recognized, in France and everywhere else, as the finest living violinist, after only a year Viotti took umbrage at the French musical public and refused to play there again, spending his time thereafter teaching and composing. During the French Revolution he lived in Hamburg and London. Apart from his violin concertos, which are discussed elsewhere, Viotti the composer is best remembered for his fifty-one Duos for two violins which are still studied by aspiring violinists, and with eventual pleasure, since they are musically inventive and pleasing to the ear. He is only known to have written one original sonata for violin and keyboard; others that may be encountered were transcribed from the Duos, some by Cherubini from Viotti's string trios. His greatest memorial may be his pupils, and theirs in France, Belgium, Austria, Germany, Russia, Japan and America—a formidable genealogy, as the tree on the next page illustrates.

The French school of violin playing was systematized in the *Conservatoire Violin Method*, compiled in 1803 by three leading French violinists of the generation after Viotti. They were Pierre Baillot (1771–1842), Rodolphe Kreutzer (1766–1831), and Pierre Rode (1774–1830). Baillot was rather a disciple and protégé of Viotti than a formal pupil. His treatise *L'art du violon* is better known than his compositions, though these include

twenty-four Preludes for violin, in all the keys, and thirty of the *airs variés*, sets of variations, which were so cultivated by composer-soloists of his generation in France. Other favourite forms were the opera fantasy, the *caprice* (such as Paganini composed), and the *étude*: French taste did not favour chamber music in sonata form, though Baillot acquired celebrity from 1814 as leader of a string quartet which gave public recitals in Paris, at a time when such events were unknown there.

Rode's great days as a violinist were before 1800, when he was introducing Viotti's later concertos to Paris, the composer having refused to play there. In 1813, when Beethoven completed his op. 96 sonata expressly for him, Rode's performance did not satisfy the composer. From other sources we learn that, after 1808, Rode's playing lost the warmth and vigour of temperament which had captivated his listeners hitherto. His concertos and twenty-four *Caprices* are still standard teaching material, and his G major Variations were given words and sung, with or without piano accompaniment, by the Italian soprano Angelica Catalani, and after her by Pauline Viardot-Garcia, as a vocalist's display-piece.

Kreutzer was the dedicatee of an earlier Beethoven sonata, op. 47 in A major, the most brilliant of the set— Beethoven hoped that it would create a stir in Paris, since he thought of making his home there, and therefore inscribed it to the leading French violinist with whom he had played sonatas during Kreutzer's visit to Vienna in 1798. Kreutzer, like Baillot, was rather an apostle than a Viotti pupil, having studied with his father, a bandsman in the Swiss Guard at Versailles, and with Anton Stamitz of the Mannheim school of composers (it was from the Mannheim violin school that Spohr and his descendant pupils also came). In Paris he was famed for the fire and fervour of his playing, for his duets with Rode—evidently the contests of admiring friends—and for the operas, mostly comic, which he composed in profusion for various theatres in Paris, not only the Opéra. His teaching pieces, forty-two *Etudes* and nineteen *Etudes-Caprices*, aim at developing the manual extension; alas, his career as a violinist ended in 1810 when he broke his arm.

It was for Kreutzer's pupil Alexandre Artôt (1815–45) that Berlioz composed his *Rêverie et Caprice* with orchestra, the first considerable piece of music to fall within this chapter's purview. It was later taken up by Ferdinand David (1810–73), Delphin Alard (1815–88, the teacher of Sarasate) and others. The first orchestral phrase, drooping with gentle melancholy, brings a new world of poetry into French violin music; the radiant

The tradition of Corelli: A teacher–pupil genealogical tree (dotted lines indicate influence). With acknowledgement to *The Great Violonists* by Margaret Campbell.

Opposite: Title-page and postural diagrams from Baillot's *L'Art du violon*.

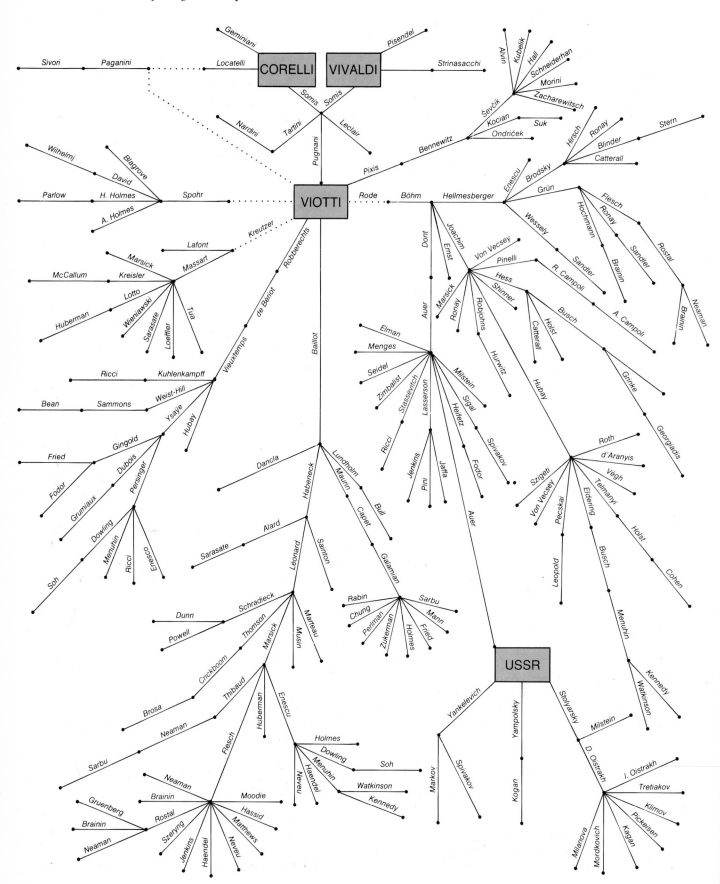

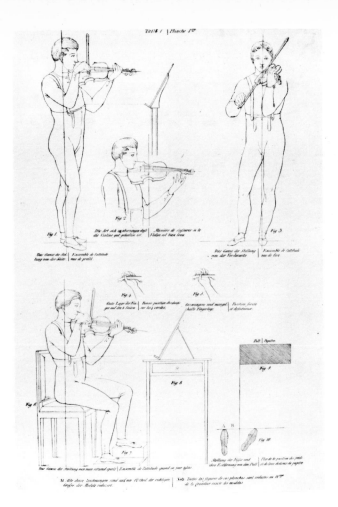

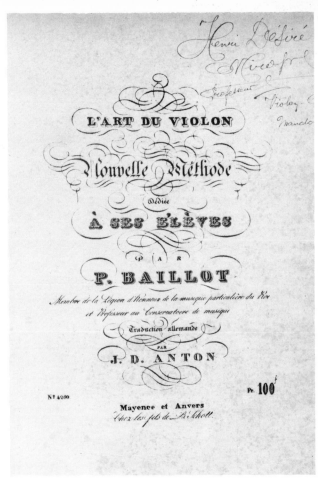

arch of the first violin entry has grace as well as fire, and the principal melody of the *Rêverie* (it was alternatively known as *Tendresse*) is utterly characteristic of Berlioz's distinctive melodic style, perhaps recalling the Love Scene in his *Roméo et Juliette*. It was planned at first as Teresa's first air in *Benvenuto Cellini*. The music begins to gather energy and pace. At first the element of faster caprice has to conflict with the attractions of rêverie, then they mingle, the slower melody against solo bravura decoration. A powerful violin passage on the G-string may recall Berlioz's admiration for Baillot in such music, as attested in the composer's *Mémoires*. The *Caprice*, when it gains control, is but mildly virtuoso though full of Berliozian fire and festivity (rather in the Capulet manner); the textures and rhythms here are elaborate, and call for vigorously controlled ensemble.

The Belgian school of violin-playing, as important as its parent in France, was instituted by Charles Auguste de Bériot (1802–1870) who completed his studies under the supervision of Viotti and Baillot, though he was too wayward and eccentric a pupil to remain with either teacher. On his travels through Europe as a virtuoso soloist, he fell in with the great singer Maria Malibran, shared concerts with her, and married her in 1835. After her sudden death, following a fall from a horse, in the following year, Heine declared that her soul lived on in de Bériot's playing, and the melodic style of his music is indeed indebted to the *bel canto* opera of Rossini, Bel-

lini and Donizetti in which she had excelled. De Bériot's particular gift as a violinist, reflected in his music, is a combination of French elegance, a German sweetness and the dazzling brilliance which he so admired in Paganini. Of his many *Airs variés*, the op. 9 is with orchestra, and the op. 2 features the fourth string retuned up to A. The sixty *Etudes* included in de Bériot's *Ecole transcendentale* op. 123 are a diverse lot, some with piano, most for violin solo: no. 12 is grandly Lisztian, no. 2 an effective fake four-part fugue in the manner of J. S. Bach. He remained director of violin studies at the Brussels Conservatoire until 1852 when his left arm became paralysed; soon afterwards he became blind. His son, by Maria Malibran, bore his father's name as a pianist, and was the teacher of Granados, Ravel and Riccardo Viñes, Debussy's favourite pianist. De Bériot senior's most famous pupil was Henri Vieuxtemps (1820–81), whose chamber music has not the authority and boldness of his concertos, though there is some structural cunning in his Ballade and Polonaise in G major op. 38.

The pupil-descendants of Viotti have been generally violinists first and composers second (Kreutzer, exceptionally, was active in the theatre and, significantly maybe, he was not a Viotti pupil). One of Habeneck's pupils was Edouard Lalo (1823–92), a Frenchman whose preference was for playing chamber music, and who forwent a virtuoso's career to form and maintain

Below: Henri Vieuxtemps

Opposite: The concert hall of the Paris Conservatoire: engraving from *L'Illustration* (1843).

the Armingaud Quartet. His success as a composer was slow to arrive, French musical taste still being as hidebound as in Baillot's day. In 1871 he was among the founders of the *Société Nationale*, a movement designed to encourage orchestral and chamber music by living French composers. The concerts of this society finally brought him to public attention, and he won fame, ironically, with an opera, *Le roi d'Ys*, and a virtuoso violin concerto, the *Symphonie espagnole*, written for Sarasate— two genres which the French in any case preferred.

Lalo's chamber music is as attractive, and in intention as serious, as might be expected: it includes two (actually three) piano trios, and a violin sonata, the latter composed in 1853 as a *Grand Duo Concertant* and published as his opus 12. The sonata is of special interest as an authentic sonata structure, twenty years before the genre became current in France through works by Fauré, Franck, Lekeu, d'Indy and others. Like them, it draws nourishment from German music, yet remains essentially French in character: unlike them, Lalo's language is essentially pre-Wagner, hardly aware of chromatic harmony, and scarcely interested either in contrapuntal elaboration—that devil, as Richard Strauss described it, which dogs all German composers. Like all of Lalo's music, the *Grand Duo* revels in rhythmic vitality and in a vigorous diatonic palette, primary colours boldly applied. The themes are personable, those of the first movement perhaps not enough contrasted for the good of the musical argument; and indeed, although the development keeps going effortlessly throughout the movement, we do not eventually remark a substantial transformation in them, as we should in the finest sonata design. The central movement is a bland, amiable set of variations, which do not try hard enough to deserve the double cadenza towards the end. The Rondo is surely the best movement, a happily chattering *perpetuum mobile* with bursts of high spirits. The work is enjoyable for both players, and the audience too: it deserves regular performance.

The *Société Nationale* worked wonders for French chamber music in general, the sonata for violin and piano included. A generation of composers, unattracted to the popular genres of instrumental music, had been languishing in obscurity in Paris, without any outlet for their creative desires. As well as Lalo, there was his compatriot César Franck; Camille Saint-Saëns was enabled to extend his range profitably, and the *Société Nationale* gave a serious spur to his young protégé Gabriel Fauré. All these produced important violin sonatas during the first decade and a half of the Society's existence. First in the field was the Society's founding secretary Alexis de Castillon, whose C major violin and piano sonata, op. 6, was premiered in 1872, just two years before his death: it is said to look forward to some of the structural new departures from sonata-form found in subsequent works of the school.

Fauré (1845–1924) composed his first violin sonata, op. 13 in A major, during 1875–6 and gave the first performance a year later with Marie Tayau (who is otherwise remembered for her experiments with a wire E-string: see also p. 42). Hubert Léonard, a Belgian pupil of Habeneck who, like Lalo, made his violinistic career unfashionably in chamber music, had given Fauré advice about the violin part (Fauré was a pianist by upbringing), and violinists ever since have warmed gratefully to the sonata; it was dedicated, however, to Paul Viardot, the violinist son of the great mezzo-soprano Pauline Viardot-Garcia, with whose daughter (Paul's sister) Fauré was unsuccessfully in love at the time. Fauré's A major sonata combines youthful ardour and French brilliance with spacious ease, and a subtle adjustment of accepted sonata-form balance which he was to develop further in the E minor second sonata op. 108 (1916–17), bringing exposition and development closer together, and doubling recapitulation as well as exposition. Some slighter salon pieces included the melodious and much-loved *Berceuse* in F major op. 16, the (for once under-inventive) Romance in B flat major op. 28, and the attractive *Andante* op. 75 in the same key, obviously more mature in manner and sound.

The second sonata, dedicated to the Queen of Belgium (herself a noted violinist) and first performed by Lucien Capet and Alfred Cortot, is a strong and highly original piece in Fauré's elliptical late style. Franck's cyclical technique of thematic reprise is effectively used in the finale of this masterly, too seldom played sonata.

It was almost ten years before Fauré's mentor Saint-Saëns (1835–1921) ventured into the same genre, though he had been friendly in his youth with George Bridgetower (Beethoven's virtuoso model at the time of the 'Kreutzer' sonata), and more recently with Pablo Sarasate. For the latter he wrote the first violin concerto, and in 1863 the irresistibly charming *Introduction and Rondo Capriccioso*. The Introduction could well be a lover's entreating serenade, so eloquently are the phrases articulated. The girl seems to answer, when the pace quickens, only to be countered by yearning questions, reinforced by a sultry Iberian, perhaps Moorish, half-cadence. Upon this, the Rondo breaks with a strutting, truculently *macho* melody that Bizet might have invented for Escamillo in his *Carmen* of ten years or so later. A fashionable Paris audience would savour the Sarasate Spanishry, the dazzling violinistics, the dapper composition—a handsome surprise at the tune's third entry, when the off-beat rhythm is shifted on to the beat. The gentler episodes hint at Mendelssohn, the frenzied coda at Chopin; there is also Spanish tourism to spare, and yet the *Introduction and Rondo Capriccioso* wears an indelible seal of authenticity, mastery that gives no

hostages at all to tourist public relations.

So it is with the other non-concerto works by Saint-Saëns for violin, with piano or orchestral accompaniment. I should mention a late and chastely exquisite *Duo* op. 132, for violin and cello, called *La Muse et le Poète* (1910). The delectable *Havanaise* op. 83 (1885) derives from the crackle of firewood on a cold evening in Brest, where Saint-Saëns was on tour with the violinist Diaz Albertini—in retrospect we can hear the snap of burning twigs in the solo violin's theme. There is another venture into musical Spanishry, the *Caprice andalou* op. 122 (1904), the opening melodious section rather conventional, the concluding *Allegro* full of sparkle. The melodist in Saint-Saëns is richly indulged in the Romances with orchestra, op. 37 in D flat (an exquisitely elaborated accompaniment by this master of the orchestra) and op. 48 in C major. Violinists sometimes include in recitals the tuneful *Andantino* from the prelude to Saint-Saëns's oratorio *Le déluge*.

Even granted the excellence of the last violin concerto, and the skill affectionately deployed in those solo pieces, the two sonatas for violin and piano seem, as if deliberately, to sum up Saint-Saëns's most serious feelings about the violin as his own musical voice, and himself as France's heir to the tradition of Viennese classicism. As a child prodigy, he had been raised on that tradition (after his debut piano recital at the age of eleven, he offered to play as encore whichever of Beethoven's sonatas the audience requested). Saint-

César Franck: drawing by G. Villa.

César Franck

Saëns was probably the master technician of nineteenth-century music, surpassing in knowledge both Wagner and Brahms whom he admired, and having a compositional ability of his own—a child of Paganini as well as Beethoven, of Mozart and Haydn, and then of Bach and other old contrapuntalists. Whatever he turned to, he made new.

So it was with his first violin sonata, op. 75 in D minor. The first two movements are linked, likewise the last two (as in Michael Tippett's third symphony, to name one later example). The music moves forward by contrapuntal interaction, more naturally and regularly than in any French nineteenth-century music before very late Fauré. The first movement changes metre and key with like ease, and thinks all the time of the two instruments as brilliant contestants intent on competition at the highest intellectual level. The object is ambitious indeed, but Saint-Saëns had the imagination and technique to do such a thing with ardent enthusiasm. His *Adagio* glows with lyrical warmth. After a pause there follows a G minor scherzo intent on surprise, and a brilliant D minor finale. It is perhaps of interest that Marcel Proust, when questioned about the origins of the 'sonate de Vinteuil' so eloquently described in *A la recherche de temps perdu*, mentioned this sonata by Saint-Saëns, rather than that by Franck, which most readers assumed to be his inspiration. The

second Saint-Saëns violin sonata, op. 102 in E flat major, makes fewer demands on its interpreters, but abounds in imaginative ideas, whether melodious, as in the first and third movements, or animated, as in the scherzo, or the middle section of the *Andante* in B major, or the *presto* conclusion of the finale's *allegro grazioso*.

The most popular of all these French Romantic violin sonatas remains that by César Franck in A major—so popular indeed that other instruments have raided it for their repertory, first the cello (condoned by the composer), then the viola, latterly the flute. Like Saint-Saëns, Franck (1822–90) was a keyboard player, as much virtuoso pianist as organist, with an enormous hand-stretch that Kreutzer would have envied: the sonata gratifies the ambitious pianist to such an extent that he must constantly fear to drown his partner, yet violinists (and predatory colleagues on other instruments) continue to find the work endlessly attractive. It is not violinistically brilliant, like the piano part in the tempestuous second movement, for example; but it gratifies a player of strong and sensitive temperament, and the work as a whole is beautifully balanced between its unassuming, quasi-improvisatory start—which quickly blossoms into a self-developing bipartite melody—and the equally bland canonic finale theme which is to draw together the intervening emotional threads. The rhapsodical third movement is inventively less assured: after two quite positive movements, the music seems becalmed, until the arrival of a new swooping theme full of passionate striving that gets nowhere. But the movement does successfully prepare for the finale, which justifies not just that theme but the rest of the thematic contents. For this is one of Franck's 'cyclic' works, which bring back music from earlier movements, eventually declaring their unity, a technique deriving perhaps from the *Leitmotif* methods of Wagner (themselves indebted to earlier composers), whom Franck greatly admired: it is put to its most persuasive purpose in the violin sonata, perhaps more naturally than in the well-known D minor symphony.

Franck's compatriot and pupil, Guillaume Lekeu (1870–94), composed a sort of sequel violin sonata, the cyclic method applied to a conventional formal mould, and with limited technical resources so that the music sounds either repetitious or improvisatory. Lekeu was soon to die aged 24, and the violin sonata does suggest that he was prevented from fulfilling a real creative talent, that is only adumbrated here.

It was another Belgian, Eugène Ysaÿe (1858–1931), who brought Lekeu's violin sonata into being. Ysaÿe was the champion exponent of those other sonatas, by

Fauré, Saint-Saëns, Lalo and Franck, and indeed an inspiring figurehead for serious French and Belgian composers, comparable in influence with Joseph Joachim in German-speaking countries. Better known today than any of Ysaÿe's six violin concertos are six sonatas for unaccompanied violin, each dedicated to an eminent fellow violinist (see also p. 187). The model was evidently J. S. Bach, the Prelude to whose Partita no. 3 in E major haunts the opening movement, entitled '*Obsession*', of Ysaÿe's second sonata in A minor, dedicated to Jacques Thibaud; its second and third movements, '*Malinconia*' and '*Danse des ombres*', treat the old *Dies Irae* plainchant. The first sonata, following Bach, is in G minor, and deals impressively in chromatic polyphony during its first two movements (there are chords of five and six constituent notes); it was dedicated to Joseph Szigeti. The third sonata, a Ballade in one movement, richly emotional, was written for Georges Enescu, the most complete musician among violinists of the present century, worthy of this noble sonata, the most frequently performed of the six. No. 4 in E minor was for Fritz Kreisler, and is notable for a Sarabande in which different typefaces are used to mark the flow of

the counterpoint; the finale is a convincing 5/4 *presto*. Sonata no. 5 in G major was for Mathieu Crickboom (second violin in Ysaÿe's string quartet): it features pictorial ideas, and a burst of 'Paganini effects' for which Ysaÿe felt obliged to apologize, 'though they are quite original', he added. No. 6, for Manuel Quiroga, is in a single movement, strongly virtuoso in character with a marked flavour of the dance.

It was Ysaÿe also who introduced the lovely *Poème* for violin and orchestra by Ernest Chausson (1855–99), a French pupil of Franck who came late to composition and died at forty-four in a bicycle accident. Chausson's Concerto is for violin and piano duo with accompaniment for string quartet, a combination which works so successfully that one wonders it was not more copied. In Chausson's few but treasurable works, as in the songs of Henri Duparc, the French Wagnerian movement soared to its zenith, unsurpassed by grander forces or dimensions. Neither composer was a violinist—and indeed little violin music of front rank was composed by French violinists of the nineteenth century, let alone the twentieth, by which time the exotic plumage of the composer-violinist is all but extinct.

Italy

An Italian musician looking for a career around 1800 could hope to become a church organist and choirmaster, an opera singer, a composer, or an orchestral musician, but hardly a virtuoso violinist: the Corelli tradition in Italy had been dispelled, and its latest scion, Giovanni Viotti, went abroad to make his career. The great violins of Cremona, many of them gathering dust in cupboards and glory-holes, began to be sought out by collectors, bought from their (usually ignorant) inheritors, and likewise exported, mainly for modernization and new use at the hands of the latest itinerant virtuosos. Nevertheless Italy had a glorious role to play in nineteenth-century violin music, thanks to one man. Niccolò Paganini (1782–1840) may appear in his historical context as some sort of sport, but his musicianship was the heritage of Vivaldi and Corelli, and Biagio Marini before them, as well as Amati and his fellow architects of the instrument in Cremona. Paganini's violin teachers were unimportant: he learned his art, he said, from Locatelli's music and from watching the virtuoso Alphonse Durand, a Viotti pupil. He was much influenced by the playing of Kreutzer and Rode. He is a characteristically prodigal son of the Viotti family, but undeniably a kinsman.

In the century of the peripatetic violin virtuoso, a circus-artist as often as a musician, Paganini stands as the archetype, the paragon of his kind. Even granted the rose-tinted memories of those who wrote about his playing, he must have been a violinist of exceptional personality as well as proficiency. Today every aspiring violin soloist sets his sights on Paganini's twenty-four *Caprices*, yet few can play them in public to anything like satisfaction—they require not only 'transcendental' technique (to borrow Liszt's epithet), but transcendental sensibility and inflammability. They must be made to appear not only difficult but vastly entertaining. That they are so is confirmed by the creative stimulus they have given to other composers, notably Schumann and Brahms. Their musical value is not more exalted than Paganini intended, nor than that of his violin concertos (discussed elsewhere in this book), nor yet his many amazing, still greatly enjoyable, operatic fantasies and *airs variés*. The Variations on the Prayer from Rossini's *Mosè in Egitto* are composed for the fourth string alone. Some say that Paganini deliberately broke his violin's three upper strings during the previous item, apologized to the audience, braced himself, and embarked upon the *Moses Fantasy*, which had been his intention all the time; others claimed that he endured

Opposite: Autograph of Paganini's *Caprice* op. 3 no. 5.

Below: Festival-concert in the Salle Pleyel in Paris, with Sarasate, Saint-Saëns at the piano, 1896.

eight months' imprisonment, with a one-stringed violin as his only recreation. The Variations have remained prime encore material for a brilliant violinist—in the early 1970s and afterwards the American virtuoso Gary Karr was even playing this work on the double-bass.

Paganini's G string trick was nothing new: Viotti is credited with inventing music for the violin's lowest string alone, and in less dramatic circumstances than those attributed to Paganini. No more original was Paganini's ruse (in the first concerto and *Le streghe*) of writing music in one difficult key, and playing it in an easier adjacent key, by retuning his violin (*scordatura* is the Italian accepted term—see also pp. 66 and 101); Mozart was employing it in his *Sinfonia concertante* K.364 for violin, viola and orchestra, which the orchestra played in E flat major, the soloists in D major. Paganini's *Caprices* at once roused the creative larceny of Schumann and Liszt who stole some of them for the piano (both paid interest in musical invention of their own). His variations on '*Di tanti palpiti*', the hit-tune from Rossini's *Tancredi*, gave the melody an extended immortality (or a bridging gap, if that opera ever becomes repertory again), and are as charming as they cause amazement at the violinist's skill. The opera-fantasy, such as Liszt's *Don Giovanni*, Chopin's

Variations on '*Là ci darem*' and on the final rondo of Rossini's *Cenerentola* (also treated by Paganini), was designed to popularize important new music among people unlikely to hear the real thing in a concert (as records do today). We do not nowadays expect independent musical enlightenment from this repertory, but it is there, and often proves illuminating as well as inspiring. Paganini's Variations on the famous *Carnival de Venise* melody hold a place in violinists' programmes, as does his '*Le streghe*' on a theme by Mozart's pupil Süssmayr. Paganini's duos for violin and guitar, which include 60 variations on the folksong 'Barucaba' that pass through all 24 keys major and minor, treat both instruments brilliantly—Paganini was a highly accomplished guitarist too—but they need special pleading by a pair of super-gifted interpreters. He played them with a guitarist named Sina.

Paganini admitted that his most remarkable feats on the violin could not be reproduced at home: he succeeded as a violin virtuoso only when faced with a large audience to conquer. Yet he was a keen chamber musician in private, who loved to lead Beethoven's string quartets (he decorated the reprises, quite spontaneously), even the latest of them, a man who revered Palestrina and Mozart's *Don Giovanni*. The circus artist

was only a part of Paganini's fascinating career. He was accounted an excellent teacher by his only pupil, Camillo Sivori (1815–94), but the latter made no comparable impression as solo violinist; he was, however, the teacher of Zino Francescatti's father. Paganini gave advice, rather than formal training, to Antonio Bazzini (1818–97), who made a successful career as a solo violinist: he took part in a famous performance of Maurer's then extravagantly popular *Concertante* for four violins and orchestra at Leipzig in 1843, when his fellow-soloists were Ernst, David and Joachim. Bazzini's best-known composition today is the *scherzo fantastique* called *La ronde des lutins*, dedicated to Ernst. He introduced the string quartet to Italy and composed six quartets himself as well as a violin sonata. From 1873 he taught composition at Milan Conservatory, where his pupils included Giacomo Puccini.

Spain

This country's major contribution to nineteenth-century violin music was Pablo de Sarasate y Navascues (1844–1908), whose name has been mentioned above in connection with Lalo and Saint-Saëns. He had evidently acquired a Paganinian transcendental technique by the age of 12, when he left home to study in Paris with Delphin Alard, from whom he acquired a classic style and an uncommonly pure tone. Thereafter his travels took him to North and South America, as well as all over Europe. His repertory was broad and large, and he was also an assiduous composer for his own instrument. His books of Spanish Dances, opp. 21–3, 26, 27 (the popular *Jota aragonesa*) and 29 (*Canto del ruiseñor*, which anticipates Granados), are all charming and poetical as well as brilliant, and are likely to have influenced his French contemporaries in their taste for pseudo-Spanish music, as well as his younger compatriots Albeniz and Falla. Sarasate's op. 25 is a fantasy for violin and orchestra on themes from Bizet's *Carmen*, a specialist's variant of this well-loved genre. Bizet's harmony and scoring are left as he wrote them; Sarasate takes the third *Entr'acte*, the *Habanera*, Carmen's taunting melody ('*Coupe-moi, brûle-moi*'), the *Séguedille*, and the *Chanson bohème*, and treats their melodic lines to all manner of elegant and dazzling embellishment, including a canonic treatment of the *Habanera* that Bizet forgot to write. A later piece, '*Adios, montañas mias*' op. 37, is a charming exercise in double-stops and 5/8 metre. The most favoured of all Sarasate's works is not at all Spanish in character: 'Gypsy Airs' (internationally known by its German title *Zigeunerweisen*) op. 20, with orchestral accompaniment, is modelled on the

Johann Schrammel and his quartet.

Hungarian Rhapsody as put together by Liszt, a slow, smouldering *lassú* followed by a dazzling *friss*. Sarasate lived to record it himself for the gramophone.

Vienna and the Austrian Empire

Paris might claim to be the musical capital of Europe during the nineteenth century, but during its first thirty years Vienna was the prime scene of action. Haydn, Beethoven and Schubert were all working there until their deaths. To conquer the Viennese public was a high priority for the itinerant virtuoso soloist, and visiting musicians were numerous: in 1790 half the soloists who played there were under fourteen years of age, and it was being said that 'to succeed one must be blind, pretty, or between the ages of six and eight years old'. As the capital of the Holy Roman Empire, Vienna was the immediate goal in particular of every ambitious young musical talent in Bohemia, Moravia and Hungary: many of the remained, like Joseph Boehm and Heinrich Ernst, or moved elsewhere, like Joachim and Reményi to Germany or Leopold Auer to Russia.

Vienna was always full of foreigners, like Haydn and Beethoven, and later in the century, Brahms. For composers and string-players, the city was, unlike Paris, a haven of chamber-music, with the tradition of the Viennese classics behind it. Here was Ignaz Schuppanzigh (1776–1830) with his string quartet which introduced the quartets of Beethoven and Schubert to the world; Schuppanzigh, a grand-pupil of Joseph Haydn, had brought to Vienna the role of violinist as *Bratlgeiger*, the sweetly beguiling café entertainer of his neighbouring Hungary. Vienna had plenty of time for the *Bratlgeiger* whether his name was Johann Strauss, Fritz Kreisler or Johann Schrammel (1850–93), who gave his name to the popular Viennese music which he and his quartet (violin, clarinet or accordion, guitar and bass) dispensed in the taverns of Grinzing, and which their successors dispense to this day. We owe this whole enchanting side of truly Viennese music to Beethoven's 'house violinist' Schuppanzigh. Brahms's generation could call on the Hellmesberger Quartet, formed in 1849 by Joseph senior of that name (1828–93), son of Georg Hellmesberger (1800–73), the violin professor who figures first in the Corelli family tree on p. 118, and father of Joseph junior (1855–1907), who was conductor of the Vienna Philharmonic Orchestra from 1900 with Gustav Mahler (another foreigner).

Opposite above: Niccolò Paganini: portrait by Georg Friedrich Kersting, 1830.

Opposite below: Paganini as paid guest at a dinner party.

Several of the Hellmesberger family were also composers, chiefly of operettas and Viennese dances.

Aspiring violinists did not have to go to Paris to learn their art and craft: there was a flourishing branch of the Viotti school in Vienna, and subjects of the Holy Roman Empire took advantage of it. The fame of Joseph Boehm (1795–1876) was largely as a virtuoso and pedagogue; as a composer he rates a mention for his solo violin Variations on a theme by Beethoven, each in the style of a named violin virtuoso, Clement, Schuppanzigh, and others. Ernst (1814–55), who came from Brno (then called Brünn), was a Paganini apostle, and a crony of Berlioz who played the solo viola part in the Russian premiere of *Harold in Italy* under the composer's direction—a work whose overt literary basis and modern idiom was to alter the course of Russian music. Ernst's unaccompanied violin *Caprice* on Schubert's '*Der Erlkönig*' used to be much admired, and his *Fantasy* on Rossini's *Otello* has successfully been revived by Ruggiero Ricci in recent years (a dazzling record that also includes Sarasate's *Carmen* and Wieniawski's *Faust* confections).

Serious music for the violin was composed in nineteenth-century Vienna by Schubert, to go no further after Beethoven. Schubert has bequeathed us three violin sonatas, misnamed sonatinas, from his boyhood, and three later great works. He composed the three early sonatas for family performance; he was brought up a violinist, though he preferred (like J. S. Bach and Mozart) to take the viola in chamber music. They are prentice works, unsure of their path and clinging to safe models, but instinct with true Schubertian warmth and outgoing naturalness. The A major Duo D.574 is an altogether more masterly, I would say Olympian, document, which announces its stature from the unhurried opening theme for piano, and conveys the pain as well as the joy that Schubert had to live with—he could reveal enough to make a desert weep, and yet he does so with such generosity of spirit (one remembers now also the second and, particularly, the third sonatas, in A minor and G minor respectively) that by the end we are all smiling in sympathy. There is more tragedy to be sensed in the C major *Fantasy* D.934, written for the Czech-born violinist Josef Slavik (1806–33, a pupil of Pixis): a work of profound elegiac poetry and stirring drama that finds unlikely yet true release in a set of variations on Schubert's song, '*Sei mir gegrüsst*'. A violinist could not discuss Schubert's music without at least passing reference to his string quartets, which range from what virtuosos called 'solo quartet', i.e. solos for first violin with three accompanists, to such splendours

of ensemble as the G major quartet D.887 and the C major string quintet D.956, works of the highest poetry which nevertheless proceed from the datum of a magnificent leading fiddler, as in the quintet's *Andante*.

After the death of Schubert in 1828, Viennese violin music knew only the glories of Brahms, who wrote for the solo violin of Joachim, now resident in Germany, and of Johann Strauss who had no solo aspirations, until the arrival of an *echt*-Wiener, the wonderful Fritz Kreisler (1875–1962), who claims two branches on the Corelli family tree. In this chapter Kreisler takes his place as a composer not so much of operetta or a string quartet as of a series of enchanting and elegant encore pieces, some pseudo-Classical and ascribed by him to earlier masters, such as Pugnani or Tartini, quite falsely, others of the post-prandial sweetmeat variety. Such are *Schön Rosmarin, Liebesleid* and *Liebesfreud*, the *Caprice viennois*—once accounted unplayable except by Kreisler (it is not technically so difficult)—the *Tambourin chinois*, and the Rondino on a theme by Beethoven. Modern violinists sometimes manage to evoke the authentic *frisson* in these pieces (Itzhak Perlman is one), but the style, that of the lofty poet-orator who can also relax completely without relinquishing an iota of musical idealism, is not easily caught. Kreisler responded to the dedication of Ysaÿe's solo sonata (see pp. 123 and 187) with his own *Introduction and Solo Caprice*, dedicated to Ysaÿe, a work both impressive and charming.

Bohemia, now part of Czechoslovakia, was close to Vienna in the Holy Roman Empire, and a country with strong musical traditions and abundant talent, particularly for instrumental music, and chamber music above all. The violin was almost a national instrument by 1800. Viotti's pupil Friedrich Wilhelm Pixis (1785–1842) soon brought the new French violin technique to Prague, and developed the national talent still further. His pupil Johann Kalliwoda dominated Bohemian violin literature in the first half of the century, though he worked chiefly at Donaueschingen in Germany. Kalliwoda's compositions exceed three hundred, 243 with opus numbers. They include a duet in A major for violin and piano op. 111, and some violin duos: the earlier works are the most creatively inventive.

The composers who made Bohemia musically famous during the century, Smetana and Dvořák, were both brought up as fiddlers, though only the latter worked professionally as a string-player, and he settled for the viola. Bedřich Smetana (1824–84) first worked as a pianist, then a conductor, but he found time to compose a D minor sonatina for violin and piano; the hero of his opera *Dalibor* is a fiddler who plays a good deal in

The Bohemian String Quartet: lithograph after Hugo
Böttinger, 1907.

the course of the opera (handsome solos for the orchestra's leader); his two autobiographical string quartets
speak, as narrators, from the first violin's desk, in the
old manner of the *concertante*—or 'solo' quartet (an
eighteenth-century, not always bad tradition which
survived long into the time of this chapter). And in
Smetana's suite so-entitled 'From my native land'
(*Zdomoviny*, 1880) we have a work of fire and boldness,
the second of its two movements most unexpected in
its sequence of striking musical events: the piece gives
unusual scope to an imaginative violinist with a strong
sense of humour.

Antonin Dvořák (1841–1904) used to play the violin
for the inmates of his father's tavern, and something
of those memories must have found a way into his G
major sonatina op. 100. He designed it for young
players, and the music has a quality of strange enchant-
ment, a romantic nostalgia for childhood without its
uncomfortable aspects (was also a speciality of Schumann). The second movement of this sonatina is
sometimes billed as 'Indian lament', a reference to
Dvořák's recent stay in America (the Indians were sup-

posedly Red); but the title, like the 'Nigger' nickname
attached to his quartet op. 95, is wholly spurious and
rather distasteful. Dvořák composed sympathetically,
and quite keenly, for the violin, as may be found in the
Romantic Pieces op. 75. Some of his violin solos with
orchestra would make good encore material, or contrast,
for a concert programme. His son-in-law, Josef Suk
senior (1874–1935), was a fine violinist and founded the
Bohemian String Quartet, greatly admired in its day;
his work as a composer began in the nineteenth century,
but he found creative maturity only after 1900. Josef
Suk, Dvořák's grandson, is a virtuoso violinist of the
present day.

The violin was as much cultivated in Hungary as in
Bohemia, but the finest exponents moved elsewhere to
seek their fortune, among them artists like Hubay,
Joachim, Auer and Reményi. Jenö Hubay (1858–1937)
is best known for his attractive '*Hejre Kati*' op. 32. His
ten *Concertante Studies* op. 89 stand out radiantly amid
other teaching material: no. 5 is a delicious waltz; no. 6
contrasts various types of touch and bowing with most
colourful effect; none is dully academic. He was a pro-

Joseph Joachim: ink drawing by Wilhelm Gertner, 1845.

EVENING CONCERT

OF

CLASSICAL INSTRUMENTAL MUSIC

AT

RADLEY'S HOTEL, BRIDGE STREET, BLACKFRIARS,

On WEDNESDAY, the 5th JUNE, 1844.

First Part.

QUARTETT IN D MINOR, No. 2 ... *Mozart*
TWO VIOLINS, VIOLA AND VIOLONCELLO.

Messrs. JOACHIM, CASE, HILL and HANCOCK.

GRAND TRIO IN D MINOR ... *Mendelssohn Bartholdy*
PIANOFORTE, VIOLIN AND VIOLONCELLO.

Dr. FELIX MENDELSSOHN BARTHOLDY, Messrs. JOACHIM
and HANCOCK.

Second Part.

FANTASIE BRILLANTE (VIOLIN) ... ... *Ernst*
Master JOACHIM.

WITH PIANOFORTE ACCOMPANIMENT.

QUARTETT IN C, Op. 59 ... ... *Beethoven*
(*Dedicated to Prince Rasamouffsky*)
TWO VIOLINS, VIOLA AND VIOLONCELLO.

Messrs. JOACHIM, CASE, HILL and HANCOCK.

To commence at Eight o'clock precisely.

Single Tickets, 5s. each; or a Family Ticket, to admit Five Persons,
One Guinea. To be had of Messrs. EWER and Co., Music Sellers,
Newgate Street; and of Messrs. PURDY and FENDT, 20 Finch Lane,
Cornhill, and 3 Oxenden Street, Haymarket, where all further par-
ticulars may be obtained.

lific composer of symphony, opera, choral and chamber music, as well as for his own instrument. The great virtuoso Liszt owed much to Paganini, but he wrote little violin music, and nothing specifically for the Italian master. His *Duo* for violin and piano on a Chopin Mazurka (*c.* 1835) is a four-movement work, spartan in style but of some interest: perhaps he played it later at Weimar with Joachim. There is an Epithalamium for the wedding of Reményi, and another *Duo* on a song by the French violinist Charles-Philippe Lafont (1781–1839), who collaborated with other celebrated virtuosos, including Paganini. Liszt essentially paid his debt to Paganini in music for piano.

Germany

Nineteenth-century violin music in Germany was dominated by three great violinists: Louis Spohr (1784–1859) who taught Ferdinand David (1810–53) who taught Joseph Joachim (1831–1907). Spohr consciously modelled his playing, from 1803, on the French style of Pierre Rode, whom he heard and met during his first concert tour of Russia with his teacher Franz Eck (who came from Stamitz's Mannheim school). He was evidently an outstanding violinist in his youth, but eventually tired of virtuosity, preferring to devote his energies to orchestral and chamber music, the composition of opera and oratorio, musical administration and conducting (he was a pioneer of the conductor's baton). Spohr was an active teacher too, who boasted 187 pupils to his name by the time of his retirement (hastened by his radical politics and insistent championship of Richard Wagner's works). Through his and disciples' influence, German musical taste was encouraged to favour earnestness in artistic effort, and to eschew empty brilliance, for better or for worse. Yet Spohr's concept of the string quartet (he composed thirty-six of them) was essentially a *concertante* one, and his musical invention tended to harmonized melody rather than counterpoint. There is more musical interest in his double string quartets and such mixed concerted works as the septet, octet and nonet. Violinists enjoy his many duos: for example the rich four-part harmony in the first movement of op. 39 no. 2, and the exercises in the *staccato moderato* that was his speciality. His first wife was a harpist, and so he regularly wrote his violin sonatas with that instrument as partner (though his op. 96, 'Memories of a Journey to Dresden and Saxon Switzerland', has piano accompaniment).

Spohr's pupil Ferdinand David from Hamburg (not to be confused with his exact French contemporary

Right: Heinrich Wilhelm Ernst: portrait by Frederick Tatham, 1844.

Below: Franz Schubert: watercolour portrait by Wilhelm August Rieder, 1825.

Félicien David) went, while still in his teens, to work as a violinist in Berlin, where he became friendly with Felix Mendelssohn, a year older and a violinist too, who had composed string symphonies for the family orchestra to play, as well as a violin sonata in F minor op. 4, too dutiful to be much fun. Mendelssohn made up for it in 1838, when he wrote a second sonata in F major, and began the E minor violin concerto. Both works were for David, by this time installed as principal violin of the Gewandhaus Orchestra which had brought Mendelssohn as conductor to Leipzig. The sonata unaccountably remained unpublished until 1953, when Yehudi Menuhin acquired a copy; it has three movements, the first jubilantly energetic, the central one a meditation interrupted by sharp dramatic contrasts, the finale a sparkling *perpetuum mobile* after the manner of Weber. (One is reminded that Weber composed six 'Progressive Sonatas' for violin as his op. 106; some of the movements are novelty numbers with fancy titles, such as '*carattere espagnuolo*' with a *bolero* rhythm, and the rondo-finales are pleasant, but Weber was clearly not a violinist, nor much interested in the instrument.)

Quartet recital at the Berlin home of Bettina Brentano, an
admirer and close friend of both Beethoven and Goethe
(seated listening); Joseph Joachim plays first violin, Graf
Flemming cello, and probably Woldemar Bargiel second
violin: watercolour by Johann Carl Arnold, 1855.

A string quartet recital in Spohr's house: drawing by Carl Heinrich Arnold (1798–1874).

Opposite: Autograph of the finale of Schumann's F-A-E sonata in A minor (violin sonata no. 3).

Under Mendelssohn's direction, Leipzig became an important musical centre in Germany. He passed on his enthusiasm for J. S. Bach to his friend David, who reintroduced Leipzig to Bach's solo sonatas and partitas, this time with additional piano accompaniments by Mendelssohn and Schumann. David formed a string quartet and Leipzig learned the quartets of Beethoven and Schubert, and the latter's magnificent string quintet, as well as new string quartets by Mendelssohn. When the Leipzig Conservatorium opened in 1844, Mendelssohn as founding director persuaded his good friend Robert Schumann to join the staff, with his pianist wife Clara. Schumann had been a law student at Leipzig University, until his attendance at a concert given by Paganini in Frankfurt determined him to devote his life to music, not the violin, which he never studied, but (like Liszt) the piano. Mendelssohn persuaded him to write songs, Liszt encouraged him into concerted chamber music. In Leipzig David urged him to compose for

the violin: to 1851 belongs the charming A minor sonata op. 105, and shortly afterwards op. 121 in D minor, which ends with variations on the chorale melody 'Gelobt seist du, Jesu Christ', foreshadowed in the previous movement.

By then another violinist had entered his life. Joseph Boehm's prize pupil in Vienna, the Hungarian Joseph Joachim, made his Leipzig debut aged twelve in a concert at which his pianist was Mendelssohn. The boy remained there to study the violin with David, and composition with Mendelssohn; Schumann was to write for him the C major Fantasy for violin and orchestra op. 131, as well as the violin concerto (which Joachim never played in public). The last music that Schumann completed, before the collapse of his mental health, was a violin sonata for Joachim, based on Joachim's musical motto F-A-E, standing for 'Frei aber einsam' ('free but alone'). Schumann wished to complete, by himself, a sonata for which two movements had been contributed,

Robert Schumann: lithograph by Feckert after a portrait by Adolf Menzel (1815–1905).

Below: Joseph Joachim, 'the last of a classic school': portrait by 'Spy' in *Vanity Fair*, 5 January 1905.

in joint homage to Joachim, by Schumann's pupil Albert Dietrich and young protégé Johannes Brahms. The latter's scherzo is an estimable movement and makes good encore material for a recitalist, especially if preceded by Schumann's last sonata.

Brahms had already made Joachim's acquaintance, when he accompanied the Hungarian-born, Viennese-trained violin virtuoso Eduard Reményi on a concert tour of Germany. It brought them to Hanover, where Joachim held a post at court, and welcomed the colleague from his native land and his shy, over-awed but clearly talented pianist. It was Joachim who introduced Brahms to Liszt in Weimar (not a success) and to the Schumanns in Düsseldorf (they had left Leipzig when Mendelssohn was recalled to Berlin). Joachim became chief mentor to Brahms, discussing each of his works as they were written, rehearsing them in private and giving first public performances of many string compositions (he fulfilled a similar function to Brahms's protégé Dvořák). When Brahms settled in Vienna, he had Joseph Hellmesberger senior and his greatly admired string quartet as eager champions of his chamber music. But the close link with Joachim remained, surviving a period of coolness in the early 1880s when the violinist's marriage broke up, and Brahms took the wife's side in the case.

Immediately after completing the violin concerto op. 77 in 1878, Brahms composed his first violin sonata, op. 78 in G major, sometimes nicknamed '*Regenlied*' because the finale is based on a Brahms song of that title; it also harks back, midway, to the ruminative theme of its slow movement, though cyclicism was not one of Brahms's foibles. The second sonata, op. 100 in A major, followed in 1886, and is more heroic in tone, with a noble slow movement and a sublimely confident finale: its nickname '*Meistersinger*' is unauthentic and feeble, connecting Brahms with Wagner through the first three notes of the sonata, which, transposed into C major, are those of the Prize Song in the opera. The third and last of Brahms's violin sonatas, op. 108 in D minor (1888), is much more Promethean in character, heaven-storming in the outer movements, sumptuously melodious in the *Adagio* (a record by Huberman suggests how dear the movement must have been to his teacher Joachim), with a gossamer-light scherzo to leaven the whole. The Hamburger in Brahms had been well *gebratlgeigert*, salamified, by Joachim as well as Reményi, before he settled in Vienna and wrote those convivial Hungarian Dances (four books, 1868–80) for piano duet which Joachim promptly transcribed for violin and piano.

Johann Strauss conducting his orchestra at a Viennese ball: lithograph after a watercolour (c. 1853) by Theo Zasche.

Below: Johannes Brahms, the last portrait: etching by W. Unger, 1896.

Th. Zasche. Johann Strauß' Kapelle beim Hofball.

In 1899 Joachim celebrated his golden jubilee as an active musician (he dated it from his appointment as leading violinist to Liszt's orchestra at the Weimar court, not from his first concerts as a wonderboy virtuoso) with a concert in Berlin whose orchestra included 44 violinists and 32 viola-players, all of them his pupils. The most famous of these was August Wilhelmj (1845–1908), whom Wagner chose to lead the orchestra at his first Bayreuth Festival, and who was principal of the Guildhall School of Music in London, from which have come generations of string players through him and his successors Flesch and Rostal. He was reputed to command the richest, most penetrating violin tone in the world; he exploited it, and earned violinists' gratitude, with his transcriptions of Schubert's 'Ave Maria' and J. S. Bach's 'Air' (as Wilhelmj made it) 'on the G string' (Bach meant it to *float* on air, a major ninth higher). Wilhelmj's detractors claimed that he only obtained this monumental sound by changing bow on every note and ignoring the composer's phrasing instructions. Joachim did himself insist on fidelity to the printed text and the spirit of the music, though in his later years his pupils complained that he allowed them no interpretative latitude at all, teaching them only his own prejudices, parrot-fashion, never using the violin to expound his ideas, but preaching them as incontrovertible gospel. He took his artistic mission seriously, and lived to see results, though he would as much loathe our concept of 'musical fidelity' as we may smile at his approach to unaccompanied Bach on early gramophone records, for which posterity must nevertheless remain eternally grateful.

Joachim's influence on violin music may date first from his years in Weimar (1849–53) where one of his colleagues was the pianist Joachim Raff (1822–82), composer of a violin sonata which other violinists accounted more taxing than any concerto, and later of a Cavatina, op. 85 no. 2, whose fulsome strains rang round many a Victorian drawing-room, and strongly suggest Joachim's prowess on the G-string; the same set of *Morceaux* includes an enchanting filigree scherzino, which may connect through Joachim with the similar scherzo of Brahms's op. 108. The music director at Weimar was Liszt, then at the height of his creative powers, and happy to have a fellow-Hungarian as his concertmaster, though Joachim will have learned more, at that age, from Liszt than *vice versa*. Raff's op. 67, *La fée d'amour*, was a favourite of Sarasate; his five violin sonatas were supervised by David; the op. 63 *Duos* for violins are based on themes by Wagner (Raff strongly espoused the new German school, unlike Joachim) and his op. 203 (he was a hard-working composer who died at sixty, worn out) is *Volker*, a cyclic tone-poem for violin and piano, still vanguard music by intention. Raff cut himself off from Joachim, on an issue of musical politics. Joachim still guided the creativity of Max Bruch, who wrote a number of violin solos with orchestra apart from his concertos (the *Scottish Fantasy*, for example, though that was destined for Sarasate). Towards the end of the century Ferruccio Busoni composed two violin sonatas, the second of which, op. 36a in E minor (1898), is a noble work indeed, three movements rolled into one, Liszt-fashion, ending with variations on a chorale melody, '*Wie wohl ist mir*' (as if in memory of Schumann's second sonata). It was composed in Berlin, and suggests the influence of Joachim, who was then still musically on the throne.

Richard Strauss was brought up to play violin as well as piano, and in 1887, aged 23, he produced a violin sonata destined for his cousin-teacher Benno Walter which later generations of violinists continue to prize for its unbridled virtuosity and heroic manner, as gratifying as it is daunting. A curiosity is the central slow movement with its fluttering, insect-like figuration for muted violin and a final quotation (more enigmatic than elucidatory) from Beethoven's *Pathétique* sonata op. 13. The sonata is no more typical of Strauss than his earlier violin concerto, but violinists are still happy to play it.

Max Reger, a prolific composer by any standards, wrote reams for the violin, which instrument he was taught by his father. His op. 1 was a violin sonata in D minor, thick in texture, Brahmsian in manner. These characteristics remained long with him, and I am sure, having examined many of his works for the instrument, that he wrote as unself-critically as many of the violin-composers from France early in the century, though his C minor sonata op. 139 is a big and fine piece of music with an eloquent finale, and other intervening works, especially those in the Baroque spirit of Bach, give pleasure. Reger seems to have succeeded best as a composer when he was most concerned to archaize, and could measure his notes and contrapuntal lines against those of J. S. Bach and other Baroque idols: his op. 93 Suite is a jolly and rich exercise in time-travelling. His violin music is well worth exploring—but selectively! Just when you have had enough of the Suite op. 103a, you find the A major second '*Hausmusik*' sonata op. 103b, so-called 'little', but actually heart-warming and full of lyrical invention, a real piece of music.

German violin music lost its way at the end of the nineteenth century, but the instrument was still being cultivated, at the highest level, in the French tradition laid down by Viotti. The composers and the violinists were no longer the same person, but two colleagues who grew up and worked together, like Brahms and Joachim. The old tradition produced one survivor, Paul Hindemith, a prolific and masterly composer of music for everybody who could play almost any instrument. He was part of the Corelli genealogical tree, and his place is in another chapter, since he composed in the twentieth century. But he allows me to link my chapter with the next one, in Germany as in France.

Poland

The violin meant little or nothing to Chopin, with whom modern Polish music begins. He wrote for it only in his G minor piano trio op. 8, and then he wondered if he should not have replaced the violin by a viola. Numer-

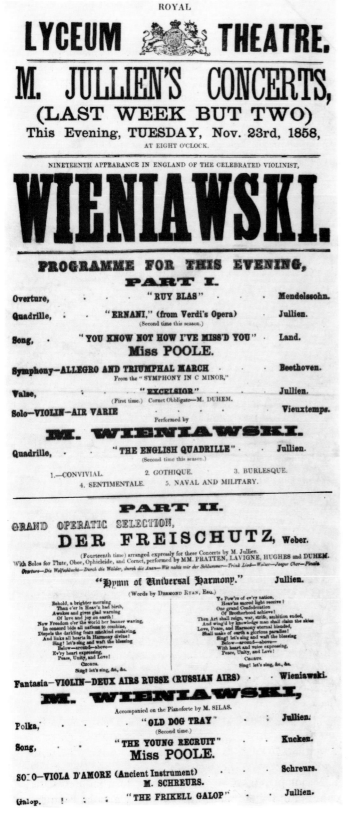

ous of Chopin's solo piano works have been claimed by violinists as recital material because the composer's melodic style derives from Italian *bel canto*, a tradition at the heart of the Corelli method from which all modern violin-playing derives (see again the tree on p. 118).

There was a reputable school of violin-playing in Poland before the nineteenth century; and Poland nourished a great violinist in Charles Lipiński (1790–1861), with whom Paganini played duets. But Polish violin music begins, in present-day repertory terms, with Henryk Wieniawski (1835–80), a wonderboy violinist who was sent to Paris at the age of eight to study with Lambert Massart. By the age of thirteen he was touring Russia, where Vieuxtemps reckoned him unsurpassed for his age; he was composing profusely too, and had fifteen opus numbers to his credit by the time he was nineteen, including the first concerto, the *École moderne* (a method incorporating ten *Etudes-caprices* of amazing originality and difficulty), and some old-time favourites such as the *Souvenir de Moscow*, originally for violin and orchestra. The *Capriccio-valse* in E major op. 7 is flashy but etching. Wieniawski's best-known piece, after the concertos, may be the *Légende* for violin and orchestra op. 17: it is harmonically quite ambitious, especially for 1860, though I prefer the Mazurka called 'Le ménétrier' from op. 19, with its mimicry of bagpipes (though *ménétrier* usually means a village fiddler), and especially the *Fantaisie brillante* on themes from Gounod's *Faust* op. 20 (1868), a clever pot-pourri which combines creative ingenuity with the pleasures of musical reminiscence.

Wieniawski held an official post in St Petersburg from 1860 to 1872, and influenced Russian violin-playing considerably: the stiff-looking but very useful 'Russian bow-grip' which produces a rich, intense and thrilling tone in high passages, derives from Wieniawski. From 1875 till 1877 he was in charge of the violin department at the Brussels Conservatoire, where he was no less influential. For the rest of his life he toured, almost compulsively. He was extremely popular in Berlin, where Joachim admired his easy left hand with something like awe. Wieniawski advanced technical mastery of the violin, during his short life, to a degree rivalled only by Paganini; he concentrated particularly on feats of derring-do: '*il faut risquer*', he declared, and his singular appeal seems to have been French schooling grafted on to Slavonic temperament. His music is not to be taken very seriously, yet he was an admired quartet player, and toured as far as America with Anton Rubinstein in sonata recitals. He wore himself out with the life of a travelling virtuoso by the time he was forty, and went back to Russia, not Poland, to die. He had friends galore

Opposite: *The Violinist at the Window*: painting by Otto Franz Scholderer, 1861.

to ease his last weeks of life, since he was much loved: his music shows us why. Wieniawski bridges, quite credibly, the gap in Polish music between Chopin and the next great composer from that country, Karel Szymanowski, who figures in another chapter.

Russia

The Paris school of violin-playing quickly made its mark in nineteenth-century Russia, where the court taste followed French fashion, even after the Revolution. Baillot played there in 1802; Rode arrived in 1803 and stayed for five years; Vieuxtemps was there between 1845 and 1852. They were all duly appreciated as brilliant soloists, and as string quartet players, for concerted chamber music found favour there (as not in France), but did not inspire Russian composers to write for the violin. Music was for early nineteenth-century Russia essentially an amateur pursuit, opera and song being preferred to instrumental music. Glinka and Dargomizhsky both played the violin, but seem never to have written solo music for it; at best they composed concerted chamber music involving the violin, more suitable for aristocratic amateur performance. Brilliant musicians had to be imported from abroad, like the above-named French violin virtuosos.

When Anton Rubinstein founded the musical conservatory at St. Petersburg in 1862, he entrusted the violin department to Wieniawski, who was followed, a decade later, by Leopold Auer (1845–1930), trainer of many great violinists, not himself a composer, but at least an inspiration to the composers of Russia. Auer was born at Veszprem in Hungary, studied with Dont in Vienna and Joachim in Hanover, and after some orchestral experience in Germany, was called to St. Petersburg, where he remained for fifty years before emigrating to the United States in 1918. At the ballet in St. Petersburg's Maryinsky Theatre, it was the custom to engage a noted virtuoso whenever the music prescribed a violin solo. Tchaikovsky made the most of the tradition in his ballet scores, especially *Swan Lake* when he knew Auer would be playing, and he wrote for Auer in other works also. Twice Auer let Tchaikovsky down, and on both occasions it was Russian-born, Viennese-trained Adolf Brodsky (1851–1929) who gave the first performance—he had taught and played in Leipzig, and was for some years leader of the New York Symphony Orchestra. Brodsky went on to be principal of the Royal Manchester College of Music and leader of a famous string quartet, but that was in the twentieth century.

Tchaikovsky is, by miles, the major Russian composer of violin music in this period. Even before the concerto, he had been asked by Auer for a new work, and obliged with the *Sérénade mélancolique* op. 26, a lovely piece of Slavonic self-pity, with two surprisingly strong, workable themes, exquisitely decorated, especially by woodwind—I say surprisingly, because both are hesitant in expression. A head of emotional steam is well generated, but the climax can sound coarse and unspontaneous; the coda shakes its head sadly at the melancholy state of affairs.

This was not, though it might have been, the original slow movement of the later violin concerto. That was composed with the practical aid of Yosif Kotek, a fine virtuoso, a pupil of Joachim and of Tchaikovsky also. Kotek introduced Tchaikovsky to his eventual protectress Nadeshda von Meck (in whose arms Wieniawski died), and was rewarded with the *Valse-scherzo* op. 34, a dazzling piece which begins hesitantly (we may think of the boy's invitation to dance in Weber's celebrated piano solo), then launches out boldly with a heady, vigorous theme that lives up to the title: the boy is swept off his feet by a star ballerina. This is a really exciting piece, worthy of the violin concerto's last movement, to which it sometimes looks forward. There is one other Tchaikovsky violin work to be mentioned: the suite with piano accompaniment 'Souvenir d'un lieu cher' (Glazunov transcribed the piano part for orchestra quite brilliantly). It begins with the 'Meditation' which Tchaikovsky dropped from his violin concerto: an enchanting piece which swoops bravely, and embellishes ardently. The Scherzo is a shadowy, almost sinister piece with a triplet theme, decidedly heady, and much athletic *spiccato* (that 'Russian bow-grip'). The *trio* section veers attractively between hesitancy and athletic dash. Kotek's good influence is noticeable. The last piece, *Mélodie*, is in the composer's most eloquent, tuneful vein, worthy of *Eugene Onegin* in its melodiousness and aching passion.

As the master of violin music in Russia towards the end of the nineteenth century Tchaikovsky, it must be admitted, had little competition. Anton Rubinstein, composer of the 'Melody in F' and a potent influence on Russian musical life, composed a *Grand Duo* on themes from Meyerbeer's *Le prophète* with Vieuxtemps, a *Romance and Caprice* op. 86 for violin and orchestra, and three violin sonatas of which the third begins with quotations from its two predecessors, though the cyclic trick is not played thereafter. The second sonata, op. 19 in A minor, looks the most inventive of the three, with a spirited first movement and scherzo. Even in perform-

Edvard Grieg.

ance it is hard to work up enthusiasm for Rubinstein's fluent, seldom quite coagulated music: the gestures are fervent, but vague and uninvolving for the most part, though some of the music is attractive.

César Cui (1835–1918) was the only member of Balakirev's *Kuchka* ('the Five') to espouse solo violin music, and of a not very demanding or committed nature. Rimsky-Korsakov composed engaging violin solos in *Sheherazade,* and in the *Spanish Caprice* (originally intended as a concertante for violin and orchestra), but did not attempt violin music, except in a *Fantasy* on Russian themes, and a *Souvenir of three Polish songs,* posthumously published, both originally designed with orchestra. An early violin sonata in A major op. 8 (1877), by Mikhail Ippolitov-Ivanov (1859–1935) uses Russian traditional tunes to modest, songful purpose. Anton Arensky (1861–1906) left two sets of four short pieces, for violin and piano, op. 30 and op. 72, further witness to the deft, decorative, frivolous imagination that we enjoy in his Trio and two-piano suites. Alexander Glazunov (1865–1936), beside a luscious violin concerto, composed the very appealing *Meditation* in D major op. 32, a broad-spanned melody, beautifully articulated and constantly eventful. Violinists and their audiences enjoy it for any number of good musical reasons.

Scandinavia

The prominent role of violin music in Scandinavian countries during the nineteenth century owes much to the flamboyant, determinedly patriotic career of Ole Bornemann Bull (1810–80), the Norwegian violinist who made an extraordinary career in Europe and the Americas as a virtuoso, was active as a conductor, and consciously used his celebrity to boost foreign interest in Norway as an interesting source of music. Bull studied with Poulson, a Viotti pupil, and later fleetingly with Spohr. Experience of Paganini's concerts determined him to do as well. He had studied the playing of Norwegian peasants on the Hardanger, a folk-violin, and adapted his Amati instrument with a flat bridge and thin strings to facilitate chords and polyphonic playing. When he heard Paganini play a duo for solo violin, Bull promptly wrote a quartet for the same instrument, and performed it to general astonishment. From a peasant Hardanger virtuoso nicknamed '*Nyllarguten*', Bull borrowed the long, heavy bow which enriched his violin tone and, being flexibly haired, made chords easier on his flat bridge. His Bach playing was much admired, and he may be the missing link between Baroque playing

and its revival in our own day: nobody else, until Arnold Dolmetsch in the present century, regretted the French modernization of those Cremonese violins mentioned at the beginning of this chapter and earlier on p. 19.

In London (1840) Bull partnered Franz Liszt in Beethoven's 'Kreutzer' sonata. In Italy he profited musically from work with de Bériot and his then mistress, the Spanish mezzo Maria Malibran. He toured America more than once, partnering the eight-year-old Adelina Patti on one circuit. He liked the easy ways of the United States, more like his own than those of south-western Europe. At home he recognized the boyish talent of Grieg, and encouraged the composer Halfdan Kjerulf. Bull's most admired composition, in his lifetime, was his *Recitativo, Adagio amoroso con polacca guerriera* for violin and orchestra. He is more likely to interest modern listeners with his Norwegian genre violin pieces, such as *Cowgirls' Sunday* and *Visit*

Ole Bull, 1875.

to a Farm in Summer, as can be heard on a currently (1984) available record which also includes the *polacca guerriera* above mentioned.

That intriguing, boldly idiosyncratic composer Franz Berwald (1796–1868), was a violinist in the Swedish court orchestra for sixteen years and wrote concertos for the instrument, but a violin and piano sonata of 1825 is lost, and a Concertino for the same instruments was not completed. We are left with a pair of *Duos* (1860) in D for violin and piano, and in B flat for violin and cello. They are certainly the work of a string player, and there are remarkable contrasts of key, and modulations, that justify Berwald's reputation as an unconventional harmonist; but they are unpretentious pieces, for domestic consumption, with strong roots in the Classical tradition that are this composer's hallmark in his more familiar chamber works and symphonies.

Violinists should know the three sonatas by Niels Gade (1817–90), a Dane who played the violin, was befriended by Mendelssohn and Schumann, became popular in Britain and later fell under the spell of Wagner, though his music does not show it. He composed three violin sonatas, of which the last is worth trying first; it is the least nationalistic, indeed close to Mendelssohn, but likably inventive. Johann Svendsen (1840–1911), Norwegian rather than the Swede his name suggests, learned numerous instruments as a boy, his father being a military band-master. He settled for the violin, and began his career, with the blessing of Ole Bull, as a soloist; study with Ferdinand David in Leipzig was to prepare him for a virtuoso career, but his interest shifted to composition and conducting. For his first instrument he composed, besides the concerto op. 6, a *Caprice* (1863) and the Romance in G op. 26, both with orchestra. This latter, perhaps his best-known work, owes its popularity to a natural tunefulness (how poetic the rising fifth at the end of the first line!) and a natural capacity to induce variety of texture and emotion constantly, but without ruffling the elegance of the music.

Svendsen's close friend Edvard Grieg (1843–1907) envied his command of symphonic forms, and all his life he exerted himself to master music on a large scale: examples to hand are his three violin sonatas. No. 1 in F major op. 8 (1865) fails at sonata form in the first movement, though the first gesture is something like a stroke of genius, and the other ideas are felicitous in themselves. The subsequent movements tend to Scandinavian folk music, song, dance, and mimicry of the Hardanger. Gade and Liszt both admired this work. Sonata no. 2 in G major op. 13 (1867) was dedicated

to Svendsen, who gave the first performance with Grieg in Oslo, and later in Paris with Saint-Saëns: here the dance element, the accents of nationalism, dominate the textbook formulas; the writing for both instruments is technically demanding, but the work is a joy to play. Grieg dedicated his sonata no. 3 in C minor op. 45 (1887—a gap of twenty years' disheartened virtual withdrawal from large-scale composition) to Brodsky, rather as a powerful player than as a dauntless virtuoso. Grieg's mind here seems outward turned, back to Germany where he had learned his trade and where the music market was chiefly booming. Perhaps that is ungenerous to a thoroughly honourable musician, but Grieg does not often sound here to be talking in his own voice, rather seeking to command the grandly authoritative tones of a Brahms. I used to find this sonata hard work as music to play, and assumed the fault was mine; subsequent years of listening to it have suggested that Grieg found it even harder work, though many pages of the central movement do speak his language with unmistakable and touching effect. His genius lay in other directions, and in the more expansive forms they embrace the piano concerto as well as the first two violin sonatas.

Christian Sinding (1856–1941) belongs on the cusp of this chapter, since much of his music was written in the present century. By 1900 he had composed two suites and two sonatas for violin and piano, which already show him set on a path of post-Wagnerian late Romanticism, enlivened with elements of Norwegian nationalism. There is real fire in the third movement of the op. 10 *Suite im alten Stil* (Heifetz used to play it marvellously), though archaizing did not otherwise suit Sinding; and the sonata no. 2 in E major op. 27 (1895) has ardour and brilliance in the outer movements, and charm in the central one, that the players can warm to. He was trained as a violinist, studying at Leipzig with Schradieck, but like Svendsen, his compatriot, he preferred composition.

Great Britain

Music flourished during the nineteenth century in the countries now known as the United Kingdom. It was choral music, to some extent orchestral music, chamber music was popular, and Charles Hallé's innovation of the solo recital soon won support. Many British composers were trained as violinists, but none made a great career as such; what violin music they composed has virtually vanished. Only amateurs bought printed music, and they shunned composers with British names. Sir Alexander Mackenzie (1847–1935) composed Scottish genre music for violin and orchestra. Samuel Coleridge-Taylor (1875–1912) brought out *Hiawatha Sketches* op. 16, carrying his successful Red Indian can-

tatas to a wider public, he hoped optimistically; he also composed a violin sonata op. 28. So did Ethel Smyth (1858–1944), her op. 7 in A minor. They made no impact, and had not the environment in which to do so. The most talented and inspired composer cannot effectively bombinate in a vacuum. Britain by 1900 was no farther advanced in violin music than Russia before Tchaikovsky, or France before the advent of the National Society.

Music arrives when it is wanted. The nineteenth century was a wonderful time for violin virtuosos, though the music they composed was seldom durably satisfying, for all the new musical resources they disclosed to other composers. These composers flourished in centres where appreciation was general and enthusiastic—in Leipzig, in Vienna, in Paris and Berlin, and later on in some smaller countries. Here the soul of the violin could freely take flight as it pleased, knowing that it would be welcomed and taken to heart. Nineteenth-century violin music cannot sensibly be reviewed without reference also to violin concertos (see pp. 159–185), the chief vehicle of the instrument in a century of astounding technical and interpretative advancement. This was the time at which concerted chamber music involving stringed instruments really spread and developed, to great purpose. It was also a great century for sales of printed music to amateur performers. By 1900 few of these were ready for the sonatas of Franck and Fauré, Brahms and Schubert: they were more likely to spend money on operatic fantasies and genre pieces by composers whose names are now deservedly forgotten. The best nineteenth-century violin music was only just good enough for the century's many great violinists. It is good that the teacher-pupil genealogical tree united so many of them, as still today, in a great and continuing tradition.

Violin Technique

Its Modern Development and Musical Decline

Joseph Szigeti.

Man views the history of the world, or of his culture, or of his own professional world, in terms of his own—the only history he really knows, first-hand. We cannot, in fact, deny the untrustworthiness of history as a discipline, nor are Schopenhauer's objections to it—in brief, the *post hoc, ergo propter hoc* fallacy—the gravest, powerful as they are.

Each of us will be able to convince himself of the circumstance that, inevitably, the reality of history as a study is unconvincing—if, that is to say, he is prepared to indulge in a simple experiment: a comparison between his own knowledge of a person, or an event, derived from personal, first-hand experience, with impressions that are the result of second- or even third-hand experience. Almost invariably, he will come to the conclusion that without first-hand experience, any real knowledge of the person or event is impossible—and that it is difficult enough to get at the truth by comparing different first-hand experiences, even though his own are, needless to add, the most detached and reliable.

It is because of man's inevitable, instinctive projection of his own history upon the world that he will never succeed in ridding himself of his fallacious belief in progress, even though by now scientific evidence compels him to accept, if anything, the contrary. Especially where life matters most to him, he will spontaneously invent evidence to the effect that things are immeasurably better than they used to be—simply because he thinks he has improved. Within our own art, admittedly, he has had to accept the fact that Beethoven is not likely to be out-Beethovened, not even by Schoenberg (if he happens to be the present writer); none the less, every technical innovation, creative or re-creative, is immediately regarded as progress, at least by those who are involved in it, either actively or receptively.

For why, otherwise, would one want to innovate? In order to make things worse? One's motives or reasons might be mistaken, of course, but once they are accepted by a lot of people, their validity tends to be accepted too, owing to what I call the democratic fallacy, according to which a truth becomes ever truer the more people believe in it. So powerful is the seemingly honourable motivation behind the democratic fallacy, behind letting the majority decide, that we readily forget—if ever we realized—that wellnigh every single important discovery in the history of mankind was made by a minority of one, and that quite a few of them were, to begin with, accepted by a minority of nil—the late Beethoven quartets, for instance, to take an example of a discovery on which no progress has yet been made, which has not, let's face it, ever been continued, though quite a few

geniuses have tried in all conscience: Mendelssohn, Brahms, Bartók, Schoenberg.

So far as musical composition is concerned, however, it is true that, Beethoven apart, the belief in progress has received many a knock in our own century, owing to the chronic contemporary crisis which started in the early years of the century with the abandonment of tonality, and has never left us. Ironically, this very disappointment, whose depth in many a musical mind cannot be overrated, has contributed, on the basis of the Adlerian 'law of compensation and over-compensation' (wrongly attributed to Freud), to our unshakable conviction that we play much better than they used to, that instrumental technique has improved out of recognition, that, technically, we would find a truly authentic performance of a work from the remoter past downright intolerable.

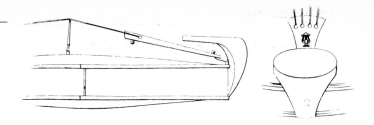

Spohr's chin-rest, which he called a 'fiddle holder',
illustrated in his *Violinschule* of 1832.

It is even said that in Bach's or even Mozart's and
Beethoven's time, things used to be out of tune, though
one can demonstrate that countless thoughts in these
composers' works depend, for their comprehensibility,
on the most sensitive intonation. I propose to prove that
on the contrary, a Bach's or Mozart's or, for that matter,
a Schuppanzigh's intonation was decidedly and
decisively better than is ours—but my proof will ensue
at a much later stage in my argument. Meanwhile, we
have to appreciate the ineluctable complexity of the
problem of progress: not only are there intended
improvements which result in deterioration, but many
a development yields both advantages and disadvanta-
ges, so that progress and regress can easily be
combined—not necessarily inextricably so, if we remain
intent upon realistic diagnoses.

Yes, even the most obvious improvements should be
viewed critically, just in case something was lost while
a major gain was achieved. In the realm of violin technique, the most obvious improvements are, of course,
those initiated, or at any rate articulated, by Carl Flesch
in *The Art of Violin-playing* (1923). We need not go into
complicated detail; the chin-held violin and the right
upper arm's upward motion as the bow moves towards
its lower half are firmly conventionalized improvements
which, it would seem, cannot possibly involve any dis-
advantages: changes of position have become
immeasurably easier ever since the left hand no longer
had to hold the violin, and bowing has become freer
and more natural.

Yet it so happens that half a century ago I knew two
violinists, both of them laughably old-fashioned in their
technique, whose tone-modulation was such that it
would be difficult to find a modern example of comparable finesse. One of them can still be heard on
gramophone records—Joseph Szigeti; the other, Oskar
Adler, the leader of the then unequalled Adler Quartet,
was Schoenberg's first quartet leader and lifelong
friend. Szigeti you could hardly watch if you had learnt
the fiddle the proper way: his right upper arm remained
chained to his chest; no doubt he had to hold a book
between his upper arm and his chest when he learnt
the violin as a boy. I am not suggesting that the
imprisonment of the upper arm contributed to his
bowing refinements, but it certainly did not harm them.

As for Adler, who often held the violin with his left
hand, to the point of finding it just as easy, or almost
as easy, to play without chin-rest, the relatively free
movement of his *left* arm did contribute to the wealth
of his bowing differentiations; he bowed, as it were, with
both arms. My first example, then, draws attention to

an improvement which, for this particular violinistic
personality, need not have taken place, while my second
does actually show a possible loss hiding behind the
modern position of the violin with all its inestimable
advantages.

The transition from the hand-held to the chin-held
violin, incidentally, must have been very gradual: it
seems that Louis Spohr (1784–1859) was the first to
introduce the chin-rest, probably because he had a very
long neck; anyhow, at his stage in the history of violin
technique, the chin must already have begun to play
quite some role, for otherwise he would hardly have
decided upon what must have been a very drastic step,
not without dangers for the instrument's own tonal
capacities. I well remember playing quartets with Adler
and Norbert Brainin forty-odd years ago, and the two
being in passionate agreement about their enjoyment of
chin-restless playing and the resulting violin tone; to
Brainin who, of course, grew up the Flesch way (taught
as he was by Flesch's principal assistant Max Rostal),
I am thus paying a quite exceptional compliment: on
purely musical grounds, he was able to free himself of
a convention which, to every other violinist, had become
second nature.

Conventions that have become second nature are the
curse of our interpretative age—technically, musically,
and in combination. The standardization of technique
has been an inevitable consequence of its rationalization
and its far-reaching separation from the music to which
it is applied. The standardization of performance has
resulted, just as ineluctably, from the mass-medial distribution of (rightly or wrongly) leading performances,
from the availability of the gramophone record, and
from the resultant arrested development of most of our
leading artists who, in the circumstances, have never
developed an independent, individual artistic conscience, and whose ideal interpretations are to be found,
not wholly within themselves, but in various places in
the outside musical world. As soon as technique parted,
moreover, at least in places, from the specific music
which it was intended to realize, interpretation itself
came, again unavoidably, under the influence of various
categories of technique.

Those of us who are old enough to have heard
virtuosos from what, by now, has become the less
accomplished past are sharply aware that the automatic
belief in technical progress is open, if not to criticism,
then to eminently concrete reservations and qualifications: with the help of the otherwise harmful
gramophone record, it is indeed possible to demonstrate
that the greatest virtuosos of that past were capable of

Max Rostal: drawing by Milein Cosman, 1949.

mediocrity has unquestionably risen: the progress of mediocrity is correlated to the regress of supremacy. It might indeed be suggested that it is mediocrity alone that has truly progressed—for it could never do without standardization anyway, so that our own age's intensified standardizations couldn't do it any harm.

Otherwise, instrumental techniques having become more conscious and, proportionately, more systematized, the illusory belief in progress has come to include the conviction that as a matter of conscious, sustained effort, we have 'improved' (extended, widened) our instrumental range of expression, both through a more rational construction of certain instruments themselves and by refining our playing with the help of an analytic inspection of its technical components. That a Stradivarius still has a far wider expressive range than any modern fiddle need not, admittedly, be proved at the present stage in the history of violin-making—but that just as invariably, modern playing habits have narrowed down the modern fiddler's potential range of expression may seem a downright incomprehensible proposition to many a modern violinist, especially if his ultra-conscious technical education has taken in such reflections on the subject as can be found in Carl Flesch's aforementioned masterpiece (for an educational masterpiece it does remain despite the unforeheard, inartistic results which certain features of his mastery are producing).

To be absolutely precise, however, it wasn't, in the first place, Flesch's highly musical observations which produced the deplorable, utterly unintended mid-twentieth-century construction of the violinist's range of expression; it was Fritz Kreisler's actual playing, at least equally inspired and musical though it sounded. When I say that it *sounded* musical I am not implying that it harboured hidden unmusicality—or rather, it did, not for Kreisler himself, but for all his plentiful conscious and unconscious imitators. For by that time, the twentieth-century performer's arrested development had started, and his artistic conscience, at least part of it, was to be found in the outside world in general and in Fritz Kreisler in particular.

Legion were the students of the violin who listened to his gramophone records over and over again, utterly unalive to the fact that as an artistic act, any performance is unrepeatable. Why? There were plenty of reasons, and from the so-miscalled musical point of view, it was his characteristic 'sweet tone' that was chief amongst them. But from the technical standpoint which, by then, had become disturbingly isolated, there was one single puzzled, baffled, mystified

technical feats which our contemporary virtuosos would find difficult to emulate. Above all, on the highest level, those past techniques persuaded and convinced through their sharply defined individuality—which, it its turn, was the result of the actual music, and its picture in the performer's ear, being the chief determinant of his technical approach.

Contemporary virtuosity, on the other hand, has become standardized to the point of unidentifiability: a Bronislaw Huberman, for instance, was (and still is) identifiable after a phrase or a bar of his particular *spiccato* or *staccato*, which will undergo surprising metamorphoses according to the musical sense he wished to make—whereas an Itzhak Perlman's very phrasing (and I'm deliberately picking one of our most individualistic violin virtuosos) needs far more time and music to be recognized, while his sheer technique is, in certain departments, absolutely indistinguishable from his fellow virtuosos'—at least one or two of them. At the same time, personal experience confirms that while the greatest of the past were undoubtedly greater than are the greatest of the present, the standard of

Bronislaw Huberman, 1939.

preoccupation—Kreisler's intriguing vibrato in quick passages, his ability to employ vibrato in the fastest scale and yet keep it crystal-clear.

When he came in, the all-pervasive vibrato had progressed well beyond the danger point anyhow; as soon as one heard and *saw* that he was capable of employing vibrato in the very places which one had learnt to keep free of vibrato in order to retain their clarity, 'Let there be vibrato!' became more unconditional than 'Let there be light!', for God divided the light from the darkness, whereas Kreisler didn't divide his vibrato from anything. There is not the remotest trace of criticism in my objectively critical observation (I heard Kreisler many times in the flesh), for his tone, more characteristic than which I can imagine none in the history of violin-playing, possessed an expressive range equalled, at that time, only by Huberman (not, for instance, by Heifetz who, needless to add, outshone him in quite a few other, technical respects, amongst which one only has to remind oneself of Heifetz's down-bow *staccato*). How Kreisler did it I don't know; the trouble is and was that nobody else knew, either, though everybody tried to imitate him. For a considerable period, the greatest virtuosos apart, clear virtuoso passages vanished from the concert scene.

Though the mania for vibrato passage work has meanwhile subsided, vibrato tone as the norm has so firmly established itself that a player will, as it were, start vibrating as he ascends the platform. The devastating influence the chronic vibrato has had on the envelopment of the right arm's expressive power cannot be overestimated. As a matter of standardized technique, the left hand has taken over a considerable part of the area of tone-production previously dominated by the right hand—but all the left hand can contribute (if you are lucky) is different types of vibrato, all of which share their doubly concealing purpose: on the one hand, that is to say, vibrato, which in itself consists of regular pitch variations, will serve to hide the left hand's less obtrusive distortions, while on the other, it has been promoted to the rank of chief tone producer, at the expense of what used to be the right hand's infinitely varied ability of tone-production and tone-modulation. In respect of tone-modulation, in particular, we have, in my lifetime, witnessed so dramatic a decline that nowadays a student of the violin is no longer able to produce a vibratoless, and hence all the more compelling tone, whose own expressive range used to be greater than is the contemporary range between vibrato and 'senza vibrato'—if, that is, the player is at all capable of bowing without vibrato, which in many cases he isn't.

When he is, moreover, one usually wishes that he weren't. Since he has never been encouraged to develop the tonal powers of his right hand without the alleged help and actual hindrance of the chronic vibrato, the tonal repertory of his right hand is so minimal, its vibrato-less bowing so artificial, that notes or motifs or passages which should ideally be played without vibrato sound far more acceptable, and are far more readily blendable and balanceable texturally, when he employs the vibrato to which he is used than when he is forced to feel naked and helpless, solely intent upon hiding his shame.

'I think', says Schoenberg, 'the tone becomes perceptible by virtue of tone color, of which one dimension is pitch. Tone color is, thus, the main topic, pitch a subdivision. Pitch is nothing else but tone color measured in one direction.'* It is the range of colour in the widest,

*Roy E. Carter's translation, from *Theory of Harmony*, p. 421 (Faber and Faber, London, 1978). Mine: 'I find that a tone makes itself felt through its colour, one of whose dimensions is pitch. Colour, then, is the big area, pitch a mere province of it. Pitch is nothing but colour measured in one direction.' (*'Theory of Harmony'* is itself a mistranslation: Schoenberg points out that this is precisely what his book is not. The proper translation of *Harmonielehre* is, simply, *Harmony*.)

Schoenbergian sense, then, which the contemporary chronic vibrato, developed as it has been from its earliest possible infusion into the child's bowing, has limited well beyond the danger point. Nor is mine empty rhetoric, for in a masterly string-quartet texture, that danger point can be demonstrated with total precision: as soon as the player in question is incapable of drastically contrasting the colours of (a) a principal part, (b) a subordinate part, and (c) an accompaniment, he has sunk beyond the danger point, into a tonal state where he is also incapable of adjusting his intonation—both in and outside the province of pitch—to the melodic and/or harmonic requirements of the moment; in fact, the modern string player has virtually forgotten that he can influence the province from outside—that he can adjust his pitch by means of a change of colour.

Likewise, the modern quartet player is no longer aware of the requirements of what one might call creative intonation—the need to use the province for purposes that lie outside it, though still within the area of colour, of course: both harmonic and melodic motion, as well as that blend which makes two instruments sound like one and that balance which, in other places, meaningfully distinguishes between yet combines the selfsame two instruments, can be decisively influenced

by pitch variations so minute that a vibrato will always destroy them. In the Classical master quartets and quintets (with the sole exception of the quasi-orchestral outer movements of the 'Emperor') as well as in all the Mendelssohn quartets (with the sole exception of the quasi-orchestral outer movements of the D major) and quintets there are countless textural junctures the audibility of whose full significance *depends* on such pitch variations—on a refinement of intonation of which, as players, Haydn, Mozart, Beethoven, Schubert, and Mendelssohn must therefore have been capable. The chronic vibrato, however, though originally an innovation, makes this refinement impossible. Why, you're lucky nowadays if a string soloist or even a string quartet has retained sufficient intonational integrity to depart from the pitches of the well-tempered clavier, and the exciting, highly individualistic intonation of, say, a Bronislaw Huberman, always at the music's service, has become a thing of the past. At the same time, it is fascinating to observe a modern violin student listening to a Huberman record: far from finding the player 'out of tune', such a listener will immediately and instinctively realize that an important means of musical persuasion has, meanwhile, been lost.

Intonation apart, the loss of vibratoless tone-

Fritz Kreisler.

production and tone-modulation has to be separately examined in the soloist's tonal world on the one hand and the paradise of Western instrumental music on the other—the string quartet and, so far as Mozart, Beethoven, Schubert, Mendelssohn, Dvořák and Schoenberg are concerned, the string trio and the string quintet. Nor, let me hasten to reassure the musicological reader, must the vibratoless early-music boys be forgotten, although God knows that musically, I would find nothing easier than to forget them—of which reckless observation more anon.

Where a player's tone needs projection, prototypically in a concerto, there will, of course, be a stronger need for vibrato than in any other part of the playing world. Yet even in the large concert hall, our merciless contemporary vibrato bears no comparison to the variety-conscious tone of leading virtuosos of the past—and not only because the variety of past has been replaced, largely, with a standardized utility vibrato the possibilities of whose intensification and reduction are minimal, but also because the type of vibratoless tone-production which will carry in a large concert hall no longer exists, for the simple reason that it does not form part and parcel of the modern student's education: he vibrates throughout his lessons, anyway. Conscientiously empirical, I should like to confine my evidence to two incisively remembered examples of such vibratoless projection from my own, unforgettable experience.

By the time I had reached my mid-teens, I was aware that the contemporary, chronic vibrato had come to stay and grow—and vibratoless tone modulation by the greatest players overwhelmed me proportionately. Huberman's performance, with Furtwängler, of the Beethoven concerto in Vienna's *Grosse Musikvereinssaal*, in the mid-thirties, was the most spellbinding interpretation of the work I have heard: not only Huberman, but even Furtwängler improvised throughout, and the success of their respective improvisations (and the partner's equally successful contribution) was invariably acknowledged by mutual or joint smiles. One such improvisatory moment occurred at the end of the first movement's cadenza, where Huberman suddenly decided to let the second subject enter without a trace of vibrato, yet with so penetrating a contained *espressivo* that Furtwängler's own smile was immediately mirrored in the faces of most listeners; throughout the passage, and indeed throughout the final, just as improvisatory climax, one found it impossible to breathe.

Also in the mid-1930s, on my first, extended visit to London, I felt a little starved musically: London was still very far from becoming a musical centre. When

Casals gave a concert at the Albert Hall, therefore, I was in a state of exceptional excitement, and his playing of Bach's first solo Suite fell on intensely receptive ears. There were several passages, all of which I could now immediately list, where he played not only without vibrato, but pronouncedly *pianissimo* at the same time—yet I, right on top of the Albert Hall (the only ticket I could afford), was able to take in every finesse of his bowing.

The string quartet and its relatives need separate consideration for two reasons—because its requirements are, so far as tone production and differentiation are concerned, immeasurably more complex, and because the history of the string quartet includes its transfer from the chamber with its potentially ideal acoustics to the concert hall, whose acoustics are so inimical to the quartet's characteristic texture that at the present stage in the history of performance, the only place where you can produce a natural quartet sound for an audience is the recording studio: in my producing days, I used to take the studio manager into the studio, place him next to the viola, and let him listen for about twenty minutes, whereafter I invited him to reproduce the balance he had heard. In the first place, of course, I had to remind the quartet to forget all about 'projecting', to play, to converse, phrasingly, as if they played at home, for and to themselves and each other. Needless to add, there are few quartets left which are capable of producing a natural quartet sound, even in such ideal circumstances.

The degeneration of the string quartet which we owe to its transfer to large concert halls is not, of course, confined to its playing, but equally affects its very composition. After Schubert, that is to say, the instances of true quartet texture become fewer and fewer; Mendelssohn is the true, intrinsic quartet's last consistent outpost. After him, while we do get such genuine quartet textures as Dvořák's E flat work and Smetana's first quartet, the fact remains that the vast majority of quartets were written with the concert hall in mind—by composers, moreover, who were not themselves quartet players, as the classics and Mendelssohn were; for a time, Mendelssohn even played the viola in Spohr's quartet. It was not until Schoenberg that true quartet sound was creatively recaptured; otherwise, the quartet had lost much of its *raison d'être*—its communication to the players rather than to an audience.

It follows that the modern, chronic vibrato has done immeasurably more harm to the genuine quartet than to works addressed to an audience in the first place—works which, far from musically resisting 'projection', have been composed with a view to it. It is the true,

Yehudi Menuhin in 1976.

largely Classical quartet sound which is crudified, sometimes beyond understanding recognition, by concert-hall projection and the age's constant vibrato alike; since its texture stands or falls by the complexity of its tonal differentiations and modulations, the normal concert hall performance results in a crudification *ad absurdum*. But while it is impossible to give an unprojecting, effective performance of a quartet in a large concert hall, the fact remains that at least some essential part of a characteristic quartet's intrinsic tonal complexity could be retained if the players had a wide enough range of expression—wide enough, that is, to produce a Huberman-like or Casals-like vibratoless projection of sound which, while not an open *espressivo* on the one hand, preserved a suppressed *espressivo*'s all the more pungent intensity on the other.

Then there is, needless to remind ourselves, the emphatic non-*espressivo* of the mere, sheer accompaniment, as distinct from the quartet's infinitely shaded subordinate parts: the murder of the Schubert A minor's opening accompaniment to nothing, its beginning before the beginning, occurred as early as the early 1930s, when the second fiddler of the Busch Quartet (of all quartets!) opened the work *molto espressivo, molto vibrato* and, accordingly, far too slowly; even in the large concert hall in Vienna where the crime took place it would have been easily possible to make this introductory accompaniment carry while adhering to a vibratoless, flowing style. I must confess that despite my tender years, I found this idiotic opening so disturbing that I immediately walked out on the Busch, regardless of what they might have had to offer later on, which, including as it did op. 135, probably was a lot. And Busch himself certainly was capable of vibratoless tone-modulation, even in his concertos, though his brilliant style never convinced: he was not a born virtuoso. For the rest, by now, composers themselves are becoming unaware of the tonal complexities and contrasts and variabilities obtainable in a string quartet texture if one doesn't think in terms of public performance in a large hall; unless the gramophone record keeps the sound of the true string quartet alive (as it could, but hardly ever does), the most developed form of instrumental music may well be dying a long, painful and nightmarish death—the worse for its nightmares being increasingly experienced as wish-fulfilments.

In my childhood, the authenticity boys and girls confined themselves to the illusion that the acoustic conditions and results of pre-Classical times can, indeed must be re-established, but nowadays the Classical string quartet itself is subjected to authentication—to murderous attempts to cure its terminal disease. Ironically enough, it all started with the authenticating endeavours of a quartet leader who combined the most anti-historical technical peculiarities, which he had doubtless developed under the influence of his venerated, yet anti-authentic brother-in-law, Arnold Schoenberg, with a passion for confining his Classical bowing of quick notes to what Haydn or Mozart or Schuppanzigh did, or is supposed to have done, when he played quartets. When, before its birth, I started coaching the Lindsay Quartet, I learnt to my horror that Rudolf Kolisch, who had coached them just before I came in, had not allowed the bow to leave the string in any quick up-and-down from Haydn up to and including late Beethoven. The musical result was, of course, catastrophic—parallel, in part, to the effect of the *sempre vibrato*: the chronic *détaché* and the *spiccato* prohibition limited the players' range of expression and, unlike their chronic vibrato, made them bow artificially rather than spontaneously.

Kolisch, the most overrated quartet player of our time (who owed his fame to what, in the 1930s and 1940s, was his unequalled knowledge of the Schoenberg quartets) had betrayed music—in that he let historical knowledge, rather than his ear, determine his quartet technique. At the same time, with amusing inconsistency, he forced the Lindsay Quartet to stick pages from the relevant pocket scores into their parts, happily forgetful of the fact that there were no pocket scores in Classical times, when you had to listen in order to know and understand. The intention was to acquaint the players with the entire quartet texture, and the predictable result was that they looked instead of listening to and remembering what they had heard: I removed those visual aids in our very first session.

The unconditional primacy of the ear is what the authenticating quartets of our own time, too, tend to abandon. As a result, instead of widening the instrument's range of expression, they narrow it down to a scratchy *non vibrato* sound produced by a kind of bowing and fingering with which hardly any of them has grown up. Their technique is not rendered more natural by the reintroduction of gut strings and the removal of the chin-rest. Let me hasten to add that I would be all in favour of a reintroduction of, at least, the gut A-string—but only if the player in question has learnt, from early on, to utilize the greater tonal flexibility of the string towards wider and subtler tone-modulation. As it is, what we usually hear is the opposite—a monotonous sound quite out of touch with the player's instinctive, spontaneous bowing impulses.

Adolf Busch: lithograph by Olaf Gulbransson (1873–1958).

We need not condemn all attempts at authenticity out of hand: there may be some which do not abandon the primacy of the ear. Yet the very desire to play authentically must remain suspect: we aren't playing in the same rooms in which 'they' used to, whence the wish to reproduce 'their' sound is, in itself, fallacious. Nor is this physical, acoustic circumstance the only reason for one's suspicions, for the sole sound we are musically entitled to produce is the sound our musical understanding demands—and the relation between sound and *our* understanding cannot conceivably be identical with the relation between sound and 'theirs'. Speaking practically and therefore testably, I would submit that all phoney attempts at changing technique for the purpose of greater musical truthfulness reduce our range of expression, whereas all genuine attempts widen it or, at the very least, aim at widening it.

As it is, let's face it, most of the authentic boys just aren't good enough as players to make their way without musicological crutches: since they can't do what others can, they have to find something, do something, which others can't do because they don't want to—and they don't want to because, quite rightly, they feel they cannot go beyond the evidence of their own ears. If the present chapter were not concerned with such evidence alone, it would never have been written: no sound here described or alluded to or defined as desirable is a sound that has not been heard.

And my life's aural experience, as a player, teacher and 'mere' listener, has fortunately been sufficiently long and wide to take in the effect of our century's division between music and instrumental technique—a complex subject which has to be examined with unfailingly concrete care. Time was when one could hear masterly players, virtuosos even, who, like Huberman and Oskar Adler, were not only self-educated in all essential respects,* but their very self-education meant that the development of their technique was determined, throughout, by the specific passages of music, the individual phrases and shapes whose realization demanded the particular technical activity which was in need of development: at that historical stage and with such individuals, the unity of musical meaning and technical accomplishment was absolute, for it was the music, its sound in the mind's ear, which created the technique.

This did not mean, of course, that the individuals in question didn't practise, or rather study, any studies—but the studies themselves, it mustn't be

*The degree to which Joseph Joachim 'taught' Huberman was minimal and superficial: Huberman had hardly reached puberty when Joachim said, 'I can't teach you any more'.

forgotten, were music: Rodolphe Kreutzer was, after all, a real composer, as was Pierre Rode, and either's studies, however specialized technically, pose well-defined musical propositions whose technical solution must make musical sense in order to convince.

The single-minded father of the isolation of violin technique, on the other hand (chiefly the left), Otakar Ševčík, wasn't a composer at all, and be it said in honour and defence of Flesch and his school (above all, of course, Max Rostal) that they regarded, indeed described, Ševčík's exercises as therapeutic poison—helpful in small dosages, deadly when freely absorbed without awareness of their poisonous nature. The separation of violin technique and music, then, can be realistically dated as from Ševčík, but although Flesch always remained heavily conscious of the need to relate technique to what it was about, his approach, the systematic isolation of technical problems, did remove technique from musical dominance. At the present moment in the history of violin technique, it is the American and Russian schools whose technical achievements are at once the best and the worst—the best in respect of their reliable, extra-musical mastery, the worst in view of their essential extra-musicality and its palpably unmusical consequences.

If we think about (read: inwardly listen to) the various categories of technical problems and difficulties with a ruthlessly musical conscience, there is only a single, well-definable category whose separation from the music it concerns will be tolerably harmless, in that extra-musical practice will not seriously affect the eventual musical performance, will not run the risk of seriously demusicalizing it—the category of virtuoso bowings, of those ostensibly brilliant, and brilliantly different types of fast successions of notes the need for which is virtually confined to outspoken virtuoso music.

Even the normal *staccato* in the violinist's strict sense (i.e. the quick succession of short notes on a single bow) hardly plays any indispensable role outside deliberate virtuoso passages, though it is true enough that, say, in more than one great Haydn quartet's first-violin part, brilliant upbeat phrases can be found in slow movements in which a *staccato* approach will prove sensible and natural; the upbeat direction of the phrase will, however, easily guide the player towards a flexible realization, even if he has spent a great deal of his past practising time on inflexible, extra-musical *staccato* exercises. But *ricochet*, for instance (invented or discovered, it seems, by Paganini), can harmlessly be practised without any music behind it, although there are again places in highly substantial music (and again even in Haydn quartets, as in the finale of the 'Bird') where this virtuoso variety of *staccato* can be used (though it certainly needn't be!). Its execution depends as much and as little on its particular musical context as, say, the execution of a trill.

But as soon as we leave the virtuoso area and enter the field of various types of quick passages, of *détaché*, *spiccato*, and *legato*, of arpeggios, scales and double-stoppings, we immediately notice the devastating effect of extra-musical practice, of systematized and abstracted technique, which ineluctably harbours anti-musicality, whether the victim is the right hand, the left, or both of them: the scales, the octaves, the thirds, the sixths, the various bowings take over the music. Its structure and hence its phrasing no longer create the technique, and in the highest circles, you quite often hear an incisive phrasing abruptly interrupted by a *spiccato* passage, which rolls off mechanically, even outside the established tempo and tempo character, until the technical exhibition is over. In itself, the exhibition is, of course, flawless—so far as its mechanical accuracy and the even distribution of its notes is concerned (which latter may, however, be musically unacceptable!).

One can actually go so far as to say that it is not easy at this problematic stage in the history of performance to go to a concert by an outstanding violinist or an outstanding string quartet in which the shaping of the music is not occasionally interrupted by stretches of technique. Now, in the technical spectrum of the right hand, if *ricochet* is at one end of the scale because its extra-musical practice won't easily harm its musical use, the kind of tone-modulation which should be of the essence of tone-production, but which the constant *vibrato* has altogether removed from the violinist's repertory, is right at the other end, in that it simply cannot be practised extra-musically at all: its every feature exclusively depends on the logic of the line which is being played. It is for this very reason that so long as it was alive, *vibrato*-less tone-modulation invariably persuaded and convinced through its musical significance: outside its specific musical meaning, it did not exist.

Tone and tone-production you can indeed practise as such, especially 'full' and *forte* tone. Significantly enough, on the level of contemporary mediocrity, you may encounter a very positive *forte*, whereas *piano*s tend to be negative—not loud rather than positively soft. For like tone variation, the character of positive, lyrical softness wholly depends on the music, which will determine the balance between an *espressivo* and its simultaneous, equally expressive containment: we are again at the other end of the spectrum, for without the specific, usually complexly soft music before you, there is nothing to practise. And it is again this kind of positive *piano* or even *pianissimo* which used to be overwhelmingly defined and characterized before the opaque *vibrato* screen came in.

The abstraction of technique, then, favourable though its influence has been on the development of accuracy and sheer fluency, inevitably de-musicalizes any technical achievement, even where a Flesch-like conscience is intent upon not allowing the separation of technique to result in its downright isolation—where everything that is being practised in the abstract, 'as such', is at the same time continually being related to the music to which it is intended to apply. For the point is that this very application is, musically speaking, a fallacy—that in it, cause and effect are exchanging roles: 'applied' to the music, the technique assumes a causative role, whereas in all solely musical music-making, it is the music that is the cause; if it is sufficiently alive in the mind's ear, its effect will be the technique required to realize it.

Nor is the musical degeneration of technique, its standardization and expressive constriction, the only result of its abstracted development. In order to replace an infinite variety of *spiccati* with a single, flawless utility *spiccato*, one has to devote a great deal of time to extra-music, and there are countless such technical departments, each of which requires sustained, demi-semi-musical attention: in short, professional musical education is having ever less to do with music. As a result, it is not only the student's expressive range which his ever-improving technique narrows down further and further, but his actual musical knowledge too—the extent to which great music is alive in him. It is a vicious circle: the less great music he knows, the fewer will be the potential musical determinants of technique, and the less he looks, listens to music to inspire his technique, the more extra-musical practice will he feel (and be told) he needs, and the less time and energy will there be to get to know music.

I have devoted much of my life to teaching, but until a year or two ago my experience of institutional teaching had been intermittent and limited: my pupils were either leading musicians, or at least youngsters who, officially, had completed their studies and were about to start either a solo career or a composing life or a quartet. It is only since I have been put in charge of all string quartets at the Yehudi Menuhin School (and occupying a comparable position at the Guildhall School of Music and Drama) that I have had an opportunity to examine and study cross-sections of contemporary musical youth—its musical minds. The effect of these studies has been one of my life's profoundest traumas.

In my early teens, I knew, as a matter of course, the greatest violin literature, the great quartet literature (including all forty-five great Haydn quartets), the greatest other chamber music, the great symphonies and concertos, the Bach Passions and the most important oratorios, as well as most operas consisting of great music (of which there are fewer than twenty)—nor was my knowledge exceptional: every deeply musical child, regardless of whether he intended to become a musician or simply considered himself an amateur and music lover, knew the most important music for his own instrument, as well as what is nowadays called the standard repertoire.

Despite the immeasurably wider availability of music and musical performances in our own time, the modern musical child or youngster is abysmally ignorant: a fiddler may know one or two Mozart and/or Beethoven sonatas, half a dozen quartets at the outside (with no late Beethoven or, at most, op. 127 among them), and whatever he happens to have come across in the standard repertory, the orchestra's and/or other instruments'. My concluding phrase is crucial: the urge to get to know all Beethoven sonatas after one has played one, to get to know his other works after one has been playingly overwhelmed by one of them, the discovery of greatness no longer plays any tangible role in the youthful mind which, quite especially if it envisages a professional future, forces itself, and is indeed compelled, to direct its musical energies elsewhere.

Before I describe the nature of the contemporary youngster's so-called musical preoccupations, let me emphasize that the disastrous absence of wide and deep musical experience from the contemporary young musician's mind is, of course, due to complex circumstances, many of them part and parcel of our mass-medial civilization and of the late and transitional stage at which we now find ourselves in the development of our musical culture. But an analysis of these circumstances would go far beyond the present essay's legitimate field of investigation as indicated by its title. What does not go beyond this area is the examination of one single source of contemporary ignorance—or, as I'd prefer to call it, contemporary emotional death, or coma. This source is the separation of technique and music which is prompting our young musician—more so than our young musical amateur—to enlist his musical energies in the service of extra-musical activities, of technical practice rather than musical study.

Even the present essay's central object of derision, the *sempre vibrato*, is acquired, not by playing contrasting cantilenas and so discovering their equally contrasting vibrato requirements, but by extra-musical practice of an all-purpose, standard vibrato. Carl Flesch himself was well aware of the musical need for different vibratos, but his own, unchanging, wide and slow vibrato, which formed part of what, otherwise, was an eminently musical, masterly technique, showed that in this dimension, at any rate, he had not himself solved the development of his technique, that it had not been born out of his musical understanding.

And the contemporary youngster simply does not possess enough understanding, doesn't know enough music, to make his technique the child and servant of musical understanding; on the contrary, when he reads a new piece, progressing as he must from the known to the unknown, he will throw his technical achievements, his *spiccati* and his scales (with their mechanical fingerings) at the music before he knows how it goes, what kind of *spiccato* flexibility and shading the line

Mischa Elman: drawing by Milein Cosman, 1965.

dictates (if any *spiccato* at all), which changes of position in his scales will produce the most meaningful articulation, characterization, and definition of his phrases.

In this sense, then, it is not only technique whose musical decline is the direct result of its impressive systematization and development, and its less impressive standardization: our title, far from overdramatizing the role of modern violin technique, is a modest understatement. For it is the very art of performance which is endangered: what has been an art is turning into a craft. But music as we know it, as its composers knew it, cannot survive without artistic performance, without which it does not, in fact, come to life (though the performance may merely take place within one's own mind). Unless drastic steps are taken to rediscover the concrete, specific musical meaning of all technique, the only way out will be, ultimately, electronic music and its instrumental imitations; performance as the tail-end of composition will have had its day.

If the string quartet is endangered by the *sempre vibrato*, music itself is endangered by extra-musical practice, and violin music more so than any other: the division between technique and music has, systematically, progressed and regressed further in the fiddler's world than anywhere else—for reasons which have to do, in the last resort, with the unnatural position of the violin (as opposed to, say, the cello). We have reached the point where our youngsters are puzzled by a choice remark of Kreisler's, which they meet with utter incomprehension: 'Practice is a bad habit.' Study isn't, and study gives birth to musical technique.

The Violin Concerto

The solo violin part of the first of Vivaldi's twelve violin concertos op. 8 ('Spring').

To tease out the origins of the violin concerto, one must delve into the origins of instrumental music itself. Until the diatonic scale superseded the church modes as the principal building-blocks of melody, it was not possible to construct abstract musical forms on a large scale. Form implies internal relationships, a structure that is coherent and intellectually satisfying; and the hierarchy of pitch relationships that the diatonic scale necessarily implied opened the way for the planning of music on a more expansive scheme, without the need for a verbal text to support and sustain it.

In the second half of the seventeenth century, then, primitive 'sonata forms' began to evolve; the trio sonatas and *sonate da chiesa* of Italians such as Maurizio Cazzati (1620–77), Giovanni Battista Vitali (1632–92) and Giovanni Maria Bononcini (1642–78) represented the first tentative steps on the road to an organization of instrumental musical form that we would recognize as the norm nowadays. Further impetus to this development came from the unlikely direction of Italian opera: the dramatic flexibility and opportunities for contrast afforded by diatonicism were rapidly recognized, and the short instrumental sinfonias that conventionally preceded each act of early Baroque operas became more elaborately sectional. In some of the opera sinfonias of Alessandro Stradella (1644–82) the dramatic contrast is heightened by dividing the orchestra into a group of solo instruments, the *concertino* (or 'little consort'), and the remaining body of strings or *concerto grosso* ('grand consort', also referred to in later periods as the *ripieno* or *tutti*). It is that contrast and opposition of little and grand consorts which is the basic thesis of all concertos.

The Baroque concerto

By the end of the seventeenth century the term *concerto grosso* had become established as the name of an instrumental form in its own right, and Arcangelo Corelli (1653–1713) renowned as its greatest exponent. Quite how early Corelli was writing *concerti grossi* remains uncertain, but there is good evidence that he was directing performances of them in 1682. Corelli's fame and influence as a violin virtuoso were crystallized in the set of six *sonate da chiesa* and six *sonate da camera* that made up his op. 5 (see pp. 70–7); but the set of *Concerti grossi* op. 6, published a year after his death, is conceived in equally violinistic terms, with the first violin in the *concertino* group dominating the solo sections. Yet despite his innovations, Corelli's influence on the Baroque violin concerto was more stylistic than formal; a whole generation of Italian composers adopted a Corellian approach to writing for the violin.

The achievement of Giuseppe Torelli (1658–1709), although parallel with that of Corelli, represents a more significant step towards fully-fledged solo concerto form. After his death Torelli's brother published a set of concertos as the composer's op. 8, in which the *concertino* was reduced to only two violins, and even on occasion to just one. Tommaso Albinoni (1671–1750) had experimented in a similar fashion a few years earlier in his *Concerti* op. 2, but Torelli's innovations went further. The concertos follow the fast–slow–fast movement plan of the Italian opera overture of the time, but in the outer movements there are clear elements of *ritornello* form, with marked distinctions between *ritornello* and episode and a scheme of keys to articulate them. In earlier works Torelli had used solo violins as *concertino* (two works from his op. 6 can therefore claim to be the earliest of all violin concertos) and primitive *ritornello* forms, but not until his op. 8 are they fused to provide all the elements of the solo concerto which the later Baroque composers required.

It was Antonio Vivaldi (1678–1741) who appropriated the concerto and the violin concerto in particular for the next twenty or more years. Vivaldi thoroughly absorbed the lessons of Corelli and Torelli, but he introduced into his concertos a brilliance and virtuosity that was quite new. Where Torelli's solo writing is moderately demanding but ultimately decorous, Vivaldi exploited every facet of violin technique and its potential for expressive nuance. He wrote some 225 solo violin concertos as well as numerous multiple violin works, but his earliest set of op. 3, entitled *L'estro armonico*, remained the most influential and celebrated in his lifetime. The twelve items in this set are divided between *concerti grossi* (eight) and solo violin concertos; the latter adopted the three-movement scheme employed by Torelli and Albinoni, and which Vivaldi was to establish as the norm for concertos for the best part of two centuries.

The flamboyance of Vivaldi the man, famous for his vanity, could no doubt be easily related to the unashamed extroversion of his concerto writing. The use of high registers, multiple stops and the insertion of cadenzas into many movements, together with the overtly expressive *cantabile* style he cultivated in slow movements, may perhaps merely reflect the fact that the violinists in Vivaldi's Venice were more expert than those in Corelli's Rome, but it nevertheless represents an important beginning for an approach to the writing of violin concertos that was to reach its apogee more than a century later in the works of Paganini.

Autograph of the solo violin part of the *Andante* from Bach's violin concerto in A minor.

In the modern concert hall the violin concertos known as *The Four Seasons* have quite eclipsed the remainder of Vivaldi's output in popularity. In fact, *The Four Seasons* are only the first four of a set of twelve concertos published in Amsterdam around 1725 as *Il cimento dell'armonia e dell'inventione* (*The Contest of Harmony and Invention*) op. 8, lively, programmatic works, delightful and easy on the ear, that were quickly and successfully mimicked in Italy and France. Vivaldi continued to write concertos up to 1730. (The composer Luigi Dallapiccola, a Vivaldi scholar himself, once observed that Vivaldi did not write 600 concertos but the same concerto 600 times.) New stars, however, were already appearing in the firmament of Italian violin playing. Chief among them were Pietro Locatelli (1695–1764) and Giuseppe Tartini (1692–1770), and it was Tartini's influence, through his activities as violin teacher and pedagogue, that was the most extensive and profound.

Locatelli's fame in his time was based largely upon his *L'arte del violino* op. 3 which contains as cadenzas twenty-four capriccios exploring every facet of technique, works which were to influence Paganini in the next century. Tartini was more productive: he wrote 125 violin concertos, whose clean-cut formal outlines were to be much admired by Bach's sons and Leopold Mozart. Through Tartini's pupils, especially Pietro Nardini and his protégé Gaetano Pugnani, a line of inheritance can be drawn to Viotti and the whole school of Romantic virtuosos in the nineteenth century.

Nevertheless it was Vivaldi, by his travels and vigorous self-promotion, who initially spread the achievement of the Italian violin school far beyond Italy itself. In Germany, and in Saxony especially, *L'estro armonico* was widely and faithfully imitated. The Venetian fashion was given a further push in 1717 when the Dresden court violinist Pisendel returned home from studying with Vivaldi, bringing with him scores of his teacher's concertos. While in the service of the court at Weimar, Johann Sebastian Bach (1687–1755) had made keyboard arrangements of nine Vivaldi concertos, including five from *L'estro armonico*. But it was not until he moved to Cöthen in 1717 to become court musician to the Prince of Anhalt-Cöthen that Bach found the artistic freedom to compose concertos of his own.

There was no liturgical music to be written for the Calvinist prince, but there was a court band of around seventeen musicians to be supplied with a repertory. The results included the six famous concertos dedicated in 1721 to the Margrave of Brandenburg, but clearly intended for the Cöthen orchestra, as well as the two violin concertos that have survived (in E major and A minor) and the magnificent D minor concerto for two violins. In the Brandenburg Concertos the *concerto grosso* principle is extended and refined, though among the *concertino* groups there are solo violin parts that demand a level of virtuosity close to that of a Baroque concerto: in the first of the set, for instance, a *piccolo* violin is *primus inter pares*, its fellow soloists being three oboes and two horns; in the second a violin shares the honours more evenly with recorder, oboe and (especially) trumpet; in the fourth the violin is partnered by two recorders that operate as an indivisible unit.

If Corelli is the model behind the Brandenburgs (even though some of them began life as more orthodox concertos for domestic consumption at the Cöthen court), in Bach's A minor violin concerto and the double concerto Vivaldi's influence is palpable. Both works stick closely to the *ritornello* organization developed by the Venetian school, yet the writing is so fluent and the solo lines of such varied interest that the formal outlines

Painting by a unknown eighteenth-century artist of a concert (possibly including a *concerto grosso*) in a Venetian palace.

of the outer movements in both works are all but obscured. The A minor concerto has a first movement dominated by the theme of its opening *ritornello* and is capped by a prodigious fugal finale, while the double concerto welds the two violins together by close imitation, in dazzling, inseparable union.

If the key sequences of these concertos do not extend beyond the limits laid down by Vivaldi, the E major work is signficantly more ambitious. It moves from tonic to dominant and back again in the course of the opening *ritornello* alone, and later in the first movement visits some quite arcane tonal regions, while the melodic invention makes do with the minimum of material from the opening theme. The slow movement, a sustained and passionate song for the soloist over an *ostinato* bass, may have followed the plan of the A minor concerto, but contained enough new formal ideas to prove a valuable source for composers in the second half of the eighteenth century as they set about reconciling concerto form with the new sophistication of sonata organization.

The Classical concerto

In the Baroque era the development of concerto form had been intimately bound with the violin, as a natural evolution from the *concertino* groupings of the *concerto grosso* and because the tonal power and expressive possibilities of the violin were more effective than those of the available keyboard instruments. After the death of J. S. Bach, however, the harpsichord concerto grew in popularity, while the *concerto grosso* itself was superseded by the solo concerto. And as the piano was developed and refined in the second half of the eighteenth century, the violin concerto very definitely lost its position of pre-eminence. The history of concerto form quite rapidly became the history of the piano

Giovanni Battista Viotti: pen and wash drawing by an unknown artist.

concerto, for Mozart's achievement in fusing the *ritornelli* of the Baroque concerto with the dramatic possibilities of sonata form was accomplished almost entirely through his series of piano concertos; his five works for violin are relatively early and pre-date the composition of his significant E flat piano concerto K.271. The bias was practical as much as artistic: Mozart was mainly a pianist who relied on his new concertos to promote his subscription concerts; he turned to other solo concerto instruments, including the violin, only to fulfil commissions.

Before Mozart, however, the violin concerto was sustained by a number of lesser figures, nowadays of historical rather than purely musical importance. Bach's sons largely continued the line of their father's concertos, cleaving to the *ritornello* principle and its array of keys, and generally not attempting to fuse with it the rudiments of sonata form already detectable in the works of Sammartini and Monn. The composers of the Mannheim school were often professional violinists, and though the Stamitz family—father Johann (1717–57) and sons Carl (1745–1801) and Anton (1750–1801)—produced a large number of concertos, many of them have been lost. Those that have survived show father and sons drawn in different directions: Johann's concertos, published in 1754, take the clear proportioning of Tartini as their model, while those of Carl, praised towards the end of the century for the expressiveness of their slow movements, lean more towards the French style that Viotti would soon capitalize upon.

Joseph Haydn's (1732–1809) concertos also date from the middle of the eighteenth century, the composer's early years in the service of the Esterházy court, and were intended for the court musicians to play. Haydn's temperament did not lend itself to self-publicity, nor towards the brilliance that since Vivaldi had been taken as the necessary concomitant of concerto writing; he was not a particularly distinguished performer himself on any instrument. But he wrote at least some violin concertos while at Esterházy. The exact number is difficult to define; several have been lost, and those that survive include works now attributed to other composers, including Carl Stamitz and Haydn's brother, Michael. A set of four violin concertos from the late 1760s is quite conservative in its echoes of the Baroque: evidently Haydn's willingness to experiment and innovate in other media was curbed in the concerto, whether as the result of temperamental disaffinity or in deference to the innate conservatism of the Esterházy court.

Michael Haydn (1737–1806) was, by contrast, far

Mʳ VIOTTI

more bold in his thinking. His violin concerto in B flat, written in 1760, includes the unmistakable elements of a development section in its first movement, for all the superficial trappings of the Baroque style it still carries. Where Bach's E major violin concerto had used a single theme for a first movement organized around the *ritornello*, a revolution in concerto form begun by Michael Haydn (and in some of his violin concertos by Karl Ditters von Dittersdorf, 1739–99) was carried to full fruition in the concertos of Mozart.

As has already been mentioned, Mozart's own revolution was wrought almost entirely in terms of the piano concerto. His five violin concertos were written in Salzburg in 1775. From 1770 he had been *Konzertmeister* to the court of the Archbishop of Salzburg, and in the violin works he attempted to fulfill at least one part of his function as leader of the court orchestra. Through his father Leopold, Mozart will have come into contact with the staples of the violinist's repertory in the second half of the eighteenth century. He would have known the concertos of Tartini and Geminiani, while during his Italian tours he might have encountered the works of more recent Italians such as Pardini and Pugnani.

Against that historical background it is not so surprising that the first of Mozart's violin works, the concerto in B flat K.207, should have been relatively traditional; in its first version it ended with a sonata-form finale, but Mozart added a rondo as a much later afterthought (K.269). The next three in the set were conceived from the start with rondo finales. The second (K.211) betrays a knowledge of the French school, but the difference in sensibility between these first two and the last three concertos is enormous: the works in G (K.216), D (K.218) and A (K.219) are in every concert violinist's repertory, while their predecessors are not (although the gap between K.211 and K.216 was only two months in chronological terms). The G major concerto begins with a theme culled from Mozart's quasi-opera *Il re pastore*, and replaces the conventional slow movements of the earlier concertos with an *Adagio* of infinitely greater profundity. In it the violin's cantilenas are embedded in a close colloquy with the orchestra; the conventional juxtaposition of soloist and accompaniment is all but dissolved. The rondo finale is of a different order of intricacy also, with episodes in contrasting tempos and metre.

Mozart's violin concertos demand every ounce of inspired musicality a soloist can muster, but technically speaking the solo writing is not, even by the standards of the time, especially demanding. Only in the D major concerto is virtuoso brilliance emphasized, and Mozart here consciously commands a wider canvas of bravura effects. (For a long time this concerto was regarded as being based on one by Luigi Boccherini, but that work has been shown to be a later forgery.) The plan of the extrovert D major is close to that of the G major, whereas the final work of the group in A major is more original in shape as well as expression. This A major concerto begins with a serenely expressive *adagio* introduction leading to an *Allegro* in which the dialogues between soloist and orchestra are expertly dovetailed with a wealth of thematic material, much of it subsidiary to the main themes. The finale reserves another surprise: the graceful minuet is interrupted by an episode 'alla Turca', complete with cymbals and droning horns. The form of the whole movement is of particular interest, for despite all the characteristics of a minuet, Mozart labels it 'Rondeau: *Tempo di Minuetto*', an attempt perhaps to reflect the elaborate structure with episodes that are as important expressively as the elements of the minuet.

After 1775, Mozart did not return to the violin concerto, save for a couple of beginnings that remained just that, and to replace movements in the earlier works he subsequently found unsatisfactory. But shortly before he left Salzburg for the last time he wrote the *Sinfonia Concertante* K.364 for violin and viola, which enshrines the lyrical essence of the violin more completely than any of the solo concertos. Mozart composed another *Sinfonia Concertante* (for wind instruments) and began two more; his precedent could have been the works of Carl Stamitz in Mannheim, who wrote several for violin and viola, one of which, in D major, is sometimes performed nowadays.

Mozart's wonderful *Sinfonia Concertante* is a double concerto in all but name; the two instruments play separately and in intimate dialogue, each turning the themes to its own account. By comparison with this inspired work the violin concertos seem positively lightweight; the material of the *Sinfonia Concertante* is developed with almost symphonic rigour in the outer movements, its textures given added weight and richness by the persistent division of the orchestral violas, and the C minor *Andante* is one of its composer's greatest slow movements. The explanation is partly to be found in the E flat piano concerto K.271 whose composition separates that of concertos and *Concertante*; here Mozart had exploited the dramatic potential of the concerto form fully for the first time. The lyrical currency of Mozart's violin concertos is not at all devalued by the more powerful emotional charge of the *Sinfonia Concertante*, but it moves the expressive possibilities of

Concert in the *Sala dei Filarmonici*, Venice: painting by
Gabriele Bella, early eighteenth century.

Below: Autograph of part of the *Andante sostenuto* of Viotti's
violin concerto in C major, *c.* 1795.

Opposite: A performance of Haydn's opera *L'incontro
improvviso* at Esterhazy: gouache by unknown artist, 1775.

the string concerto on to a different plane entirely, opening the way for the series of great, universalizing violin
concertos the next century was to produce.

By the time Beethoven (1770–1827) came to write his
only violin concerto (an earlier work in C major from
his Bonn years before 1792 survives as a fragment), the
form had been developed out of all recognition in
Mozart's mature piano concertos and in Beethoven's
own earlier concertos. But Beethoven's violin concerto
in D op. 61 shows another important influence, that of
Giovanni Battista Viotti (1755–1824), whose twenty-
nine concertos for the instrument are as crucial to the
development of the classical violin concerto as Mozart's
piano concertos are to the history of that form.

Viotti was generally regarded as the finest violinist
of his time (see also pp.116–17); he called himself
'*élève du célèbre Pugnani*' and continued the tradition
begun by Tartini and Nardini, which in its turn had
stemmed directly from Corelli and Vivaldi. Italian by
birth, Viotti spent his adult life largely in Paris and later
in London, and accordingly his violin concertos can be
divided into two groups. The nineteen concertos written
in Paris, though musically inferior to the later 'London
concertos', were nevertheless more influential in creating a French school of violin playing, in which Viotti's

pupils Pierre Rode (1774–1830), Rodolphe Kreutzer (1766–1831) and Pierre Baillot (1771–1842) took leading parts, and continued the tradition in numerous concertos of their own.

Viotti's concertos are essentially Italianate; they place great reliance on a sweet-toned *cantabile* style. But there is a French cut to many of the themes; dotted rhythms are common, and the martial quality of the *ritornelli* points to the same source. Slow movements are *romances*, with themes that recall popular song; finales are *rondeaux*, specifically intended to end the concerto in as brilliant a manner as possible. Yet even within this basic framework Viotti shows considerable ingenuity. Every opportunity is taken to colour the solo line with sparkling bravura, to the extent of interpolating minature cadenzas between the sections of the first movement, and introducing a solo episode in both exposition and recapitulation, principally intended to generate further excitement. Similarly the finale *rondeau* could be made to accommodate a variety of genre-pieces; in concerto no. 13, for example, it takes the form of a lively *polacca*.

Viotti's London concertos, more substantial and less purely decorative than their forerunners, have lasted longer in the repertory. No. 22 in A minor was much admired by Joachim and Brahms, while the later works look forward to the Romanticism of Paganini and his followers. By the time these concertos were written, however, Beethoven's own violin concerto had been performed and had opened yet another new path for the further development of the form.

When Beethoven completed his concerto in 1806, he had already included the instrument in several other works for soloist and orchestra. The triple concerto for violin, cello and piano op. 56 (1804) is marginal Beethoven and its violin part not especially rewarding: the work revolves around the cello, which is given most of the important thematic statements. Of more interest to the concert violinist are the pair of Romances for violin and orchestra, in F op. 40 and in G op. 50. It has been suggested that they were intended as possible slow movements for the C major violin concerto from the early 1790s which Beethoven did not complete. The key of either would have been appropriate in the context, the orchestrations call for similar forces, and he might well have turned to the Viotti model for a slow movement at that stage of his career. The Romances contain nothing to validate their later publication date of 1802: they are elegant lyrical effusions, idiomatically concentrating on the upper registers of the instrument

Programme for the concert on 23 December 1806 in the *Schauspielhaus an der Wien* at which Beethoven's violin concerto was first performed, with Franz Clement as soloist.

and descending to the lower strings only for specific expressive effects.

Neither the Romances nor the triple concerto bears directly upon the Beethoven violin concerto itself. This noble work has become accepted as one of the greatest concertos of any age, and is a landmark in the history of the form, even though it was slow to win acceptance from public or performers because of its lack of fashionable brilliance. In essence it is a lyrical work, but the singing qualities of the solo instrument are contained within a strict formal structure. In the first movement, almost for the first time, concerto and sonata-form principles are wholly synthesized: the modulation from the D major tonic to the dominant is delayed until the soloist's entry, thus adding powerful intensity to the drama of the solo exposition, while the home key of the concerto is continually soured by the minor, lending a delicate astringency to the violin's singing lines.

Beethoven had completed three of his piano concertos before the composition of op. 61; he had begun the G major concerto also, but interrupted it to write the violin work at top speed. Certainly the way in which the first movement unfolds seems entirely spontaneous; there is nothing self-conscious about its consummate formal control. In stark contrast to the careful pattern of keys in the first movement, the *Larghetto* forgoes modulation altogether. It takes the form of five paragraphs, each in G major, in which a statement of the main theme is complemented by the soloist's filigree decoration. Slow movement and finale are linked; the finale returns to the major–minor ambiguity of the first movement, and its rondo form finds room for a G minor episode to counterbalance the first movement's development in the same key.

Beethoven's concerto is essentially symphonic. It places greatest weight on thematic development and structural coherence. As a prototype for the great 'symphonic' concertos of the nineteenth century it was of critical importance, but it nevertheless emphasized a profound dichotomy in the development of the form which was to persist throughout the century and which reflected the Romantic movement in two opposed ways.

The Nineteenth Century: Spohr

The significance of Beethoven's violin concerto took more than a quarter of a century to permeate through succeeding generations. The premiere in 1806 was given by Franz Clement and subsequent performances were sporadic: in Berlin in 1812 by Luigi Tomasini, by Bail-

lot and Vieuxtemps in the 1820s and 1830s. By the time Joseph Joachim took up the work and performed it under Mendelssohn's baton in Leipzig in 1844, Mendelssohn's own violin concerto was completed, and the next stage in the evolution of the 'symphonic' concerto had been established.

In the first decades of the nineteenth century, however, Viotti proved a more potent and relevant influence. Though the concertos of Louis Spohr (1784–1859) belong geographically to the Germanic tradition, they show the clearest debts to Viotti, inherited through Rode. Their style is that of the French violin concerto, with notably expressive slow movements and no shortage of bravura passage-work. But the orchestral accompaniment is far more organic than anything in Viotti; there is a symphonic breadth to some of them that suggests Beethoven as a model. Spohr left fifteen violin concertos, as well as a number of double concertos involving violin and a concerto for string quartet and orchestra. They span some forty years: the first pre-

Louis Spohr.

dates Beethoven's concerto, the last was written in the year of Mendelssohn's. In several of the concertos, the soloist becomes a quasi-operatic protagonist: in no. 8 in A minor, subtitled *in mode di scena cantante* and intended for a visit to Italy in 1816, the violin line is conceived in terms of dramatic vocalise with a lengthy recitative to follow the opening orchestral tutti; in no. 12, in A major, the orchestral introduction is transformed into an accompanied recitative.

In the nineteenth century the popularity of Spohr's tuneful and accessible concertos far outstripped that of Beethoven's. Yet they only nibbled at the edges of the problems of concerto form, unwilling to incorporate bravura display into a musical conception more frankly organic, but at the same time recognizing the structural rewards of symphonic organization. The dichotomy in the concerto tradition needed a more radical polarization, and this was provided by the music and colourful personality of Niccolò Paganini (1782–1840).

Paganini and the Virtuoso Tradition

Paganini wrote a vast quantity of music for violin and orchestra—sets of variations on Italian operatic themes, arrangements of folk tunes—as well as at least six concertos. There is evidence that he composed at least two more which have not survived, and the solo violin parts in many of his other orchestral works have also been lost. None of the concertos was published during his lifetime, for a vital ingredient of the myth surrounding Paganini the performer was his inaccessibility; even copies of the orchestral parts were strictly controlled. The music relied on Paganini's exclusive advocacy for its popularity; and there is no doubt that the composer reinvented much of the solo line for each performance, so that the written-out score in practice was little more than the framework for an elaborate improvisation against an orchestral backdrop.

What we read in the score today is thus only the bare bones of the Paganini concertos, yet even in skeletal form they show the background of the French violin school from which they were developed. Paganini is known to have played concertos by Kreutzer and Rode, treating them in the brilliant and cavalier fashion he treated his own music, recasting the solo lines in his own style and never hesitating to provide additional episodes when he deemed them appropriate. From these models he took the sectional form of his first movements, with the recapitulations drastically compressed, as well as the attention-grabbing finales, with their leaning towards popular melody. He grafted on to it a knack for writing happily ingratiating tunes and an essentially theatrical concept of the soloist's role. The brilliance of the violin writing far outshines anything from the French school; the operatic experience of the early years of Paganini's career, when he gave recitals in the intervals of theatrical events, had left an indelible mark.

The concertos represent the mature Paganini. An unnumbered E minor concerto dates from 1815, and the first of the numbered series (in E flat, though usually transposed to D) was probably written two years later. They do not have the deliberately, one might almost say intimidatingly, pedagogic intent of the twenty-four *Caprices* op. 1, written in the first decade of the century, but are a heady mixture of devastating pyrotechnics—trills, chords and harmonics—and broad lyrical effusion. The first concerto mingles theatricality with sweet-toothed *cantabile* in the elaborate fantasia that makes up the soloist's second entry in the first movement; on the other hand the slow movement of the fifth concerto in A minor seems to be a sincerely felt, authentically Romantic creation. Paganini's concertos are

Opposite above: Interior of the *Schauspielhaus an der Wien*, coloured engraving, 1825.

Opposite below: Autograph page from Beethoven's violin concerto.

Beethoven: portrait by Joseph Willibrord Mähler, *c.* 1804.

KING'S THEATRE

SIGNOR

PAGANINI'S

Nine'th

GRAND CONCERT:

This Evening, Friday, July 15, 1831.

PROGRAME

PART I

Symphony in E - - - - - - Mozar

Duetto alli idea Signor Rossini, (Ill barbiere di siviglia)

Grand Concerto in e myir in three parts composed and Performed by

SIGNOR PAGANINI.

1. Allegro Marziale
2. Adagio Cantabile Spianato
3. Polacca Brillante

Aria ah arieal giomo Mademoiselle Beck semiramide - Rossini

Duetto questo acciro signor Petalli and signor Curioni.

Pervaldo ed Isolina Marlachi Overture semiramide - Rossini.

PART II

Grand Variations di u n Canto Appassianato and variation on a tema

Marziale compos d & performed on

ON ONE STRING

the Fourth String b Signor PAGANINI

Grand Variations Brilliant with an orchestrial Accompanament performed on the Piano-forte by Mademoiselle Debellvile.

Pianiste to h r h the Princess Frederice of Russia her First Appearance in this country

Aria ah s estinto signora Petralia - - - - - Rossini

Larghetto recitativo and Variations on the Cavatina Panti Palpititi, composed and performed For the first time in this Country by

SIGNOR PAGANINI.

Overture Final Don Giovanni - - - - - Rossini,

Conductor - - Signor M. Costa
Leader. - - Signor Spagnoleti

The Prices of Boxes will be the same as on Opera Nights.

ORCHESTRA AND STALLS.........................£1 1s 0d.
AD ISSION to the PIT...............................0 10 6.
ADMISSION to the GALLERY......................0 5 0
To commence at Half-past EIGHT o Clock, and the Doors to open One Hour before the Performance

J. H. COX, Printer, 14, Garden Row, London Road, Southwark

170

nowadays valued chiefly for their virtuoso flamboyance, an estimate little different from that which prevailed in the mid-nineteenth century, when his catchy melodies inspired and furnished innumerable salon pieces. Yet he was the archetypal Romantic, whose influence extended far beyond the essentially limited tradition of violin playing which he developed (see also pp. 124–126).

Within Paganini's own lifetime, the first signs of that tradition manifested themselves in the concertos of Charles de Bériot (1802–70) and Henri Vieuxtemps (1820–81). In delineating any genealogy that stems from Paganini one must remember that only two of his concertos were published in the nineteenth century, and those (the E flat and B minor) did not appear until 1851; it was the manner more than the letter of Paganini's music that proved so influential.

De Bériot wrote two concertos in the 1820s that showed the progressively increasing importance of Paganini-style brilliance. The first bears all the trappings of the French violin school inherited from Viotti, Kreutzer and Rode; the second, which reached London in 1835, parades the full range of virtuoso technique—harmonics, *scordatura*, left-hand *pizzicato*—designed as a vehicle for de Bériot's own talents. He wrote ten concertos in all. The later ones relaxed their technical demands in favour of lyrical sweetness, and two of these, nos. 7 and 9, have remained on the fringes of the teaching repertory.

Vieuxtemps was de Bériot's most celebrated pupil, and shared his enthusiasm for Paganini. He met his idol in London in 1834, and his first violin concerto appeared six years later to the accompaniment of lavish praise from the French critics, including Berlioz. Vieuxtemps's concertos, seven in all, rapidly found a niche between the consuming virtuosity of Paganini, the ingratiating sweetness of de Bériot and the unfashionable classicism of Viotti and his disciples. The French public was given an alternative to the Germanic Spohr and embraced it enthusiastically. Yet Vieuxtemps's achievement went beyond mere opportunism, for he set about nothing less than reinvigorating the French violin concerto. His fourth, in D minor (1850), recast the form into four movements, with an impassioned first movement and big cadenza, a rhapsodic slow second movement, and a sparkling scherzo and finale. Berlioz described it as 'a magnificent symphony with violin'. In its successor, in A minor (1860), Vieuxtemps took his innovations yet further, paring down the form to a single movement with a slow section embedded in it.

Only Heinrich Ernst (1814–65) carried on strictly where Paganini had left off. Ernst had achieved celebrity by memorizing some of his master's unpublished compositions by ear and performing them with similar brilliance. Among his own compositions, alongside a host of virtuoso variations for violin and orchestra, there is a *Concerto pathétique* (1844) in F sharp minor which demands a technique even more advanced than Paganini's, yet whose musical qualities impressed even the demanding Joseph Joachim, who described Ernst as the greatest violinist–musician of his generation.

Henryk Wieniawski (1835–80) was the last significant figure in the nineteenth-century virtuoso tradition. Thereafter the lines of descent blurred into the nationalist works of Lalo and even Saint-Saëns. But Wieniawski's two violin concertos, in F sharp minor (1853) and D minor (1862), have proved to be more permanent than those of any of his predecessors except Paganini. In them, Wieniawski combined the technical *éclat* of the virtuoso tradition and Slavonic colouring from his native Poland with an authentically Romantic mode of expression. The second concerto, with its rich melodies and highly idiomatic violin writing, has worn the better; the first promotes brilliance at the expense of formal cohesion, but the later work balances the elements of the style more equably. It is still cherished as one of the finest examples of a genre that was always likely to prove ephemeral.

Opposite: 'Signor Paganini during one of his Performances at the Kings Theatre, June 1831': lithograph, 1831.

Felix Mendelssohn: painting by Eduard Magnus, 1845.

Mendelssohn and beyond

Vieuxtemps made his name as an interpreter of the Beethoven concerto in the 1830s, but its idiom had virtually no effect on his own concertos or those of any of his fellow virtuosos. The bravura tradition seemed almost hermetically sealed from any developments within the mainstream of music in the first half of the nineteenth century; it was self-generating and ultimately self-fulfilling. It was left to Felix Mendelssohn (1809–47) to create a new symphonic tradition for the violin concerto, even though with hindsight the concertos of Spohr may be seen as the 'missing link' between Beethoven and Mendelssohn.

Mendelssohn's E minor concerto cost him a great deal of time and labour. As a teenage prodigy he had written a violin concerto in D minor (1822, but unpublished until it was edited by Yehudi Menuhin in 1952) and a concerto for violin, piano and string orchestra also in D minor (1823), in which his debt to the classical concerto form of Mozart is clear. His work on the E minor concerto lasted for nearly seven years between 1838 and 1844, and it was first performed a year later by Ferdinand David in Leipzig, conducted by Niels Gade. The great care which Mendelssohn lavished upon it was justified, for as well as dramatically reshaping concerto form, it is an enduring masterpiece. The lengthy orchestral and solo expositions of the traditional concerto are cast off in favour of an opening that plunges directly into the argument of a tightly constructed sonata movement that has as its centrepiece the main cadenza. Conciseness is emphasized by linking the first movement and *Adante* by means of a luminous chord progression, and joining that second movement to the finale with a meditative bridge passage. The limpid, essentially small-scale scoring is far removed from that of Beethoven's concerto, but the unity of structure owes much to that example. Mendelssohn's work enshrines much of the same lyrical quality of the violin as Beethoven's. While the finale looks back to the elfin prettiness of the younger Mendelssohn's string octet and the incidental music to *A Midsummer Night's Dream*, the *cantabile* of the opening theme and the song-form of the central *Adante* give no doubt of his Beethovenian intentions.

If Mendelssohn's example brought the violin concerto back into the ambit of the Romantic symphonic tradition virtually single handed, his influence on succeeding generations was made more potent through the achievements of his protégé Joseph Joachim (1831–1907). Joachim was the motivator and inspiration of most of the great concertos of the second half of the

nineteenth century, and his championing of the Beethoven concerto (for which he wrote some notable cadenzas) was instrumental in establishing the work in the repertory. Robert Schumann (1810–56) was one of the first to respond to Joachim's talents. In the last year of his creative life (1853) he wrote two works for violin and orchestra, the single-movement *Fantasie* op. 131 and the D minor concerto.

Neither represents Schumann at his best; the *Fantasie* does not treat the partnership of soloist and orchestra with any distinctive drama, and the level of the melodic invention is nothing out of the ordinary. The concerto is hardly better, though its subsequent history is fascinating. Schumann asked Joachim to advise him on the practicalities of the violin part; the 22-year-old modestly declined and so received the score unaltered. By the time Joachim came to discover serious deficiencies in it, Schumann's health had disintegrated and he was unable to contemplate any revisions. In conjunction with Clara Schumann, Joachim decided to suppress the work, because it was not 'equal in rank to so many of his glorious creations'. After his death, the manuscript was sold to the Prussian State Library in Berlin on the understanding that it would not be performed until 100 years after Schumann's death.

The old Gewandhaus, engraving *c.* 1840.

Opposite: Brahms and Joachim.

There it remained until 1937, when the d'Aranyi sisters, great-nieces of Joachim, claimed to have received instructions in a spirit message from Schumann to rediscover and play an unpublished work of his for violin. These instructions Jelly d'Aranyi obeyed, and the first performance of the concerto was given by her in London in 1938. It would be comforting to report that this bizarre chain of events unearthed a forgotten masterpiece, but it remains one of the least convincing of Schumann's major orchestral works, weak in its formal structure and laboured in its working out.

The first of the concertos (G minor) of Max Bruch (1838–1920) also owed inspiration to Joachim. Bruch wrote nine works in all for violin and orchestra, including three concertos, a *Konzertstück* and the *Scottish Fantasy*: of these only the first concerto of 1868 (and marginally the second) have found a permanent place in the repertory, together with the *Fantasy*, but the popularity of the first concerto effectively swamps that of the other two. Its enormous success lies neither in originality nor profoundity but in the undoubted charisma of its themes and the warmth of its rhetorical style, with a first movement punctuated by luscious solo recitatives for the violin and given the title of *Vorspiel*

(Prelude). The three movements are linked, following Mendelssohn's model, though there is a fully fledged sonata-form slow movement which has become a popular lollipop in its own right, and a finale whose Hungarian-style main theme is a pre-echo of the same movement in Brahms's concerto; the link may be Joachim himself, who was Hungarian by birth.

Bruch's second concerto in D minor (1876) is more original; an extensive *Adagio* and a sonata-form finale are linked by a recitative that recalls Spohr's operatically influenced concertos. It is more prolix than its predecessor and virtuosity is consistently favoured over musical rigour; the concerto is, however, worthy of more than occasional revival, and at least as deserving as the *Scottish Fantasy*, completed four years later and intended for the virtuoso Sarasate (though Joachim's advice on the solo part was also sought). The *Fantasy* is a rambling five-movement affair, said to have been inspired by the novels of Sir Walter Scott. The Scottish influence includes a prominent harp in the scoring and a handful of folk tunes woven into the movements; its demands on the soloist are considerably more exacting than those of any of the concertos.

The collaboration between Joachim and Johannes

Brahms (1833–97) proved the most fruitful of all. Brahms's concerto op. 77 (1878) was the result of detailed consultation between composer and soloist, while the double concerto op. 102 of 1887 was a (largely successful) attempt by Brahms to heal a rift that had developed between them after the failure of Joachim's marriage. In some ways Brahms's violin concerto is the most perfectly reconciled of all his concertos, bringing together his lyrical gift with his ability to construct works of grandly organic cohesion. It is also the most authentically 'symphonic' of all violin concertos, and perhaps because of this, as well as an inordinately difficult solo part, was condemned as unplayable after the first performance—Hans von Bülow, otherwise a champion of Brahms, declared that whereas Max Bruch had written a concerto *for* the violin, Brahms had written one *against* it.

Brahms originally designed the work with four movements, the scheme that he preserved for the B flat piano concerto, which he was working on at the same time. In the violin concerto, however, he replaced the central two movements by the hymnic *Adagio* we now know, and it has been suggested that the scherzo which now appears in the B flat piano concerto may have originally been written for violin. The Beethovenian model is faithfully developed. The considerable difficulties it presents to the soloist are never superficial decoration, but arise out of the conception of the work itself. Joachim wrote cadenzas for the concerto, and they remain the most widely used today.

The double concerto for violin and cello is one of the most haunting and fugitive works in the solo repertory of either instrument. It was composed in 1887, at a time when Brahms was absorbed by Baroque music, and much of the solo writing suggests an attempt to recapture the spirit of the *concerto grosso* in a late nineteenth-century style. Many passages are strenuously polyphonic, and the problems of balancing two such tonally disparate soloists are reflected in the light orchestral touch. Again perhaps in a gesture of reconciliation to Joachim, the finale's main theme has a Hungarian flavour; that movement as a whole is the most substantial of the work.

Dvořák's A minor concerto (1879–80) was the last major solo work to be written expressly for Joachim, but it was one that left the violinist largely unmoved; he never played it in public, and the first performance was given by another violinist in Prague in 1883. It is not on the same level as the same composer's concerto for cello, but significant nevertheless for its nationalistic traits, and a wealth of attractive and rewarding writing for the solo instrument.

Nationalism

Dvořák's concerto preserved strong links with the central European tradition personified by Brahms, but it was also symptomatic of a number of works from the last quarter of the century in several countries. The concertos of Edouard Lalo (1823–92) did not even confine themselves to a single nationalist flavour. As a French citizen of Spanish descent he followed a high-pressure concerto in F minor (1872) with the popular *Symphonie espagnole* (more concerto than symphony) written for Sarasate. Lalo's work is intriguing, for it manages to combine elements of several tendencies. In many respects it belongs with the virtuoso concertos of the French school, but it is organized formally along symphonic lines in which Schumann's influence is occasionally detectable. The themes do have undeniable Spanish outlines; the orchestration is exceptionally colourful. It has proved a more durable work than many of its kind, far more than Lalo's own later attempts to exploit assorted nationalisms in his *Concerto russe* (1879) and *Fantaisie norvégienne* (1878).

France in the last half of the nineteenth century also produced the three concertos of Camille Saint-Saëns

(1835–1921)—in A (1859), C (1879) and B minor (1880)—and the *Poème* for violin and orchestra of Ernest Chausson (1855–99). The third alone of Saint-Saëns's violin concertos has achieved anything like the popularity of the same composer's concertos for piano. It is a charming if relatively conventional three-movement work, of less technical asperity than its predecessors, whose singular curiosity is a strange chorale inserted into the finale which seems to recall Wagner's *Lohengrin*. Chausson's delightful *Poème* (1896) is based upon a short story by Turgenev and was inspired by the playing of Ysaÿe. The mood of the work is heavily Romantic, and it proved to be a watershed in Chausson's development; in the last three years of his life Debussyan impressionism brought with it a more limpid style.

Elsewhere in Western Europe the concerto tradition proceeded in fits and starts. The Hungarian violinist and composer Károly Goldmark (1830–1915) produced two violin concertos in the same cheerful, highly coloured idiom that has kept his symphonic poem *Rustic Wedding* in the orchestral repertoire. There are also examples of the genre from Feruccio Busoni (1866–1924), a con-

certo in D major finished in 1897 which displays a debt to the German Romantic tradition rather than any forward-looking tendencies, and even from Richard Strauss (a violin concerto in D minor op. 8 dating from 1882).

The history of the Russian violin concerto in the nineteenth century is similarly patchy. Only Pyotr Ilyich Tchaikovsky (1840–93) showed interest in the concerto form; there is a *Fantasy* on Russian themes by Rimsky-Korsakov (1887) and a violin concerto by Arensky, but Tchaikovsky's single violin concerto in D op. 35 (1878) stands apart. It followed a couple of occasional pieces for violin and orchestra, a *Valse-scherzo*, and the *Sérénade mélancolique* composed for Leopold Auer, who was to be the dedicatee of the concerto. Auer's reaction to such a demanding gift was ambivalent; though he was to play the work many times in later life, he declined the privilege of giving the first performance. The premiere eventually took place in Vienna in 1881, played by Adolf Brodsky, and it provoked from the critic Eduard Hanslick one of his most vituperative reviews. Yet the concerto prospered in Germany at least.

Pyotr Ilyich Tchaikovsky, 1880.
Below: Leopold Auer.

It was a product of one of the most turbulent periods in Tchaikovsky's turbulent life, shortly after the devastating fiasco of his marriage, but it scarcely betrays a hint of this personal tragedy. Throughout its pages there is a celebration of the lyrical quality of the solo instrument as comprehensive and exuberant as that in Mendelssohn's work, which it follows in some crucial formal aspects, not least in the structure of its first movement (the cadenza comes before the recapitulation). It is, however, also a considerable feat of virtuoso daring, and the quality of its melodies marks it out for enormous popularity. Tchaikovsky's violin concerto broke little new ground, but it spawned a number of imitations, not least in the work of Alexander Glazunov. That belongs, though, to the following century.

The Twentieth Century

No dramatic stylistic revolution attended the first decade of the twentieth century. The violin concertos written up to the end of the First World War consolidated and recapitulated the achievements of the nineteenth-century Romantic tradition; radical composers of the period initially eschewed a medium with such conventional associations.

The concerto in D minor by Jean Sibelius (1865–1957), written in 1903 and substantially revised two years later, was very consciously produced against the background of the models of the great symphonic concertos. While a student, Sibelius had cherished ambitions of a career as a concert violinist, and his early training informs much of the bravura writing in the concerto, which integrates passage-work of real excitement and brilliance into a thoroughly organic structure. The concerto separates the second and third symphonies, marking a transitional period in which the rhetoric inherited from the Romantic symphonies of Tchaikovsky was discarded in favour of a more terse, elliptical mode of utterance. It crystallizes this ambivalence; there are passages that look forward to the introspective and highly personal idiom of the fourth symphony, at the same time as it recalls a much more grandiose and essentially nostalgic manner.

As a pupil of Rimsky-Korsakov, Alexander Glazunov (1865–1936) was content to use the language established by his nationalist forebears. His violin concerto in A minor (1904) has remained the most successful and popular of his works, a fusion of Tchaikovsky and Balakirev into a genuinely seductive (if faintly academic) style. Carl Nielsen's (1865–1931) approach in his concerto is a good deal more relaxed, though its propor-

Jean Sibelius: portrait by A. Gallen- Kalella, 1894.

tions are ample enough. Yet the grand, heroic designs of Brahms or Dvořák did not appeal to Nielsen: he kept such humanistic strivings for his symphonies. The violin concerto followed the third symphony, *Sinfonia espansiva*, in 1911. Even if the virtuoso demands on the soloists are fairly routine, the work has an unusual and original shape: two extensive slow introductions are followed by faster movements. Alongside Nielsen's later concertos for flute and clarinet, it seems less sharply characterized, and has perhaps been neglected in favour of more colourful works from an unusually rich period of concerto writing.

The influence of Brahms, though more than tinged by that of Wagner, is strongly felt in the massive concertos of Max Reger (1873–1916). Reger's music has a historical significance that has consistently outstripped its popularity; his prodigious output of works for violin includes one concerto, completed in 1908. The highly chromatic language of Reger, significantly extending the boundaries of tonality, was influential on the Second Viennese School and on Arnold Schoenberg (1874–1951) in particular. In the evolution of the twelve-note system the traditional concerto form played no part, and Schoenberg's single violin concerto is a relatively late work, completed in 1936. It remains one of the most difficult works in the repertoire—Schoenberg half joked that to play it successfully would require a violinist with six fingers—yet the bravura is more than decorative. The form is Classical in outline, opening with a fully-fledged sonata movement. It is a work still written very much within the tradition of the German Romantic concerto, but there is never any suggestion of the deliberate nostalgia of the kind found in the 1924 violin concerto of Hans Pfitzner (1869–1949). Pfitzner and Schoenberg represented the opposite poles of German music in the first decades of the twentieth century, positions that their supporters defended with vigorous polemic. Yet it was a Schoenberg pupil, Alban Berg (1885–1935), who in 1935 demonstrated in a violin concerto the expressive potential that many conservatives had denied was possible within the framework of the twelve-note system.

Berg's concerto is arguably the greatest written for any instrument in the twentieth century. Its instant popular success doubtless owed a good deal to its overt and elegiac programme: dedicated 'to the memory of an angel', it was intended as a requiem for Manon Gropius, daughter of Alma Mahler, who had died of polio at the age of 18. Berg revealed that the concerto's four movements are designed as a biographical portrait—birth, teenage delight in dancing, the catastrophe of illness, death—but at the same time he linked his own fate with it; he was to die within a year. The finale closes with quotation of a Bach chorale, *Es ist genug*, whose opening pitches form the first four notes of the twelve-tone row on which the work is based. The music is conceived very much within the tradition of the symphonic concerto stemming from Beethoven, whose orchestra is a full partner in the dialogue, but the work does not stint its virtuosic demands (even though, for the most part, they arise quite naturally out of the progress of the musical argument). Berg had earlier written a chamber concerto for violin, piano and wind instruments (1925), which remains the most refractory of his works, though the central *Adagio*, for violin and wind alone, is a fine example of his complex and highly wrought expressive style.

179

Autograph piano score draft of a page from the last
movement of Berg's violin concerto: the violin enters with
the theme of Bach's chorale *Es ist genug*.

Alban Berg in November 1935 (left) and Manon Gropius (right).

Neoclassicism

The reaction against the rich, rhetorical manner of German Romanticism that began in the years immediately after the first World War proved immensely fruitful for the violin and for the violin concerto in particular. The Neoclassical style came to embrace several originally distinct evolutionary strands and crossed many national boundaries.

The archetypal Neoclassical concerto was the violin concerto in D (1931) of Igor Stravinsky (1882–1971). Stravinsky took advice from the violinist Samuel Dushkin, and studied the major works of the concerto repertory. Apart from the choice of key, D major, which had been favoured for the violin since Beethoven, the study seems to have had little direct bearing on the result, which is more closely related to Stravinsky's own earlier concerted pieces, such as the *Capriccio* for piano and orchestra of two years earlier. The gestures of the violin concerto cannot be accused of the blatant 'time-travelling' that was one of the criticisms made of Neoclassicism at the time: no *objets trouvés* can instantly be recognized. Yet the spirit of the music, the sharp, clear outlines and busy, motoric textures all testify to that eighteenth-century spirit to which Stravinsky had paid more overt homage in his ballet after Pergolesi, *Pulcinella*.

Stravinsky developed his Neoclassicism while living in France between the first and second World Wars, and the two violin concertos of Sergey Prokofiev (1891–1953) were also first performed during his self-imposed exile in the same country. Prokofiev had prefigured Neoclassicism in his precocious *Classical Symphony* (1917), and the composition of his first violin concerto dates from the same period, though it was not performed

for some six years. It has the mixture of acidulated lyricism and sweet-sour dissonance that became Prokofiev's stock-in-trade. Though he disapproved of what he called Stravinsky's 'pseudo-Bachism', it is in the Neoclassical school that Prokofiev's two concertos for violin (the second followed in 1935) can be most easily placed. Their crisp, lean textures and incisively angular solo writing owe little to the Germanic tradition, and a good deal to the chic insouciance required of composers by the Paris of the 1920s and 1930s.

Other French concertos of the same period were generally lightweight; the composers of 'Les Six' shunned such a serious genre, with the exception only of Darius Milhaud (1892–1974), who produced two violin concertos in the 1920s. Maurice Ravel made an orchestral arrangement of his brilliantly virtuoso *Tzigane* (see also p. 189). German Neoclassicism was a more serious and scholarly affair, in which Baroque forms and mannerisms were carefully imitated. In his set of seven *Kammermusiken* Paul Hindemith (1895–1963) was at pains to revive the spirit of the *concerto grosso*, using ensembles inspired by the Brandenburg Concertos of J. S. Bach. The fourth *Kammermusik* (1925) is a violin concerto with a *ritornello*-form first movement, even if its non-functional harmonic progressions betray its modernity. In 1939 Hindemith wrote a second violin concerto, this time with an explicit title, in which the model is the nineteenth-century symphonic concerto, though still with a *concertante* element informed by his earlier explorations. The violin concerto of Kurt Weill (1900–50), too, is one of its composer's least ingratiating compositions. It dates from the end of the period of his study with Busoni (1924) and uses a wind ensemble in place of a full orchestra; there are echoes in the music of Hindemith and Stravinsky and, in the central set of three linked nocturnes, of Mahler's seventh symphony.

Elsewhere in Europe, Neoclassicism proved as easily assimilable: in the 1943 concerto of the Czech Bohuslav Martinů (1890–1959), and the works of several minor Italian composers including Ottorino Respighi (1879–1936: a *Concerto gregoriano* of 1921), Alfredo Casella (1883–1947) and Gian Malipiero (1882–1973). American composers of the 1930s especially found in the style a solution to the problems of writing accessible music at a time when the social pressure to strike a populist stance was most urgent. But the finest and most durable violin concerto of the period from the United States is better described as Neoromantic than Neoclassical. Samuel Barber (1910–82) wrote a single violin concerto in 1941 in a vein that recalls the *Adagio for strings* which was extracted from his string quartet and made into a

Right: Stravinsky by Picasso, 1920.

Below: A Christmas card drawn by Hindemith.

popular success by Toscanini; it is an effortlessly lyrical piece which sets more store by succulence than aggressive bravura. Barber's may have been a non-developing art, but it carried an effective emotional punch, though later American composers chose to pursue a more consciously nationalistic line.

Neither Béla Bartók (1881–1945) nor Karol Szymanowski (1882–1937) can be comprehensively described as Neoclassicists, in the first case because Bartók's achievement was too wide-ranging for such cosy classification, in the second because Szymanowski's style underwent several profound changes in the course of his career. If there are elements in Bartók's second violin concerto (1938) that can be assigned to Neoclassicism, they are matters of mood rather than of construction. One of the most tautly argued and gripping of his orchestral masterpieces, it is built around two large-scale sonata-form movements that make extensive use of variational procedures; at its centre is an explicit set of variations. The solo part is exceptionally demanding, and for all the textural brittleness it displays, in evolutionary terms the work is a symphonic concerto. After Bartók's death another violin concerto dating from 1908 was published and performed. It provides a reminder of his early high-flown, almost Straussian Romantic style, chromatic with a violin part rich in double-stopped thirds and sixths. Two Rhapsodies for violin (1928) also appear in orchestral versions, which follow the Hungarian rhapsody *csárdás* plan of an introductory *lassú* followed by a more vigorous *friss*.

Szymanowski's two violin concertos are separated by sixteen years. The first (1916) remains one of the freshest and most neglected concertos in the twentieth-

century repertory, and is the finest work of Szymanowski's 'impressionist' period. Its scoring and solo writing are quite unlike those of any other concerto, ambiguous of tonality and texture, violin and orchestra intimately entwined. In the second concerto (1932) outlines and gestures are far more conventional. Szymanowski's late music reverted to a nationalistic style in which folk materials played an important part. There is greater emphasis on traditional bravura in the second work, and a reliance on motoric figures lacking something of the vitality and spontaneity of the first.

British violin concertos

The roundabouts of fashion and the profound changes in musical language which European music underwent in the first half of the twentieth century were regarded with characteristic phlegm and insularity by composers working in Britain at the time. Yet among the works of Elgar and Walton especially are to be found violin concertos that stand comparison with almost any of their contemporaries. Edward Elgar's concerto (1910) can be considered Brahmsian to a fault, but it is sustained by a stream of poetic ideas that are authentically memorable in their own right. The accompanied cadenza in the finale, which requires the orchestral strings to imitate the sound of an Aeolian harp, is an exceptionally explicit programmatic image in a composition that is

generally more abstract than any other of Elgar's large-scale works of the period, though the epigraph '*Aqui está encerrada el alma de . . .*' has provided several generations of Elgarians with yet another unsolved mystery.

The violin concerto of 1916 by Frederick Delius (1862–1934) is accounted by Delians the most successful of his concerto essays (a double concerto, for violin and cello, dates from the same year). Delius's essentially rhapsodic style did not lend itself to the rigour of large-scale symphonic construction, and there is a tendency even in the concerto to lapse into amorphous meditation, although this is offset by some decidedly effective bravura passages. In the work of E. J. Moeran (1894–1950) Delius's example is not always completely expunged; Moeran's violin concerto of 1942 is an ingenious synthesis of lyrical outpouring and harmonic warmth, with a satisfying structural framework. The *Concerto accademico* (1925) of Ralph Vaughan Williams is some kind of attempt at an English Neoclassicism, a concerto for violin and strings modelled on those of J. S. Bach; it is less successful and less popular than his poetic rhapsody for violin and chamber orchestra composed four years earlier, *The Lark Ascending*.

The highly scented rhapsodical style of his earlier music is all but absent in the 1937 violin concerto of Arnold Bax (1883–1953); it is a well-proportioned work made with an unfailingly light touch—a concerto after the manner of Mendelssohn, say, rather than Brahms. The clean-cut textures and hard-edged figurations of Benjamin Britten's concerto of 1939 present yet another set of influences in which technical glitter is softened by elegiac reflection; Britten's occasional nods towards Neoclassicism were invariably tempered chromatically by his awareness of the second Viennese school, and of Berg in particular. Britten's concerto is exactly contemporary with that of William Walton (1902–83), whose violin concerto, written for Heifetz, is one of the handful of orchestral works on which his reputation rests. It represents a fascinating fusion of the 'English symphonism' of Elgar with an angularity and glitter derived from the music of Stravinsky and Hindemith, even if neo-classical tendencies are confined principally to the shaping of themes and sonorities.

The concerto by Roberto Gerhard (1896–1970) also belongs here, for it was one of the first works he completed on settling in Britain after the Spanish Civil War. It is a transitional work, linking Gerhard's early nationalist scores with his later style found upon serialism. Atonal, tonal and serial writing mingle in the concerto, while the instrumental sonority has the bright sheen that was to make his later music so superficially attractive.

Developments since 1945

The multi-faceted evolution of musical history in the years before the second World War split after 1945 into still more overlapping strands. As a form linked inextricably to the tradition of tonal music and to the institution of the symphony orchestra, the violin concerto found itself generally outside the field of the most significant developments. The total serialists, for instance, wrote no music remotely corresponding to received ideas of what constitutes a concerto, although *Varianti*, for solo violin, strings and woodwind (1957) by the Italian composer Luigi Nono (b. 1924) at least returns to confront the problems of setting a solo instrument against a heterogeneous ensemble. But a number of important concertos can be found among the more conservative styles.

In Soviet Russia, for instance, the concertos of Aram Khachaturian (1903–78), Dmitry Kabalevsky (1904–81) and Dmitry Shostakovich (1906–75), all composed for David Oistrakh, added significantly to one portion of the repertory. Shostakovich's two examples represent distinct phases in his development. The first, written in 1948 but not performed until 1955 after the death of Stalin, belongs with such 'public' works as the tenth symphony;[*] the second, from 1967, is more intimate and lucid, sandwiched between the outrage of the thirteenth and the despair of the fourteenth symphonies. The Soviet tradition has been continued distinctively in three concertos of Alfred Shnitke (b. 1934), the most recent of which, mingling elements of atonality and diatonicism, unmistakably recalls the idiom of Berg.

The younger generations of Polish composers have also tackled the concerto, but with fresher, less circumscribed ideas, as demonstrated by the *Espressioni varianti* (1959) of Tadeusz Baird (b. 1928), the seven concertos of Grazyna Bacewicz (1913–69), and especially the *Capriccio* for violin and orchestra (1967) and the violin concerto (1976) of Krzysztof Penderecki (b. 1933). The *Capriccio* is representative of Penderecki's early style in its orchestral and soloistic effects, but the later concerto celebrates his new-found Romanticism, a return to the style and techniques of the nineteenth century.

A similar Neoromanticism informs the concerto of H. K. Gruber (b. 1943), but here the evocation is specifically Viennese and the instrumental colours are

---

[*] As an interesting by-product of Stalinist double-think Shostakovich's first violin concerto has two opus numbers: 77, assigning it to 1947–48; and 99, placing it in 1955. The composer himself made contradictory statements, sometimes preferring the earlier opus number, at other times stating that it belonged to the later period.

Yehudi Menuhin and Sir Edward Elgar in 1932.

Shostakovich and David Oistrakh.

applied with a light and ingratiating touch. Hans Werner Henze (b. 1926) has so far written two violin concertos. The first (1947) introduced serial working into his previously Neoclassical style; the second (1971) calls for bass-baritone soloist and pre-recorded tape in addition to the violin, and includes a setting of a propagandist poem by Hans Magnus Enzensberger.

In Britain conservative traditions have kept the form alive. There are concertos by Lennox Berkeley (b. 1903) and Iain Hamilton (b. 1922), while Michael Tippett's triple concerto for violin, viola and cello (1981) is one of the most successful of his purely instrumental works. Among younger generations of British composers, the concertos of Alexander Goehr (b. 1932) and David Blake (b. 1936) are especially noteworthy. The former (written in 1962) uses an orchestra of Brahmsian sonority to express music of Stravinskian severity of gesture; the latter (1975) has an Italianate warmth initially unexpected from a composer whose primary impulse has been serial. The 1971 violin concerto of Hugh Wood (b. 1932) belongs within the same

Schoenbergian tradition, yet the plan is in the conventional three movements, with a central scherzo and *trio* that recall traditional usages.

The relative thinness of the concerto repertory of the last thirty years—few works have become established internationally in that period—is a consequence both of a lack of interest in the medium among composers and of a lack of top-flight violinists willing to take up and champion new music. One reason may have led directly out of the other, for as a new generation of performers demonstrate their musical and technical abilities to cope with any demands made of them, so composers are showing signs of renewed interest in what seemed quite recently an outmoded form. At the time of writing, John Cage (b. 1912—see also pp. 205 and 209) is currently engaged on a major work with orchestra for Paul Zukovsky; Elliott Carter (b. 1908) has been commissioned to write a concerto for the Norwegian violinist Ole Bøhn. The rise of Neoromanticism in central Europe, too, is as likely to give rise to violin concertos as it is to newly fashionable symphonies.

The Twentieth Century

Ysaÿe at an acoustic recording session, *c.* 1905

During its youth in the seventeenth and eighteenth centuries, the violin became the main vehicle of musical exploration and development—a burgeoning of activity which reached its height of musical and technical sophistication in such masterpieces as Bach's solo sonatas and Partitas. In the late years of the eighteenth century, however, this role of protagonist was gradually taken over by the relatively new and fast-developing piano. Whereas in pre-Classical times the composer-violinist had naturally taken the centre of the stage, his place was at first partially and then decisively usurped by the composer-pianist (who was as likely as not unable even to play the violin, and who therefore turned for advice on the subject to eminent virtuosos). The twentieth century has not neglected the violin; but it has not, by and large, been a Golden Age for violin music—although no less rich than previous centuries in its abundance of great performers.

An important body of music none the less, both good and great, has been composed for the violin in this century, much of it conceived in such a way that it could not exist without the specific resources and sonorities of the instrument. Some of the works examined in this chapter are chamber or orchestral music, but most of the examples we will consider are of music for solo or accompanied violin which extends both the technique and resource of the instrument while still faithfully serving the composer's own musical concept. These last qualities will provide our working definition of what constitutes 'good violin music'.

The Belgian violinist Eugène Ysaÿe is both an exceptional figure and, as a violinist-composer of notable influence and stature whose career extended well into the twentieth century, an exception to the rule. He was a strictly trained, conventional Romantic virtuoso who had the imagination to move with his times, and his role in the history of the violin is comparable with that of Busoni's in the development of the piano. Each composer summed up the technical state of his art; and each fired his sophistication with a subjective, eager seeking after the new which continually informed and redirected his work. Ysaÿe was born in 1858 and died in 1931. His career, like Busoni's, straddled the turn of the century. Among the works written expressly for or premiered by him were the violin sonatas of César Franck and Guillaume Lekeu, Debussy's string quartet, Fauré's piano quintet and Chausson's *Poème* as well as his concerto for violin, string quartet and piano.

As a composer, Ysaÿe's finest contribution to the repertory is a set of six solo sonatas op. 27 (1924). Interestingly enough, this music was inspired not by the composer's own playing (or even intended for his own performance) but by hearing the Hungarian virtuoso Joseph Szigeti playing unaccompanied Bach (see also pp. 122–3). The range of Szigeti's playing, its intellectual rigour and expressive depth, made a powerful impression on Ysaÿe, and set him thinking along new lines about their common instrument:

When one hears an artist like Szigeti who is able to accommodate his playing to the rectangular lines of the great Classics as easily as he can to the expressive melodies of the Romantics, one is forced to consider how absorbing it would be to compose a work for violin while keeping ever before one the style of one particular violinist.

On publication, each of the sonatas was dedicated to a well-known colleague—the first to Szigeti, and the other five respectively to Thibaud, Enescu, Kreisler, Crickboom and Quiroga—but the Neoclassical rigour of Szigeti's playing can be counted the strongest influence on Ysaÿe's usually lush and easygoing harmonic style.

As in much of the most ingeniously worked violin music, the striving after contrapuntal textures in what is primarily a monodic medium leads the composer to exploit or develop novel technical solutions. The *Grave* of the first sonata in G minor maintains a two-voiced discourse, weaving melodic threads and hints of voice-leading even through the arpeggios of its climax and into the ghostly *tremolo sul ponticello* coda. Other noteworthy technical features include the *pizzicato* quadruple-stops which start the *Danse des Ombres* of the second sonata; the Sarabande of the fourth, which contains an inner melodic voice played in left-hand *pizzicato*; the rapid alternations of sixths and tenths in passagework in the third sonata; the headlong rushing octave *glissandi* of the sixth; and the use of harmonics melodically throughout.

The chromatic shifts and oblique harmonies that characterize some sections (the *Allegro* of no. 3, the opening movement of no. 5, '*L'Aurore*') are not just a legacy of Ysaÿe's compositional mentor César Franck, but signs of a liberation of violin technique codified and to a great extent pioneered by Otakar Ševčík (1852–1934: see also p. 154). More renowned as a teacher than as a performer, Ševčík's most notable achievement was a radical reworking of left hand technique. Fingering had traditionally been based on diatonic scales; he expanded the technique by inventing countless studies based on new chromatic fingerings, thus freeing the left hand from many severely limiting conventions of the past, and enabling rank-and-file players to cope far more securely with the chromatically charged harmonies

Fig 1

Fig 2

Fig 3

Claude Debussy and his first wife Rosalie (Lilie) Texier in 1902.

of late Romantic composers. Without Ševčík's work, it is doubtful whether Ysaÿe's music, or indeed the orchestral works of Richard Strauss and Debussy, could have joined the repertory as quickly as they did.

Ysaÿe's six solo sonatas can be seen both as a summary of, and as a springboard for, violin technique at the start of the twentieth century, in much the same way as Paganini's works had at once defined limits and encouraged creative exploration in the nineteenth. When compared to Paganini's *Caprices*, however, Ysaÿe's sonatas demonstrate a more fluid technical layout, and less reliance on repetitive figures and sequential patterns to extend the composition. The various technical resources (*pizzicati*, harmonics, complex stoppings and arpeggiations) form an organic part of each of the sonatas; bravura for its own sake takes second place to the prime considerations of consistency, clarity and re-creative musical imagination. These requirements will become the hallmarks of good performing, and composing, in the decades to come.

They are qualities called for especially in the interpretation of Claude Debussy's single sonata, composed in 1917 in the last months of his life. It is a harmonically elliptical and in some respects emotionally restrained work: Ysaÿe's vocal, introspective style would have suited it well. The violinist had enjoyed a close relationship with the composer in earlier years; Ysaÿe's ensemble gave the first public performance of Debussy's string quartet in 1893, and the *Nocturnes* for orchestra were first conceived with an important solo part for violin. One can still perceive a ghost of this early version in certain passages of the final orchestration: the short, recurring cor anglais solo, for example, and the serene melody played first by flute and harp, then by solo violin, viola and cello against an elaborately divided, shifting background of strings, near the close of the first *Nocturne*.

A remarkable feature of Debussy's later orchestral violin writing is the equal emphasis it places on the three elements of colour, melody and rhythm. A glance at the last movement of *La Mer* (1903–5) shows all these elements clearly differentiated. The very first violin entry (fig. 1) is a gentle *tremolando* six-part chord, shimmering behind brass solos; at the climax of the movement (fig. 2), the melody is reinforced by both second violins and violas; for the final coda (fig. 3) powerful string triplets off the main beats push the orchestra forward, up to and across the bar-lines. *La Mer* marks the climax of a crucial chapter in the history of the violin: for here the nineteenth century's orches-

tral hierarchy of instrumental voicings, based on the format of the Classical string quartet and extending to all orchestral writing—principal melody on first violin, harmonic filling and bass-line for the rest—is at last constructively, decisively overturned.

To these three elements, Debussy's violin sonata reintroduces a fourth, more traditional and intimate in character: the violin as singer. Much of the opening movement is written on the stave, within a soprano's range. The hesitant and ambiguous opening pages, which withhold from the listener any clear information about tempo and metre for as long as a composer could dare without risking collapse, have the *parlando* character of a recitative, even when delivered in strict time. The second movement soars and swoops in more conventionally 'violinistic' fashion. The third achieves a convincing balance between the two styles; the tenderest melodies are sung on the violin's lowest string, while the climaxes fly up to brilliant high registers.

This assignation of musical characteristics to the highest and lowest strings of the instrument, and the resulting exploitation of the contrast between them, is a natural and traditional expressive device. No composer used it to greater effect than Maurice Ravel in his *Rhapsodie de Concert, Tzigane* (1924). The music starts with a long, unaccompanied cadenza, full of heavy Magyar accents, expressive *portamenti* and *rubati*. For the first 28 bars the violin plays entirely on the G-string. Ravel's brilliant depiction of a central-European gypsy fiddler then moves from imitation to apotheosis. The G-string solo is repeated and elaborated using octaves, sixths and slashing chords to raise the tension and the pitch. In good gypsy style, *Tzigane* proceeds to a series of short variations on a simple melodic fragment, the piano accompaniment functioning merely as an imitation of the cimbalom. This brilliantly ersatz-Hungarian music was composed for Jelly d'Arányi, who also commisioned more authentic works in the same genre from Bartók.

Pastiche of this sort was an important ingredient in Ravel's musical personality. One might argue that the second, piano-accompanied half of *Tzigane* doesn't transcend its model, which the opening violin solo surely does. The bluesy slow movement of his 1927 violin sonata is perhaps a better example of an outside influence absorbed and reworked in entirely personal terms. Repeated *pizzicato* chords give the impression of a casual guitarist, and the piano interjections (pitched in A flat, a semitone higher than the violin's G major, but in a lower octave) have a cool acerbity that deftly and economically evokes the atmosphere of jazz. Ravel's professed aim in this sonata was to emphasize the

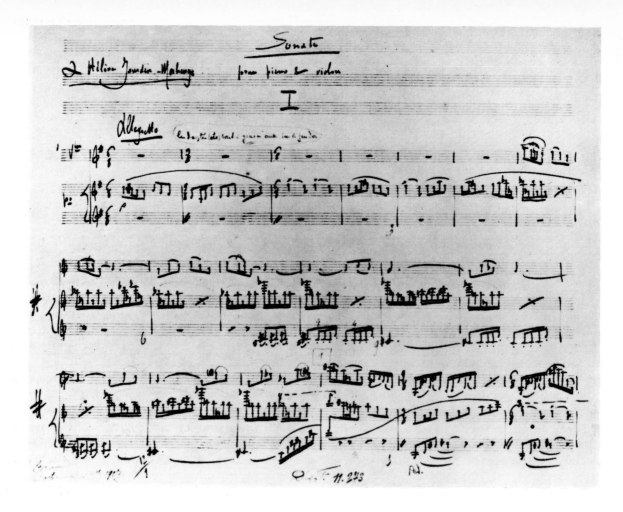

differences, both of character and technique, between the two instruments. Though they share the same melodic material, the composer establishes a manner of diction which at once separates violin and piano and allows them equal status. There are few unison statements: the climax of the opening movement, for example, unites a violin tremolo against single piano notes. The carefully notated *glissandi* of the second movement Blues further heightens the disparity, as do the *glissandi pizzicati* towards the close of the movement.

Ravel's earlier sonata for violin and cello (1920/1) was composed, by contrast, according to principles of unity and integration. Long melodies contrapuntally worked, intertwining figures and a linear voicing of repeated arpeggios—a weaving effect evoked by a single thread of sound, also found in Ysaÿe's solo sonatas of 1924—all contribute to a work of great subtlety and charm.

The 'separate but equal' principle demonstrated by Ravel's sonata for violin and piano became, during the next decade, the Neoclassical ideal. Stravinsky's remarks concerning the conception of his *Duo Concertant* (1931) are not just characteristic of the man but also summarize a general view shared by many of his contemporaries:

After the violin concerto, which is orchestral as well as instrumental, I continued my researches into the domain of the violin and turned to its functions in the chamber-music ensemble. For many years I had taken no pleasure in the blend of strings struck in the piano with strings set in vibration with the bow. In order to reconcile myself to this instrumental combination, I was compelled to turn to the minimum of instruments, that is to say, only two, in which I saw the possibility of solving the instrumental and acoustic problem presented by the strings of the piano and those of the violin. Thus originated the idea of the *Duo Concertant* for violin and piano. The mating of these instruments seems much clearer than the combination of a piano with several string instruments, which tends to confusion with the orchestra.

Note the order of instruments in the composer's description; the work is for 'violin and piano', yet the piano's percussive string articulation is still the dominant feature of the partnership. Stravinsky's preference for composing at the piano is strongly felt even here.

Paring down the range of colour also implies a similar distillation of melodic ideas. The opening *Cantilene* of the *Duo Concertant* has only two thematic tactics, a rapid, arhythmic piano tremolo and a sharply defined, rising and falling violin fanfare. When the violin begins a long sequence of two-part chords, a slow melody moving principally by step, the piano takes over the fanfare material, extending it, but in parrot-fashion, never really developing it. This format, now established, is repeated in the subsequent *Eglogue*. A meandering progress, flowing in one long, unmeasured bar, is swiftly cut off by a quick dance, reminiscent of the composer's

Opposite: Autograph of the first page of Ravel's violin sonata (1927).

Maurice Ravel.

Below: The first night of *L'Histoire du Soldat*: detail from a watercolour by Théodore Strawinsky (the composer's son), aged 11: Ernest Ansermet is the conductor.

earlier *L'Histoire du Soldat*. The second *Eglogue* recalls the Arias of Stravinsky's violin concerto (both this and the *Duo* were written in close collaboration with the American violinist Samuel Dushkin, who toured with the composer during the 1930s). There is a convincing reconciliation of opposites in the final movements. During the *Gigue*, both instruments move in parallel, and the violin's left hand *pizzicati* form a bridge to the percussive piano attacks. In the final *Dithyrambe* the instruments again share the same material and register, the piano's top line often next to the violin's, exchanging carefully notated ornaments and short-spanned scales. It is worth noting that these last two movements are the most conservative of the *Duo*.

Such chaste expression of keyboard and string concord is in striking contrast with Stravinsky's earlier work featuring solo violin, *L'Histoire du Soldat* (1918). Here the violin is one voice of a septet (double-bass, clarinet, bassoon, cornet, trombone, percussion), but in most movements it is the dominating voice. The three dances, Tango, Waltz and Ragtime, are in effect violin solos with decorative commentaries from the other treble instruments and discreet accompaniment from the percussion and bass. The writing is far less well-groomed than in the Dushkin collaborations, for here Stravinsky uses the instrument to fulfill a variety of functions, harmonic and rhythmic as well as melodic—but the collision of such a multitude of roles brings its own excitements and rewards. As the primary voice in a strikingly contrasted ensemble, the violin in *L'Histoire du Soldat* is used to spectacular effect; the stage version of the work, after all, presents the Devil as a virtuoso violinist.

In all its brilliance and originality, *L'Histoire du*

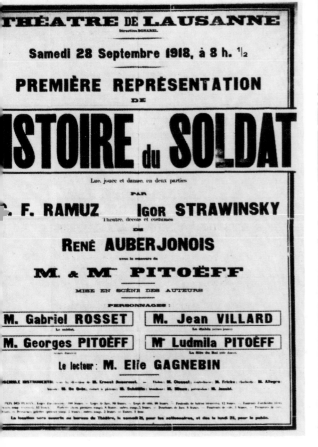

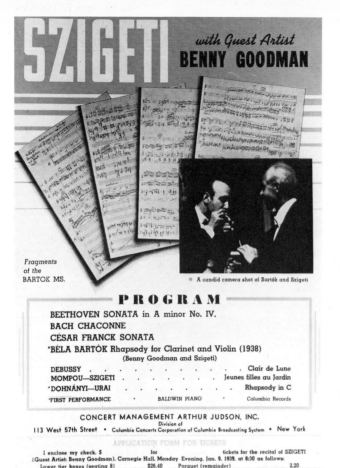

Fragments of the BARTOK MS.

A candid camera shot of Bartók and Szigeti

PROGRAM

BEETHOVEN SONATA in A minor No. IV.
BACH CHACONNE
CÉSAR FRANCK SONATA
*BÉLA BARTÓK Rhapsody for Clarinet and Violin (1938)
(Benny Goodman and Szigeti)

DEBUSSY . . . . Clair de Lune
MOMPOU—SZIGETI . . . . . . Jeunes filles au Jardin
*DOHNÁNYI—URAI . . . . Rhapsody in C
*FIRST PERFORMANCE · BALDWIN PIANO · Columbia Records

CONCERT MANAGEMENT ARTHUR JUDSON, INC.
Division of
113 West 57th Street · Columbia Concerts Corporation of Columbia Broadcasting System · New York

APPLICATION FORM FOR TICKETS

I enclose my check. $ _____ for _____ tickets for the recital of SZIGETI
(Guest Artist: Benny Goodman), Carnegie Hall, Monday Evening, Jan. 9, 1939, at 8:30 as follows:
Lower tier boxes (seating 8) $26.40 Parquet (remainder) 2.20

Soldat is ample demonstration that a composer-pianist can invent new roles for the violin-especially, it would seem, when the piano is absent. The other great composer–pianist who most significantly developed the violin's resources in this century was Béla Bartók. Much of his finest and most characteristic writing for the instrument is to be found in the six string quartets and the two concertos, but the two sonatas for violin and piano, dating from 1920 and 1923, also contain much that is worthy of note.

Bartók's invention was inspired by folk music, but unlike Ravel's pastiche of urban folk music in *Tzigane*, his folk inspiration influenced the construction rather than the manners of his music. Rhythmic and intervallic cells derived from the folk songs Bartók painstakingly transcribed take charge of and shape its very roots. This is associated, especially in the second sonata, with the use of pentatonic and whole-tone scales (contasted pairings of whole-tone scales cast off all sense of tonal anchor at one point in the second sonata's second movement), and with a stylistic expressionism that brings the sound of the music very close to that of the Second Viennese School. The piano writing of both sonatas uses a variety of arpeggiations, solidifying into sharp percussive attacks and angular repetitions, but rarely resolving into simple melody. This is reserved for the violin, and the use of coloristic effects in the part (*tremolo sul ponticello* and the like) never really contradicts the melodic emphasis.

After the two sonatas, Bartók wrote a pair of more conventional Rhapsodies (both published in 1929) and a set of 44 pedagogical Duos (1930). The simplicity and elegance of these works, which make use of Hungarian folk melodies in a more direct way than either of the sonatas, show the deep understanding of violin technique that he had developed by this time. The works were composed at the instigation of the German teacher Erich Doflein, who describes the processes of simplification and distillation the composer went through to achieve his result:

. . . I succeeded in winning Bartók's agreement to the whole idea of writing educational pieces . . . Soon, much to our gratification, Bartók sent us some duos. These pieces now form the last section of the cycle. However, they proved too demanding for the kind of players we had envisaged. The ensuing correspondence was one of the great experiences of my life. We defined the skill that could possibly be achieved in any one stage in a beginner's development and the new tasks he had set himself including fingering in the left hand and bowing in the right. From then on, for a whole year, we received further consignments from Bartók, which gradually became simpler and easier . . . Bartók's progress towards the simplest examples developed within him an even stronger sense of the accessible and the specific. Thereby he reached that ideal state of mind in which the observer may well ask: does the composition determine the task or the task the composition?

Bartók's solo sonata (1944) is his last work for the violin

Szigeti and Bartók outside the Liszt Academy in Budapest, *c.* 1927. *Photo © G. D. Hackett, New York.*

Letter from Bartók to Yehudi Menuhin about the sonata for solo violin (30 June 1944).

and summarizes his contribution to it. Written at the end of his life for Yehudi Menuhin, it consciously seeks out the stylistic framework of a Bach solo sonata, using Baroque forms as an example and precedent for Bartók's own sonorous operations. Though it was not over-enthusiastically received at its premiere, audiences and critics have never had any doubts about the sonata's stature.

The opening *Tempo di ciacona* uses a recurring left-hand *pizzicato* as a reference point, and the composer gives this singular sound a structural as well as a harmonic function. It is both a singularly violinistic touch and an integral part of the music's construction. Doflein's observations about task and composition certainly apply to this demonstration of Bartók's 'orchestration' of a single violin. In terms of technical layout, open, or low-position, fingered strings in rapid alternation with more complex double-stops (a device beloved of cadenza writers of every century) are used in the *ciacona* so pervasively that an illusion of two-part counterpoint twisting over a lower pedal bass is magi-

Autograph of part of Bartók's sonata for solo violin.

cally conjured. The *Fuga* extends this principle within a still more rigorous form, and makes frequent use of alternations between the upper and lower strings, thereby encouraging the performer to characterize the fugal theme in a variety of ways. At its close, the theme on the G-string dances obsessively around an open-string drone maintained by the D- and A-strings—a fine example of imaginative voicing: the G-string in this high position carries strongly against its more resonant but thinner-toned companions.

After these complex textures and strong contrasts, the ensuing *Melodia* inhabits the same grey landscape as the *Adagio* of the *Music for Strings, Percussion and Celeste*. Although it unfolds in a single, virtually unbroken strand, the melody is framed by a variety of delicate effects, each isolated from the other. Muting darkens the instrument's colour and makes all the more ghostly the contrast between high melodies normally played and their continuation in insubstantial harmonics. The use of trills and tremolos pitched a tenth below the primary part has two results: it reduces the feeling of pulse by adding a quick, unmeasured movement to the slower progress, and it necessarily makes the execution of the passage more hazardous, less forthright.

The mute stays on at the start of the concluding *Presto*, and is only removed for the ebullient, *parlando* Hungarian melody that contrasts with the primary subject. The start of the *Presto* is a famous instance of Bartók's use of quarter-tones (another being the cadenza of the second violin concerto). Here they were conceived as an integral part of the main theme, a wedge-shaped sonority moving outwards through quarter-tone steps eventually spanning the interval of a major second. In the published version, edited by Menuhin, conventional semitones are substituted, so that the wedge shape spans a minor third. Bartók excused his original idea to Menuhin as being 'of a colour-giving character', and authorized the change. But the first, more compressed wedge lends a far greater sense of expectancy to the opening, and provides a stronger contrast later on when the material is pushed out over a wider span. It is unfortunate that the only published edition does not even acknowledge the existence of this first, highly effective and characteristic idea.

Bartók was not the only composer in the years between the wars to be interested in folk music. From the violinists' point of view, the Rumanian Georges Enescu (1881–1955) was undoubtedly the most interesting of this group, since he was a virtuoso of great repute and the teacher of Ferras, Gitlis, Grumiaux and Menuhin. As a composer he was not of great significance. His three violin sonatas are, as one would expect, expertly laid out for the instrument, but the first two at least (1897 and 1899) contain little that is original or arresting. The third (1926) is a more mature work, composed '*dans le caractère populaire roumain*'. The premise engenders a plethora of major seconds in every melodic phrase, drowning the music from its opening bars in a powerful brew of gypsy kitsch. Ravel's sense of direction and pacing at the opening of *Tzigane* seems positively austere when compared with the sprawling, formless progress of Enescu's first two movements. The finale progresses more steadily; but a serious lack of harmonic cohesion finally undermines unquestionably eloquent intentions. Perhaps the objectifying focus of a model or collaborator might have helped Enescu, as Szigeti's example a few years earlier had tempered the lush impulses of Ysaÿe. The crucial lesson of Enescu's third sonata is that 'violinistic' writing, however grateful to play, is not by itself enough to guarantee fine music.

A good deal of Czech music for violin was written during the same period—parallel with the school of playing fostered by Ševčík's work in Prague. Among numerous compositions by Vítěslav Novák (1870–1949), Josef Suk (1874–1935), Oskar Nedbal (1874–

Georges Enescu.

Right: Bartók in 1922.

Below: Jack Benny and Szigeti in a scene from *Hollywood Canteen*, 1944 (see page 236).

Sergey Prokofiev: drawing by Henri Matisse

1930) and Bohuslav Martinů (1890–1959), the sonata by Leos Janáček is pre-eminent. Its strikingly youthful idiom (although it was finished in 1914, when Janáček was sixty) and its vein of vibrant fantasy—supported by a great degree of thematic integration which unites both the accompanying tremolo figuration and the tenderest solo melody within a single musical frame—ensure for it a place among the violin masterpieces of the century.

The Polish composer Karol Szymanowski produced a small body of violin music, all of it worthy of attention. His violin sonata of 1904 has the melodic grace of his earlier music, innocent of the later harmonic explorations. The *Nocturne and Tarantella* of 1914 and the three *Mythes* of 1915 are more characteristic of his mature style, which critics tend to classify as 'impressionist' or 'decadent' according to their perspective. This last work especially, written for the Polish virtuoso Paul Kochansky, deserves a more prominent place in the repertory. Also of interest, chiefly to players, are Szymanowski's ingenious variations op. 40 for violin and piano on three of Paganini's solo *Caprices* (nos. 20, 21 and 24) dating from 1918.

Looking eastwards, it is surprising that the excellent group of violinists nurtured by the Moscow Conservatory around the turn of the century did not inspire a more substantial contemporary Russian repertoire for the instrument. Soviet composers often collaborated with leading virtuosos—Khrennikov and Khachaturian wrote concertos for Leonid Kogan, and Oistrakh advised Shostakovitch, Kabalevsky and Myaskovsky on theirs—but this collaboration cannot be said to have produced, in the field of sonatas, especially outstanding results.

Prokofiev's two sonatas, the first written over eight years (1938–46), the second an adaptation of his flute sonata (1946), are notable exceptions in a fairly arid Soviet field; both are highly coloured and individual works, conceived in a fast-moving, conversational style. In the first sonata, the bite and snap of the violin writing fully matches that of the piano. Joseph Szigeti wrote of it: 'A certain adventurousness is needed to bring off some *pizzicato* effects which the composer imagines, but which fail to materialize with orthodox means.' We can see that Debussy's gift of equal status to the atmospheric and rhythmic aspects of the violin has gradually created, here and in the music of Stravinsky and Bartók, a new, percussive role for the instrument. Bartók's special *pizzicato* effect, pulling the string so far away from the instrument that it slaps against the fingerboard when released, is one extreme example of this development. Another is the tricky plucked effect in Prokofiev's first sonata mentioned by Szigeti.

Prokofiev's solo sonata op. 115 (1947) is deliberately simple and strongly contained music, written in the

10.20   A Recital

SOPHIE WYSS (soprano)
ANTONIO BROSA (violin)
BENJAMIN BRITTEN (pianoforte)

ANTONIO BROSA AND BENJAMIN BRITTEN
Sonata in G, Op. 30, No. 3 . . Beethoven
1. Allegro assai ; 2. Tempo di minuetto, ma molto moderato e grazioso ;
3. Allegro vivace

10.40   SOPHIE WYSS

Ich ging mit Lust durch einen
  grünen Wald
Phantasie   } Mahler
Um schlimme Kinder artig
  zu machen

The Birds . . . . Britten
Daphne   }
Through gilded Trellis } . . . . . Walton

10.55   ANTONIO BROSA AND BENJAMIN BRITTEN

Suite for Violin and Pianoforte,
Op. 6 . . . . Britten
1. Introduction ; 2. March ; 3. Moto
perpetuo ; 4. Lullaby ; 5. Waltz

(First performance of complete work)

Benjamin Britten's Suite for violin and piano was begun in Vienna in November, 1934, and completed in London in June, 1935. The violin part affords the soloist plenty of opportunities for a display of virtuosity, and the idiom throughout is distinctly 'modern'. The work is among those chosen for performance at the forthcoming International Contemporary Music Festival in Barcelona.

'open' key of D major and intended primarily for teaching purposes. The main material of each of the three movements is diatonic: only in the five variations of the middle movement does a surprising, charming Neoclassicism (reminiscent of *Romeo and Juliet*) emerge.

Other Soviet works include sonatas by Karen Khachaturian (1957), Evgeny Golubev (1953), Dimitri Shostakovitch (1969) and Galina Ustvolskaya (1966). Alfred Shnitke's short first sonata (1963) and his quixotic second (*Quasi una sonata*, 1968), which juxtaposes tonal and atonal harmonies, are a glimmer of light at the end of this fairly dark tunnel.

Virtually all of the composers of the twentieth-century English musical renaissance wrote a single major sonata for violin and piano each. Only the cosmopolitan Delius broke this mould, writing three beautiful but constrained works (1905–15, 1924, 1930)—although one senses that Delius really aspired to a more thickly textured, more richly coloured and shaded medium than the violin and piano as the ideal vehicle for his ideas.

The standard of British string playing at the start of the century was not uniformly high, and British teaching hardly matched the work of important European pedagogues like Auer, Ysaÿe and Flesch. Virtuosos visited London and other major concert centres, but a significant difference of sound and attack can be heard if the old recordings of Albert Sammons, for example, are compared with those of Kreisler or the young Milstein. Sammon's playing is softer and more pliable; but the tone is not as emphatically 'centred' as that of his European counterparts.

That is not to call Sammons a 'lesser' player. Beecham often remarked that the tonal quality he obtained from the strings of the London Philharmonic Orchestra in the 1930s, when Sammons led it, suited Delius's orchestral writing perfectly, while the more vibrant and pressured sound produced by Auer-influenced European string sections made such delicate music wilt. But the softness and subtlety of the playing of the British school rarely led to the production of major virtuosos; nor did it match up to the fierce, percussive demands made by composers like Bartók or Stravinsky. Just as Liszt's piano music not merely presupposed, but actually called into existence, the modern concert grand, so those composers summoned

197

Ralph Vaughan Williams and Frederick Grinke.

Opposite top: William Walton: portrait by Michael Ayrton, 1948.

Opposite below: Schoenberg in 1930.

the metal E-strings, the sharper percassive attack and faster *vibrato* of the twentieth-century violin.

Of Edward Elgar's sonata (1918), only the middle *Romanze* is fully worthy to stand beside that composer's fine violin concerto: elsewhere a desire to write 'good violin music', liberally larded with arpeggios, renders the texture monotonous and the harmonic progress laborious.

Benjamin Britten's Suite for violin and piano dates from his twenty-first year (1934/5). A serious piece, sparkling with youthful energy, it is set out as a series of fantasies on a motto, the notes E, F, B and C, which permeates both the opening March and the *Moto perpetuo*. By using a pair of semitones separated by an augmented fourth as his basic material (intervals which fit fairly comfortably under the fingers and across the strings), Britten is able to spin out a good deal of difficult but well-crafted and playable passage-work. After a stratospheric and rather curious *Lullabye*—the quiet, high-altitude writing is certainly hypnotic, and must

test any player's concentration—there is a final movement which casually mixes fragments of the motto into a dry and witty *Waltz*. Towards the end, a short slow passage reinforces the motto's domination.

Like Bartók's solo sonata, William Walton's sonata for violin and piano (1949) was written for Yehudi Menuhin. It is cast in two movements, both predominantly Romantic and vocal in style (an original scherzo third movement was removed and combined with another short work, to make the *Two Pieces* of 1949/50). Although Walton was never a prolific composer, this sonata was written after an unusually unproductive period of his career: except for the immediately preceding string quartet, he had composed little of consequence since 1939. It is therefore surprising to find long sections of the second movement using Schoenberg's twelve-tone technique. A set of twelve pitches, including all the semitones of the tempered scale, makes up an *ostinato* against which a series of variations unfolds; the movement ends as the sonata began, unambiguously in

B flat major. This brief flirtation with a then controversial technique was apparently not the stimulus Walton was seeking, and the experiment was never repeated.

Though he was the leading British composer of his generation (and an archivist of folk song almost of the distinction of Bartók), Ralph Vaughan Williams produced only one violin sonata, late in his life (1954). It was first played by Frederick Grinke, an exceptional musician who, like Louis Krasner in the United States, did much to encourage new work. An ample, expertly constructed piece, it nevertheless lacks the energy and cohesiveness that makes the similarly late sonatas of Debussy and Ravel so compelling.

The music that has been dealt with up to this point reflects the development of a tradition, the expansion of a heritage. The significant musical revolution of the first half of the twentieth century, Arnold Schoenberg's establishment of twelve-tone compositional principles, was primarily concerned with the harmonic process. (Only later, and especially after the second World War, did it begin to influence the realms of structure, timbre, dynamics and articulation.) As a result, it is to be expected that the preferred vehicle of Schoenberg's revolution would be the piano, and that his new system would not substantially alter the nature of writing for the violin.

The requirements of composers, none the less, have always necessitated changes in playing technique. Schoenberg's granting of equal compositional status to each of the tempered semitones paralleled similarly

Below: Louis Krasner, backstage during the rehearsal for the premiere of Schoenberg's violin concerto with the Philadelphia Orchestra under Stokowski.

Right: Anton Webern: black chalk drawing by Egon Schiele, 1918.

important changes in violin fingering. As Ševčík's Prague-based work had given greater freedom to the left hand, so Carl Flesch's *Art of Violin Playing* (published in Berlin in 1923) recommended neatly fingered chromatic runs, as opposed to the untidier confection of small slides between fingerings and irregular shifts traditionally used to accommodate such passages. (As always, such changes should not necessarily be regarded as 'improvements': different techniques suit different styles.)

A few of Schoenberg's compositions show a positive disdain for the instrument's capabilities. In the Chamber Symphony op. 9 (1906) he optimistically expects the first violin to carry important material which must be clearly heard against a ten-strong wind section, including many instruments with far weightier timbres. Even the finest players and most careful conductors find this a risky balancing act.

Later, after composing the violin concerto (1936), which he described as needing 'a six-fingered violinist', Schoenberg wrote his *Fantasy* for violin and piano (1949). (Both were first played by Louis Krasner, an American virtuoso who also premiered Berg's violin concerto.) The *Fantasy* is both more classically simple and more expressively relaxed than his earlier works.

Since the violin part was the first one to be composed, it is not surprising that the violin always leads: the full title of *Fantasy for violin with piano accompaniment* is no exaggeration. The difficulties of the music are not, as it were, athletic. It can be played by a musician who is not a virtuoso: but it is hard to conceive of a good performance by a player who reverses those attributes. The problems are ones of tuning wide leaps and awkward intervals, of balancing chords in which one of the notes is a harmonic and the other produced normally. The work is in one movement, divided into five sections; the music moves smoothly, with a sense of emotional inevitability not always associated with the composer's earlier, expressionistic works, and the condensed repeat of the opening section at the end provides a convincing frame for the whole. As with much of Schoenberg's later music, we discover in it a decidedly Viennese grace and lilt as soon as we accustom ourselves to the 'radical' harmony.

In 1910, while he was still Schoenberg's pupil, Anton Webern composed his *Four Pieces* for violin and piano op. 7. This remarkable work predates the majority of the compositions so far mentioned, but it belongs in very essence to the twentieth century. Though contemporary with such late-Romantic effusions as Mahler's eighth

The Rosé Quartet: etching by Max Oppenheimer, *c.* 1930.

symphony and Richard Strauss's *Rosenkavalier*, it is the distillation of an entirely contrary aim. Webern's four movements are respectively nine, twenty-four, fourteen and fifteen measures long; together they last no more than five minutes. Within each movement, shifts of tempo and articulation further fragment the material; the players' perception and control of the music are constantly challenged by split-second changes of dynamic.

It is not surprising that the violinist who intended to give the premiere of Webern's op. 7, the distinguished Arnold Rosé (Mahler's brother-in-law and a leader of the Vienna Philharmonic), cancelled his appearance at short notice—though to his credit, Rosé later played the work with Webern accompanying him at the piano. The uncomfortable character of the music is easily explained: for both violin and piano are here

The second of Webern's *Four Pieces* op. 7.

stripped entirely of their rhetorical heritage. The two instruments are used purely as *sources of sound*, without thought for their repertory of effects and figurations, traditions and manners. But the *Four Pieces* are also fine violin music. The difficulties presented by Webern's dynamic scheme could hardly be realized so accurately or so purely by any other solo instrument—it is the bow arm's ability to change speed, pressure or attack that makes the physical sounding of such ideas possible without wholesale orchestration. One could hardly imagine this line (see below) rendered by the flute, oboe or clarinet, or even by a combination of the three.

The use of the violin and other string instruments principally as a sound-source, freed from the preconceptions of their traditional repertoire, is an easier imaginative leap for a composer to make when more than one instrument is involved. Stravinsky's massed *glissandi* harmonics in *The Firebird* (1910) and the very opening of Mahler's first symphony (1885–1888), which confronts the listener with a still, immovable wall of A's spread over some six octaves, are examples of such a technique applied to a large string section. A later

instance is the *Epode* of Messiaen's *Chronochromie* (1960), in which each of the twelve violins, as well as four violas and two cellos, play a different bird call in individual rhythm. This dawn-chorus multiplicity suits the uniform tone colour of massed strings especially well. If the same notes were played, for example, by contrasting pairs of woodwind, the dissimilar overtone structures of each instrument would over-colour the sound, resulting in a uniform brown texture, like mixed plasticine. If the composer balanced the woodwind more carefully, they might risk resembling another famous dawn chorus in Ravel's *Daphnis et Chloë*. So Messiaen's solution is both practical and novel: even if in some ways it inevitably recalls the common ancestor of all such coloristic effects, the seething arpeggios with which Wagner depicted Loge's Magic Fire in *Die Walküre*.

Hindemith was the German-speaking composer most removed from Webern's ground-breaking aesthetic. An accomplished violinist and extremely prolific writer, he seems now as a composer to have been locked within an honest but ultimately barren tradition. The linear classicism of his two solo sonatas op. 31 (1924) has little

Hindemith playing the violin: drawing by Benedikt Dolbin, 1928.

Charles Ives's confrontation at the turn of the century was a classic example:

Generally speaking, this [third] sonata was a slump back due, I am certain, to a visit in Redding in August 1914 from a typical hard-boiled, narrow-minded, conceited prima donna solo violinist with a reputation gained because he came to this country from Germany with Anton Seidl as his concertmaster. He has given concerts at Carnegie Hall (forty years ago), where he played the usual kind of program and everybody applauded, etc. etc. Mrs Ives knew him at Hartford, and as I'd had so much trouble with musicians playing my music, we thought it would be a good plan to get one of the supposedly great players. Before finishing the third sonata, I wanted to have the first and second played over.

The 'Professor' came in and, after a lot of big talk, started to play the first movement of the first sonata. He didn't even get through the first page. He was all bothered with the rhythms and notes, and got mad. He said, 'This cannot be played. This is awful. It is not music, it makes no sense.' He couldn't even get it after I'd played it over for him several times . . . After he went, I had a kind of feeling which I've had off and on when other more or less celebrated (or well known) musicians have seen or played (or tried to play) my music. I felt (but only temporarily) that perhaps there must be something wrong with me . . . I began to feel more and more, after seances with nice musicians, that, if I wanted to write music that, to me, seemed worth while, I must keep away from musicians.

(Memos)

Indeed, by his own standards, Ives's four sonatas are, seen as a whole, somewhat tame. The violin writing has none of the exuberant freedom and zany self-assertiveness that makes the second string quartet so individual. For the most part the instrument is well behaved, singing New England hymns with simple expressiveness. The piano rumbles through a greater range of sonorities, but again the music seems thinner, in both texture and content, than that in the best Ives piano parts. The impression is of sonatas designed to travel no farther than the front room parlour. Ives admits as much in his *Memos*: 'The last movement (of the third) especially shows a kind of reversion. The themes are well enough, but there is an attempt to please the soft-ears and be good.'

Two violin sonatas composed in 1923 by George Antheil (1900–59) shed their inhibitions much more eagerly. An American pianist–composer who was also part of the Parisian avant-garde in the 1920s, Antheil's recently resurrected sonatas are the incarnation of percussive violin writing. They were written for Olga Rudge, then Ezra Pound's mistress. Pound (who

of the freewheeling extravagance of Ysaÿe's exactly contemporary work; nor does their invention compare with that of Bartók's equally severe neo-Baroque composition of twenty years later. The four sonatas for violin and piano hark back to the tonal and rhythmic certitudes of the world of Brahms, without any of that composer's beguiling sweetness. They can perhaps be cited as examples of a composer-violinist whose imagination was circumscribed rather than fired by close contact with his instrument. (Hindemith was an equally good violist, cellist and keyboard player, and no mean conductor.)

An entirely different kind of circumscription is to be seen in the perennial twentieth-century conflict of composer-composer with performer-performer.

contrast between the violin and the piano, both stringed instruments, is fundamentally a gestural one—between stroking and striking. Using a great variety of bow strokes, the violin can be made to produce many different types of attack; it can also prolong its sounds and give them a variety of tone colours and inflections, such as swelling and fading or becoming more, or less, intense. On the other hand, the finger of the pianist strikes a key that catapults a felt-covered hammer up to the string more or less suddenly and forcefully, depending on how the key is struck. Once the hammer has started the string vibrating, the player has no further control over the sound—which immediately begins to die away—except that he can cut short this decay by raising the finger from the key, activating the damper.

Carter's intentions are not far from Stravinsky's in the conception of his *Duo Concertant*, but the plan of execution is far more detailed and exhaustive. For the first 80 bars or so, the two instruments could not be more differently treated. The piano's inability to sustain long-held chords is called to notice by the very first violin note, an expansive open D bowed 'with many changes of colour and character'. The violin moves quickly through many different rhythms and articulations, the expressive nuances of the line pointed by specific verbal instructions. During all of this the piano behaves rather stiffly, diffidently, like a wallflower at a party. Then suddenly, in the space of about ten bars, the partners begin to dance, sharing and exchanging rhythmic and intervallic patterns. The piano part, too, begins to explore a comparably wide variety of articulations and densities.

In the course of the work, the violin focuses on one aspect of its part after another—and often on two or more aspects at a time—playing in *rubato*, rhythmically irregular style, while the piano constantly plays regular beats, sometimes fast, sometimes slow. Toward the end, while the violin is involved in a very fast and impassioned music, the piano becomes more and more detached, playing a series of regular rhythmic patterns, each successively slower than the previous one. As the piano reaches a point of extreme slowness, the violin is heard increasingly alone, isolating for a few measures at a time the various elements of its part, with the quiet and more lyrical aspects given more prominence than previously.

It is worth noting that the remarkable sense of intimate exchange to be found in Carter's *Duo* is achieved more by what might be called narrative than by coloristic means. Extreme effects are avoided; great importance is placed instead on each instrument's characteristic diction, as distinct from its rhetoric. The very independence of the two partners serves to

reckoned himself to be something of a music critic at the time) was enlisted to turn pages for the accompanying Antheil, and then to contribute a solo on the tom-toms during the wistful, modal coda at the close of the second sonata. Both works are colourful and eclectic, full of toccata-like repetitions and fierce dissonances. Perhaps the most arresting feature of the first sonata is the use of a rapid piano *glissando* to wind the music up to a high pitch of tension. Later, unpredictable stops and starts give the music the animation of a badly projected, speeded-up silent film.

Experimental futurism of this sort played little part in the rest of American violin literature. Apart from Antheil's blessedly loony tunes, many good American composers, including Henry Cowell (a sonata written in 1945) and Aaron Copland (his sonata of 1943), seem to have been almost as inhibited as Ives was at the start of the century.

Elliott Carter's *Duo* (1974) represents a notable break from this confinement; and not surprisingly, its principal concern is to examine, and at once to contrast and reconcile, the fundamental natures of the two instruments. The composer recounts that

It was considered a matter of great importance that the expression and thought arise from the unique sound and performance techniques . . . of the piano and the violin. There was a desire to get down to the physical origins of musical sound and take off from there . . . In the *Duo*, the

John Cage.

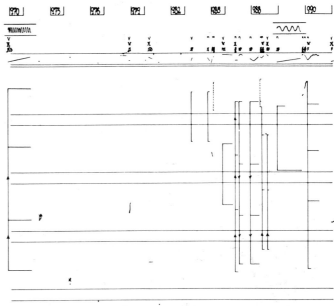

intensify their points of mutual agreement, yet also to motivate the progress of the music as a whole.

John Cage is another American composer who has, on a few valuable occasions, returned to fundamentals. Since Cage's main aesthetic premise has always been to have no premise, the musical results are by their nature less susceptible to analysis than Carter's, but no less thought-provoking. His *Nocturne* (1947) and *Six Melodies* (1950), both for violin with piano, are works conceived in what will probably come to be labelled the composer's 'second period': that time during and just after the second World War when a preoccupation with small gestures, and quiet, reposeful sounds, was paramount.

The *Nocturne* floats comfortably in a warm bath of whole-tone chords and incantations; in *Six Melodies* the violin plays, without *vibrato*, in 'white', disembodied tone, a sequence of mechanically repeated tunes. Tricky rhythmic irregularities are worn gracefully. The flat, modest sound of these *Melodies* comes as close as music can to resembling the calm, primary-coloured geometry of Mondrian's paintings.

After this, Cage produced a series of pieces that questioned the very act itself, and all its associated operations, of performing music. *59½″ for a string player* (1953) and *26′ 1.1499″ for a string player* (1955) are graphs of playing instructions written in time-space notation (that is, two centimetres horizontally on the page equals one unit of the metronome mark given). The production of tones on each of the four strings is

separately graphed, as are sounds to be made on the body of the instrument and bow pressure. Few conventional symbols are used, for the aim is to represent not the result the player should achieve, the goal of performance, but rather to indicate, precisely, various physical activities of playing. In these works, dislocation of the instrumentalist's traditional performing criteria is all but complete. The *why* disappears entirely, and the *how* takes its place.

In recent years Cage has formed a productive association with one of the few virtuoso violinists willing to maintain active collaborations in the field of new music, Paul Zukovsky. A startling fruit of this partnership is the six-minute-long *Chorals* of 1978. The music is a version for violin of an earlier abstract made by Cage of Erik Satie's *12 Petits Chorals*. The result is a sequence of simple notes, unisons and 'beats' (produced by playing conventionally tuned simple intervals, octaves, fifths and fourths microtonally wrong, so that the oscillations beat against one another). In performance, the piece sounds dangerously like a very adept innocent's first encounter with the instrument. But when *Chorals* is played with a sure technique, the surprising juxtaposition of 'acceptable' sounds (the single tones) with the sort of piercing intervals that have been strenuously banned from violin playing and from Western music itself for so many centuries, has a delightful and refreshing effect.

More stable and, as a result, more consonant-seeming use of microtonal tuning has been made by the

From Boulez's *Domaines* (1968).

Opposite: A page from the full score of *Pithoprakta* by Xenakis.

Hungarian composer György Ligeti. His *Ramifications* (1968/9) for 12 solo strings tunes half the ensemble of players a quarter-tone higher than normal pitch. The paradoxical result of such pervasive *scordatura*, less shocking than Cage's, less purely colorist than Bartók's, is a uniquely homogeneous texture. The density and almost tactile quality of the sound is enhanced by the busy, rushing counterpoint as each instrumental voice tumbles over its companions with lemming-like intensity. As in Messiaen's *Chronochromie*, the uniform tonal qualities of the instruments contribute markedly to the effect: a heterophony of movement within a stable, homogeneous timbral frame.

There is a similar density to the texture of *Violin Phase* (1967) by Steve Reich, although the music is tonal in character and more calmly articulated. The work is intended either for solo violin with a shifting background of pre-recorded tape, or for a quartet of violinists. The background consists of the 'phasing' (gradual movement in and out of perfect synchronization) of a simple repeated melodic pattern, which overlaps in a kind of 'phased canon', or round, to produce still denser chords and patterns cross-hatched with slowly shifting interior lines. The soloist joins in this aural weaving to provide subtle reinforcement and connection, and is free after a while to abstract notes from the shifting background, to point out chance aural coincidences, or to propose other connections between overlapping phrases. This music has the strength of being entirely self-referential: it creates its own context, and then, with various degrees of freedom, constructs its own self-commentary. Although Reich provides a written-out part that can be played as it stands, he also invites the inclusion of considered alternatives.

The avant-garde of post-war Europe tended by and large to ignore the solo violin in favour of brighter and more percussive colours and instruments. The first wave of total serialism indeed, associating the violin too closely for comfort with its legacy of 'expressiveness', avoided it entirely. Since the attentions of Pierre Boulez and Karlheinz Stockhausen have been directed mainly towards piano-based chamber ensembles, the violin appears chiefly in their orchestral works. One may note (see below) a characteristically Boulezian violin shape from *Domaines* (1968). The doubling of lines creates an effect far stronger than that of simple reinforcement, while the fast grace notes and brilliant trills are beautifully laid out for the instrument. One might also note that the violin has played a significant part in Stockhausen's dreams, if not in his solo music. The extraordinary double curtain of gauze and sound, coloured aurally and visually a deep mauve, which is fundamental to his orchestral theatre-piece *Trans* (1971), could never have been conceived without the sustaining power of stringed instruments.

A great part of the music of Iannis Xenakis (who, like Stockhausen and Boulez, was also a pupil of Messiaen) is similarly indivisible from the nature and potential of the violin. Pitch flexibility and density are essentials, as they are in Ligeti's *Ramifications* and Messiaen's *Chronochromie*, since the plan of Xenakis's music in the 1950s was literally architectural.

His work at that time, in music as well as building design, was concerned with the flow of large vectors around fixed points. Every powerful shaft of sound is made up of a large number of smaller sounds, constructed either of points (attacks) or lines of sound (often string *glissandi*): compare the graph of string *glissandi* at bars 52–5 of *Pithoprakta* (fig. 5) with Xenakis's designs for the Philips Pavilion made in the same year (fig. 6). *Pithoprakta* (1956) is scored for 24 violins, eight cellos, six double-basses, a pair of percussionists and two tenor trombones, each with an individual part (fig. 4). In the pages of this score, string

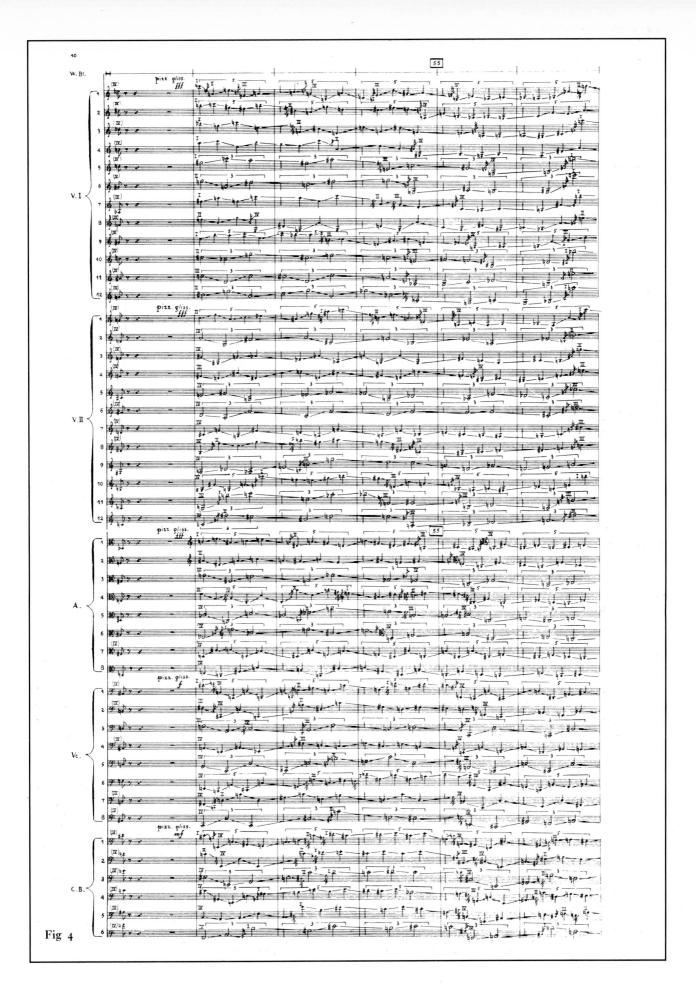

Fig 4

Graph of bars of 52–5 of Xenakis's *Pithoprakta*.

Right: Part of Xenakis's design (1956) for the Phillips Pavillion at the Brussels World Exhibition, 1958.

Opposite: Violinist at the window: Henri Matisse, 1917–18.

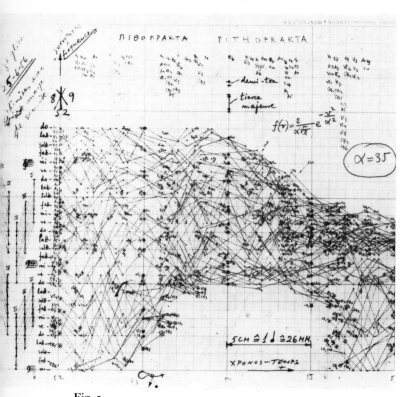

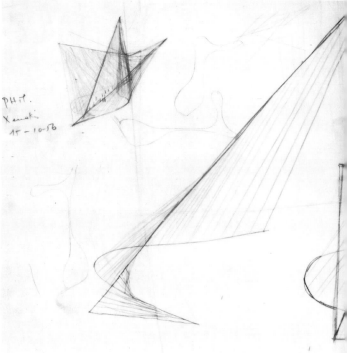

Fig 5

Fig 6

instruments are freed still more decisively than they had been by Webern's op. 7 from their traditional harmonic and melodic roles; and in this sense *Pithoprakta*, as well as the earlier *Metastasis* of 1954, have both proved seminal works of the second half of the twentieth century.

In a series of works for string or string-dominated ensemble, among them *Syrmos* (1959) and *Aroura* (1971), Xenakis has further explored and refined the potentials of violin writing. He has developed in this radical body of work a new violin rhetoric, at times governed by mathematical theory (for example, that concerning the behaviour of large masses) but always of unusual expressive potential: towering arches, fierce *glissandi*, bird-like swoops, clouds of tiny *pizzicati* and powerful strides of parallel but rarely uniform movement. Two works for solo violin, *Mikka* (1971) and *Mikka S* (1976), bring these expressive aims within the range of the single instrument. The violin is once again renewed, as it had been in the music of Bach, Ysaÿe and Bartók, by an instinctive return to contrapuntal texture and to the myriad sonorities which can exist within a single gesture.

Such new and original perspectives have, it would seem, successfully stimulated greater interest in the violin, especially among younger composers. Recent works by Reinhard Febel (*Polyphonie*, 1980), Robin Holloway (sonata, 1982), Oliver Knussen (*Autumnal*, 1976/7), Rolf Gehlhaar (*Naïre*, 1983), Ladislaw Kupkovic (*Morceau de genre*, 1968; *Souvenir*, 1970) and Yuji Takahashi (*Sieben Rosen hat ein Strauss*, 1982) all attest to the continuing validity of the violin as a compositional medium. *All the trees they are so high* (1977) by the young British composer Michael Finnissy is another recent example of a fresh and imaginative response to the instrument. A wandering folksong, cut with Bartókian quarter-tones, is spun out over a ground of open-string drones; two 'cadenzas' follow, the first fast and light, the second more stately in pulse but no less rapid in movement. It is a short work, but the variety of articulation is exceptionally wide: the drones and the breathless quality of the cadenzas suggest the ghost of a post-tonal folk fiddler.

That the violin is able to encompass, at this mature stage of its life, so wide a range of musics and attitudes, is testimony to its undiminished vitality and potential. Not long ago, John Cage wrote: 'Paul Zukovsky . . . asked whether I would consider making him a . . . work for the violin. I am now engaged in that work. But in order to do it, I study under Zukovsky's patient tutelage, not how to play the violin, but how to become even more baffled by its almost unlimited flexibility.'

From Folk Fiddle
to Jazz Violin

Fiddlin' Jake and George Baize at the Ozark Folk Festival,
Eureka Springs, Arkansas, 1952.

Grass roots and the Fiddling Devil

The fundamental musical instrument is, of course, the
human voice, which almost all men and women are
endowed with. Following in the voice's wake are those
wind instruments—pipes, flutes, trumpets, horns—
which emulate the construction of the human vocal
organs in applying wind from the player's lungs to
produce a vibrating column of air. Wind instruments
which introduce reeds, such as oboes, combine the
human feature of a vibrating column of air with the
vibrating strings of the vocal chords; vibrating columns
and vibrating reeds on man-made instruments may
enlarge vocal resources, but do not introduce any
radically different principle.

Though the origins of bowed string instruments are
shrouded in the mists of antiquity, it would seem that
they represent a slightly more advanced stage of musical
consciousness, in that in them duality is more overt. A
singer, driving air through the vocal chords, remains
a unity; a fiddler, scraping a bow held in one hand over
strings attached to a wooden frame held in the other,
is a duality—relatable to, though less crude than, the
twoness of the drummer's stick and the sphere of air
enclosed within the drum's membrane. Similarly the
bow agitates, through the agency of the string, a volume
of air enclosed within the body of the violin: with the
difference that the bow, operated by the right hand, is
not a relatively insensitive promoter of action like the
drummer's stick, but a life-force in its own right.

Instruments of the viol and violin family are characterized by the fact that they produce musical sounds
from an interaction of two forces: the passively female
form of the instrument, the parts of which (belly, back,
shoulders, rib, neck) are named after the human body,*
and the active male will of the bow. Herbert Whone,
in his fascinating book *The Hidden Face of Music*, has
discussed why and how the triumph of the violin
coincided with the flowering of humanism in Europe's
post-Renaissance:

Whether we see the word 'violin' as coming from 'vol'
(German root) or 'vil' (Italian root), the violin is essentially
to do with will. The playing of the violin is the enactment
of life itself. The bow, operating on the right side, the side
of power, stimulates the universal female womb (left side),
giving life to all potential forms within it, symbolized by the
fingers of the left hand. With the substance wooed by the
will, and the ensuing form vitalized, the work is complete—
a perfected man in whom every second of consciousness, like
every second the bow is on the string, is a second in time
and in eternity. The raw polarized drum and stick has
become a marriage of instrument and bow.

This explains why in the more primitive folk-cultures
bowed string instruments are less conspicuous than
human voices and pipes, and are used mostly to play
drones rather than to articulate melody or define
rhythm. Folk consciousness, rooted in man's presumed
unity with Nature, would like to efface duality if it
could: whereas duality is inherent in the fact that the
will of the fiddler's bowing right hand attacks on the
right side the previously unravished bride of quietude.
The age-old, world-wide legends that associate fiddling
humans—from spell-weaving gypsies to necromantic
Tartini and Paganini—with the devil cannot be
fortuitous. Violin-scraping gypsies always were and still
are regarded as magicians, black rather than white; of
their nature they are tawny outsiders beyond the pale
of social conformity, mysterious in belonging to
another, indeterminate and darker race. Often they gravi-
tate from the enclosed, self-contained rural community
to the periphery of cities; their music corrupts folk
music's pristine (pentatonic, additive-rhythmed) sim-
plicities with the taint of harmonically-tending tonality.

Folk fiddling in the obscurer regions of central
Europe still reflects this today. A startling concatenation
of rural tradition with urban pop, with gypsy outra-
geousness as catalyst, may be heard in an Albanian
example which amounts to a jam-session for folk clarinet
and folk lute, with urban violin and accordion.[1] The
reed instrument takes the main line, ornate, screechy,
bibulous; the accordion and lute provide a discreet
background; the violin, low in register and dark in
timbre, comments insidiously on the clarinet's squawky
ecstasy. A similarly gypsyish, orient-inclined tang is
found in middle-European fiddling whether or not gypsies are present—as is evident in wedding dances played
on violin and clarinet in the frontier lands between
Albania, Jugoslavia and Greece.[2]

To our ears at least, this music sounds dangerously
inebriated. Tempi are very fast, whirling the dancers
like dervishes; violin and clarinet gibber in a rasping
heterophony, high and strained, like strangled birds.
The tone-colour of reed and string instrument is
similar: rawly penetrating, on edge with microtonal distonations. The violinist uses virtually no *vibrato*, and
employs double-stops to drone-like rather than
harmonic effect. Across the border into Greece the folk
fiddle reflects similar traditions, but in styles that sound

---

*But, interestingly enough, only in English. In other European languages,
the parts of the violin are denoted by a neutral, technical vocabulary that
ignores the parallels entirely.

Hardanger fiddler Søren Nomeland.

Below: fiddle and lyra players leading a Cretan wedding procession.

to us less distraught, possibly because life is less climatically arduous, and links with the Mediterranean past are warmer and stronger. Wedding dances may be highly ornamented, but are comparatively fluid in line and dulcet in tone;[3] when a more primitive rebec-like fiddle produces a thin, pinched tone it does not lacerate.[4] The reiterated rhythmic patterns—often irregular, in various permutations of fives and sevens—generate an excitement that is both stimulating and ordered in its hypnotic repetitiveness. It is interesting, perhaps significant, that 'spontaneous' peoples, living close to the earth, relish dancing in additive metres, especially magic fives and sevens, whereas we products of ordered civilization seldom advance, among the uneven numbers, beyond three; and even then we often feel the metre in sixes (two times three) or twelves (four times three), thereby affirming our preference for symmetrically marshalled twos, fours and eights. The collocation of uneven and even is noticeable in the merry music of cafés and radio networks such as one can hear nearly everywhere in present-day Jugoslavia. In such musics[5] corporeal energy is undiminished, and rhythms may intermittently explode in erratic ebullience. But the violin line tends to be unambiguously diatonic, without microtones except in the crude form of sobs and scoops, while the tone is open, even sweet, seeking after 'Western' expressivity. Even in these relatively commercialized areas one lights, however, on the occasional wild throwback as in a *Pravo tivesko*[6] played with traditionally scrawny tone and indeterminate pitch, the line noodling around an unchanging nodal point. The bowing is short, thrustfully stabbing; central Europe here merges not only with the 'outsiderism' of the gypsies but also with quasi-oriental Turkey.

The Northern Fiddle: a music of sea and sky

It is possible that the origins of the bow—applied to stringed instruments originally devised to be plucked rather than scraped—are in the Orient: which would accord with our account of bowed-string music's gypsy-like subversiveness. The origins of the fiddle, in anything resembling the forms we recognize, are obscure, though northern countries may establish strong claims to precedence. Ancient fiddle-like instruments, at first plucked rather than bowed, were known in Sweden as *talharpa*, in Finland as *jouhikantele*, in Wales as *crwth*, in Ireland as *cruit*, and in the Shetlands as *crot*, *gue* or *goe*. As early as the sixth century we find a reference to an Irish *fidel*-like instrument, almost certainly plucked, but with four strings like the modern violin.

Peruvian folk fiddler with harp (played upside-down as the player walks). The violin seems to have been introduced into Latin America by the Jesuits in the seventeenth century, and was taken up notably by the Cora and the Peruvian Indians.

Norway and Scotland: countries which, from the sixteenth to the nineteenth century, were culturally interlinked, and remained small and cohesive enough to permit, even promote, interfusion of rural with urban culture. In Norway there are still two distinct instruments reflecting the two disparate yet complementary rural and urban worlds. The folk or Hardanger fiddle (*hardingfele*) remains prevalent in western Norway and in the mid-country valleys. It is related to the *landeleik*, the oldest and most rudimentary, lute-like instrument of Scandinavia, which had a long narrow case without neck, one melody string stretched over the fingerboard, and a number of open strings used for drones. The melody was plucked with the fingers of the left hand, while the right hand accompanied with a plectrum on the open strings. The Hardanger fiddle shares with this primitive instrument the short neck and the sympathetic strings; the flat bridge makes double-stops easily negotiable, and the short bow lends itself to rapid articulation rather than to expressive cantilena. The basic strings are four in number, as on the modern violin, but are usually tuned E, A, D, A or E, A, E, A (from the top downwards)—arrangements that accord readily with drones either on single notes or on double-stopped fourths and fifths.

Although there are links between fiddle tunes and folk songs, especially repetitive songs of a lullaby-like nature, the music created for and by this instrument is basically dance music. The *gangar*, *springar*, *halling* and *pols* are triple-rhythmed dances characterized by an outward-directed vigour. The resonance of the *hardingfele*, agile in line, tremulous in sonority, has a grandeur apt to open spaces and perhaps reminiscent, like the sung ballads, of magical and mythological events. Though the old, heroic bardic tradition is, in vocal music, almost obsolete, if one listens to Magne Mannheim's *hardingfele* version of *A so sulla ho mor* after hearing it sung by Talleiv Roysland, one can recognize how the genius of the instrument transcends the sung words.[7] In *Kvenneslatten*, a *springar* dance played by Gunnar Dahle, the heroic qualities of this music become wilder, more dangerous; weirdly whining microtones and oscillating, dissonance-disturbed drones suggest wizardry and the fabulous elements in Viking mythology, so that the cooler Nordic tradition approximates to fervent gypsy outlawism.[8] Trolls and goblins seem active too in a *hardingfele* trio, *Myllagutens bruremarsj*,[9] and to a lesser degree in Kjetil Londal's *halling*, *Sevliden*,[10] and Torleiv Bjorgum's *gangar*, *Tveitlien*.[11] In such fabled forms does the fiddling devil appear in northern climes, chattering in eldritch

The Scandinavian and Celtic *crwth*-style instruments had anything from two to six strings, though if there were more than four, the extra strings were placed not on but at the side of the fingerboard, to be plucked or possibly bowed as occasion offered. There can be no precise date at which the bow's dominance over the strings was irrevocably affirmed. It seems probable however that this occurred decisively in Celtic Britain, migrating thence to Scandinavia and so to the East. On reflexion it makes sense (since bowed string instruments represent a comparatively late stage of evolution) that the folk fiddle should be a northern and western phenomenon. Oriental folk consciousness eschews duality so far as is possible; northern-western folk consciousness is more prepared to accept and cope with it, if not to revel in it. Though for some centuries fiddles were used, in Britain and Scandinavia, in emulation of voices, flutes and bagpipes, it was inevitable that their nature as a duality of bow and strings with soundboard should eventually be manifest.

The transitional process is strikingly evident in

213

abandon rather than murmuring with gypsy guile. Grieg, whose recourse to Nordic mythology was usually regressive, late in his life made an astonishingly immediate re-creation of this wild undercurrent to Norwegian folklore in the form of arrangements of Hardanger fiddle music for piano. His *Slåtter* can be compared with the folk-song arrangements of Bartók, for Grieg does not attempt to sophisticate or sentimentalize the music's drones or its telescoped tonics and dominants and acrid tritonal arabesques with ripe piano sonorities and nostalgic chromatics, but skilfully and accurately translates the sharp, crackling sound of the village fiddle to the parlour piano.

The Norwegian *fiolin*, as distinct from the Hardanger fiddle, is in effect our modern violin, which tended to oust the *hardingfele* in the eighteenth century. Since, however, expressive intensity is not the aim, it may be held in any position the player finds convenient: to the neck, in the modern way, but also to the forearm, the chest, or between the legs, like a viol. The music for *fiolin*, though less wild and devil-tainted than *hardingfele* music, is by no means cosily domestic. Ola Opheim, playing *Bess leiken*, displays a pure, sweet tone in a line of convoluted arabesques around contours that are basically pentatonic.[12] Drones are intermittently employed, but do not produce the tangled web of heterophonic dissonance such as characterizes Hardanger fiddle music. Often the tunes spring from the nature of the instrument in a modern way, since the figurations are arpeggiated across the strings. The effect is free, open, airy, relatable to the mountaineer's yodel, as in Hilmar Alexandersen's version of *Gammal vals fra Innherad*.[13] The lyrical but non-opulent timbre enhances the effect of open-air spaciousness. There is a parallel here with Shetland fiddle music, and it is profitless to argue about which influenced which. We may regard them as complementary musics, reflecting similar historical traditions and a comparable way of life. Geographically, the Shetlands are as close to Scandinavia as they are to Scotland, and were once part of a Danish empire. It is not surprising that the Shetlands fiddle should be played in much the same way as the Norwegian *fiolin*, with the same variety of holding-position and a similar reedy tone. Many Shetland fiddle tunes may be identified with Scandinavian prototypes: the *Muckle reel of Finnigarth* crops up in Norway as a *halling*, the *Shetland's bride's march* is identical with a Hardanger wedding dance, while *The merry boys o' Greenland* and *Shaalds o' Foula* are versions of country dances from North Jutland and Sweden.

The remoteness of the Shetland Islands from the mainland, and therefore from notated and printed music, no doubt helped to preserve the music's folk integrity, and to foster in it an archaic flavour that often resembles *hardingfele* as much as it does the *fiolin*. *Grieg's pipes* and *Black Joe*, as played by Andrew Polson,[14] preserve the raw, open sonority of the fiddle's Shetland predecessor, the *gue*; while *Auld swarra*, a slow air played by Tom Anderson, is as erratic in rhythm and as troll-infested in sonority as all but the craziest examples of *hardingfele*.[15] The tuning used in most Shetland fiddle music, and prescribed in the early Scots manuscript collections, is E,A,E,A or E,A,D,A as in Scandinavian fiddle musics. Again the tuning encourages an open-air resonance, and we should mentally hear the music within its human and natural context. In the case of reels and other dances it is an impulse to solidarity, appropriate to seasonal ceremonies within a crofting and fishing community geographically isolated, usually wind-buffeted and often tempest-tossed; in the case of the slow airs it is evocative of man's ultimate loneliness, at once heroically grand and scary. The social and the individualized musics are complementary. Arpeggiated triadic tunes springing naturally from fiddle technique may jollily band together groups of isolated folk, but the players exploit, even in dance music, the traditional tone and resonance of open strings. The lonely majesty of the slow airs, evocative of the empty space within which Shetland folk live their lives, cannot be effaced; even as we tipsily dance we are aware of the vulnerability of social institutions against the vast backcloth of sea and sky. Shetlanders engaged on whaling expeditions meet the ocean in all its immensity; small wonder that even their most institutionalized social music should betray tremors of uncertainty! Thus the vigorous up-bow stroke of Andrew Polson's reel playing is compromised by slight hesitancies and syncopations, especially in the first 'turning' of a tune. After the initial statement he and his community gradually gather confidence; in the tiny hiatuses, however, the 'reality' of the music, and of life, is manifest.

Implicit here is a point of general relevance to folk fiddling, which is entirely dependent on bowing techniques. All folk fiddlers play exclusively in the first position; the vitality and variety they create is thus dependent on the duality of strings and bow. The left hand does no more than find the notes; the bow dictates the way in which a note is attacked and quitted, its timbre, tone variation and precise duration. Regional differences between folk fiddling styles are conditioned by the bowing technique favoured. Some articulate

Gypsy band of violins, cimbalon and bass in north-east Hungary, 1968.

melodic details subtly, others encourage rhythmic flow and lilt; the best—among which we may include Andrew Polson—manage to do both simultaneously. We see here how technique, as always, can never be separated from function; and are reminded that function may be both physical and metaphysical (see also pp. 146–157). The activity of the folk fiddler's bowing arm promotes energy that keeps his fellows going; at the same time it asks questions as to where they're going, and why. A good folk fiddler is a servant of his community and at the same time the voice of its morality and conscience. The 'marriage of instrument and bow' is both a festivity and a potential sacrament.

This being so, it is not surprising that a high proportion of the fiddle music thus far referred to should be associated with weddings: the dances effect both an erotic and a social union of the twoness of bow and string, with a hint of the Fall that, as Christian took precedence over pagan concepts, was presumed to be inherent in sexuality. Weddings are one of the few surviving ceremonies in which pagan customs, such as the scattering of rice or confetti, still flourish, even in our mechanized urban environment. For us the sacramental meanings of what we do are mostly forgotten; but not only in Albania, Jugoslavia and Greece but also in northern Norway and the Shetlands, sacraments may still be active, withstanding the threat of 'progress'. Over the years, in the Shetlands, European quadrilles, waltzes, two-steps and foxtrots have percolated by way of radio into the traditional reels; and as social junketings began to take place in specially built 'community centres' as well as at home and in the pub, the fiddle has been reinforced or even replaced by louder instruments such as accordion, piano and electric guitar. Even so, the Shetlands are sufficiently remote, and the old traditions deeply enough rooted, for such modern importations to remain superficial; progress may seem relishable, but the past cannot be radically destroyed. Only in Ireland, especially southern Ireland, has the

ancient Celtic fiddle tradition been equally durable; and since the currents of Hibernian legend and mythology run both wider and deeper, it has produced music still more magically poetic.

The life and the truth of myth: the fiddle in Old Ireland

Few would challenge the view that there is no richer tradition of folk music than that of the Irish Celts, especially as manifest in songs to words both Gaelic and English, and in the closely related music for Irish pipes. In the Shetlands vocal music does not substantially survive, while pipe music is virtually non-existent. In Ireland the fiddle tradition is hardly separable from song and from pipe music. A superb metamorphosis of heroic Gaelic song into terms of the fiddle is created by Sean Moriarty of Killarney in his version of *The brown thorn*, a love-song so potent in verbal imagery and in lyrical span that it was known among old-timers as 'the king of all songs'[16].

While Sean's ornamentation is effectively violinistic, its relation to Gaelic vocal decoration is unmistakable, and both vocal and violin ornament suggest an analogy with the runic decoration on Celtic crosses. For reasons which must delve into our ancestral subconscious memory, the effect of this intricate ornamentation is highly and deeply magical: highly because the whirling convolutions of arabesque do not destroy the monolithic grandeur of the stone cross, nor the *superbia* of the ancient tune, but rather give them wings, seeking release from crucifixion in whatever form it may take; deeply because the serpentine interlacings of pattern ward off evil and bring good luck, since witches and warlocks are compelled to follow the threads to their labyrinthine ends. (As the childhood spell puts it, 'Twist ye, twine ye, even so, Mingle threads of joy and woe'.) Visually, the ornamentation on the cross is a paean to the prodigal beauty of the natural world, and at the same time a maze, drawing us to the centre of the universe. Aurally, the decoration in the violin line twitters and quavers like birds, beasts and insects, like the purling stream and the wind in the trees, while at the same time it averts the evil eye by tangling us in the intricacies of its patterns much as do, and for the same reason, the complexities of a Persian carpet or the simpler but similar magic of the child's cat's cradle. If this seems fanciful, so is the music: the wonder and mystery it engenders belong to a world older and stranger than that of our rational consciousness. In its mingling of extreme ornamental elaboration with purity and sweetness of tone this music

Padraig O'Keefe, fiddling patriarch of Glauntane.

A dance on Brandon Pier, Co. Kerry, *c.* 1935.

reminds us now of melismatic oriental cantillation, now of plainchant, the austerely doctrinal music of the Christian Church, and now of the melodies of the troubadours, sophisticated poet-composers who sang of love frustrated and transcended in monodic styles that are both occidental and oriental, elitist and popular. Such complexity, inherent in such simple spontaneity, is the ultimate flowering of a folk culture.

The range and variety, the magical heights and the depths, of Irish folk fiddling we may most comprehensively examine in the playing of the great Tommy Potts, as recorded on his disc *The Liffey Banks.*[17] Tommy was born and reared in the Coombe area of Dublin, learning his music—significantly for voice and pipes as well as fiddle—from his father, 'who was very clear and precise' about the right way to play things, although he had never received any formal training in music. Tommy found this grounding in convention and tradition valuable, yet at the same time restrictive:

As I progressed in making sound on the fiddle I found I was stirred in thought and feeling . . . I have no recollection of observing anything of like reaction in the players of the time. The nearest on the point of influence on me were Luke Kelly, fiddle (though he was not a great player), Mrs Sheridan—she was quite distinctive—and Seamus Mahoney. Also if I may say so, my brother Edward, who improvised well. The others had what they called 'very nice touches', but they used the same notes all the time without intensity or emotion. The harp-like clumping of notes in slow airs appealed to me deeply and I developed it somewhat in my air playing. Seamus Mahoney was serious minded in his playing: I consider this a great thing. Mrs Sheridan's playing was of the sweet, plaintive, drawling kind. Well, this covers the fiddle players, but there were pipers too. The best of those I heard were Jem Byrne of Mooncoin, Jimmy Ennis, father of Seamus Ennis, Johnny Doran, John Kearney from Longford and of course my father and my brother Edward (who was better on pipes than he was on fiddle). So I praise God for the gift of playing the fiddle, for I see in it a very poor reflection of the unbroken music of Heaven.

Tommy's comments reaffirm the point made earlier about the folk fiddler's simultaneously physical and metaphysical function; and to me his reflection of the heavenly music seems, in his slow airs, far from being 'poor'. In his marvellous version of *The dear Irish boy* marvels are indeed evoked as folk convention is transmogrified by the power of 'art'. Fantasy is created in the suddenly spurting, suddenly poised phrases and in the elaboration of the arabesques which resemble those of the great Gaelic singers both in contour and in colour, the tone being sweet yet reedy, with *vibrato* applied only occasionally, as a special, deeply pathetic effect,

as in Baroque string playing. The melodic line seems profoundly Irish in its waywardness and whimsicality, always on the brink of comedy, yet at the same time seraphic, soaring into the heavens. No less enthralling is Tommy's version of a Gaelic love-song, *An Buachaill Caol Dubh* (another Irish boy, this time dark and slender): wherein the convolutions of melismatic decoration surge onwards, only to be intermittently 'braked' by the double-stops that serve to mark the periods of the original half-submerged tune. Less ecstatic but no less poignant is another slow air, *An Raibh Tu aggCarraig?* (*Were you at the rock?*), a love song which acquired religious connotations as a lament of Irish priests on the run from persecution. Here the rhythm is more spasmodic, and the double-stops, especially on fourths, are stronger than the flow of the tune, creating abrupt cessations of breath. The music comes out as darkly mysterious, yet pure and cool: a negative complement to the winging flights of the two pieces referred to above. Simpler, more moderately paced airs, such as *Billy Byrne of Ballymanus*, Tommy plays with the same vocal 'speaking' tone, akin to Irish vocal idiom, but with a lilt that carries the body with it. The slow airs owe their self-communing intensity partly to the waywardness of their rhythm, intermittently pausing in meditation, to start off again on a different and often surprising tack. Quicker airs have a pulse which involves the individual communally with his fellows—though

Johnny Doherty from Donegal: fiddler, songster and
itinerant entertainer.

The ship comes home, which Tommy describes as a lullaby, gives some odd lurches to its baby-dangling three-
four metre. Again we may observe Tommy's impatience
with routine; the baby troublesomely becomes his, not
merely an anonymous offspring of The Folk.

If Tommy Potts's versions of airs are deeply affiliated
with Irish vocal, especially Gaelic, styles, his playing
of dance music is no less closely related to the Irish
pipes. It is possible that the Celtic pipes (both Irish and
Scots) have antique links with central Europe and the
Orient, and both are close to vocal tradition. The nasal
tone of the pipes resembles folk vocal production; and
bagpipe figuration is of its nature pentatonic. The
pipers' grace-notes have a vocal source but display still
greater agility; pipers learned from singers, who
reciprocally embraced the stylizations of pipe music. All
these qualities are translated by Tommy Potts into
fiddling terms. The lilt of quick symmetrical triple
rhythms in reels and jigs encourages dancers to worship
the earth by stamping their feet upon her, while at the
same time denying temporality in the very continuity
of the patterns they create; this music has no seams,
no beginning, middle or end, except an end imposed
upon it by its function, since it stops when the dancers
get tired. Even so, Tommy's tone and timbre, recalling
both the tenor voice and the pipes, give a personal
flavour to communal function: as is evident in his
version of *My love is in America*, a reel on the heartfelt
theme of alienation from homeland and true love. The
tune noodles around itself, trying to break away,
uttering momentary sighs, even whimpers, as energy is
frustrated. Thus a dance is made to contain the
contradictory qualities of fortitude, hope and regret. In
Tommy's version of *Crawley's reel* the variations of
dynamics and colour are so subtle that one hardly thinks
of the performance as functional at all; it *could* be
danced to, but many might prefer just to listen since
there is so much to occupy the ears, mind and senses.
Similarly *The fisherman's lilt*, as played by Tommy,
encapsulates in a dance the mix of trepidation and
terror, jeopardy and jubilation that a fisherman
experiences, as the melody ripples on, with occasional
shifts in its modality. *The drunken sailor* imbues a dance
with mystery, tingling in false relations between minor
and major seventh in a basic Aeolian mode. At Tommy's
higher pitch it sounds like B flat minor; his version of
The star of Munster, a reel composed, according to
Seamus Ennis, in honour of a beautiful woman from the
heroic 'days of yore', rings in a radiant F sharp major.

The equilibrium which Tommy Potts discovers, in
his playing of jigs and reels, between communal
function and personal feeling qualifies him as a supreme
master: one who gives to his music 'the vitality and
spirit that will make people want to dance', as Matt
Cranitch has put it. 'Good tone, in the accepted sense
of the word, is not important, nor is it necessary to have
a good fiddle. What makes a good fiddler is not too different, in many ways, from what makes a good piper:
there must be rhythm and verve in the playing, with
just the right amount and mixture of ornamentation—of
course in fiddling this includes bowing technique.
Having said that, you have to realize that a good fiddler
is so much more than the sum total of all the techniques
and ornamentation.' Tommy Potts uses all the conventional decorative techniques: 'rolls' which produce
quick tremors, usually in pentatonic minor thirds
around the melody note; the insertion of rapid repeated
notes or of flowing triplets into the line; drones
incorporated within and through the tune, creating arbi-
trary dissonance; 'cut' notes or *acciaccature* produced
by a flick of the third finger; slides, unison double-stops
and slow *vibrato*. But what makes Potts's playing so
impressive is that, even when he plays functional music
for dancing to, we are still aware of the individual man
who creates the magical slow airs. Mostly it is a matter
of his personal adaptation of the singer's or piper's
ornamentation to the stringed instrument; a momentary
hesitation in rhythm, or an imitation of a singer's glottal
stop, may individualize a communal experience.
Dancers to Tommy Potts's music are not allowed to
forget that, even as they move in togetherness, they are
particular and peculiar human beings. A community is
not an abstraction but a concourse of individual men
and women.

Tommy Potts in 1972.

Tommy Potts's talent is exceptional enough to make us question how far the word 'genius' can be applied to the concept of folk tradition. Yet folk music is after all made by folk; and the common denominator of what is often thought, felt, expressed and accepted must be a precipitate of the responses of many varied people, some highly and others only minimally endowed with vitality, sensitivity and wisdom. A more representative notion of the nature of the southern Irish fiddle may perhaps be got from a disc of County Kerry fiddlers devoted to the playing of Padraig O'Keefe, Denis Murphy and Julia Clifford.[18] The father figure of them is Padraig, who came from Glauntane and died in 1963. When he plays a slow air like *O'Donnell's lament* he communes with himself in the traditional rhapsodic vein, oblivious of the pulse of time; but his tone, compared with Tommy Potts's, is raw, and his free rhythms do not flow, like Tommy's, in air borne ecstasy. Similarly, when he plays a dance like *Callaghan's hornpipe*, he spins a long serpentine line, 'circular' in having no beginning, middle or end, but he doesn't infuse it with a similarly personal tone. Nor is that his intention; he wants rather to involve us in communal action, and does so by carrying us into a state of trance. When he does make a number consciously 'personal', like *The old man rocking the cradle*, it joins the category of 'stunt' pieces of illustrative intent. Folk fiddlers relish these jokey exercises, which cannot be dismissed as 'mere' entertainment. *The old man*, in which Padraig mimics the noise of the crying babe by muting the sound of his fiddle with a doorkey held between his teeth, is a piece of peculiar pathos; the broken contours of the air, the microtonal wails, make a generalized as well as specific comment on the human condition.

More commonly, however, these Kerry fiddlers stress their role as servants of the community rather than as individuals within it; interestingly enough, they often play the quick dances—jigs, slides, hornpipes and polkas rather than reels—as duets in erratic unison, since in this form they make more noise and may be more easily moved to. The raucous tone and the fortuitous dissonance created by imperfect coordination evoke the wild world in which we live and momentarily rejoice. Compared with Tommy Potts's music, however, the effect—in for example the polkas *The top of Maiol* and *The humours of Ballydesmond* or the acrobatic *Chase me Charlie*—is childishly simple if more-than-childishly intoxicating.

On the whole this relatively extrovert quality typifies northern Irish fiddling also, as we may hear by comparing Tommy Potts's version of *The blackbird* with that of John Doherty of Donegal. Tommy begins with the second strain or 'turn' of the well-known tune but never arrives at a straight statement of it, dissolving it rather in sweet-toned lyrical arabesques. The tweeting and carolling bird takes over from the human burden of the unsung words: whereas John Doherty, on his disc *Pedlar's pack*,[19] plays the tune so that it is immediately recognizable, and discovers references to its avian implications only obliquely. His tone is tender, his ornamentation related to that of vocal music; unlike Potts, however, he is prepared to offer the tune at its face value, which is considerable. On this disc Doherty appears as story teller and singer as well as a fiddler. Being an itinerant entertainer, he naturally favours numbers which are directly communicative, whether because they are music for moving to (his versions of the hornpipes *High level* and *Madam Vanoni* have tremendous physical bounce), or because they are stunt pieces like *The fox-chase* and *The hunt of the hare*. These cannot have much musical substance since imitative effects are their principal point, and melody is never allowed to flow nor rhythm to gain cumulative energy. None the less the effects may be poetic: the barking fox, baying hounds and fanfaring horns create an aural landscape, just as *The Atlantic sounds* 'lull into my brain' and evoke the murmurous ocean within sound of which Doherty and his community lived. The effect is fleeting, not durable; we are invited to live in the moment while it lasts, which is not long. Perhaps it is this recognition of mutability that makes John Doherty's fiddling here so startlingly reminiscent of the fiddling pedlar-soldier in Stravinsky's *L'Histoire du soldat* (see also pp. 191–2).

The Shetlands fiddler, Bobbie Jamieson, who played for his first dance in 1907.

The Fiddler comes to town: eighteenth-century Scotland

At least up to the eighteenth century, folk fiddling in mainland Scotland must have been comparable in character and intention with that of the outer islands, except that it was still more directly affiliated to bagpipe tradition than was Irish fiddling. From the fifteenth to the seventeenth centuries we hear of legendary folk fiddlers such as James Widderspune, 'the fitheler that told tales and brocht fowles to the King' (James IV); or Patrick Birnie, reputedly the composer of the celebrated air, *The auld man's meer's dead*; or the notorious Strathspey fiddler James MacPherson, a freebooter and highwayman who became a martyr-hero, after romantic escapes and escapades, before he was finally hanged—his appropriately bold tune, *Macpherson's Farewell*, said to have been fiddled on the gallows, survives in manuscript.

The story of the mainland Scots fiddle after the early eighteenth century differs, however, from that of the musics so far discussed, and does so because of Scotland's peculiar geographical and sociological position.

The Effigie of PATIE BIRNIE.
The Famous Fidler of Kinghorn;
Who gart the Lieges gawff and girn ay;
Sit till the Cock proclaim'd the Morn:

Tho baith his Weeds and Mirth were pirny,
He reck'd those Things were langestworn.
The brown Ale Barrel was his Kirn ay;
And faithfully he toom'd his Horn.

Interrelationships between folk, pop, and art music work best when the barriers between them are least clearly defined, as was the case in England through the Middle Ages and up to the late seventeenth century. Scotland, in her golden age of the High Renaissance, proved no exception. By the eighteenth century most of the centres of European civilization had established sharp differences between folk music, which tends to be monodic, orally transmitted, amateur, unselfconscious, inexpensive, relatively static; and art music, which tends to be polyphonic or homophonic, notated, professional, self-conscious, subject to the vagaries of fashion. Though not as distant as the outer islands, mainland Scotland was sufficiently remote from Europe for her folk traditions to retain their vigour; and at the same time her few centres of urban civilization were advanced enough, consequent on her Renaissance heritage, to encourage cultural sophistication. So ambivalence flourished: her fiddlers were originally folk musicians, like those of Shetland and of rural Ireland; they played with the archaic reedy tone, and with the ornamentation related both to Scots folk song of the grand ballad tradition and to the ancient bagpipe art of *pibroch*. Yet the growth of towns gave them economic opportunities such as a rural society could not offer, and within these urban communities class distinctions were in part whittled away.

Though most of the players were amateurs of working

A highland wedding at Blair Atholl: painting by David
Allan, 1780.

if not labouring class, Scots fiddle music became a
middle-class phenomenon. Reels and strathspeys,
written down in manuscript books and later printed,
were relished by the rising middle class and even by
the aristocracy. Imperceptibly, the local tradition of
fiddle music merged into the violin music of Europe,
which had become a vogue in polite (and even fairly
impolite) urban circles. Many folk fiddlers turned
professional; some earned their living by playing genteel
European music of Corellian and Handelian vintage.
Yet the folk flavour of their music was not, even as late
as the nineteenth century, obscured. As David Johnson
has put it in his brilliant study of music and society in
eighteenth-century lowland Scotland:

Folk music flourished when its repertory remained the same,
classical music [i.e. art music] flourished when its repertory
developed; folk music was peculiar to Scotland, classical
music was common to Europe; folk music required no
formal education for its propagation, classical music required
a great deal of it. Upper-class Scots in the eighteenth century
used each kind of music in ways corresponding to, and

symbolized by, these functional features. In folk music they
found an expression of conservatism, of national identity,
and of community with all classes of fellow Scots; in classical
music they found an expression of progress, of participation
in Europe, of community with the educated classes.

The fiddle-violin music that evolved from this
ambiguous situation is fascinating and may be unique—
for such comparable modernizations of tradition as one
comes across in recordings from Finland, Norway and
Sweden seem to be more thorough-going and musically
more damaging, probably because they happened much
later.[20] In Scotland, however, one finds an eighteenth-
century musician such as James Oswald, a collector and
publisher of folk songs who was at once a folk fiddler
and a literate violinist. He composed courtly minuets
embellished with Corellian graces and paid Handel the
compliment of direct imitation, if not quotation. Yet the
tunes of his elegant dances preserve modal, often pentatonic contours by the simple expedient of dropping out
notes, especially leading notes, from the diatonic scale;
and evidence suggests that he played his genteel pieces

Niel Gow: portrait by Henry Raeburn (1727–1807).

unaccompanied, with the traditional reedy tone with which he performed strathspeys and reels.

This fusion of folk fiddle with polite violin reached an apex in the music of Niel Gow, the supreme master of eighteenth-century mainland tradition (though some of his five sons, notably Nathaniel, run him close). Born in 1827, described by Burns as a 'short, stout-built, honest highland figure' and so pictured in the beautiful portrait by Raeburn, Gow was household musician to the Duke of Atholl at Blair Castle, with which the Gow family maintained a connection through several generations. Though his music was printed and is academically violinistic in idiom, Gow still composed and usually played monodically, employing the characteristic upbow technique whereby the folk fiddler effects the famous Scotch snap by a jerk of the wrist. Even as notated, his melodies tend to begin in gapped pentatonic formation, sometimes filling in the gaps for repeats; many of his tonal procedures, such as the so-called 'double tonic' whereby phrases are repeated sequentially without modulation a tone apart, spring partly from unconscious reminiscences of modality, partly from the spontaneous movements of the fingers on the strings. These progressions may prove troublesome when the tunes are harmonically accompanied at a piano, as increasingly happened when the music was accepted, and relished, in polite society. It seems probable that the music of Gow's sons and of later players such as William Marshall, Robert Petrie and Captain Fraser of Knockie was also conceived monodically, since their tunes frequently end, or rather stop, off-key in a manner alien to harmonic tonality. Even so, in their work the old gapped scales begin to be enervated by chromaticism, while corporeal vigour is to a degree tempered so that melodies may more easily fit into an implicit if not explicit harmonic scheme. Gradually the rich ambivalence between modality and modern tonality is effaced; the inclusion of chromatic decoration itself suggests that tone and timbre were intentionally rendered more 'expressive'.

This is more damagingly evident when the music of the Gows and of their contemporaries and successors is enthusiastically performed by today's professional Scots violinists. A tone too plangent, a technique too streamlined, and the addition of an oompah accompaniment on piano, sometimes reinforced by string bass, tend to denature the music; yet the tunes are so strong and the rhythms so infectious that they still offer stimulus to minds and senses, as well as to leaping limbs and dancing feet. Ron Gonnella has recorded an impressive *Tribute to Niel Gow*,[21] using only a discreet accompaniment and a violin technique which, if closer to eighteenth-century civility than to folk virility, is nonetheless clean, bright, and impeccable in intonation. He groups the pieces, which include numbers by Nathaniel, Neil junior and John Gow as well as their illustrious father, in 'sets' as the family would have done throughout the eighteenth and nineteenth centuries, when serving as household musicians at Blair. Usually a slow air or a march is succeeded by a strathspey and a reel or sometimes a jig. The marches hint at bagpipe style in their twittering ornamentation, but acquire, through the precision of violin articulation, considerable ebullience; plainly diatonic in tonality, they are irresistible calls to physical action. The strathspeys are quick dances in which gapped scales and archaic modalities are fairly common, especially in the work of Gow the father. Melodic and rhythmic energy are generated by the tunes' pronounced upbeats and abrupt lifts, usually with a flurry of pipe-style ornament; in *Niel Gow's recovery* and in Nathaniel's *Mrs Macdonald of Clan Ranald* the upward spurts and swoops have the agility of electric eels.

Musically, the highlights of the Gow's music are the

A Shetlands wedding procession, headed by fiddlers Bobby Thompson and Jimmy Man, and guitarist Sunny Morrison, August 1963.

slow airs, as is the case with the more 'primitive' Irish fiddlers. The latter of course inherit and adapt the tunes from traditional sources, whereas the Gows' airs are composed music, plainly diatonic yet flowing in noble arches, often in a lilting dotted rhythm; they seem appropriate to open spaces rather than to an eighteenth-century drawing room. The initial statement of the tune is conventionally followed by two or three variations which embroider it eloquently without impairing its majesty. Niel Gow's *Lady Anne Hope's favourite air* is particularly spacious, haunting in its simplicity yet luxuriant in its flow. His famous *Farewell to whisky* maintains the heroic strain through vestiges of heartfelt (if not explicit) chromatic harmony. Harmonic implications are naturally stronger in airs by later members of the family, such as Nathaniel's *Lament for the death of his brother*, a superbly shaped melody whose rising and falling clauses subtly define the latent harmonic progression and retrogression. In *Cam' ye by Atholl?* by Neil Gow junior (unlike his father, he spelled his first name in the conventional way), latent inner parts become patent, played in multiple stopping or on a second violin, whether or not piano chords offer sup-

port; a comparably rich texture appears in Nathaniel's very grand *Caller Herring*. Yet the tunes themselves never surrender the bold, open quality of Scots folk song; in *Miss Lucy's compliments*, for instance, the wide leaps characteristic of violin idiom give the melody a winging eloquence, relatable both to *pibroch* and to the more bardic types of Scots song. Again, the quasi-eighteenth-century violin civilizes folk tradition without denying its spontaneous splendour. However celebrated and materially successful the Gows became in polite society, their music never allows us to forget that the father was the son of a village weaver, and the sons were proud of their heritage.

The urbanization of folk music does not necessarily involve such a consciously 'artistic' evolution as that which occurred in Scotland. In this context a brief note on Northumbrian fiddle music is called for: for though that became and still is closely associated with Tyneside cities, it calls on much traditional rural material played in traditional fiddle styles, modified mainly by the influence of the mellow sonorities and piquant figurations of the Northumbrian smallpipes. The 'magical' elements characteristic of old-style, and especially Irish,

Dr Humphrey Bate and the Possum Hunters, *c.* 1932.

fiddling have largely disappeared; the tone, like the Geordies who play the music, is raw and tough, no-nonsensical, and the rhythm in the functional dance music eschews any subtleties that might impair its efficacy. None the less Colin Ross's fiddling with the admirable High Level Ranters has the virility of genuine folk tradition, whether in a loping 9/8 number like *Shew's the way to Wallington*, which seems to be related to an Irish slip-jig, in numbers resurrected from the printed Northumbrian Ministrelsy like *The Hexamshire lass* and *The lads of Alnwick*, or a colliery 'rant', like *Whitman's reel*.[22] The most enlivening features of these numbers— the gawky tritones in *Shew's the way*, the awkward leaps of diminished sixth and octave in *The Hexamshire lass*, and the rhythmic ambiguities of *The lads of Alnwick*, which appears to be a march in 3/4!—probably spring from Northumbrian pipe idiom. The oddities seem completely spontaneous: the High Level Ranters tell us that they have made of *Dance to your daddy*, a fisherman's baby-dandling song, a 'semi-Hardanger arrangement', and they do so with total conviction. The piece transports a wild Scandinavian landscape to a Newcastle pub, where performers and listeners may unquestioningly accept and enjoy it.

The Old Fiddle in a New World

When Europeans, especially the British, emigrated to the New World they took with them their most popular and portable instrument, the fiddle, and the extensive repertory of tunes which, between the seventeenth and the nineteenth centuries, they played on it. Basically the country fiddle in America, as in Ireland and Scotland, was and is an ordinary violin used in styles more typical of the functional techniques of Europe's Middle Ages and Renaissance than the lyrically expressive techniques of the eighteenth and nineteenth centuries. Since expressivity was not the goal, the instrument could be held, like the Shetland and Irish fiddle, in any way convenient to the player. For the white American country fiddler, as for the medieval and Renaissance peasant, the instrument was an impetus to physical movement. Played with a flat bridge and sometimes with an arched bow, it was adept at marking metrical accents and at reinforcing sonority by the use of open-stringed drones, but was relatively inefficient at sustaining melody. It had lost touch with the ancient and mysterious fiddle traditions that precariously survive in the remoter reaches of Ireland, and had never had contact with the semi-civilized traditions of the violin music of eighteenth-

A Glasgow fiddler playing from the notes.

century Scotland. What the American country fiddle was called upon to do, it executed brilliantly; in so doing it complemented (at the opposite pole) the vocal music that was being fashioned in the new-found land.

White American singers sang the old British songs or made up new ones in response to their new environment. Both new and old singers, in the arduous conditions of pioneer life, preserved long established traditions, yet rendered them more pinched and niggardly. An Almeda Riddle in the Carolina mountains, an Aunt Molly Jackson, a Sarah Ogan Gunning, or a Nimrod Workman in the Kentucky or Virginia mining areas all sang with an austerely deadpan laconicism, the line relatively unadorned, as unfluent as they were materially unaffluent, a monody of deprivation. The Old World's experience is here pared to its bare bones, holding on for grim life. As complement and perhaps by way of compensation, the settlers' instrumental music abandons everything to the hedonism of the present moment, manifest in whirling limbs. Such music is 'innocent', as compared with the singers' 'experience', but it is not necessarily escapist, if only because its sheer speed may entail an element of hazard.

Southern fiddle styles varied regionally, though all betray their roots in Celtic tradition. Especially close to the Old World is Luther Strong's performance,

recorded in Kentucky in 1937, of *The last of Sizemore*, a Scots reel prompted by a notorious local hanging.[23] Here the drone-dominated texture and the wailing pentatonic arabesques in E A E A tuning recall something of the mystery of old Celtic style. More normally Kentucky fiddling fosters, in the face of odds however desperate, a kind of White Euphoria, its tunes very fast, its tone guilelessly open. Alva Greene's version of *Hunky Dory*[24] is typical of this jolly domesticity, which is boosted not only by drones but also by 'fiddlesticks'— a rhythmic *ostinato* tapped on the strings with a pair of knitting needles. A further process of domestication is revealed in a version of *That's my rabbit* made by the Walter family, who came from Nicholasville, Kentucky.[25] The fiddle tune is accompanied by 'found instruments' such as jug and washboard as well as by parlour piano and guitar. Even the most famous of Kentucky fiddlers, Arthur Smith, whose virtuosity brought him some national celebrity on the radio during the 1930s, never allowed pyrotechnics to threaten his music's sense of homeliness. It is relevant to note that although Smith also played traditional reels, he was especially partial to rags, which were the Southern black man's attempt at a 'civilized' music to compete with that of his white masters. Arthur Smith's *Peacock Rag* is an effective compromise between the black rag's dandified elegance and the brash vitality of white country fiddle.[26]

But old-time fiddle music fascinates most when it chances most. Recorded in the late 1920s, the obscure Carter Brothers offer an appropriately tipsy version of *Give the fiddler a dram*, in which excitement derives from the players' notable *failure* to co-ordinate their lines.[27] As with the less crude heterophony of the Irish fiddlers referred to earlier, it would seem that technical virtuosity may imply a degree of emotional complexity too, since one cannot walk a tightrope without at least a tremor of fear. The music of the Georgian Fiddlin' John Carson—the earliest country musician to be commercially recorded—bears this out.[28] When he sings with his fiddle, his vocal style—whether he is singing an old ballad like *The honest farmer*, or a relatively new lonesome railway-train number like *I'm nine hundred miles from home*—is traditionally scrawny, while his fiddle part, raucous with open-string chords and bagpipe-style drones, is far from merry. But when he lets loose with his fiddle, using his voice mainly for intermittent shouts or for calling the numbers in a square dance—as he does in *Corn licker and barbecue*, *Sugar in the gourd*, *Engine on the Mogul*, or in an extraordinary mixolydian, dervish-like version of *Cotton-eyed Joe*— the music is a corybantic release, comparable with the

225

orgiastic excesses of gospel music. The near-crazy zest of such performances produces a music that is no longer merely a noise for dancing to, but a ritual act simultaneously social and personal. White fervour acquires something of the immediate reality of the black blues; and indeed black influences permeated white instrumental music irresistibly, whether or not the players were willing to admit it. This is evident in the work of all the Georgian fiddle bands who flourished in the 1920s and 1930s, such as the Home Town Boys, the Georgia Organ Grinders or Earl Johnson's Clodhoppers (who give a breathtaking performance—very fast, with bouncing *spiccato* and inebriated slides—of the popular nineteenth-century hit, *Sourwood Mountain*[29]). Johnson himself had some training as an 'art' violinist, unlike Fiddlin' John Carson, an empiricist whose mistakes are the essence of his genius. Nonetheless, Johnson's technical competence did not affect the folk integrity of his music; it reinforced rather than dampened his fervour.

In a neighbouring Southern state, Louisiana, we find a minor tributary of 'euphoric' country fiddle which seems poles apart from the rabid Georgians: even geographically so, for the Acadians were originally French Canadians who, exiled from their home in the eighteenth century as a consequence of the British-American wars, settled in Louisiana. In that amiable climate they continued to speak French or a *patois*

derived therefrom, and cultivated a smilingly relaxed music that matched their physical environment. Their music, perhaps because they were 'foreigners', is the most eclectic on the American continent; folk songs and old *contredanses* from seventeenth- and eighteenth-century France blend unselfconsciously with Southern American mountain songs, Tin Pan Alley hits, cowboy songs, Tex Mex dances and Negro blues. Formally, the Cajuns (as they came to be pronounced in their new land) favoured the French waltz and two-step; yet both are often served with a Spanish or Latin American sauce, and are liable to be metamorphosed into jigs which sound like 'continental' versions of Irish reels, or into American hoe-downs—which had in any case already absorbed European quadrille, *Schottische* and polka. Vocal production is more French and Latin-American than North American, high and slightly fierce, as contrasted with the relaxed instrumental sonorities of guitars, banjos and French-café-style accordions. Melodically, the fiddle remains the leading instrument. A Floyd LeBlanc, a Wallace 'Cheese' Reed or an Austin Pitre play waltzes, jigs and stomps in a bright, sharp style clearly affected by the Southern American country fiddling heard in neighbouring states, but with a warmth and vivacity that are just as clearly European. Wallace Reed's *French jig*, *Waltz of the wayside*, *Rabbit stomp* and *Empty bottle stomp* are virtuoso

Opposite: 'The Dixieliners', Sam McGee, Fiddlin' Arthur
Smith and Kirk McGee, *c.* 1938.

'Summer evening in a French village': Mississippi 'Cajuns'
dancing.

performances that are nonetheless easy listening.[30]
Cajun music seems to be virtually oblivious of pain and
danger. Its undeniable charm needs a social context:
wine and women should accompany this song.

Cajun fiddle music is American really only by adoption and by courtesy. Nonetheless if we regard it as the
opposite pole to the wild Georgian and Arkansas fiddle,
we might say that in purely musical terms the most
rewarding American fiddling effects a compromise
between Georgian savagery and Louisianan amiability.
We may take as an instance the Kessinger Brothers of
West Virginia, who favour a moderate, almost jogging
tempo as compared with that of the whirligig Georgians,
and a tone which, if less warm than the Cajuns', is pure
and penetrating. What prevents their music from
degenerating into Southern indolence is an occasional
omitted or added beat which lends the music an uneasy
edge. Related to the Kessinger tradition is the work of
a much younger man, J. P. Fraley, most active in his
native East Kentucky during the 1960s and 1970s. Playing to the guitar accompaniment of his wife Annadeene,
he creates a lyrical line as pure as the Kessingers', but
more moving in its irregular rhythms (not altogether
distinct from the *notes inégales* of French Baroque
tradition) and in its microtonally distorted pitch. Though
the modal tune is not old and sounds American rather
than Irish or Scots, Fraley's performance of *Wild rose
of the mountain* preserves or re-creates something of the
other-worldly quality of the ancient tradition.[31] But this
is not, of course, music of the future or even the present.
Fraley's music is an anachronism, a creation of revivalist
fervour remarkable for the immediacy of its conception
and presentation.

Although American fiddle music had deep roots in
the Irish and Scots traditions which Fraley resuscitates,
it was from the start as ethnically varied as the continent
that produced it, and became more so as the fiddlers
increasingly co-operated with plucked string players on
clawhammer banjo, guitar and mandolin. The development is neatly illustrated by a comparison of the two
finest of the string bands that proliferated in the 1920s
and 1930s. Gid Tanner and his Skillet Lickers,[32] playing
Skillet Licker breakdown and *Back up and push* in 1931,
create a 'rip-roarin' free for all' directly in the tradition
of the Georgian fiddle band. Clayton McMichen and
Lowe Stokes fiddle with short, stabbing bow-strokes,
both emulating and stimulating body movement; Fat
Norris's banjo functions mainly as a rhythm instrument; Gid Tanner sings high and strained, often in
falsetto, while blind Riley Puckett fills in with his
celebrated three or four chord runs on guitar. Old folk
songs, Yankee military tunes, hymns and minstrel
dances are all grist to the Skillet Lickers' fast-pounding
mill, and genres are not differentiated. If we then listen
to Charlie Poole and his North Carolina Ramblers playing (a year earlier) *Milwaukee blues*,[33] we can note that
the bucolic abandon typical of the Skillet Lickers is here
more tightly, and much more 'artistically', controlled.
The piece is not in fact a blues, but a story-song with
the familiar railway background. Fred Harvey provides
a steady guitar bass, which could hardly be further
removed from Riley Puckett's double- and quadruple-
time capers, above which Odel Smith's fiddle, played
with relatively long bow strokes, is bluely expressive,
even 'artistic', rather than a mere encouragement to
bodily movement. Charlie Poole's banjo also functions
as a melody instrument, not merely as rhythmic
support; it is from the sophisticated interplay between
the two melodic parts and the beat that the incipiently
jazzy, urban impact of such resolutely diatonic music
derives. The jazzy flavour preserves a hint of danger:
Georgian savagery, however, has been disciplined.

The Skillet Lickers and the North Carolina Ramblers
started, back in the 1920s, as servants of their
community; their influence spread as they were heard,
on radio and records, by a far wider and more ethnically
varied audience. Later groups made their names as
much by radio and the record industry as by the
communities they came from and at first worked in; the
message changed with the medium. The music of the
most influential of the Blue Grass bands, the Monroe
Brothers, presents the Old Times not merely as a way
of life to be relished, but also as a panacea for the
nervous and physical stresses of big city life. The Monroe

Opposite: Gid Tanner, The Skillet Licker, in 1956.

Brothers' songs cover the conventional themes of Love, Home, Mother, Country, God and Disaster; even when the tunes are modally inflected, they are strongly moulded by white evangelical hymnody, the solo line boosted by two or three 'backers' in cosy parallel thirds, sustained by rigid four-bar phrases in common or three-quarter tempo, and a mean diet of two or three rudimentary chords. Only very occasionally—Wade Mainer's version of *Little Maggie*[34] is a case in point—is a modal flat seventh allowed to affect the harmony, or to encourage folk-like microtonal distortions in the fiddle part. Normally cheeriness is unremitting, to the point of inanity.

As American string bands grew more whole-hogging in their cultivation of the White Euphoria, fiddles ceased to be the only or even the main tune-bearers. In the Monroe Brothers' band, violin is merely one strand of an elaborate texture embracing guitars, banjos, mandolins, dobros and occasionally harps. As early as 1938 the Delmore Brothers recorded in South Carolina a Depression song which hit back at the misery of being *Fifteen miles from Birmingham* with blues-inflected vocal springiness, guitar-pickin' liveliness, and most of all with sprightly, elastic-rhythmed fiddling. By 1945 country string-band style was being overtly modified by the influence of urban jazz, as in the Monroe Brothers' *Why did you wander?*,[35] whose words deal cornily with a broken love, and promise pie in the sky when the lovers are celestially reunited. The music ironically reverses the burden of the words, which Monroe himself sings in a high, hard, often falsetto tenor to his own accompaniment on a very loud, forty-year-old mandolin, while Lester Flatt lets loose cascades of liquid guitar figuration and Earl Scruggs plays lead on five-string, pickin'-style banjo. Charlie Wise's flickering line on folk fiddle is no more than a descant to enhance the excitement. The breathtaking speed and acrobatic virtuosity are like a jazz break: at such hair-raising speed misfortune is impossible! Faithlessly wandering women and Death himself are annihilated in this dangerous Present, as the pickin' and pluckin' drive onwards in desperate jubilation. Such tipsy abandon is all we are likely to know of a heaven in which lover and beloved will be once more together, as they were in their 'old mountain home'. The number is purest wish-fulfilment, and the wish is momentarily attained. Time is effaced in whirling arms and flying feet; heaven is here and now (and nice work if you can get it!). Musically there is no suspicion of a 'wander'; home is precisely now in the euphorically improvised moment.

From American fiddle to Jazz Violin

In Blue Grass bands the fiddle has thus become subservient to the whole concourse of instruments. Contemporary with the Blue Grass band, however, another string-band genre evolved in which the violin remained central. Its origins are related to the dance music of the Texan–Mexican border country, where the spoken language is in part Spanish and where tango rhythms subtly infuse the waltz and two-step common to white country and cowboy music. This gives a sexy lurch to the *bailes* bands' performance even of such traditional white country numbers as *Turkey in the straw*, which Bernardo Roybal rechristens *El Cutilup*.[36] Tempos are moderate to perky, and the music resolutely cheerful and diatonic, rigid in metre except for an occasional added or elided beat that seems to be due more to carelessness than to craft. The violin tone is harsh but self-confident; the sonority, resonant with parallel thirds, makes for togetherness, generating a daft bonhomie occasionally tempered by the pungent tones of accordion. Bob Dylan, in the 'desert' numbers on his disc *Desire*,[37] poetically re-creates the sonorities and rhythms of Tex-Mex music with a harsh, sun-burnt acridity entirely apt to the fierceness and fecklessness of his Wild West words. Dylan's harmonica is a haunting substitute for Tex-Mex accordian, electric keyboards brilliantly emulate bar-room calliopes, and Latin-American percussion is vibrant, dry as the desert air. Scarlet Rivera plays Mexican folk-fiddle with dionysiac zest and with just the right degree of acid distonation.

A far more interesting hybrid genre, however, had already sprung from a fusion of white cowboy music, coffee-coloured Tex-Mex music and black jazz, and flourished initially in the South West. A considerable proportion of the music which came to be known as Western Swing remains music of the White Euphoria in the usual evasive sense; when Bob Wills and his Texan Playboys perform *I wonder if you feel the way I do*,[38] doleful verses about the familiar faithless woman promote a jogging, blandly diatonic tune which the whinings of steel guitar tinge with comedy rather than with passion and pain. But as a fiddler, Bob Wills, who had his greatest success between the mid-1930s and the mid-1940s, made out of euphoria something at once more positive and more dangerous. Playing a traditional country tune like *Cotton-eyed Joe*[39] with trumpet, piano, bass and electric guitar as well as the conventional fiddle and banjo, he creates a mini-powerhouse suggestive of the then contemporary Big Band. Wills plays violin, fairly expertly, rather than folk fiddle, yet favours a

flutey rather than an 'expressive' tone; edgy blue distonations occur even when he mates jazz vivacity with cowboy corn in numbers like *Ride on, my little pinto*, or with Tex-Mex kitsch in *Spanish two-step*, or *San Antonio Rose*, the song that made him famous and (for a while) rich. Negro pulse, Mexican-Spanish lilt and cowboy broadness blend together in this extrovert music, which is the South West's complement to the South East's Blue Grass. Like Blue Grass, it marks a significant phase in the evolution of American popular music both positively (its body energy is real and therefore infectious) and negatively (the moment of happiness passes even as it is being celebrated). White Euphoria triumphs in no discreditable sense: for the liveliness, if it lacks the more durable truth of black jazz, is true while it lasts. The music is good for listening as well as dancing; its pleasure, if skin-deep, enhances rather than anaesthetizes. It is no accident that Blue Grass and Western Swing both reached their peaks in the aftermath of the Second World War. Far from being

provoked by fear or desperation, they reasserted man's pride in his (still living) body, which was something worth celebrating, in those still dark days.

In Blue Grass and Western Swing white men exploited elements from black jazz in the interests of the White Euphoria. Meanwhile black men made their own music on country fiddles, imbuing it with the darker reality implicit in their Afro-American music. In *Yodelling blues*,[40] Van Edwards plays a primitively bleating fiddle line over Wade Ward's banjo and Earl Edwards's guitar, while intermittently breaking into falsetto yodels that recall white Jimmie Rodgers. What emerges is a hesitant compromise between white country music and black blues—fortuitously or not, the number was sometimes known as 'Hesitating blues'. The Johnson Boys' *Violin blues*, recorded in 1928, a year before *Yodelling blues*, is closer to black jazz in so far as Nap Hayes's violin line intersperses wailing scoops and sobs with double-stopped train noises, both typical of the primitive blues of small-town rurality. But since

229

the combination of violin with guitar and mandolin derives directly from black-faced minstrel shows in which whites emulated and probably guyed black prototypes, there may be an element of compromise here too.

The violin line in this number, though wailful, is pervasively sweet, even saccharine, which in part explains why the violin was not a favoured instrument in the heyday of Negro jazz; its native lyricism and relatively quiet sonority were less relevant to the black experience than were harsher, voice-aspiring horns. It is significant that the finest black performer to play the violin, Stuff Smith—who was born in Ohio in 1909 and played with many illustrious early jazzmen, including Louis Armstrong, Jelly Roll Morton and the brilliant though little-known Alphonse Trent band—ignored the violin's most idiomatic qualities. Though he played in city clubs both in New York and in Europe, and specialized in jazz standards of the 1920s and 1930s, in many ways he resembles an old-time country fiddler, using very short bowing, brief phrasing, and a dry rather than mellow tone like a muted trumpet or the laconic, throwaway sax sound of Lester Young. On a superb disc,[41] cut in 1967 just before his premature death, he weaves melodic lines that are never nostalgic or self-indulgent; even his version of *Yesterdays*, one of his rare numbers in slowish tempo, fragments the tune into touching yet intermittently comic whimpers which contain an inner electric charge. In his habitual uptempo numbers he often abruptly halts the compulsive momentum by double-stops again reminiscent of the old country fiddlers, as in the horn-like parallel fourths towards the end of *Sweet Lorraine*. His long version of *Cherokee* begins low and hollow in sonority, but spurts into ever more recklessly chirruping roulades, damped by sudden hiatuses. Always the spring of the lines, however fragmented the phrases, carries us forwards in jazzy exuberance; the melodies speak intimately to us, even as the swinging rhythm carries us out of ourselves. Stuff Smith is perhaps the only truly great jazz performer to speak through the medium of a bowed string instrument, as distinct from the plucked guitar or bass.

But Stuff Smith, though essentially a jazzman, is hardly representative of the tradition of jazz violin, in so far as one exists. A more typical figure is Eddie South, a black man who significantly had formal musical training in Europe before entering the dusty world of Chicago jazz during the late 1920s. His conventionally assured technique encouraged him to exploit the violin's natural resources of ripe tone and lyrical line, while his experience of gypsy fiddling in Bucharest no doubt suggested how the violin's proclivities could be combined with the improvised fervour of jazz. It cannot be an accident that South's finest work was achieved with the gypsy guitarist Django Reinhardt. Particularly impressive is an improvised *Eddie's blues* of 1937, in which South's tender tone-colouring is tinted with piteously blue slides and scoops, while the melodic line, invigorated by Django's potent guitar, soars with splendid lyrical élan.[41] A version of *I can't believe that you're in love with me*, dating from the same year, is of more extended scope, investing a standard with unexpected melodic allure and rhythmic verve.[42]

Contemporary with black Eddie South was a white violinist, Joe Venuti: a European of Italian descent, associated in his early days with Bix Beiderbecke and Red Nichols, Paul Whiteman, the Dorsey brothers and the Teagarden brothers, and finally with Benny Goodman—all of them white jazzmen whose activities alternated between jazz and Tin Pan Alley. Venuti won his reputation deservedly, however, through his collaboration with another guitarist, Eddie Lang, whose seductive tone and swing he perfectly complemented on his bowed instrument. Venuti's technique is even more orthodox and his tone more 'European' than South's, though some of the numbers which he and Lang created in the 1930s have achieved the status of jazz classics: one thinks of the rip-roaring *Wild dog*, or *Black satin*'s persuasive vein of romantic nostalgia.[43] For some tastes Venuti seems too squeakily aggressive or too plangently expressive; though a genuine jazz player, he lurks in the doorway of the cocktail lounge, as Stephane Grappelli, another European with a superficially similar style, on the whole does not.

Grappelli also owed his early fame to collaboration with a guitarist—the same supreme Django Reinhardt with whom Eddie South performed. Though not himself a gypsy, Grappelli was a white, French improviser of a genius measurable against Reinhardt's. Together they were the soloist mainsprings of the celebrated Hot Quintet of Paris during its vintage years in the 1930s, the other members of the quintet merely offering harmonic and rhythmic support on two guitars and string bass. During those golden years Stephane's violin line was less lyrically mellow than Eddie South's, but still more air-borne. Riding over Django's driving pulse and wonderfully varied textures, Grappelli takes Gershwin's *I got rhythm* (or the thematically triter *Them there eyes*) at ear- and mind-bending speed.[44] Yet he can also, in a version of *It was so beautiful*, cunningly delay his entry before floating into a line that winds, wanders and wonders in an adolescent dream of love, the tone fine-spun and sustained, the rhythm still swinging.

Stephane Grappelli.

Today, nearly fifty years later, Grappelli is still playing many of these numbers with undiminished agility and ever-enhanced subtlety of nuance, though there can be no substitute for his creative antiphony with the gypsy guitarist, long since dead. Grappelli's position in jazz history is of some documentary interest. There is no doubt of the jazz authenticity of his playing yet, being also a European who elegantly plays a European instrument with civilized connotations, he bridges gulfs and demolishes barriers, the more so in that he has become, over the years, the most commercially successful of all jazz violinists.

In a sense we have to recognize that Grappelli is a survivor from a vanished era. The violin never mattered greatly to jazz and is now virtually obsolete; having been electrified in the jazz-rock era, it is no longer the same European instrument. In folk-rock or 'electric folk' groups like Fairport Convention and Steeleye Span even the folk fiddle itself has been electrocuted. A genuine folk fiddler like Dave Swarbrick, who started in pubs and clubs with his acoustic fiddle, in concert at first used amplification and then the electrophonic violin, absorbing the jazz influence of Grappelli into a sound-world which re-creates for young people the pre-industrial wellsprings of being; thus the young use technology to hit back at a world they never made. A more conscious example of technology employed against itself occurs in the work of Jean-Luc Ponty, the jazz electric violinist who during the 1970s worked with the intrepid rock iconoclast, Frank Zappa. Though Ponty's electric violin blares like an electrified jazz horn, it sometimes sounds like a vastly magnified and mechanized recreation of the most primitive kinds of folk and jazz fiddle; he is closer to Fiddlin' John Carson than he is to J. P. Fraley, to Stuff Smith than to Eddie South. It would seem that our industrial conurbations are denying themselves 'subjective' expression, though not for the same reasons as did Irish and Scottish peasants, or poor white and poorer black Americans. Occasionally, as in *Pamukkale*,[45] the bleakly impersonal sophistication of Ponty's music is oddly affecting; more frequently, as in the Zappa numbers, its streamlined imperviousness at once stimulates and scares us. Though this is a valid voice of our mechanized future, one cannot help rejoicing that Stephane Grappelli *is* a survivor. In so far as he found himself in improvised collaboration with a gypsy, he takes us back to the theme with which we began. There may still be a tipsy gypsy fidder lurking in the heart of every brilliant violinist, and perhaps deep in the hearts of us all.

Folk Violin Discography

1   Folk music of Albania, recorded and edited by
    A. L. Lloyd: 12T 154, side 2 track 10

2   Folk music of Jugoslavia, recorded and edited by
    Wolf Dietrich: 12TS 224, side 2 tracks 4, 9, 10

3   Folk music of Greece, recorded and edited by
    Wolf Dietrich: 12TS 231, side 1 track 10

4   Ditto side 2 track 6; and Greek Folk Music:
    LLST 7188, tracks 14, 15, 16

5   Lado: Zagreb: LPY V 59

6   Tanec: PGP LPV 1210, side 2 track 1

7   *I heim og festleg lag*: Norwegian folk music: LPNE 3,
    side 2 tracks 8, 9

8   Ditto, side 1 track 6

9   Ditto, side 1 track 4

10 Ditto, side 1 track 7

11 Ditto, side 1 track 5

12 Ditto, side 2 track 7

13 Ditto, side 1 track 2

14 Shetland Fiddle Music, recorded and documented by
    the School of Scottish Studies, University of
    Edinburgh: TNGM 117, side 1 tracks 2, 3

15 Ditto, side 1 track 5

16 World Library of Folk and Primitive Music, edited
    Alan Lomax: Ireland AKL 4911, side 1 track 4; and
    the vocal music on tracks 3, 8, 9

17 The Liffey Banks: traditional Irish music played by
    Tommy Potts: CC13

18 Kerry Fiddles: music from Sliabh Luachra, played by
    Padraig O'Keefe, Denis Murphy and Julia Clifford:
    12T 309

19 Pedlar's Pack: John Doherty of Donegal: E.F.D.S.S.
    LP 1003

20 Compare the very primitive, three-note-scale Finnish
    wedding music for solo fiddle on FA 3005 with any of
    the Finnish fiddle-band music on RCA LSP 10367

21 A Tribute to Niel Gow, played by Ron Gonnella:
    LILP 5085
    Also Niel Gow's *Farewell to whisky* played by Bobby
    Harvey on ZLP 2086

22 Northumberland Forever: ILT 186, side 1 tracks 1,
    10; side 2 tracks 1, 3, 5

23 That's my rabbit: traditional Southern instrumental
    styles NW 226 side 2 track 1

24 Ditto, side 2 track 2

25 Ditto, side 2 track 4

26 Ditto, side 2 track 8

27 Echoes of the Ozarks: County 518, side 1 track 4

28 Fiddlin' John Carson: Rounder 1003 and County 544,
    side 1 track 3 for *Cotton-eyed Joe*

29 Georgia Fiddle Bands: County 544

30 Folksongs of the Louisiana Acadians: Arhoolie 5015
    Nathan Abshire: Arhoolie 5013, side 2

31 Wild rose of the mountain: East Kentucky fiddle music
    played by J. P. Fraley: Rounder 0037

32 Blue grass for collectors: APMI 0568, side A track 4
    and side B track 4

33 Going Down the Valley: vocal and instrumental styles
    in Southern folk music: NW 236, side 2 track 2

34 Ditto, side 2 track 9

35 Hills and home: thirty years of Blue grass: NW 225,
    side 1 track 1

36 Dark and Light in Spanish New Mexico: NW 292,
    side 2 tracks 2–6

37 Bob Dylan: Desire: CBS 86003

38 Western Swing: Old Timey LP 117, side 1 track 6

39 Country Music South and West: NW 287, side 2 track 8

40 Let's get loose: Folk and popular blues styles: NW 290
    side 1 tracks 3, 4

41 One o'clock Jump: Stuff Smith: MPS 545 114

42 Django Reinhardt and his American friends: CLP 1907,
    side 1 tracks 1, 7, 8

43 Joe Venuti: Violinology: RCA 740 110, side 1 track 6,
    side 2 track 1

44 The Quintet of the Hot Club of France 1935–39:
    ECM 2051 Stephane Grappelli: I hear music:
    Victor 730 107 and Stephane Grappelli 1972, 1973,
    et seq. (Pye)

45 Jean-Luc Ponty: Canteloupe Island: BND 4018

A Chronology of Violinists

Joseph Joachim Hungarian, b. Kittsee 1831, d. Berlin 1907 (*Hellmesberger/Bohm*). Joachim and the illustrious pupils who made up his school were the springboard for violin playing as we know it today. Joachim was the most famous violinist of his time, and is a legend in the history of the instrument. Although few violinists alive today will have heard him in person, his influence is still to be found everywhere in the violin world. His cadenzas to the Brahms and Beethoven concertos are still regarded by most players as unsurpassed, and his collaborations with the composers of his day (see pp. 134–138) were crucial to the course of violin music in the nineteenth century.
Recordings Joachim came to the gramophone at the end of his long career when the gramophone was at its very beginning. The sound is very poor in these early recordings, but we have five sides of Joachim playing the violin—and they are violin history. To modern ears, his solo Bach, warmly Romantic yet Classically poised, is probably the most instructive.

Pablo Sarasate Spanish, b. Pamplona 1844, d. Biarritz 1908 (*Alard*). Sarasate (real name Martin Sarasate) was one of the last of the great composer–virtuoso violinists, and Joachim's most serious rival. He left behind him a legacy of elaborate virtuoso compositions in his native Spanish style, which have dominated the repertoire of the genre ever since. He came to the classical repertoire only in his mid-twenties—but with such success that composers instantly formed a queue to dedicate new works to him: Lalo his violin concerto and *Symphonie Espagnole*, Bruch his second concerto and *Scottish Fantasy*, Saint-Saëns a concerto. Sarasate avoided the works of Paganini, chiefly, it is said, because his very small hands could not encompass the wide stretches the music demanded. Small hands or no, he was a sensation wherever he played.
Recordings In 1904 Sarasate made several recordings, seven of his own compositions, others including his arrangement of Chopin's Nocturne op. 9, and the *Praeludium* from Bach's E major Partita. These have been re-issued from time to time in LP collections. The sound is primitive, but the magic of the playing is unmistakeable and irresistible—even dating as it does from a time when Sarasate's health and technique were beginning to fail.

Leopold Auer Hungarian, b. Veszprem 1845, d. Loschwitz 1930 (*Dont/Joachim*). Where would the history of modern violin playing be without the name of Leopold Auer? Until a decade or so ago nearly every top-flight violinist had been at some time or another an Auer pupil. It would be difficult to imagine the violin scene without such names as Heifetz, Milstein, Zimbalist, Elman, Brown, Seidel, Rabinoff—to mention only the best of one of the greatest violin schools of all time.

A distinguished violinist himself, Auer was appointed Wieniawski's successor as professor of violin at St. Petersburg in 1868. He was the original dedicatee of Tchaikovsky's violin concerto, but decided it was too difficult—the concerto was eventually re-dedicated to its first performer, Adolf Brodsky. He abandoned his concert career for teaching, a step for which the violin world and the history of violin playing must be forever grateful. He continued to play in public, however, and made his Carnegie Hall debut in 1917 at the age of 72.
Recordings After a concert at Carnegie Hall in 1920 to celebrate his 75th birthday, Auer made a record of two works, Tchaikovsky's *Melody* and Brahms's Hungarian Dance no. 1 in G minor. Only five copies were made of this disc. It has been transcribed onto LP and issued in the 'Masters of the Bow' series by James Creighton of Canada. The original disc is a 'Victor Special Record' with no number, and the five copies were presented to Heifetz, Zimbalist, Elman, Eddy Brown and F. Steinway.

Otakar Ševčík Czech, b. Horaždovice 1852, d. Pisek 1934 (*Bennewitz*). Violinists came from all over the world to study with Ševčík, who was reputed to have had over 5,000 pupils, some of whom became top international performers. Names like Kocian, Kubelik, Daisy Kennedy, Morini, von Vecsey, Zacharewitch, Schneiderhan and Marie Hall all testify to his qualities as a teacher, although some of his pedagogic and technical theories are somewhat discredited today. No recordings of Ševčík are known to exist.

Jenö Hubay Hungarian, b. Budapest 1858, d. Budapest 1937 (*Joachim*). Hubay was a prince among violinists, whose approach to his art reflected his elegant life-style. The highly critical Carl Flesch called him 'a noble violinist of outstanding technical and musical qualities'. Perhaps a finer performer than teacher, his pupils nonetheless included Szigeti, Telmanyi, von Vecsey and the conductor Eugene Ormandy, who has directed so many fine violin concerto recordings.
Recordings Hubay recorded no major works, but only minor pieces together with some of his own compositions (he was a prolific composer of genre pieces). His first records were made around 1934 when he was already in his mid-seventies, but are nevertheless (e.g. his own *Violin Maker of Cremona*) fine illustrations of his rich sound and perfect articulation.

Eugène Ysaÿe Belgian, b. Liège 1858, d. Brussels 1931 (*Vieuxtemps/Massart*). Ysaÿe was a giant among fiddlers. He was a fiery performer who wooed his audiences with the brilliance of his passage-work and the luxuriance of his tone-colour. In 1881 he arrived in Paris, where he joined the coterie of young composers gathered around Debussy, Franck and Chausson—all three of whom later dedicated works to him (see also pp. 123 and 187). A description by the English critic

Arthur Symons of his playing in 1907 was characteristic of the enthusiasm Ysaÿe aroused: 'A marvellous passage of double-stopping in one of the Beethoven cadenzas was played as if one's teeth met in a peach . . . He floats on the surface of a river of pure sound, and dreams; every note like drops of water . . .' His pupils included Persinger, Gingold, Newman, Solway.

Recordings Ysaÿe left us twelve sides of acoustic 78s, together with two known test-pressings; there is also a reference to further test-pressings of a complete Mozart concerto whose whereabouts has never been disclosed. Most fascinating of all the discs released is perhaps the finale from the Mendelssohn concerto (all have been transferred to LP).

Willi Hess German, b. Mannheim 1859, d. Berlin 1939 *(Joachim)*. As a teacher, Hess influenced the career of many fine players of his generation. Busch studied with him in Cologne, Henry Holst was also a pupil, as was Kulenkampff, perhaps the closest to Hess in style.

Carl Flesch Hungarian, b. Moson 1873, d. Lucerne 1944 *(Marsick)*. The school of Carl Flesch is as crucial to the history of modern violin playing as Leopold Auer's was before him. The list of Flesch pupils reads almost like a *Who's Who* of the twentieth-century violin. For several decades there were probably more Flesch pupils on the international scene than from any other school: Haendel, Hassid, Rostal, Neveu, Odnoposoff, Szeryng, Gimpel, Goldberg, to name but a few. His contribution to the advancement of violin playing cannot be overestimated, both as a teacher and as the author of a two-volume work *The Art of Violin Playing*, a book on violin fingering, and his *Memoirs*. Every violinist should be given Flesch's *Memoirs* as compulsory reading: a fascinating and richly instructive collection of portraits and first-hand observations, every one of them closely relevant to performance. Flesch was also a pioneer of the master class.

Recordings Private and commercial discs are still being reissued. His Handel Sonata no. 4 is a notable for its crispness and delicacy. Two legendary performances of the concertos of Brahms and Beethoven held in a private collection have not yet been made available to the public. Flesch made many recordings for the Edison phonograph, several acoustic records, and a number of others dating from the late 1920s and early 1930s.

Fritz Kreisler Austrian, b. Vienna 1875, d. New York 1962 *(Hellmesberger)*. So much has been written about this gracious musician, who at one point in his life put down his violin to enter the medical profession. We are fortunate that, in the end, the violin won. Over his long career Kreisler was idolized by music lovers, violinists and it seems, indeed, by everyone he met. He started making gramophone records in Berlin as far back as 1904, yet was reluctant to broadcast, until finally persuaded by the conductor Donald Voorhees in 1944. All over the world, he was 'the violinist who makes everyone happy': few could resist the joy of his violin sound and the joy and integrity of his music making.

Recordings Kreisler recorded a great variety of music, some pieces several times over, and many of his own compositions.

Landmarks in the history of the gramophone are his Beethoven and Brahms concertos, and his Schubert Duo with Rachmaninov.

Jan Kubelík Bohemian, b. Michle 1880, d. Prague 1940 *(Ševčík)*. Kubelík was called the 'modern Paganini' of his time. His playing was of the highest technical order, and exceptionally dry in its tonal quality. It is hard to judge it today; contemporary writings nearly always refer to his technical abilities without considering his artistic merit (his programmes seem to have consisted chiefly of Paganini and Paganini-style showpieces).

Recordings Kubelík made many 78s but, with few exceptions, does not come over particularly well on record. He did make some electrical recordings, which seem to exist only as test pressings. He is rumoured to have once recorded a whole concerto.

Jacques Thibaud French, b. Bordeaux 1880, d. air crash on French mountain 1953 *(Marsick)*. Thibaud was one of the greatest—perhaps the greatest—of all French violinists. A child prodigy, he originally intended to be a pianist; but after hearing the Beethoven concerto at the age of seven he turned to the violin, and two years later was championed by Ysaÿe. His career was long, and he was always popular. Much of his concert-giving was also devoted to the Piano Trio which he founded in 1905 with Cortot and Casals, and which soon became world-famous. His performances of the Bach, Beethoven and Mozart concertos brought him acclaim; but it was in the music of Lalo, Chausson, Franck and Saint-Saëns that he most excelled. Sonata recitals with Cortot were also an important feature of his career.

Recordings Thibaud made a great number of recordings over the years, but they are for the most part now collectors' items. There have been reissues from time to time, mostly of his Trio performances. His recording of the Brahms double concerto op. 102 with Pablo Casals remains one of the outstanding sets of all time.

Georges Enescu Rumanian, b. Liveni 1881, d. Paris 1955 *(Hellmesberger/Marsick)*. Enescu was a capable pianist, a good composer, but above all a great violinist and a great teacher. His playing was first and foremost a spiritual experience; his sound seemed to come from a region which most other violinists have searched for in vain. While Enescu played, all else was forgotten. His influence is with us still, and will be so for many years, for his life work lives on in his pupils. All who came into contact with him were overwhelmed by his spiritual force. Enescu had many pupils who, in a sense, never left him until his death: Menuhin, Haendel, Neveu, Ferras and Bustabo are only a few of the great names who came under his spell.

Recordings Enescu's recordings are sadly few. His performance on record of Corelli's 'La Folia' sonata is sublime: no violinist should miss the opportunity to hear it at least once in his or her lifetime. He can also be heard as the accompanist to Menuhin's recording of the Paganini *Caprice* no. 6 op. 1, and as the conductor of many of the young Menuhin's concerto records. Enescu and his most famous pupil can also be heard playing together in Bach's double violin concerto—an unforgettable disc.

Bronislaw Huberman Polish, b. Czestochowa 1882, d. Nant-sur-Corsier, Switzerland 1947 *(Gregorowitch/Joachim/ Marsick)*. Huberman played the violin 'like a god and a gypsy' at one and the same time. A musician of great intellect and unswerving integrity, he took an unusually long time to learn a work. 'I must live the piece before I can play it beautifully. That moment may come when I am playing it upon the stage for the first, the fifth, or the tenth time. But if it does not come, I discard the composition, no matter what pains its mastery may have cost.' He was essentially a self-trained violinist, having received no formal tuition after the age of eleven (his lessons with Joachim and Joachim's pupil Markees in 1892 lasted only nine months). At fourteen he played the Brahms violin concerto in Vienna in the presence of the composer, and Brahms was deeply moved by his interpretation. In 1936, assisted by Toscanini and other leading musicians, he founded the Palestine Philharmonic Orchestra, which later became the Israel Philharmonic. Carl Flesch criticized him severely in his *Memoirs*, deploring many aspects of his technique and style; but for most others, musicians and non-musicians alike, he was one of the great violinists of modern times.
Recordings Huberman was one of the first violinists ever to make records: as early as 1903 he is reputed to have recorded two sides of Sarasate's arrangement of a Chopin Nocturne. His 'Kreutzer' sonata with Ignacy Friedman is one of the finest performances on record, as also his memorable Beethoven violin concerto, and two live broadcast recordings of the Brahms (1937 and 1944, both with the New York Philarmonic). His *Symphonie Espagnole* shows another aspect of his playing, richly coloured, warmly romantic.

Louis Persinger American, b. Rochester 1887, d. New York 1966 *(Ysaÿe)*. The name of Persinger enters the violin hall of fame above all for his having nurtured the talents of two of the most outstanding players of our day, Yehudi Menuhin and Ruggiero Ricci. Persinger was best known for his remarkable ability to teach gifted children: Menuhin wrote of him, 'The milk of human kindness may not lubricate a soloist's career; but it made Persinger an ideal teacher, at least for someone thirsty for instruction'. For a time he was leader of the Berlin Philharmonic Orchestra, and in 1915 became leader of the San Francisco Symphony Orchestra. After the death of Auer, he succeeded him at the Juilliard School in New York.
Recordings There are only four extant recordings of Persinger, but perhaps at some future date private recordings now held by pupils or relatives may be made available. We are fortunate that he also recorded a master-class on the interpretation of the Mendelssohn violin concerto (available on LP). Persinger can also be heard as the pianist accompanying the young Menuhin on some of the latter's early 78s.

Albert Spalding American, b. Chicago 1888, d. New York 1953 *(Lefort)*. No list of the great violinists who have made outstanding contributions to the advancement of violin play-

ing would be complete without the name of Albert Spalding: a poet of his instrument, who wooed his audiences with gracious style and heavenly sound. Spalding played mostly in the United States in his later years, after many successful world tours. No one who heard him could fail to respond to his gentle magic.
Recordings There is, happily, a lot of Spalding on record. The best of his violin concerto interpretations is perhaps Spohr's no. 8—a work that might have been written for him. His early 78 of his own transcription of Schubert's 'Hark, hark the lark' is a milestone of violin recording.

Efrem Zimbalist Russian, b. Rostov on Don, 1890 *(Auer)*. Zimbalist was, with Mischa Elman, for many years his rival, one of the first two important violinists to emerge from Auer's school. He started his concert career early, and by the age of eighteen was established as an international virtuoso of worldwide fame. His exceptionally catholic repertoire included much contemporary music, and his recital programmes frequently included premieres. In 1941 he became director of the Curtis Institute of Philadelphia, where he had taught the violin since 1928 and established a high reputation as a teacher. He is said to have one of the finest private collections of violins in the world.
Recordings Zimbalist made many recordings, chiefly of small genre pieces. His acoustic 78s of the Bach double concerto with Kreisler were in the catalogue—and still in demand—long after the advent of electric recording. Other notable discs were his Beethoven Romance in G played with the Japanese Broadcasting Symphony Orchestra, and Ysaÿe's solo sonata no. 1. Some private tapes have also been preserved of a Brahms concerto dating from 1946, and another of the Sibelius concerto from 1944.

Adolf Busch German, b. Siegen 1891, d. Vermont USA 1952 *(Willi Hess)*. Busch was greatly admired as a soloist, especially in the Beethoven and Brahms concertos, but his outstanding importance was as a player and director of chamber music. His String Quartet (formed in 1919) and later his Trio with Rudolf Serkin and his brother Hermann were famous for their inspired and lucid performances, especially of Beethoven and Schubert—and the Busch Chamber Players were renowned for their playing of Baroque works. He was also a distinguished teacher. It was to Busch that the young Yehudi Menuhin was sent after leaving Persinger.
Recordings So many splendid Busch recordings are available today, many issued on LP, that the listener is almost spoiled for choice. Chamber music apart, there are several fine sets of sonata recitals; and also some notable live recordings, including the Busoni violin concerto (recorded in 1936), a Brahms double concerto with Hermann (1949) and a Beethoven concerto (1942). It is interesting to note that there are now more recordings available of this artist in the catalogues than when he was alive.

Mischa Elman Russian/American, b. Talnoye 1891, d. New York 1967 *(Auer)*. Elman was Auer's favourite pupil. He made his public debut in Berlin at the age of thirteen, and from then on his career took unstoppable wing. He was never a profound interpreter of the classics, but rather a violin-magician whose alchemy of timbre and phrase was irresistible, and uniquely his own. He was called 'the Star of Melody', and with justice—for to Elman the violin was first and foremost a singing instrument. His tone was unmistakable: rich, dark and mellow, sensuous and infinitely expressive. Almost uniquely among violinists, his genius never dimmed: he was still playing public concerts, at the height of his powers, in the last month of his life.

Recordings There has never been any shortage of Elman material on disc. He recorded most of the popular repertoire, starting as early as 1908, and during his lifetime sold more than two million records. Many consider his Tchaikovsky concerto the finest of all time. There are no poor Elman records; every one is a delight.

Joseph Szigeti Hungarian, b. Budapest 1892, d. Lucerne 1973 *(Hubay)*. Szigeti, like Huberman, was much loved and above all much respected—a violinist of passionate devotion and integrity. He was a tireless champion of new works, and gave many first performances. Prokofiev and Bloch dedicated a concerto to him, and he was the co-dedicatee (with Benny Goodman) of Bartók's *Contrasts*. His books, *Violinist's Notebook*, *Szigeti on the Violin* and an autobiography *With Strings Attached*, should be on every student's reading list. We can still *see* him playing—he appeared in the film *Hollywood Canteen*.

Recordings Szigeti made his first recordings as far back as 1908, and continued to record throughout a very long career. To single out only a few: his Mozart recordings are very fine, his Brahms concerto with Harty is a great performance, as is his Mendelssohn concerto. Many have been transferred onto LP.

Eddy Brown American, b. Chicago 1895, d. Budapest 1974 *(Hubay/Auer)*. Brown's reputation was made mostly in America, although in his youth he played in most of the world's major concert halls. Unusual is the fact that he was taught by two masters from such widely differing schools. From 1933 onwards he was a frequent broadcaster on American radio, an important activity which he cultivated alongside his concert career.

Recordings Unfortunately none of Brown's recordings of the major concertos was commercially issued—what we have, apart from a very fine performance of Grieg's sonata op. 13 recorded in 1939, are chiefly genre pieces and encores. In later years he did record one or two larger works with his colleagues Rabinoff and Totenberg. More interesting is the fact that in the mid-1920s he is known to have recorded the Tchaikovsky and Mendelssohn violin concertos with the Berlin Philharmonic. Part of the Mendelssohn was issued but the remainder exists only in test pressing: both are very fine. The Tchaikovsky test pressings have been issued by Tom Clear of New York on a private label. It is interesting to note that Brown's versions would seem to be the first complete recordings of these concertos ever made.

Georg Kulenkampff German, b. Bremen 1898, d. Schaffhausen 1948 *(Hess)*. Kulenkampff was one of the most cultivated players of his day. His tone, famously warm and burnished like a cello's, was a joy to hear; his musicianship was unostentatious, impeccably refined. He was appointed leader of the Bremen Philharmonic at twenty, and later became Professor at Berlin University. On the death of Carl Flesch he was appointed his successor at the Lucerne Conservatory. He toured widely with Edwin Fischer and Enrico Mainardi. His death at the early age of fifty was a sad loss to the German violin school.

Recordings Kulenkampff gave the first performance of the Schumann violin concerto, and recorded it soon afterwards. Other notable achievements were recordings of the Beethoven concerto and Spohr's concerto no. 8 in A, op. 47.

Zino Francescatti French, b. Marseilles 1902 *(Paganini/Sivori)*. Francescatti came from a musical family of distinction: his father had studied with Sivori, the only authentic Paganini pupil, and his mother was a music teacher. He could never decide which of his parents gave him the more lessons. With his father he studied a great deal of Paganini, but the classics were not neglected: he played the Beethoven concerto in public at the age of ten. He played a 1727 Stradivarius (the 'Hart') with exceptional sweetness and warmth of phrase, and latterly in his career often played in a duo with the pianist Robert Casadesus.

Recordings Francescatti has made a great number of records, many of notable quality. Some of his early 78s especially are well worth hunting for—for example, the Kreisler *Recitative and Scherzo-Caprice*; of the later recordings, his Vitali Chaconne and Tartini's *Art of the Bow* are fine examples of his cultivated style.

Jascha Heifetz Russian, b. Vilna 1902 *(Auer)*. Since the end of the first World War, it would seem that there has never been a time when Heifetz was not the undisputed 'King of Violinists'. Even before that, his fame had spread: when Kreisler heard him in 1913 in Leipzig, he remarked to Zimbalist: 'You and I might just as well take our fiddles and break them across our knees'. He has been the most important single influence on violin playing since Paganini: and not necessarily always a good one. According to Flesch in 1923, many young fiddlers 'possessed by the devil of speed and trying to establish records' learned habits from Heifetz which ultimately destroyed them. The personality, both as musician and man, is enigmatic: some have found it compelling but cold; others, irresistibly seductive; all acknowledge it as technically beyond compare. Heifetz gave his last public recital, to an audience mainly of violinists who had travelled from the four corners of the globe to hear him play, in Los Angeles in 1972.

Recordings Heifetz made more records than any other violinist except Menuhin, who has continued recording during the ten years or so since Heifetz retired. Every Heifetz recording is a thrilling experience—but if one stands out above all, it is that of the Bruch *Scottish Fantasy*. If all other recordings of Heifetz's were lost, this one alone would suffice to explain to future generations exactly in what way and how far Heifetz raised the standard of violin performance.

Ivan Galamian Armenian, b. Tabriz 1903, d. New York

1981 (Capet). In his youth Galamian gained a reputation as a virtuoso, and made several successful European tours in his early twenties. But from an early age his principal interest had been teaching: after periods of residence in Paris and the Curtis Institute in the USA, he was appointed to the Julliard School in New York, where he remained to build himself a reputation comparable only to Leopold Auer's in St. Petersburg. His best-known pupils include Rabin, Perlman, Zukerman, Kyung-Wha Chung.

Nathan Milstein Russian, b. Odessa 1904 (Auer). Milstein was one of Auer's younger pupils, and the last great star of his school alive today. He has been one of the concert platform's most consistently reliable performers: as impressive a violinist in the 1980s as he was more than half a century ago. His Bach and Brahms are formidable, his Beethoven (especially the concerto) monumental.

Recordings He has recorded several concertos more than once, and while the first one is good, the second version is always better—what more can one ask of any artist? His early Brahms concerto with the Pittsburgh Symphony Orchestra under Steinberg was one of the best on LP in its time; his more recent recording of the same concerto with the Vienna Philharmonic under Jochum is one of the finest of all the many versions available. His recordings of the two Prokofiev concertos also deserve special mention.

Erica Morini Austrian, b. Vienna 1904 (Ševčík). This phenomenal violinist started learning the violin when she was three, entered Ševčík's class at the age of eleven, and made her public concert debut in Vienna the same year, closely followed by a debut in Berlin. Nikisch, who conducted her, said, 'She is not a wonder-child; she is a wonder and a child'. Before the second World War in Europe, and after it in the USA, a flawless technique, combined with the tonal charm and sweetness of the Viennese school, ensured for her a dazzling career.

Recordings All Morini's many recordings, including most of the big concertos, are impressive. Her account of Sarasate's transcription of the Waltz from Gounod's *Faust* is a characteristically seductive example of Morini pyrotechnics.

Gioconda de Vito Italian, b. Martina Franca 1907 (Principe). Gioconda de Vito was a violinist of great distinction and charm, who gave memorable readings of all the major concertos, especially the Brahms. She devoted much of her time to teaching, first at the Accademia di Santa Cecilia in Rome, and after 1949 in London. To the regret of her many admirers, she retired from the concert platform at the early age of 54 in 1961.

Recordings Most notable of her numerous recordings is the Brahms concerto—her oft-declared favourite—with the Philharmonia Orchestra under Rudolf Schwartz; 'off the air' recordings have also been made available of both her Brahms and Mendelssohn violin concertos with Furtwängler, the first dating from 1953.

David Oistrakh Russian, b. Odessa 1908, d. Amsterdam 1974 (Stolyarsky). Oistrakh was born into a musical family: his father, a poor accountant, played the violin and trained the local opera chorus; his mother was a singer and an actress. His career was established in the Soviet Union in the late 1920, but he did not play abroad until 1946, and made his debut in western Europe in the 1950s. His success was immediate and sensational. At the peak of his powers at this time, all who heard him agreed that his playing was perfection itself. After his New York debut in 1955, an American critic described him as 'a warm, enkindling sensitivity with head and heart inextricably linked'—words which were echoed for many years subsequently, until his regrettably early death at the age of 66

Recordings Oistrakh has recorded a wide range of the violin repertory, and his performances are of extraordinarily consistent quality. All are warmly recommended.

Benno Rabinoff American, b. New York 1910 (Auer). Rabinoff was one of Auer's favourite pupils, and the only one for whom he ever conducted. He played mainly in the USA, often recitals with his pianist wife Sylvia: he was a virtuoso of the Auer school, and recognizably a sibling of Heifetz. He liked informality and played often with friends and colleagues such as Eddy Brown and Roman Totenberg, with both of whom he made several recordings.

Recordings There appears to be only two commercial recordings of Rabinoff playing alone: one a collection of pieces by Sarasate, Kreisler and de Falla, and the other of Ravel's *Tzigane*. Both these contain some of the most beautiful violin playing ever committed to disc.

Szymon Goldberg Polish, b. Włocławek 1909 (Flesch). Always in demand as both concerto soloist and recitalist, Goldberg is renowned for his playing of Bach, Beethoven and Mozart. A child prodigy, he played the Paganini D major concerto in public at the age of twelve and two years later was engaged as soloist with the Berlin Philharmonic Orchestra in the same work. His playing has been described as 'refined, intimate and of noble intensity', and his technique as 'devastatingly secure'. He has frequently appeared with the Netherlands Chamber Orchestra as director and soloist, and is also a sensitive performer of Bartók, Hindemith and Berg.

Recordings Goldberg's recordings of the violin classics are numerous and noteworthy; his performances of the concertos of Berg and Milhaud are already modern classics of their kind. His sixteen Mozart sonatas with Radu Lupu are a notable achievement.

Ricardo Odnoposoff Argentinian, b. Buenos Aires 1914 (Flesch). An outstanding violinist at a very early age, he made his public debut at five, and was only twelve when he took his first lessons with Flesch. He won many prizes before sharing joint first place with David Oistrakh in the Eugène Ysaÿe Competition in Brussels in 1937. He has had a hand in the training of many fine violinists in the public eye today.

Recordings Odnoposoff made many recordings, most notable of which are perhaps a Paganini concerto no. 1 and an LP *The Magic Violin*. His record of the Tartini 'Devil's Trill' sonata is sensational, in particular his playing of the cadenza.

Wolfgang Schneiderhan Austrian, b. Vienna 1915 *(Ševčík/ Winkler)*. As a young player Schneiderhan was billed as 'Wolfi' and made some gramophone records under this name, touring Europe from the age of eleven. In 1938 he founded a string quartet which played a leading role in the musical life of Vienna for some years. He was for a short time principal violin of both the Vienna Symphony and Vienna Philharmonic Orchestras. Schneiderhan's warm, sweet tone and elegant style have endeared him to audiences worldwide. *Recordings* There are many recordings by this fine artist: notably a complete set of all the Mozart concertos, and an outstanding Beethoven concerto. It is interesting to note that while most violinists today play either Joachim's or Kreisler's cadenzas to the Brahms concerto, in both his versions of this work on record Schneiderhan uses the cadenza by one of his teachers, Winkler.

Yehudi Menuhin American, b. New York 1916 *(Persinger/ Busch/Enescu)*. Yehudi Menuhin's lineage must be unique among musicians: in his youth he learned from and worked with many of the greatest musicians of the century—Ravel, Persinger, Ysaÿe, Enescu, Beecham, Busch, Walter, Elgar, Bartók, to name only a few—by and large before reaching the age when most children are ready to leave school. The young Menuhin clearly had the sensibility and sensitivity to absorb these influences, for his playing from a very tender age was extraordinarily mature. His name was internationally known almost before he had the strength to tune his own fiddle. He quickly became, like a handful of the greatest violinists before him, a legend—not merely in his lifetime, but before a third of his life was past: and is still today regarded by performers and audiences alike with as much awe as affection. Teaching has always been close to his heart: the school in England that bears his name, founded in 1963, has already provided a comprehensive musical education for hundreds of talented young string players. *Recordings* Menuhin started recording in 1927 when he was only eleven years old, and has since made records with most of the greatest orchestras and conductors—more indeed than any other violinist past or present. His recording of the Bach double concerto with Enescu and his Elgar concerto performed under the direction of the composer in 1932, are two immortal peaks of an incomparable range. His first 78 of Schubert's *Ave Maria* (1933) demonstrates what must surely be the most perfect violin sound ever to be transferred to the grooves of a disc.

Oscar Shumsky American, b. Philadelphia 1917 *(Auer/ Zimbalist)*. Born of Russian parents, Shumsky began studying the violin at the age of three, and at the age of eight played a Mozart concerto with the Philadelphia Orchestra under Leopold Stokowski, who called him 'the most astounding genius I have ever heard'— a sentiment echoed later by David Oistrakh, who hailed Shumsky as 'one of the world's great violinists'. He subsequently became the youngest student ever accepted by Leopold Auer, and Fritz Kreisler, who took special interest in his early development, predicted an important future. After some years as a soloist, widely admired, he decided not to follow the path of an international virtuoso, but instead to give only occasional short tours of his homeland, devoting the rest of his time to teaching. Shumsky is *par excellence* a 'violinist's violinist': his rare concerts are usually sold out, a great proportion of the seats taken by fellow artists who have come to hear one of the last great representatives of the Auer school still at the height of his powers. *Recordings* Shumsky's complete sets of the Ysaÿe solo sonatas, the Bach solo sonatas and Partitas, and Mozart's sonatas (with Arthur Balsam) have been justly acclaimed. The first volume of his projected complete works of Fritz Kreisler has been recently (1983) released.

Ruggiero Ricci American, b. San Bruno 1918 *(Persinger)*. Two years after launching the young Yehudi Menuhin, Louis Persinger brought another prodigy before the public of San Francisco: accompanied by his teacher at the piano, the seven-year-old Ruggiero Ricci played a recital of works by Saint-Saëns and Wieniawski, rounded off with the Mendelssohn concerto. He gave his Carnegie Hall debut at ten, and at fourteen made the first of many triumphant tours of Europe. When he appeared in Budapest under Dohnányi, Kreisler called him the greatest musical genius since Mozart. 'A blazing violin talent', his flame burns as brightly today as it did more than fifty years ago. *Recordings* Ricci's many records are a treasury of violin playing; his Paganini *Caprices* are beyond all present competition. Ricci is the showpiece fiddler *par excellence* ('I love the violin as Kreisler played it: I would infinitely rather hear *Liebesleid* played well than Beethoven played badly')—but for all his virtuosity, no less an artist of deeply serious perception and integrity. His Bruch, Mendelssohn and Tchaikovsky concertos should be on every collector's—and music lover's—shelf.

Guila Bustabo Canadian, b. Manitowoc 1919 *(Persinger/ Enescu/Hubay)*. This remarkable prodigy could read music at the age of three, and a year later made her debut with the Chicago Symphony Orchestra; at eleven she was the soloist in Wieniawski's first concerto with the New York Philharmonic (her name is unaccountably omitted from most violin books and dictionaries of music). At Toscanini's urging, she made her first tour of Europe at the age of fourteen. In Finland she played the Sibelius concerto for the composer, and later Wolf-Ferrari wrote his concerto for her. Her rise to stardom was meteoric, but her international career was curtailed by the war and some of her best years were lost to us. She plays regularly in Europe, and currently holds the post of Professor of Violin in the Conservatory of Innsbruck. *Recordings* Judged by the records that she has made, sadly few in number, Miss Bustabo is unarguably a world-class violinist. Her recordings have long since disappeared from the general catalogues, but thanks to the efforts of the private collector Tom Clear of New York, they have all been reissued by him from his collection. Technically she stands with the very few. Her recording of the Sibelius concerto is particularly commanding.

Ginette Neveu French, b. Paris 1919, d. air crash over Azores 1949 *(Flesch/Enescu)*. From an early age, the violin playing of Ginette Neveu 'had the impact of a volcano': a performer of powerful dedication, intense and passionate, her tone, like her physique, exceptionally large and strong. She made her debut at the age of seven playing the Bruch first concerto; at sixteen she won first prize in Warsaw—a competition in which David Oistrakh came second! During the three years following the Second World War she had the concert world at her feet, and toured the USA and Europe with dazzling success. At the age of thirty, at the height of her career, she was killed in an aeroplane crash over the Azores on the way to America. Clutching her precious Stradivarius to her chest, 'she died as she lived, with the wheels of her life in full motion'.

Recordings Fortunately, Neveu started recording a few years before she died, so that some examples of the major works from her repertoire survive. All are good; several are very fine. All were made before the age of the LP, but have been transferred and collected together as one boxed LP set. There is no doubt that, had she lived, Neveu would have been one of the great violinists of our age.

Isaac Stern Russian, b. Kriminiesz 1920 *(Brodsky/Blinder)*. Stern was the child of a great tradition: although Naoum Blinder is not one of the most famous names in violin teaching, he was trained by Adolf Brodsky, who in turn was taught by Hellmesberger, thus forging a direct link, through his teacher André Robberechts, with Viotti. Stern made his debut at the age of fifteen with the San Francisco Symphony Orchestra, and after seventeen took no more formal lessons. Since then he has played with every major orchestra in the world under almost every great conductor. A great violinist, man and mover, his interests and activities have always extended beyond the concert hall—into politics, concert-promoting, musicology and, especially, teaching.

Recordings Stern's phenomenal discography, almost as large as Menuhin's, embraces virtually all of the major works for violin. Particularly worth seeking out are his 78s of the Mendelssohn concerto with Ormandy and the Tchaikovsky concerto with the Philadelphia Orchestra under Hilsberg (1951); of his later LP recordings, his Viotti concerto no. 22 is outstanding.

Arthur Grumiaux Belgian, b. Villers-Perwin 1921 *Dubois/Enescu)*. An outstanding virtuoso of the Franco-Belgian school. At the age of six he was accepted at the Conservatoire of Charleroi, from which he graduated five years later with the highest honours. The war interrupted his career, but after 1945 his reputation quickly spread throughout Europe. A landmark at this time was his performance, the first in Europe, of William Walton's violin concerto, a work which (although it was originally written for Heifetz) Grumiaux subsequently made very much his own. Three years after a triumphant American debut in 1951, he gave the premiere in Paris of the then newly discovered violin concerto no. 4 of Paganini, which he also recorded. He has been Professor of the Violin at the Brussels Conservatoire since 1949.

Recordings Among his many fine achievements for the gramophone is a complete set of the Mozart concertos with the Vienna Symphony Orchestra under Paumgartner and Moralt. Other notable discs include The Vieuxtemps concerto no. 4 with the Lamoureux Orchestra under Rosenthal, and the Saint-Saëns concerto no. 3 with the same combination. His recording of the Berg concerto with the Concertgebouw under Markevich has been described as 'the greates performance of that work on disc'.

Joseph Hassid Polish, b. Sulwalki 1923, d. Epsom 1950 *(Flesch)*. The career of this wonderful violinist lasted only three years, from 1938 to 1940: many words have been written of his mental illness and untimely end, and of the great loss it represented to the world of music. Hassid played with fire in his heart and with fire in his bow. Had he lived he would certainly have ranked with the greatest violinists of all time. Both Kreisler and Huberman were deeply impressed with the young Hassid, as was his teacher Flesch, who rated him as one of the most promising pupils he ever taught.

Recordings Hassid was to have made the first recording of Walton's violin concerto and another of the Elgar concerto, but this was not to be. What we do have are eight short pieces on four 78 records which leave us in no doubt of his genius—most memorable of these, perhaps, is an electrifying account of Elgar's *La Capricieuse*.

Leonid Kogan Russian, b. Ukraine 1924, d. Moscow 1982 *(Yampolski)*. After David Oistrakh, Kogan was considered the foremost Soviet violinist of the post-war era: a more tautly disciplined and 'intellectual' musician even than Oistrakh, his technical command was faultless, and his finest performances combined noble power with admirable stylistic integrity. After studying with Abram Yampolski (a pupil of Auer) at the Moscow Conservatoire for five years, he won first prize at the 1947 International Youth Competition in Prague, four years later also winning first prize at the Ysaÿe Competition in Brussels. He was first heard in England in 1955, and in America in 1957. Both his son and his wife (Elizaveta Gilels, sister of the pianist) are well-known violinists.

Recordings Kogan was a favourite recording artist both in Russia and in the West. Of his many discs, the most outstanding must surely be that of his Paganini concerto no. 1 in D major, with Paganini's original cadenza.

Ida Haendel Polish, b. Chelm 1928 *(Flesch/Enescu)*. At the age of four, Ida Haendel was accepted without fees at the Chopin School of Music in Warsaw, where her teacher was Michalowicz, an Auer pupil who had also taught Huberman; three years later she travelled to Paris to study with Flesch. Nothing in her playing has ever been stale or predictable: she approaches each new performance as a fresh task with its own unique demands. Her technique is formidable; her interpretations are forthright but unpretentious, broadly romantic but classically poised.

Recordings Outstanding of Ida Haendel's many recordings—in her own as well as her admirers' estimation—is perhaps the Brahms concerto conducted by Celibidache.

Michael Rabin American, b. New York 1937, d. New York 1972 *(Galamian)*. Considered by Galamian to have been the most gifted violinist he ever taught, Rabin died at the age of thirty-five, at the height of a brilliant but troubled career, undermined by drug addiction and mental illness. There are poignant parallels with the career of Carl Flesch's brilliant pupil Joseph Hassid. His playing, both in public and on record, radiates unquenchable vitality and joy, and his technique unshakeable authority. Had fate not intervened, Rabin, like Hassid, would surely have become one of the great musicians of our day.

Recordings We are fortunate that Rabin has left us many fine LP recordings, in some cases even two versions of the same work. His LP entitled *Mosaics* is superb; his Wieniawski first concerto is one of the most exuberant ever recorded; his first recording of the Paganini concerto no. 1 with Goossens is a thrilling tour de force. From his '*In Memoriam*' LP one might choose the Paganini *Moto Perpetuo* as an ideal example of the Rabin style.

Salvatore Accardo Italian, b. Naples 1941 *(Astruc)*. Accardo is Italy's most distinguished living violinist. At the age of fifteen he won first prize in Genova's Paganini Competition, and soon established a successful and widely-travelled career. He is a capable all-round musician of unusually catholic tastes and sympathies: the technique is excellent, the tone full if somewhat dry, the musicianship uneven but, at its best, commanding and original.

Recordings Of the many records by Accardo available today, his performance of the Sibelius concerto, and concertos by Vivaldi, are outstanding; his account of the three Schubert sonatinas is also warmly recommended.

Itzhak Perlman Israeli, b. Tel Aviv 1945 *(Galamian)*. At the top of the list of today's younger virtuosos stands the name of Perlman. A victim of polio at the age of four, which severely affected his walking, he began violin lessons soon afterwards at the Shulamit High School in Tel Aviv, and by the age of ten had given numerous public recitals. He won a scholarship to the Juilliard School in the USA in 1958, and five years later made his debut in Carnegie Hall. His warm, burnished tone, directness of musical expression and brilliant technique have brought him international recognition.

Recordings Perlman's recorded output has been prolific, and of an exceptionally high standard. Outstanding are a Beethoven concerto with Giulini (also available on video) and a Paganini boxed set which contains the 24 *Caprices*, the first concerto, and a bonus of Sarasate's *Carmen Fantasy*.

Kyung-Wha Chung Korean, b. Seoul 1948 *(Galamian)*. Like Perlman, Kyung-Wha Chung is another major talent from the Galamian school, who gained an international reputation very quickly after her European debut in 1970. Her playing has been much admired for its vitality, polish and expressive warmth; one of her most satisfying orchestral partnerships has been with the conductor André Previn in both concerts and records.

Dong-Suk Kang Korean, b. Seoul 1954 *(Galamian)*. Kang has been described by some who have heard him as already one of the world's great violinists. His flawless technique and perfect bow arm certainly produce one of the most beautiful violin tones to be heard anywhere today. He has studied at the Juilliard School with Ivan Galamian, and with Zino Francescatti and Leonid Kogan.

Anne Sofie Mutter German, b. Rheinfelden 1963 *(Honigberger/Stucki)*. The youngest to join this list of illustrious players. Up to the age of ten she was taught by Erna Honigberger and since by Aida Stucki, both of whom were in turn Flesch pupils: Mutter continues the tradition of a great school. The conductor Herbert von Karajan took her under his wing at an early age, and concerts with his orchestra have been her principal concerto training ground.

Discography

Introduction

This list sets out to provide no more than one of many possible reference points for the collector of violin recordings. Each individual will build up a library for many different reasons. As it grows, the collection becomes a personal reference point—just as a library of books reflects the owner's individual taste and needs.

Most collections start with recordings available in the record departments of any good store; then, as interest grows, the collector branches out into dealers' lists and the second-hand markets. The pursuit becomes more rewarding as it continues. In the same way that the violinist learns to read the music on the printed paper, the listener, whether a violinist or not, must learn to read the sounds printed on the gramophone record. Just as the history of the violin is contained in books such as this one, so also is the history of the sound of violin playing and performing style written in the grooves of the record.

The gramophone has now been established for over 100 years, and offers a unique archive of study and listening material. No serious violinist and musician can ignore what has gone before. Leopold Auer told each one of his students to go out and listen to as many great violinists as they could. The gramophone affords us just that opportunity without stirring from our living room.

Had we any records of Paganini today, we would not need to rely on contemporary writings, but could judge the quality of his performance and technical achievements for ourselves. It is true that the primitive acoustic recordings of Sarasate or Joachim for example, do not give us entirely satisfactory sound-pictures; but in the case of the former we can at least hear the *manner* in which he played his own compositions, and in the case of the latter we can hear, imperfectly but clearly, as it were in a black-and-white photograph, a style that laid the foundations of violin playing as we know it today.

Since the discovery by R. Glaspole of the recordings of Marie Soldat-Roeger, we now also have the opportunity to hear a first-generation Joachim pupil playing some of her teacher's repertoire, but with the technical advantage of better recorded sound.

It is strange that Kreisler would not entrust his unique sound to radio until the mid-1940s, yet was happy to make records as early as 1904. As a result we have the opportunity to hear the young Kreisler. Anyone who has heard his acoustic record of 'Chanson sans paroles' will realize how tragic our loss would have been had it not been recorded.

An interesting recent development has been the increasing availability on LP of live recordings taken from studio broadcasts. These originate from many sources. Mainly taken directly 'off the air', many great performances have survived in the libraries of many private collectors, and after the expiry of copyright have been gathered from every part of the world by specialist record companies. We can now hear, for instance, two versions of the Brahms violin concerto played live in concert by Huberman (1937 and 1944)—a great violinist whose performance was admired by the composer, but who never recorded the work for a commercial company. Many broadcasting companies in the past, however, failed to preserve their broadcasts of great players—as is proven by the lack of material of the great Georges Enescu, who must have broadcast many performances of the major concertos, none of which survive in the archives of the world's broadcasting stations.

Many great performances have been garnered in this fashion by specialist record companies—most notably perhaps by the Rococco Company of Toronto owned by James Creighton, who is also the author of the *Discopaedia of the Violin*, the serious violin recording collector's bible. Other companies which have added substantially to the 'live performance' lists are *I Grandi Interpreti*, the Bruno Walter Society, and Pearl Records. More recently we have seen large collections issued by the Furtwängler Society, the Bruder Busch Society, and a magnificent collection of live performances by Toscanini with many renowned soloists. Such discs are usually more expensive than those of the major recording companies; our compensation is that many of these performances are unique and never commercially recorded.

This discography is not a comprehensive buyer's guide: many more exhaustive works are available on the subject. Its intention is principally to motivate the serious listener and the serious student of the violin to investigate more fully the range of interpretations on record—to look backwards, as well as to the present. This may require some effort on the part of the seeker: but the rewards are manifold, and the way full of excitement and surprises.

In some cases a recording of a work is recommended simply because it is an excellent example of a particular artist—even though it may not be the 'best' recording available. One such is Zoltán Székely's 1939 recording of the Bartók violin concerto. There may be other, finer performances; but this is a live concert recording of the premiere, by the violinist who commissioned the work, and therefore of special interest. Since record numbers vary so much from issue to issue, and from country to country, they have not been included in the list.

Bach Double concerto in D minor. DAVID and IGOR OISTRAKH, Royal Philharmonic Orchestra/Goosens
The discography of this much-recorded work is vast. Some of the most successful have been made by the following combinations: Menuhin and Enescu, Kreisler and Zimbalist (an acoustic recording which remained in the catalogues

until the end of the war), Stern and Schneider. Among more recent versions, the Oistrakhs' is hard to match.

Bach Concerto no. 1 in A minor. YEHUDI MENUHIN, Bath Festival Chamber Orchestra dir. Menuhin
The 78 recording by Huberman and the Vienna Philharmonic Orchestra under Dobrowen, which held its own in the catalogues for many years, was superbly played, and well recorded for its time (1934).

Bach Concerto no. 2 in E. major SZYMON GOLDBERG, Philharmonia Orchestra/Susskind
There were also many fine versions before this, including a performance by Yehudi Menuhin and the Paris Symphony Orchestra/Enescu.

Bach Solo sonatas and Partitas. NATHAN MILSTEIN; ARTHUR GRUMIAUX
Starting points for comparison would be Michael Rabin's performance of the C major sonata, Heifetz's last version of the G minor Sonata, any of the six recorded by Georges Enescu, and if a set can be found, the 12-year-old Yehudi Menuhin playing the C major sonata, which he recorded in 1929.

Barber Concerto op. 14 (1941). ISAAC STERN, New York Philharmonic Symphony Orchestra/Bernstein
This fine recording by Stern has not as yet been bettered.

Bartók Concerto op. posth. (1896). DAVID OISTRAKH, Moscow Radio Orchestra/Rozhdestvensky
Yehudi Menuhin's recording with the New Philharmonia Orchestra/Dorati is a fine alternative.

Bartók Concerto no. 2 in B minor (1938). YEHUDI MENUHIN, New Philharmonia Orchestra/Dorati
We are fortunate that Hungaraton have copied and reissued the original acetates of the world premiere on 23 March 1939 given by Zoltán Székely with the Concertgebouw Orchestra under Mengelberg. Another splendid version, dating from the 1950s, is by Ivry Gitlis with the Vienna Symphony Orchestra/Horenstein.

Bartók Solo Sonata (1944). YEHUDI MENUHIN
This solo sonata was written for and first performed by Yehudi Menuhin. There are several other fine versions, notably by André Gertler, who also worked with Bartók, and by Ivry Gitlis.

Beethoven Concerto in D op. 61 (1806). ITZHAK PERLMAN, Philharmonia Orchestra/Giulini; GEORG KULENKAMPFF, Berlin Philharmonic Orchestra/Schmidt-Isserstedt (Recorded 1936)
For many years the Kulenkampff version was considered to be definitive. Predictably, a much-recorded concerto: both Fritz Kreisler's and Bronislaw Huberman's wonderful recordings should also be heard. The Perlman is also available on video.

Beethoven Romance no. 1 in G op. 40 (1803), Romance no. 2 in F op. 50 (1805). DAVID OISTRAKH, Royal Philharmonic Orchestra/Goossens
Oistrakh's playing in these two Romances is outstanding.

Beethoven Violin sonatas, complete. JASCHA HEIFETZ with Emanuel Bay (Brooks Smith in the 'Kreutzer' sonata only); JOSEPH SZIGETI with Claudio Arrau
All fine performances, matching the standard set by Fritz Kreisler with Franz Rupp in the mid-1930s. The Heifetz and Szigeti interpretations differ widely, but each has its notable qualities.

Beethoven Triple concerto in C for violin, cello and piano op. 56 (1805). DAVID OISTRAKH, Mstislav Rostropovich and Sviatoslav Richter, Berlin Philharmonic/von Karajan
While not strictly a solo violin concerto, this work cannot be overlooked by a serious violin record collector. Another inspiring performance is by the Beaux Arts Trio with the London Philharmonic Orchestra/Haitink.

Berg Concerto (1935). ANDRÉ GERTLER, Philharmonia Orchestra/Kletzki; JOSEPH SZIGETI, Symphony Orchestra/Mitropoulos (live 1945)
The work was commissioned by Louis Krasner, who gave the first performance; he also recorded the work with the Cleveland Symphony Orchestra/Rodzinski.

Berlioz Rêverie and Caprice op. 8 (1839). YEHUDI MENUHIN, Philharmonia Orchestra/Pritchard
For many years the only available version of this work was by Joseph Szigeti on 78s, which still remains a memorable performance.

Bloch Concerto (1938). ROMAN TOTENBERG, Vienna State Opera Orchestra/Golschmann
The first performance on record, by Joseph Szigeti with the Paris Conservatory Orchestra/Munch, is still worth hunting for.

Brahms Concerto in D op. 77 (1878). ANNE SOFIE MUTTER, Berlin Philharmonic/Von Karajan; ITZHAK PERLMAN, Chicago Symphony Orchestra/Giulini; ALBERT SPALDING, Vienna Tonkünstler Symphony Orchestra/Loibner (live 1952)
With so many very fine recordings of this concerto there can be no 'best' performance. Others highly recommended are by Ginette Neveu with Philharmonia/Dobrowen; Heifetz with the Chicago Symphony Orchestra/Reiner; David Oistrakh with French National Radio Orchestra/Klemperer.

Brahms Double concerto for violin and cello in A minor op. 102 (1887). ISAAC STERN and Leonard Rose, New York Philharmonic Symphony Orchestra/Walter; ADOLF BUSCH and Hermann Busch, French National Radio Orchestra/Kletzki (live 1949)
The standard here was set by an early recording of Jacques Thibaud and Pablo Casals with the Barcelona Symphony Orchestra conducted by Cortot—an unforgettable recording still available on LP transfers.

Brahms Violin sonatas op. 78 in G, op. 100 in A, op. 108 in D minor. ISAAC STERN with Alexander Zakin
This very fine set has lost none of its magic. Also of great interest is the set by Georg Kulenkampff and Georg Solti, now transferred to LP.

Britten Concerto no. 1 in D (1939, rev. 1958). MARK LUBOTSKY, English Chamber Orchestra/Britten
This sensitive performance is conducted by the composer. A more recent recording by Ida Haendel is an excellent alternative.

Bruch Scottish Fantasy op. 46 (1880). JASCHA HEIFETZ, New Symphony Orchestra of London/Sargent
Of all the records of the violin ever made, this one is perhaps the most perfect. Heifetz's performance is without fault. Not to have heard this record is not to have experienced the real thrill of perfection: like a good wine, one can never have enough. Many are of the opinion that if all other recordings of the master were destroyed, this one alone would provide living proof of the sublime heights to which Heifetz took the art of violin playing.

Bruch Concerto no. 1 in G minor op. 26 (1868). YEHUDI MENUHIN, Philharmonia Orchestra/Susskind; GUILA BUSTABO, Concertgebouw Orchestra/Mengelberg (live 1940)
This recording by Menuhin is one of the longest-surviving LPs of any artist in the catalogue—and what a grand performance it is! Bustabo's sensational performance was recorded during the war from a broadcast.

Bruch Concerto no. 2 in D minor op. 44 (1878). ITZHAK PERLMAN, New Philharmonia Orchestra/Lopez-Cobos
A superlative performance from Perlman. The old version by Jascha Heifetz with the RCA Victor Symphony Orchestra/Solomon is still very exciting.

Busoni Concerto in D (1897). ADOLF BUSCH, Concertgebouw Orchestra/Bruno Walter (live 1936); JOSEPH SZIGETI, RAI Symphony Orchestra/Previtali (live 1952)
Busch was at his prime when this recording was made. Both these performances were recorded from live broadcasts.

Chausson *Poème* op. 25 (1882). ISAAC STERN, Orchestre de Paris/Barenboim
For the truly classic performance of this work, we must go to the LP transfer of Georges Enescu, given with piano accompaniment—transcendental violin magic from another time and place, recorded in 1928.

Corelli Sonata 'La Folia' op. 5 no. 12. RUGGIERO RICCI with Dennis Nesbitt (*viola da gamba*) and Ivor Keyes (harpsichord)
There are many commendable recordings of this work, as a glance through the catalogues will reveal. The definitive recording must still be that which Georges Enescu made in 1925, and which has been transferred to LP many times: positively a violin masterclass in itself, and not to be missed.

Debussy Violin sonata (1917). MAURICE HASSON with Michael Isador
Joseph Silverstein, under the direction of Michael Tilson Thomas, has also made an immaculate recording.

Delius Concerto (1916). ALBERT SAMMONS, Liverpool Philharmonic Orchestra/Sargent
Of the few recordings made of this concerto, that of Albert Sammons is by far the most sympathetic.

Dvořák Concerto in A minor op. 53 (1879). ITZHAK PERLMAN, London Philharmonic Orchestra/Barenboim
Perlman's performance of the Dvořák concerto is one of his finest records. Also very good is Joseph Suk's account with the Czech Philharmonic Orchestra/Ancerl.

Elgar Concerto in B minor op. 61 (1909). ITZHAK PERLMAN, Chicago Symphony Orchestra/Barenboim
Can the first recording of the Elgar concerto with the young Yehudi Menuhin and the London Symphony Orchestra conducted by the composer ever be surpassed? It is one of the monuments of the gramophone, dating from 1932, and still available on modern transfer.

Enescu Violin sonatas, no. 2 in F major op. 6, and no. 3 in A major op. 25. GEORGES ENESCU with Dinu Lipatti
The finest recording of these sonatas is undoubtedly by the composer himself, accompanied by Dinu Lipatti.

Ernst Concerto in F sharp minor op. 23 (1849). AARON ROSAND, Orchestra Radio Luxembourg/de Froment
This concerto was in the repertoire of many violinists in the early part of the century, but now more rarely performed; Rosand's playing has a splendid period bloom.

Franck Sonata in A op. 26 (1886). KYUNG-WHA CHUNG with Radu Lupu
A work which always benefits from the collaboration of two fine soloists; there have also been wonderful performances recorded by Jacques Thibaud with Alfred Cortot and Yehudi Menuhin with his sister Hephzibah.

Frankel Concerto op. 24. MAX ROSTAL, Beromunster Radio Orchestra/Schmidt (live—no date available)
Benjamin Frankel's concerto is one of those of which we have no commercial recording, but only an LP transcription of a live broadcast.

Glazounov Concerto in A minor op. 82 (1904). ERICA MORINI, Berlin Radio Orchestra/Fricsay
A warm and stylish performance; but for a truly dazzling account of this work, we must turn to one or other of the Heifetz recordings, the 78 version with the London Philharmonic/Barbirolli or the LP version with the RCA Victor Symphony Orchestra/Hendl.

Goldmark Concerto in A op. 28 (1878). NATHAN MILSTEIN, Philharmonia Orchestra/Blech
Ruggerio Ricci offers an excellent alternative performance with the Orchestra of Radio Luxembourg/de Froment.

Grieg Violin sonatas, no. 1 in F major op. 8, no. 2 in G major op. 13, and no. 3 in C minor op. 45. ALAN LOVEDAY with Leonard Cassini
Mention should also be made of the very sensitive recording of the sonata no. 2 made by Eddy Brown in the USA with C. Adler, and of Arthur Grumiaux's fine performance with G. Sebrok.

Gruenberg Concerto op. 47 (1944). JASCHA HEIFETZ, San Francisco Symphony Orchestra/Monteux
There is little chance of hearing this concerto anywhere other than on this record, superbly played by the violinist who gave its first performance.

Handel Violin sonatas, no. 3 in A, no. 10 in G, no. 12 in F, no. 13 in D, no. 14 in A, and no. 15 in E. ALFREDO CAMPOLI with George Malcolm (harpsichord)
Of the many recordings listed in the catalogue of these sonatas, Alfredo Campoli's is especially pleasing. Others from the past to look out for are Yehudi Menuhin's versions of nos. 13 and 14 with George Malcolm, and no. 15 with H. Endt; Carl Flesch has recorded sonata no. 14, and Georges Enescu no. 13.

Haydn Concerto no. 1 in C (1765). ISAAC STERN, Columbia Symphony Orchestra/dir. Stern
The magnificent version by Szymon Goldberg on 78s is also a rare and lucky find.

Hindemith Concerto in D (1940). IVRY GITLIS, Westphalian Symphony Orchestra/Reichert
Also recorded by David Oistrakh with the London Symphony Orchestra, conducted by the composer.

Holst Concerto for two violins (1929). EMANUEL HURWITZ and KENNETH SILLITO, English Chamber Orchestra/ Imogen Holst
A rare, modern recording of this interesting, idiomatic concerto.

Hubay Concerto op. 99 (1907). AARON ROSAND, Orchestre Radio Luxembourg/de Froment
Yet another virtuoso concerto seldom performed in the concert hall, which Aaron Rosand was the first to record.

Joachim Concerto in D minor op. 11 'in the Hungarian style'. CHARLES TRAGER, Louisville Orchestra/Mester
A neglected virtuoso concerto, fiendishly taxing for the soloist, which we have to thank Trager for preserving on record.

Khachaturian Concerto in D (1940). IGOR OISTRAKH, Philharmonia Orchestra/Goossens
The cadenzas played in this recording are by Igor Oistrakh's father, David.

Lalo *Symphonie Espagnole* op. 21 (1873). KYUNG-WHA CHUNG, Montreal Symphony Orchestra/Dutoit; IDA HAENDEL, Czech Philharmonic Orchestra/Ancerl
Historically, the early 78 set of Menuhin is also a valuable addition to any serious collection.

Lipiński Concerto no. 2 op. 21 ('Military'). IGOR IWANOW, Polish National Philharmonic Orchestra/Rowicki
This was the first recording of the concerto, and is a performance of great spirit.

Martinů Concerto no. 2. JOSEPH SUK, Czech Philharmonic Orchestra/Neumann

Mendelssohn Concerto in D minor (1822). ARTHUR GRUMIAUX, New Philharmonia Orchestra/Krenz
First recorded by Yehudi Menuhin with the Philharmonia Orchestra/Boult—an exceptional performance.

Mendelssohn Concerto in E minor op. 64 (1832). NATHAN MILSTEIN, Pittsburgh Symphony Orchestra/Steinberg; GIOCONDA DE VITO, Radio Italiana Torino Orchestra/ Furtwängler (live 1952)

Perhaps the most frequently recorded of all violin concertos. The years have seen endless great recordings—greatest of all perhaps Yehudi Menuhin's with the Orchestre des Concerts Colonne/Enescu.

Mozart Concertone in C major for two violins K.190. EMANUEL HURWITZ and ELI GOREN, English Chamber Orchestra/Davis

Mozart Concerto in B flat, K.207. DAVID OISTRAKH, Orchestre des Concerts Lamoureux/Haitink

Mozart Concerto in D, K.211. ANNE SOPHIE MUTTER, Philharmonia Orchestra/Muti
A distinguished earlier version by Wolfgang Schneiderhan with the Berlin Philharmonic Orchestra/dir. Schneiderhan is part of a complete set of Mozart concertos.

Mozart Concerto in G, K.216. DAVID OISTRAKH, Philharmonia Orchestra/dir. Oistrakh; JOSEPH SZIGETI Orchestra conducted by Mitropoulos (live 1949)
We must return to the mid-1930s and listen again to the young Yehudi Menuhin with the Paris Symphony Orchestra/Enescu for a definitive reading of this concerto.

Mozart Concerto in D, K.218. TIBOR VARGA, Chamber Orchestra/dir. Tibor Varga; BRONISLAW HUBERMAN, New York Philharmonic Symphony Orchestra/Walter (live 1942)
Outstanding among the many earlier recordings of this popular concerto have been: Fritz Kreisler with the London Philharmonic Orchestra/Sargent; Johanna Martzy with the Bavarian Radio Chamber Orchestra/Jochum; Yehudi Menuhin with the Liverpool Philharmonic Orchestra/Sargent.

Mozart Concerto in A, K.219 ('Turkish'). GYÖRGY PAUK, Württemberg Chamber Orchestra/Faerber
One of the most frequently recorded of Mozart's violin concertos, it would again be invidious to single out a 'best' performance; unusual and interesting is the recording by Theo Olaf with Symphony Orchestra/Goehr.

Mozart *Adagio* in E, K.261. WOLFGANG SCHNEIDERHAN, Berlin Philharmonic Orchestra/dir. Schneiderhan
Another beautiful performance of this *Adagio* was recorded by Jean Pougnet with Symphony Orchestra/Goehr.

Mozart Concerto in E flat, K.268. YEHUDI MENUHIN, Bath Festival Orchestra/dir. Menuhin
There is also an exceptional version by Jacques Thibaud conducted by Sir Malcolm Sargent.

Mozart Concerto in D, K.271a. YEHUDI MENUHIN, Bath Festival Orchestra/dir. Menuhin
David Oistrakh with the USSR State Philharmonic Orchestra/Kondrashin has also made an eloquent recording of this work.

Mozart Concerto in D, K.294a ('Princess Adelaide'). LOUIS KAUFMAN, Netherlands Philharmonic Orchestra/ Ackermann
The first recording of this work was by Yehudi Menuhin with Paris Symphony Orchestra/Monteux.

Mozart *Duo* no. 2 in B flat, K.424 for violin and viola. JOSEPH FUSCH and Lillian Fusch

The classic performance of this *Duo* by Szymon Goldberg and Paul Hindemith is also one that should not be missed by any serious connoisseur of the violin.

Mozart Violin sonatas. SZYMON GOLDBERG with Radu Lupu

Do not overlook either the old 78 set of these sonatas played by Szymon Goldberg with Lili Kraus.

Nussio Concerto. GUILA BUSTABO, unnamed orchestra conducted by the composer (live 1972)

This, the only recording of the Swiss composer Otmar Nussio's concerto, is taken from a live radio broadcast.

Paganini 24 *Caprices* op. 1. RUGGIERO RICCI; MICHAEL RABIN; ITZHAK PERLMAN

These three recordings of all the 24 *Caprices* set the highest standard. The latest addition to the long and distinguished list of complete *Caprices* is that of Shlomo Mintz. Among the dozens of superb recorded performances of single *Caprices* since the early years of the century, special mention should be made of Giula Bustabo (no. 5), Oistrakh (no. 1) and Menuhin (no. 24).

Paganini The six violin concertos

The only artist to offer Paganini's concertos complete in one boxed set is Salvatore Accardo with the London Philharmonic Orchestra/Dutoit. More stylish and exciting performances of single concertos have been made by: Leonid Kogan, no. 1 in D, op. 6 (outstanding); Ruggiero Ricci, no. 2 in B minor op. 7; Henryk Szeryng, no. 3 in E, op. 63; Arthur Grumiaux, no. 4 in D minor (1829); Franco Gulli, no. 5 in A minor (1830).

Prokofiev Concerto no. 1 in D op. 19 (1914). NATHAN MILSTEIN, Philharmonia Orchestra/Giulini

Another version that held its own for many years was that of Joseph Szigeti with the London Philharmonic Orchestra/Beecham.

Prokofiev Concerto no. 2 in G minor op. 63 (1935). NATHAN MILSTEIN, New Philharmonia Orchestra/De Burgos

The first recording of this concerto, a thrilling performance by Jascha Heifetz with the Boston Symphony Orchestra/ Koussevitsky, should also be heard.

Ravel *Tzigane* (1924). ITZHAK PERLMAN, Orchestre de Paris/ Martinon

No one should miss the 78 recording of this work by Ginette Neveu, which has also been transferred to LP.

Reger Solo sonatas, no. 1 in A minor, no. 3 in B flat, no. 7 in A minor. HYMAN BRESS

Reger's three unaccompanied sonatas are wonderfully played by this artist.

Saint-Saëns Concerto no. 2 in C op. 58 (1879). IVRY GITLIS, Orchestre National de l'Opéra de Monte-Carlo/ van Remoortel

Saint-Saëns Concerto no. 3 in B minor op. 61 (1880). KYUNG-WHA CHUNG, London Symphony Orchestra/ Foster

Outstanding older interpretations are those by Louis Kaufman with the Netherlands Philharmonic Orchestra/ Van den Berg, and Zino Francescatti with the New York Philharmonic Symphony Orchestra/Mitropoulos.

Saint-Saëns *Introduction and Rondo Capriccioso* (1870). JASCHA HEIFETZ, London Philharmonic Orchestra/ Barbirolli

This 1937 recording comes from the same session as the Havanaise (see following entry), one of the most outstanding of Heifetz's career. Two fine versions which also deserve mention are by Alfredo Campoli with the London Symphony Orchestra/Fistoulari, and by Ida Haendel with the National Symphony Orchestra/Cameron.

Saint-Saëns *Havanaise* op. 83 (1887). JASCHA HEIFETZ, London Philharmonic Orchestra/Barbirolli

Heifetz made this superb recording in 1937: together with the Saint-Saëns *Introduction and Rondo Capriccioso*, it is among the greatest he ever made.

Sarasate Carmen Fantasy op. 25. ITZHAK PERLMAN, Royal Philharmonic Orchestra/Foster

A performance of immense virtuosity, immaculately recorded.

Sarasate *Zigeunerweisen* op. 20 no. 1. JASCHA HEIFETZ, London Philharmonic Orchestra/Barbirolli

Another disc from his 1937 session with Barbirolli. There is also a 1936 recording by the young Ruggiero Ricci of positively breathtaking accuracy and speed.

Sarasate Works for violin and piano

Of the many smaller pieces by Sarasate there are numerous recordings by first-class players to choose from—but the starting point would be the collections recorded by Ricci of this music, whose style it suits so well.

Schoenberg Concerto op. 36 (1936). WOLFGANG MARSCHNER, South West German radio Orchestra/Gielen

Schubert Rondo in A, D.438 (1816). SUZANNE LAUTENBACHER, Württemberg Chamber Orchestra/ Faerber

The divine playing of this work in 1937 by Henri Temianka stands out as a pinnacle among the great violin recordings of all time.

Schubert *Rondo brillant* in B, D.895. SALVATORE ACCARDO with L. Lessona; YEHUDI MENUHIN with Hephzibah Menuhin

The wonderful Menuhin performance dates back to 1937.

Schubert Fantasia in C, D.934. GYÖRGY PAUK with Peter Frankl; BRONISLAW HUBERMAN with Roubakine (live 1944)

The 78s by Adolf Busch with Rudolf Serkin should not be neglected.

Schubert Sonatinas, no. 1 in D, D.384, no. 2 in A minor, D.385, no. 3 in G minor, D.408. SALVATORE ACCARDO with L. Lessona

There are excellent recordings of the sonatinas also by Szymon Goldberg with Radu Lupu, and Arthur Grumiaux with Paul Crossley.

Schumann Concerto in D minor (1853). HENRYK SZERYNG, London Symphony Orchestra/Dorati

This concerto was lost for many years, and was not given its premiere until November 1937 by Gẹorg Kulenkampff, who recorded it shortly afterwards with the Berlin Philharmonic Orchestra/Schmidt-Isserstedt—a version which is still today unsurpassed. Another performance was recorded by Menuhin a few months later in the USA.

Shostakovich Concerto no. 1 in A minor op. 99 (1948). DAVID OISTRAKH, Leningrad Philharmonic Orchestra/ Mravinsky

Shostakovich Concerto no. 2 in C sharp minor op. 129 (1967). DAVID OISTRAKH, Moscow Philharmonic Orchestra/Kondrashin

Sibelius Concerto in D minor op. 47 (1905). PINCHAS ZUCKERMAN, London Philharmonic Orchestra/ Barenboim; GUILA BUSTABO, Berlin State Opera Orchestra/Zaun

One recording that should definitely be heard is the early LP of Isaac Stern with the Royal Philharmonic Orchestra/ Beecham. Both Heifetz's recordings must also be very highly rated (a set on 78s with the London Philharmonic and a later LP version with the Chicago Symphony Orchestra/Hendl.)

Spohr Concerto no. 8 in A minor op. 47 ('*Gesangsscene*') (1816). JASCHA HEIFETZ, RCA Victor Symphony Orchestra/Solomon

This composer's most popular surviving violin work has had two other memorable performances on record: by Georg Kulenkampff with the Berlin Philharmonic Orchestra/Schmidt-Isserstedt; and by Albert Spalding with the Philadelphia Orchestra/Ormandy.

Szymanowski Concerto no. 1 op. 35 (1922). KONSTANTY KULKA, Polish Radio Symphony Orchestra/Maksymiuk

Roman Totenberg's with the Poznan Philharmonic Symphony Orchestra/Wislocki is another fine version of this unjustly neglected concerto.

Szymanowski Concerto no. 2 op. 61 (1932). CHARLES TRAGER, Polish National Philharmonic Orchestra/ Satanowski

Tartini Sonata in G minor ('Devil's Trill'). ALFREDO CAMPOLI with Eric Gritton

This has always been a very popular work for recording artists. Older versions by Yehudi Menuhin, David Oistrakh, and Nathan Milstein are an indication of differing styles of interpretation of music from this period.

Tchaikovsky Concerto in D major op. 35 (1878). NATHAN MILSTEIN, Vienna Philharmonic Orchestra/Abbado

It would be impossible to list all of the fine recordings that this concerto has enjoyed. But try to hear the magnificent 1931 set of 78s made by Mischa Elman with the London Symphony Orchestra/Barbirolli.

Vieuxtemps Concerto no. 4 in D minor op. 31 (1850). ITZHAK PERLMAN, Orchestre de Paris/Barenboim

Jascha Heifetz was the first to record this concerto in 1937 with the London Philharmonic Orchestra/Barbirolli.

Vieuxtemps Concerto in A minor op. 37. ITZHAK PERLMAN, Orchestre de Paris/Barenboim

No recording has come even near the perfection of the 1949 version on 78s by Jascha Heifetz with the London Symphony Orchestra under Barbirolli. Leonid Kogan's performance is another also highly recommended.

Viotti Concerto no. 22 in A minor. LOLA BOBESCO, Orchestre d'État du Palatinat Rhénan Redel; YEHUDI MENUHIN, New York Philharmonic Orchestra/Mitropoulos (live 1955)

The Bobesco is well played and she uses the Ysaÿe cadenzas. A version which should not be overlooked is that of Isaac Stern with the Philadelphia Orchestra/Ormandy. The Menuhin performance is taken from a live broadcast from Carnegie Hall, and conveys an atmosphere and a sense of occasion seldom heard on a recording.

Vitali Chaconne in G minor. ZINO FRANCESCATTI, Zurich Chamber Orchestra/de Stoutz

The version on 78s by that grand lady of the violin Gioconda de Vito with the Philharmonia Orchestra/Erede and H. Dowson (organ) is also a classic.

Vivaldi Four concertos ('The Four Seasons'). WOLFGANG SCHNEIDERHAN, Lucerne Festival Strings/Baumgartner

Since this work has become so popular it has been recorded more often than many of the major Romantic concertos. An older version worth hearing is that by Reinhold Barchet recorded with the Stuttgart Chamber Orchestra/ Munzinger.

Walton Concerto (1939). KYUNG-WHA CHUNG, London Symphony Orchestra/Previn

This concerto was written for Jascha Heifetz, who recorded it first with the Cincinnati Symphony Orchestra/Goossens and then again with the composer and the Philharmonia Orchestra—the first is the better of the two.

Wieniawski Concerto no. 1 in F sharp minor op. 14 (1870). ITZHAK PERLMAN, London Symphony Orchestra/Ozawa

A very exciting record was made of this concerto by the young Michael Rabin with the Philharmonia Orchestra/ Boult.

Wieniawski Concerto no. 2 in D minor op. 22 (1870). IDA HAENDEL, Prague Symphony Orchestra/Smetacek

Itzhak Perlman has also made brilliant recordings of both the Wieniawski concertos on one disc. But again we must turn to Jascha Heifetz for the most confident dashing performances of all.

Wolf-Ferrari Concerto in D op. 26. GUILA BUSTABO, Munich Symphony Orchestra/Kempe (live 1972)

This is an LP transcription from a broadcast. Bustabo co-wrote this concerto with Wolf-Ferrari, and our thanks must go to the American collector Tom Clear for making an LP available in a limited edition.

Ysaÿe Solo sonatas (published 1924). MICHAEL RABIN; DAVID OISTRAKH; EFREM ZIMBALIST

These important and effective sonatas are unfortunately very badly represented in the modern catalogues. A complete set by Oscar Shumsky is an elegant and welcome exception.

Glossary

Accidentals   The signs by which notes are *chromatically* moved upwards or downwards by a *semitone*—e.g. the sharp (♯) raises the note by a semitone, the flat (♭) lowers it by a semitone, the double-flat (♭♭) lowers it by two semitones (one tone), and the double-sharp (×) raises it by two semitones. The natural sign (♮) contradicts a previous ♯ or ♭, restoring the note to its 'natural' condition.

Arpeggio   Italian, *arpeggiare* meaning 'to play the harp'. The notes of a chord played in rapid succession, either in regular time or freely. Thus *arpeggiando*, 'arpeggiated'.

Atonality, atonal   A modern term for music not written in a specific *key*.

Bar   The space between two 'bar-lines' drawn through the musical *stave* to indicate the metrical divisions of the music; also called 'measure', especially in USA.

Bariolage   French term: the playing of high notes in high positions on the lower strings (1) to vary tone-colouring or (2) to facilitate the performance of rapid high passage-work without changing positions. Also the alternation of the same note on an open string and a stopped string.

Baroque   A loose musical term, of limited use except as determining a chronological period (but without implying any kind of stylistic continuity or homogeneity). Subdivided further as: early Baroque, 1580–1630; middle Baroque, 1630–80; late Baroque, 1680–1730; and even '*Baroque tardif*', 1730–1750/60. Similarly *Classical*, used loosely to denote the period of Haydn, Mozart and Beethoven; and *Romantic*, the nineteenth century, after *c.* 1830.

Basso continuo   See *continuo*

Blue notes   Especially in jazz; notes of the scale, especially the third and seventh, played deliberately out of tune to produce a clash, or an ambiguity, between major and minor *tonalities*.

Bout   The part of the body of the violin, either 'upper bout' or 'lower bout', above or below the waist (itself sometimes called the 'middle bouts').

Cantilena   A sustained, flowing melodic line, especially when played *cantabile*, or in the manner of singing.

Canzona, canzone   Usually an instrumental piece in a *polyphonic* style, originally *canzona francese*.

Classical   See *Baroque*

Clef   The sign (e.g. 𝄞 or 𝄢 :) in front of the key and time signatures at the beginning of each composition, repeated on each *stave* to show the position of notes on each stave. The 'G clef', 𝄞 , placed on the third line of the stave, for example, indicates that the note on that line is G.

Chromatic   From the Greek *chromatikos* meaning coloured. The harmony or scale which uses all the semitones of the scale—i.e. all the notes available in traditional Western music, as opposed to *diatonic*.

Col legno   Italian, 'with the wood': a direction to strike the strings with the wood of the bow.

Concord   The sounding together of notes in harmony, satisfying the ear as being 'final in itself.' No following chord is required to give the impression of resolution.

Consonance   The purely intoned sounding together of notes capable of producing *concord*.

Continuo   Abbreviation of Italian *basso continuo*: a system of shorthand notation for keyboard instruments used from the early seventeenth to the mid-eighteenth centuries by which instead of writing out the full harmony, the composer provided the accompanist only with a bass line together with figures and *accidentals* to indicate the broad harmonic movement (thus also '*figured bass*'). The term often denoted the instrument itself, usually harpsichord, which played the *continuo* part.

Counterpoint, contrapuntal   The art of combining two or more independent melodic lines. The general practice of counterpoint as a mode of composition is called *polyphony*.

Détaché   The violinist's basic bow-stroke: smooth and even, drawing the sound without leaving the string, the bow-changes inaudible at all speeds and *dynamics*.

Diatonic   The harmony or scale (as opposed to *chromatic*) that uses the notes proper to the major or minor keys or scales only, without deviation.

Discord   The opposite of *concord*: the sounding together of notes which does not satisfy the ear as being 'final in itself', or requires a following chord to give the impression of resolution.

Dissonance   The sounding together of notes producing *discord*; the opposite of *consonance*.

Dominant   See *tonic*

Dynamic   The relative volume of musical notes or combinations of notes; the gradations of softness and loudness in music.

Enharmonic   In modern usage, a term applied to changes of notes or *keys* only as a matter of terminology—i.e. C sharp major to D flat major, or E flat to D sharp. On the piano or other instrument using the well-tempered tuning system, such pairs of notes are actually the same; but on string instruments there is, at least subjectively to the player, a minute but important difference between them.

Favola per musica   Italian, meaning 'story for music': early term for opera of a legendary or mythological nature; often a story of that kind in dramatic form written specifically to be set to music.

Figured bass   See *continuo*

Fioriture   Italian word, literally 'flowering, flourishes, decorations'. Ornamental figures elaborating a plainer or simpler melody, often improvised.

Flautato   Italian, 'fluted': a whispering sonority produced by drawing the bow across the string without pressure, using only its own weight.

Heterophonic   Literally, 'made up of a number of voices or parts'. In non-Western music, the simultaneous performance of a melody and of variants or decorations of it, without regard to 'Western' harmonic sense.

Homophony, homophonic   Term (from Greek, literally 'alike-sounding') applied to music in which the individual lines making up the harmony have no independent significance.

Intonation   The tuning of notes, and the way that they are played or sung according to the ear's perception of what is, or is not, 'in tune'.

Key   The *tonality* of a piece of music that is based on particular major or minor scale, and accepts harmonic relationships deriving from the notes of those scales. The first note of the scale gives its name to the key—i.e. 'the key of G major', 'the key of B flat minor'.

Key signature   The arrangement of sharps or flats at the beginning of each line of music indicating which notes are to be consistently sharpened and flattened, and also showing the key (e.g. one sharp, F sharp = G major or E minor; four flats, B, E, A, D flat = A flat major or F minor).

Leading note   See *tonic*

Legato   Italian, 'tied', 'bound': a form of *détaché* bow-stroke in which many notes are played (bound together) in a single stroke.

Martelé   Fast, brief, energetic strokes, usually (though not exclusively) played with the upper half of the bow.

Measure   See *bar*

Mediant   See *tonic*

Metre   The rhythmic patterns produced in music by notes of varying length combined with strong and weak beats—similar to the metrical 'feet' (spondees, dactyls, trochees etc.) in poetry.

Mixolydian mode   The sequence of white notes on the piano, beginning on G. This mode thus has a sharp third and sixth, but a flat seventh. See also **modes**.

Modes   The scales, made up of various groupings of the 'white notes' of the keyboard, which became established in the Middle Ages and were accepted, at least in theory, as the basis of Western music until the sixteenth century. They were given Greek names, such as 'Dorian', 'Phrygian', 'Lydian', '*Mixolydian*', 'Ionian'.

Monody   A *monophonic* melody or note-sequence.

Monophonic   Single-voiced, one melodic part only.

Motive, motif   A brief melodic or rhythmic figure, too short to be called a theme or a tune.

Neapolitan key   The distant key of the flattened supertonic (e.g. B flat in the key of A minor), which came into vogue in the seventeenth century especially as part of a closing cadence; later used for more elaborate and dramatic effect, especially by Schubert.

Obbligato   Italian, meaning 'obligatory', 'compulsory': applied to an instrumental part that is essential, in the sense that it performs an important soloistic function, and is not merely optional.

Pentatonic   The various forms of five-note *modes*—one of which is represented on the piano by the black notes of the keyboard. Any 'gapped' scale that omits two of the normal seven notes of the ordinary *diatonic* scales. Of all scalic formulae the pentatonic are those mostly derived from the acoustical facts of the harmonic series; that is why they form the basis of primitive music everywhere, and of most sophisticated music that is melodically conceived.

Pitch   The 'height' or 'depth' of a musical sound according to the number of vibrations that produces it; also the standard by which notes (usually in relation to the A above middle-C) are to be tuned in relation to each other. It is not an absolute: the pitch of A, for example, has varied over the centuries and from country to country—although today, by international agreement, it is generally standardized at 440 cycles per second.

Pizzicato   Italian, 'plucked': when done with the right hand, *pizzicato* produces a banjo- or guitar-like effect. It can also be done with the left-hand fingers.

Polyphony   Literally 'many voices': two or more melodic parts co-existing (see also *counterpoint*).

Portamento   The effect of carrying on from one note to another with a slight slide; also called scooping.

Register   A set of pipes (organ) or strings (harpsichord) brought into action to produce a particular *tone (2)* or *dynamic*; also the different parts of the range of the human voice, e.g. 'head register' or 'chest register'.

Ricochet   See *staccato*

Ripieno   Italian (literally 'full', 'filling' or 'stuffing'), meaning an instrument or instruments subordinate to the soloist or leader. In the eighteenth-century *concerto grosso* the string players other than the soloists are *ripieni*.

Ritornello   Italian, literally 'little return': originally a refrain, or a recurring instrumental piece in a stage work—applied from the eighteenth century onwards to the orchestral *tutti* in concertos, especially in rondos where the same theme returns many times.

Romantic   See *Baroque*

Rubato   Italian word, literally 'robbed'—thus *tempo rubato*, 'robbed time': playing out of strict tempo for expressive purposes, covering a very broad range of manners and styles.

Semitone   The smallest interval normally used in Western music—i.e. the interval between a black note and an adjacent white note (or the intervals between the four white notes with no black note between them, B/C and E/F, on the piano).

Serial music   See *twelve-tone music*

Spiccato   A short, bouncing bow-stroke, using the elasticity of the bow-hair and the string, which enables the bow to leave the string between each stroke: usually played in the middle of the bow.

Staccato   A bow-stroke in which each note is separate, and which can be played at great speed, up- or down-bow, sounding like a succession of *martelés*. In 'flying *staccato*', the *staccato* bow leaves the string between each note (also called *ricochet*).

Stave   The five horizontal lines on which music is written.

Stretto   Italian, literally 'narrow', 'tightened', 'squeezed'. A device in fugal writing whereby the entries of the various subjects are drawn closely together, and appear either simultaneously or in overlapping sequence.

Sub-dominant   See *tonic*

Sub-mediant   See *tonic*

Sul pont(icello)   Italian, 'on the bridge': a direction to play with the bow very near to (not actually on) the bridge, producing a characteristic nasal, rustling sonority.

Sul tasto   Italian, 'on the fingerboard': a direction to play with the bow high up on the strings over the fingerboard.

Supertonic   See *tonic*

Tonality, tonal   Strictly speaking, tonality is the relationship between tones that are inherent in acoustical facts, so that the term covers all scale formulae, from the *pentatonic* to the *chromatic*. In practice, however, tonality has become associated with the tempered major and minor scales of the eighteenth and nineteenth centuries, and their 'functional' behaviour to one another. The word is virtually synonymous with *key*, but also means more specifically the feeling of a definite key suggested by a piece or passage of music (see also *atonality*).

Tone   (1) The term used for pure musical notes not containing harmonics, each harmonic being itself a tone; (2) the quality and timbre of a musical sound; (3) the interval between first and second, second and third, fourth and fifth, fifth and sixth, sixth and seventh notes of the *diatonic* major scale: i.e. two *semitones*.

Tone-row   A translation of the German word *Tonreihe*, to designate the 'rows' of twelve notes on which twelve-note or *twelve-tone* compositions are based; also known as series.

Tonic, dominant, sub-dominant   The main or first note of a *key* (or first 'degree of a scale'), and the fifth and fourth notes respectively above it. Tonic, dominant and sub-dominant *triads* condition the basic *tonal* relationships of Western music in its most rudimentarily harmonic form. The other degrees of the scale are the *supertonic* (second), *mediant* (third), *sub-mediant* (sixth) and *leading note* (seventh).

Triad   A chord of three notes composed of two superimposed thirds—e.g. C-E-G, G-B-D, F-A♭-C, B-D-F♯.

Tritone   The interval of the augmented fourth (i.e. B to F, or C to F sharp, progressing upwards).

Tutti   Italian meaning 'all'. Term to designate the singing and playing together of all the forces in a performance; or frequently also the purely orchestral passages of a concerto where the soloist is silent, whether the whole orchestra happens to be playing, or only part of it.

Twelve-tone music, twelve-tone harmony   The system of composing on which the later works of Schoenberg, and other subsequent composers, are based, that abolishes *keys* and with them the predominance of certain notes of the scale (especially *tonic*, *sub-dominant*, *dominant* and *mediant*)—using instead the twelve notes of the chromatic scale, each of which has exactly the same importance as any other. In order to ensure that no note assumes even temporary predominance, a 'series' of all twelve notes in any chosen sequence is employed, in which each note must appear only once—thus *serial* composition and *serial* music.

Whole-tone scale   A musical scale progressing by nothing but whole *tones*, without *semitones*—e.g. C-D-E-F♯-G♯-A♯, or D♭-E♭-F-G-A-B.

Bibliography

GENERAL

1897 **Erlich, A.**, *Celebrated Violinists, Past and Present*, London Strad Library; 3rd edition 1913

1901 **Moser, A.**, *Joseph Joachim: A Biography*, translated L. Durham, London, Wellby

1925 **Bachmann, A.**, *An Encyclopedia of the Violin*, London, Appleton; reprinted 1966, New York, Da Capo

1930 **Flesch, C.**, *The Art of Violin Playing*, New York, Carl Fischer

1933 **Straeten, E. van der**, *The History of the Violin*, 2 vols., London, Cassell; reprinted 1968, New York, Da Capo

1940 **Farga, F.**, *Violins and Violinists*, London, Barrie and Rockliff; reprinted 1969

1948 **Brook, D.**, *Violinists of Today*, London, Rockliff

1951 **Lochner, L. P.**, *Fritz Kreisler*, London, Rockliff

1957 **Flesch, C.**, *The Memoirs of Carl Flesch*, trans. Hans Keller, London, Rockliff; reprinted 1973, New York, Da Capo; Harlow (Essex), Bois de Boulogne

1967 **Szigeti, J.**, *With Strings Attached*, New York, Alfred A. Knopf

1972 **Applebaum S. and S.**, *The Way They Play*, 10 vols., New York, Paganiniana Publications

1976 **Menuhin, Y.**, with **Primrose, W.**, and **Stevens, D.**, *Violin and Viola*, London, Macdonald

1980 **Campbell, M.**, *The Great Violinists*, London, Granada; New York, Doubleday

1980 *The New Grove Dictionary of Music and Musicians*, 20 vols., London, Macmillan

THE ANATOMY OF THE VIOLIN

1939 **Bessaraboff, N.**, *Ancient European Musical Instruments*, Boston, Museum of Fine Arts; reprinted 1964, October House

1963 **Hill, W. H., A. F. and A. E.**, *Antonio Stradivari*, New York, Dover

1979 **Sacconi, S. F.**, *The 'Secrets' of Stradivari*, Cremona, Libreria del Convegno

THE BAROQUE AND CLASSICAL VIOLIN

This list does not include primary sources, for which reference should be made to *The New Grove Dictionary of Music and Musicians*: bibliographies under Violin II and Violin III; and all composer entries.

1922–4 **La Laurencie, L. de**, *L'École française de violon de Lully à Viotti*, Paris, Librairie Delagrave; reissued 1971

1923 **Moser, A.**, *Geschichte des Violinspiels*, Hesse, Leipzig; revised and enlarged, Schneider, Heidelberg, 1966

1946 **Meyer. E. H.**, *Early English Chamber Music*, London; revised by D. Poulton and reissued, London, Lawrence & Wishart, 1982

1956 **Robbins Landon, H. D.**, and **Mitchell , D.** (eds.), *The Mozart Companions*, London, Faber

1959 **Newman, W. S.**, *The Sonata in the Baroque Era*, Chapel Hill, University of North Carolina Press

1963 **Newman, W. S..**, *The Sonata in the Classic Era*, Chapel Hill, University of North Carolina Press; revised 1972

1965 **Boyden, D. D.**, *The History of Violin Playing from its Origins to 1761*, London, Oxford University Press

1966 **Winternitz, E.**, *Musical Instruments of the Western World*, London, Thames and Hudson

1971 **Arnold, D.** and **Fortune, N.** (eds.), *The Beethoven Companion*, London, Faber

1972 **Nelson, S. M.**, *The Violin and Viola*, London, Ernest Benn; New York, W. W. Norton

1973 **Loft, A.**, *Violin and Keyboard: the Duo Repertoire*, 2 vols., New York, Grossman

1980 **Ratner, L. G.**, *Classic Music: Expression, Form, Style*, London, Collier; New York, Schirmer

1984 **Walls, P.** and **Stonewall, R.**, articles in *Early Music*, August 1984

THE VIOLIN CONCERTO

1952 **Hill, R.** (ed.), *The Concerto*, Harmondsworth, Penguin

1959 **Hutchings, A.**, *The Baroque Concerto*, third edition 1973, London, Faber

1969 **Emery, F. B.**, *The Violin Concerto*, 2 vols., New York, Da Capo

1971 **Rosen, C.**, *The Classical Style*, London, Faber; revised edition 1976

1972 **Blume, F.**, *Classical and Romantic Music*, London, Faber

1979 **Abraham, G.**, *The Concise Oxford History of Music*, Oxford University Press

1982 **Abraham, G.** (ed.), *The New Oxford History of Music*, vol. VIII, *The Age of Beethoven 1790–1830*, Oxford University Press

THE NINETEENTH CENTURY

1929 **Cobbett, W. W.** (ed.), *Cyclopaedic Survey of Chamber Music*, London, Oxford University Press; 2nd edition 1963

1936 **Pulver, J.**, *Paganini and the Romantic Virtuoso*, London, Herbert Joseph; reprinted 1970, New York, Da Capo

1940 **Farga, F.**, *Geigen und Geiger*, Zürich, Müller Verlag; English edition translated by E. Larsen, *Violins and Violinists*, 1950, London, Barrie & Rockliff; 2nd edition 1969

1957 **de Courcy, G. I. C.**, *Paganini the Genoese*, 2 vols., Oklahoma, University of Oklahoma Press

1972 **Kollneder, W.**, *Das Buch der Violine*, Zürich, Atlantis Verlag

1973 **Wechsborg, J.**, *The Violin*, New York, Viking Press; London, Calder and Boyars

1975 **Melkus, E.** *Die Violine*, Berne, Hallwag

THE TWENTIETH CENTURY

1966 **Flesch, C.**, *Violin Fingering*, London, Barrie and Jenkins

1969 **Szigeti, J.**, *Szigeti on the Violin*, London, Cassell, reissued 1979, New York, Dover

1971 **Slonimsky, N.**, *Music since 1900*, 4th edition, London, Cassell

1971 **Xenakis, I.**, *Formalized Music*, Indiana University Press

1973 **Loft, A.**, *Violin and Keyboard : the Duo Repertoire*, vol. 2., New York, Grossman

1974 **Ysaÿe, A.**, and **Ratcliffe, B.**, *Eugène Ysaÿe*, London, Heinemann

1977 **Carter, E.**, *The Writings of Elliott Carter*, edited by E. and K. Stone, Indiana University Press

1978 **Moldenhauer, H.**, *Anton von Webern*, London, Gollancz

1979 **White, E. W.**, *Stravinsky*, London, Faber

THE FOLK VIOLIN

1966 **Collinson, F.**, *Traditional and National Music of Scotland*, London, Routledge and Kegan Paul

1968 **Malone, B. C.**, *Country Music U.S.A.*, Texas, American Folklore Society

1972 **Johnson, D.**, *Music and Society in Lowland Scotland in the 18th Century*, London, Oxford University Press

1974 **Whone, H.**, *The Hidden Face of Music*, London, Gollancz

1977 **Baggelaar, K.** and **Milton, D.** (eds.), *The Folk Music Encyclopaedia*, New York, Thomas Y. Crowell; London, Omnibus

1978 **Canainn, T. O.**, *Traditional Music of Ireland*, London, Routledge and Kegan Paul

1979 **Klingman, D.**, *American Music, a Panorama*, New York, Schirmer

1983 **Hamm, C.**, *Music in the New World*, New York, W. W. Norton

DISCOGRAPHY

1936 **Darrell, R. D.**, *The Gramophone Shop Encyclopedia of Recorded Music*, New York, The Gramophone Shop; reprinted 1948

1951 **Lochner, L. P.**, *Fritz Kreisler* (with discography), London, Rockliff

1951 **Sackville-West, E.**, and **Shawe-Taylor, D.**, *The Record Guide*, London, Collins; revised edition 1955

1956 **Magidoff, R.**, *Yehudi Menuhin* (with discography), London, Robert Hale

1974 **Creighton, J.**, *Discopaedia of the Violin*, 1889–1971, Toronto, University of Toronto Press

1975 **Greenfield, Layton and March**, *Penguin Stereo Record Guide*, Harmondsworth, Penguin; second edition 1977

1982 **Greenfield, Layton and March**, *New Penguin Stereo Record Guide*, Harmondsworth, Penguin

Acknowledgements

The publishers wish to thank all private owners, museums, galleries, libraries and other institutions for permission to reproduce works in their collections. Further acknowledgement is made to the following (the illustrations are identified by page reference, *t* representing top, *b* bottom, *r* right, *l* left, *c* centre):

Agency for Public Information (Government of Jamaica), Kingston 8*c*; Akademische Druck- u. Verlagsanstalt Graz (from *Denkmäler der Tonkunst in Österreich*, vol. 25, H. F. Biber, 'Violinsonaten II', 1959, p. 82) 70; Archiv für Kunst und Geschichte 134, 137*t*, 143, 150, 179, 182*l*, 190 (Editions Durand), 199*b*; Ashmolean Museum, Oxford (Hill Collection) 28, 33, 40, 45, 51; photo Clive Barda 152; Bartók Archívum, Budapest 195*r*; Bayerisches Nationalmuseum, Munich 59, 89 (Hansmann), 105 (Hansmann), 108; BBC Hulton Picture Library 123, 149; BBC Publications 197; J. & A. Beare Ltd 54; Dr Erich Alban Berg 181; Biblioteca Nazionale, Turin 53; Bibliothèque Nationale, Paris 66*tl*, 78*t*, 189 (Trela/Ziola); Bildarchiv Preussischer Kulturbesitz, Berlin/BRD 173; © copyright 1976 by Boosey & Hawkes Music Publishers Ltd, reproduced by permission of the publishers 207; British Library, London 10*tl*, 67, 71*b*, 74, 78*b*, 79, 94*r*, 96, 99, 107, 109*h*, 111*tl*/*b*, 126*r*, 158, 164*b*; Trustees of the British Museum, London 104, 112*l*, 162, 201; Casa Goldoni, Venice (Giacomelli) 161; Christie's 48; Civico Museo Bibliografico Musicale, Bologna (Archiv für Kunst und Geschichte) 76*t*; Claddagh Records (Tommy Potts) 219; Comhaltas Ceoltóirí Éireann (photo Conor Sinclair) 218; photo Peter Cooke 220*r*; Giancarlo Costa 188*t*; photo D. Coutts 223; Robert Craft 191*bl*; photo Malcolm Crowthers 204, 205*l*; Deutsche Staatsbibliothek, Berlin/DDR 135; Dover Publications Inc (from J. Camner, *The Great Instrumentalists in Historic Photographs*, 1980) 186; Lucy Durán 10*r*, 212*b*; Mary Evans Picture Library 121; Fotomas 71*tl*, 82, 103; Jacques Français 171; W. H. Freeman & Co, San Francisco (after C. M. Hutchins, 'The Physics of the Violin', *Scientific American*, ccvii, Nov. 1962)/Macmillan Publishers Ltd 46; photo Jos Gansemans 8*l*; Germanisches Nationalmuseum, Nuremberg 12, 77; Gesellschaft der Musikfreunde, Vienna (Costa) 169; Giraudon 66*bl*; Goethemuseum, Frankfurt (Edelmann) 133; photo Malcolm Green 225; Frederick Grinke 198; copyright 1962 by Henmar Press Inc, New York, reprinted by permission 205*r*; W. E. Hill & Sons 29, 32, 36, 41, 44, 131, 132*t*, 177; Historisches Museum der Stadt Wien 111*tr*, 132*b*, 168*t*; Louis Krasner 200*l*; Leggatt Brothers, London 81; photo Les Leverett 224, 226, 229; Macmillan Publishers Ltd 68*br*; Irène Magaloff 192*r*; Meyer Collection, Paris (Ziolo) 92, 203; MGM/UA (British Film Institute) 195*b*; Mittet Foto Oslo 212*t*; Mozart Museum, Salzburg 93; Musée de l'Homme (photo M. du Buisson) 8*r*; Musée Lambinet (Bulloz) 112*r*; Musée Antoine Lecuyer, St Quentin 97; Musée du Louvre, Paris (Lauros-Giraudon) frontispiece; Musée National d'Art Moderne, Paris (SPADEM) 209; Museo Civico, Cremona 27, 42, 43; Museo Correr, Venice (Denis Stevens) 65*r*; Museo Teatrale alla Scala, Milan (Costa) 101; Museum Boymans-van Beuningen, Rotterdam 91; Museum für Geschichte der Stadt Leipzig 174; National Galleries of Scotland, Edinburgh 221 (by kind permission of the trustees of the late Mrs Magdalene Sharpe Erskine), 222; Peter Newark's Western Americana 227; Novosti Press Agency 185; National Portrait Gallery, London 80, 85 (Fotomas), 188*t* (Mrs Michael Ayrton); Nationale Forschungs- und Gedenkstätten Weimar 109*t*; Österreichische Nationalbibliothek, Vienna 60, 66*r*, 113, 127, 136*t*, 166, 168*b*, 178*b*; Palazzo Pitti, Florence (Scala) 69*b*; Patrimonio Nacional, Madrid 111*l*; copyright 1972 by Edition Peters Leipzig (P–9153a), reprinted by permission 188; Pinacoteca di Brera, Milan 7 (Giraudon), 75*l*; Pinacoteca Querini Stampalia, Venice (Scala) 73, 164*t*; Princeton University Library (courtesy of William H. Scheide) 86; Private Collection 13, 52 (photo Victoria and Albert Museum, London), 84 (Goodman), 117 (Bulloz), 119, 122 (Ziolo), 125, 129*b*, 130, 136*b*, 137*b*, 145, 148, 157, 170, 180 (original source reproduced by kind permission of the Music Department of the Österreichische Nationalbibliothek, Vienna, F21 Berg 27, f. 17 and Universal Edition (Alfred A. Kalmus Ltd)), 182*r* (Faellet/Ziolo), 193*r* and 194 (Mr Peter Bartòk), 195*l*, 196*l*, (Trela/Ziolo, SPADEM); photo David Redfern 231; photo Mary Remnant 10*bl*, 15, 69*t*; Ricordi & Cie 124; photo Henry Ries 146; Rijksmuseum, Amsterdam 76*b*; Roger-Viollet 120; Royal College of Music, London, 57, 98, 100, 126*l*, 139, 142, 172, 184, 196*r*; David Rubio 89; photo Balint Sarosi 215; Scala 14, 17; Robert-Schumann-Haus, Zwickau 115; Scottish National Portrait Gallery, Edinburgh 220*l*; Society for Cultural Relations with the USSR 178*t*; Sotheby & Co. 55, 56, 72; South American Pictures (photo Tony Morrison) 213; Staatliche Kunstsammlungen, Dresden 102, 129*t* (Deutsche Fotothek); Staatsbibliothek Preussischer Kulturbesitz, Berlin/BRD 87, 160, 176; Städelsches Kunstinstitut, Frankfurt (Artothek) 141; Städtische Galerie im Lenbachhaus, Munich 154; Théodore Strawinsky 191*br*; Mrs Sivvy Streli, Innsbruck 200*r*; Theatermuseum, Munich 165; Tiroler Landesmuseum Ferdinandeum, Innsbruck 65*l*; Topic Records 216; Universal Edition (Alfred A. Kalmus Ltd) 202; Universal Edition (London) Ltd 206; Universitätsbibliothek, Heidelberg 11*r*; University of Arkansas, Fayettville (photo Dwight Nicols) 210; University College, Dublin (Department of Irish Folklore) 217; University of London Library 68*tl*; University of Toronto Press (from E. Leipp, *the Violin*, 169) 9; Verlag das Musikinstrument, Frankfurt (from *Alte Meistergeigen*, Bd III, 1979) 37; Württembergisches Landesbibliothek, Stuttgart 88; Iannis Xenakis 208.

Index

Note: page numbers in *italics* refer to illustrations and/or captions. Where confusion might arise between page numbers and, for example, opus numbers, the page numbers are prefaced by 'p.' or 'pp.'